Types and Shadows

ALSO BY ROY STRONG

Splendours and Miseries
Diaries: 1967–1987

Scenes and Apparitions
Diaries: 1988–2003

Types and Shadows

DIARIES
2004–2015

ROY STRONG

W&N
WEIDENFELD & NICOLSON

First published in Great Britain in 2020
by Weidenfeld & Nicolson

1 3 5 7 9 10 8 6 4 2

© Oman Productions Ltd 2020
Edited by Johanna Stephenson

A CIP catalogue record for this book
is available from the British Library.

HB ISBN 978 1 4746 1733 8
eBook ISBN 978 1 4746 1735 2

Typeset by Input Data Services Ltd, Somerset

Printed and bound in Great Britain by Clays Ltd, Elcograf S.p.A.

Weidenfeld & Nicolson

The Orion Publishing Group Ltd
Carmelite House
50 Victoria Embankment
London, EC4Y 0DZ
An Hachette UK Company

www.orionbooks.co.uk

FOR

JOHN SWANNELL

Friend and photographer

But for whom this volume would not exist

CONTENTS

PREFACE

In the case of the previous two volumes of these Diaries I have always observed a ten-year gap before going into print. Such sensitivity seems, however, to have been abandoned in recent years, particularly by those who have held political office and, once shorn of it, can't wait to burst into print right up to the present moment.

My decision to produce the third volume, going as far as 2015, is a reflection of my own age. By the time that this volume appears I will be eighty-five and therefore, as my years ahead will be finite, I have a desire to be the one who makes the final selection. As with its two predecessors, in this volume the Diary entries go in stops and starts. I was pretty regular from 2005 to 2008, when the entries abruptly stop for a reason it would be tactless to disclose. That my Diary was resumed at all I owe to the photographer John Swannell, who, billing me as this period's Mr Pepys, was horrified to discover that I had stopped. So it resumes again in the autumn of 2010, by which time a laptop had come my way and the copy, as a consequence, multiplied. Later I reverted to my old habit of scribbling in a blank notebook or on endless pieces of scrap paper. That method, it seems to me, suited my desire to capture 'types and shadows', set scenes and reflections.

I have trespassed into 2015 with a few entries publishable now. In fact these three volumes find me in the end a happy and grateful man. I print as the Epilogue to this life saga an account of my investiture with the Order of the Companions of Honour in the spring of 2016, a wholly unexpected award which moved me greatly.

As in the case of the previous two volumes, the debt to my editor, Johanna Stephenson, is untold as each time we make a journey through time. To her I add all those at Weidenfeld & Nicolson, headed by Alan Samson and Lucinda McNeile, who have seen the saga through to its end. This volume records my life subsequent to my wife's death in 2003. She was a dedicated photographer of absolutely everything. Suddenly I found myself looking for pictures for the first time, at which point all sorts of friends sprang to my rescue, headed by the dedicatee, John Swannell, the painter Jonathan Myles-Lee and my inspirational trainer, Jonty Williams. To them and others I am most grateful.

As in the case of the previous volumes of Diaries, I reiterate for those who may be miffed by this or that turn of phrase that all that you read here is what I heard and saw at a particular moment in time. My views now would probably be very different. I need hardly say that Puck's invocation at the close of *A Midsummer Night's Dream*, beginning 'If we shadows have offended . . .', says it all.

ROY STRONG

2004

This begins a new phase in my life as a widower. Julia had died on 10 October of the previous year.

8 JANUARY

The launching of RMS Queen Mary 2

This was a case of 'Come back the Odeon, all is forgiven'. How the décor of this ship was reached I know not. Its predecessors were all monuments to the taste and style of their time. This one is down memory lane with sham Art Deco by the mile (literally), with much gold and scarlet and mirror glass. It is difficult to divine the target audience for this maritime aberration, which looks from the outside like a vast block of council flats dislodged and floating out to sea.

The arrival was chaos and the light refreshment produced the worst sandwiches ever: grated cheese, hard-boiled egg and onion – and they had to be asked for. But the launch itself was a monument to showbiz technology. No trace of the old days with a be-toqued

Queen Mary bashing a bottle and off. We sat in what amounted to a vast temporary auditorium with a stage, a military band, the Royal Choral Society and the Royal Philharmonic Orchestra. It was a spectacular in the midst of which the Bishop of Winchester said a few prayers and the Queen, in cerise and using a stick (she had had a knee cartilage operation recently), dubbed the vessel. So we had lots of patriotic music, fanfares, a good singer who did her stuff and Lesley Garrett, whose hair was a matted fright, singing 'Amazing Grace'. But it was all very slick, with ticker tape and projections, and the ship literally unveiled as vast curtains fell to the ground, followed by a bravura firework display to round it all off fronted by Beethoven's 'Ode to Joy'. The ubiquitous Michael Buerk did the honours well.

But what a contrast to its predecessors, which had been showcases of British design and art. The old *QE2* was the work of Colin Anderson, with Hugh Casson bringing in the artists and designers. The *QM2* is just retro-decorator's décor. It is odd to have launched a ship that will go through the twenty-first century with décor that doesn't even go back to the post-war *QE2* but to the 1920s.

It was, however, a great party. Angela Rippon, Alan Titchmarsh, Alan Whicker and Terry Waite were among those I talked to. I was so exhausted by the time dinner had finished that I missed the show, where things, I heard, went awry with Mozart dissolving into Lloyd-Webber and then Madame Butterfly appeared, sang and then found herself marooned as some of the machinery failed. Dancers reeled on, whirling around her. Disconcerted, she decided that she had better get off the stage somehow and made her way to the wings, where her dress caught on the scenery. There was a terrible rip and half of it was torn off her as she at last made her exit.

22 JANUARY

Julia's service of thanksgiving

The day of Julia's service. Up at 6.45 a.m. and to the Abbey for the eight o'clock service with David Hutt celebrating and Julia remembered. I got to St Paul's, Covent Garden, about 9.45 a.m. The flowers were fine: huge branches of pussy willow, rosemary, buttercup yellow narcissi and apples, all in terracotta pots or baskets. I rearranged them to frame the altar. David Hutt arrived and we went through everything. As I tried out the pulpit, a figure appeared and stretched up his hand holding a tiny posy of winter garden flowers with a little card attached: 'To a very special lady . . .' It was the Queen Mother's page. I was so touched.

Last week there was the crisis of Robert Tear being ill but the Royal Opera House sprang to and produced John Mark Ansley, a quite wonderful singer. He sang Lensky's aria in Russian from the gallery at the back. I had to go to the Garrick Club in order to arrange the seating for the lunch and then dash back. It was a grey, lustreless, wet day. *The Times* and *Telegraph* appeared, along with a photographer. I retreated into Mark Oakley's office, where we all assembled in a somewhat pell-mell and muddled way. Antonia [Fraser] was in brilliant cerise, rather wonderful but quite thrown when I told her that Mary Henderson was dying. Alan Bennett arrived, looking like a 1950s provincial university student with a marvellous head of still-brown hair; Patrick Garland was in a corduroy suit; Patricia Routledge in blue beneath swathes of black capes; and John Tooley, besuited as usual. David Hutt, Mark Oakley and Wesley Carr put on the works, all in copes.

You could watch the church fill up on the television monitor. There came the moment when the decision was taken to fill the choir stalls and later they carried in the churchyard benches. I would reckon that there were some four hundred and fifty there, jammed. It was a huge turn-out.

Off we went on the dot and, because everything had been talked through in terms of movement and pauses, the result was flawless. The flow of it was perfect, and so also was the service sheet, sepia on ivory, with Julia's drawings of Souci, baskets of apples, cats, the garden and wellington boots. There was also the contrast of poetry, prose, communal and solo singing, and varieties of voice, from Patrick's slightly Gielgudian to Alan Bennett's North Country. It was touching laying that great sheaf of rosemary festooned with blue and yellow ribbons on the altar at the opening. It brought our house and garden right into the rain-sodden Metropolis. So there it was – the welcome, 'We plough the fields and scatter', the laying of the sheaf on the altar by me and my reading of the opening passage of *The Laskett: Story of a Garden.* Then came Patrick reading Andrew Marvell, Lensky's aria, John Tooley's address (a trifle too long, but fine), a hymn, Alan reading Patrick's account of Julia's set for *Brief Lives*, music from *Onegin* again (the organist adequate, but at sea from time to time), Antonia reading the Gospel with Christ the Gardener, David with the prayers and Patricia reading 'Remember me . . .' Then the hymn 'Now thank we all our God . . .' and finally the Dean's blessing. And then it was over. I'm told that it was marvellous and I just know that all of it was so *her*.

The lunch at the Garrick went off with no problems. I'm never sure whether Harold [Pinter] might take umbrage or be awkward. But he was in radiant form and I put him between John Tooley and Alexandra Bastedo. It worked! He even sprang up and thanked me. I was truly touched.

The day went on and on and on. Down to the Abbey for a meeting about royal peculiars and the government inquiry. Everything was going well, it seems. Then Evensong followed by the Audit Dinner. I found myself next to Garfield Weston's son. It must be extraordinary to own Fortnum's, Selfridges and Heal's. So there was much talk as to how to revive the latter and not do it on a retro basis.

28 JANUARY

John Cornforth re-enters my life

It was as though life had gone backwards, as if I was to pick up pre-marital threads of existence, although all of us were three decades older at least. In John Cornforth's case not only three decades but seemingly as many stones in weight. He is now enormous and his beaming features are sunk into a halo of pink flesh.

The flat in Clarence Gate Gardens was virtually the same, although infinitely more cluttered, floor to ceiling with prints and pictures and every sort of horizontal surface with things. It was claustrophobic and I longed for the light. Everyone now had to eat in the kitchen, which is no monument to modernity or cleanliness. I shuddered when I saw the grimy pans from which dinner was disgorged. But it was all so well meant, a kindly rescuing job of me, although at times I felt that it was he who needed rescuing!

This was a life lived as though nothing had changed and by shutting out the real world and where we'd got now in terms of email and the Internet. I think that John thought that my life and diary were blank, whereas, on the contrary, my problem was how to get through it all. Old bachelors like this must have existed in Victorian times, shuffling around their littered apartments. His interests and preoccupations were still where they were all those years ago: interior decoration in the eighteenth century, the wealth and other taxation problems and their impact on historic houses, etc. There have been no new intellectual horizons. He left *Country Life* ages ago and they treated him well, but the subtext of it since he left is largely one of disapproval.

There we sat, going down the list of all those we used to know and still do, on and off, from my pre-marital days. It was as though I was passing some sort of test. All I could feel was, yes, they did figure from time to time but my life had moved on three times since – with marriage, the V&A, leaving the V&A and now, with Julia's death, a fourth time. Each occasion has brought a new configuration of life and people, which, in fact, I've found enriching. I felt an affection for this old Cheshire Cat purring in his nest, but I don't want to end up like that.

3 FEBRUARY

The garden

There's no escaping it. It is going to have to be all change like everything else in my life. First the box disease and now the leylandii beetle. The decision had to be taken to remove the huge 65-yard-long hedge along Elizabeth Tudor Avenue. It cost £6,000 to take it out but they did a splendid job owed, as usual, to Steve Tomlin. One cannot but deny that it is a huge change. The division between the main garden and The Folly has been dissolved. In gardening one must be positive and always look for new opportunities. I'd been training pieces of topiary here and there, so I moved them all into the new space as a topiary chequerboard. It already looks exciting. The huge border seen over the golden privet, beech and *Acer campestre* hedge was reversed. Suddenly there's a wonderful opportunity to make a stunning flower border, so I etched in a wave-like line to echo the waves of the ER beech hedge. We started to move out shrubs and put things like box in. Meanwhile, the Nutcracker garden had to be sorted out; the *Rosa* 'Wickwar' and much else was removed. The trouble was that Julia planted just about everywhere. I felt a tinge of guilt and remorse as Shaun [one of my gardeners] and I pronounced a death sentence on some of the trees, but when they were dug up they had no root. They couldn't grow there, struggling up to get some light, so brave decisions had to be made. After thirty years a garden calls for radical reappraisal. Somehow it is all change. The result is a far greater clarity in the structure and the plants are seen to advantage and given the space they need to grow properly. Inevitably the snowdrop garden and walk reduce me to tears.

7 FEBRUARY

Early spring flowers

I worked in the garden, planting up the new great border with box accents. It began to look very exciting, with its bold curves and the glossy green box domes within re-echoing the topiary chequerboard that has replaced the vast leylandii hedge. Gardening never ceases to amaze me, how quickly disasters open up eyes and possibilities. I can't wait to see the border this summer and I rushed up to the local garden centre and bought up a mass of herbs, along with old-fashioned plants like hollyhocks and lupins. And the David Austin roses left over from replanting the Rose Garden – 'Eglantyne', 'William Morris' and 'Windflower' – I also scattered through the border.

Everywhere I looked there were swathes of snowdrops and aconites like ribbons and pools of white and yellow running through the garden. Every so often I was overcome with memories of Julia – this is her season, along with the autumn – and grief seized me.

9 FEBRUARY

Windsor, the College of Arms and a check-up

This was not an easy week. The first time I presented the Laskett book before an audience it was a sell-out with a waiting list at Methvens in Windsor. I didn't anticipate how difficult I would find this. After all, I'd read that opening passage flawlessly at both Julia's funeral and the service of thanksgiving. But at Windsor there were moments when my voice broke and I paused, wondering whether I could go on. It was a terrible strain, my emotions pounding and grief tugging at me. But I got through it, although I nearly didn't finish reading the epilogue of the book, faltering before the last paragraph about death and my ashes and the orchard and the blessed rosemary. But I made it. It was a wonderful audience and I made them laugh with other bits from the book and I was jolly with the questions. They all knew what I was going through. On analysing it afterwards I wondered why I had found it so difficult. On the other occasions when all of us gathered there we were paying tribute to Julia. On this occasion the focus was not on her but me, and I realised the huge affection in which that audience held me and the thought overwhelmed me.

It was also the evening of the Beaton show at the National Portrait Gallery. The Gallery had never told me, and I was quite upset about that, but it had not been intentional. So I felt that I ought at least to go to the dinner and I'm glad that I did. They are always so sweet to me. Sandy Nairne is a terrific success and I feel a glow at having contributed to the ascent of both him and Charles Saumarez Smith, both of whom have done the place proud. The next generation of Smileys were there, he a mild, portly man, very surprised when I said that Cecil terrified me. He did. She was a barnstormer who said that 'We in the family didn't think anything of him', to which I replied that families were like that, as I know.

On Thursday I worked all day at the College of Arms on coronations and went again to the National Portrait Gallery to do a dialogue on Cecil Beaton with Sandy Nairne to a full house, much to my surprise. Sandy thought that it was a wow, but I really couldn't judge. Afterwards various kindly ghosts from my past came up, which was touching. We had supper and Pim Baxter, their lively fundraiser, joined us and we talked of the Gallery's plans for its 150th celebrations. When I realised that they could have Trafalgar Square, I said 'Grab it' and put on an enormous people's day with artists like Hockney doing portraits and masks of the famous available to wear, all the fun of the fair. And, yes, do the grand fundraising evening but away from the other event because that is the balance and reflects where we are now.

I had what we call my first MOT with Dr Nigel Scott-Moncrieff, who seemed to think that I was a model for my age! But I then fell down in Piccadilly outside Fortnums and ripped my trousers and found myself later in Harvey Nichols buying a suit by a Japanese couturier. It is a knock-out, but I shouldn't have.

The task of clearing Julia's workroom at Morpeth Terrace is a deeply eroding experience. I stuffed black bin bag after black bin bag, on and on and on. I can't hang on to all those boxes labelled 'Arab faces', 'Austria', 'Country dancing', 'Old wallpaper', etc., etc. I now have to decide what to do with her design archive. More and more I think that it should go to the Theatre Museum, where it would be kept intact in a central, accessible repository. I can't see the sense of keeping it myself. All of this calls for a degree of urgency as they will be redoing Morpeth and installing another bathroom, as well as creating my bedsitter in London.

On Tuesday I went to the launch of Simon Thurley's Hampton Court book in the Wellington Arch, an eccentric venue. I'm glad that

English Heritage now has Apsley House and that the Wellingtons have been defeated. This was a nerve-racking event, for there was gathered the art and architecture mafia. Simon is a perky, small-built man whose energy seems boundless. I hope that he doesn't burn himself out. Charles Saumarez Smith was there, quite a portly figure these days, and also the journalist Simon Jenkins. And then there was someone quite small who kept on smiling at me and winking and I couldn't think who it was. He came up, covered me with kisses and I introduced him to someone as Wayne Sleep. Oh dear, it was Jasper Conran. Well, he took it bravely and he's so engaging and bright and more than over the top. And he collects Tudor pictures. 'I don't like your father,' I said. 'I know,' was the reply. But Jasper's an original and they're rare.

6 MARCH

The folly of saying 'yes'

I want to get on with things but I can't. People come at me and I've said 'yes' to everything, realising that it was necessary but it was also a mistake. So here I am, in London for a second weekend. The previous one had been a pile-up, from a Geoffrey Robinson *New Statesman* lunch, to introducing Brian Allen at the Royal Geographical Society for the first World Monuments Fund in Britain lecture, to a reading from the Laskett book at the Orange Tree Theatre in Richmond. I hadn't taken in that the latter was theatre-in-the-round, seats and a scaffold gallery encircling the performer. In a split second I had to re-orchestrate the reading into this form of theatre, arranging chairs and thinking how I could move around and face all four sides. It worked but I was done in afterwards.

But to revert to where I started. Today was good works day for the Buckinghamshire Gardens Trust: a lecture on The Laskett garden to a sell-out house at Waddesdon. There's something immaculate about any Rothschild house, which always has everything – taste, style, attention to detail, also in a way a generosity – but somehow humanity is always missing. I can't quite explain this. Perhaps it has just got lost amidst so much borrowed plumage.

This is an expensive arcadia, but we were bidden to lunch at The Pavilion, which I recall from the cluttered days of Dolly de Rothschild and Miss Brassey. Jacob is a year younger than me. He's softened at the edges from our last encounter and I felt that I'd been asked out of a genuine sense of kinship in a weird way. The Pavilion is beautiful, ordered and symmetrical, an elegant juxtaposition of old and new, like bought *boiserie* with a Giacometti chandelier. Everything was spotless, but I longed for signs of a newspaper or a magazine. But they were all in welcoming mood, headed by Jacob of the supreme intelligence and the hangdog face. I felt no pressure to pay court, as so many do. But Mary Keen appeared, larger and layered and blustering. She must have been paying court, for she had driven the whole way here for lunch from Cirencester. Whatever for? It's such a release to be out of all that kow-towing. Who cares? I don't want anything from Jacob and he wants nothing from me. Odd really. But it's good to see all that porcelain and the rest of it used and loved and appreciated. They all carolled how marvellous Jacob had been in the National Trust series on television that week. I saw it. I didn't find it that pleasant. He emerged like a twentieth-century Duca di Mantova with a sycophantic court.

16 MARCH

Coastal Command commemorated

Things can go wrong, even at the Abbey. This was the great day of
the service to mark the dedication of a memorial to the RAF Coastal Command. The RAF grandees were festooned with medals and
their womenfolk hatted. The ceremony was to begin in the cloister,
where the Dean was to dedicate the handsome memorial. I nobbled
Chris Chivers, who told me: 'You stand here', indicating a cross of
sticking plaster on the floor. 'When the procession starts, you follow
the Royal Suite.' Alas, much of this was not to be, nor also for many
others, as panic set in when Prince Michael of Kent arrived ten minutes before his scheduled royal arrival time and the Queen no less
than fifteen minutes before hers. Unheard of! The Lord Mayor of
Westminster arrived after the Queen and therefore missed the line-
up. I got into position next to David Burden, who was on a crutch
(a victim of tobogganing), and could glimpse the flurry of copes on
the kerbside without. Down the line the royals went, the Duke of
Edinburgh saying what a picture I made in my ruff and robe against
a tapestry of RAF flags. Then the presentations went wrong as the
line-up of the diplomatic representatives had been reversed and poor
David Hutt found himself presenting someone who was someone
else! Things then began to get badly out of sync. The Abbey bells
had been timed to peal joyfully at 11.30 a.m., when Her Majesty
arrived; but by now we were fifteen minutes in advance, so when
the Dean found himself in the midst of the bidding prayers the bells
suddenly burst forth, drowning him out. We were meant to process
up the nave to the hymn 'All people that on earth do dwell', but it
was long over by the time we got there. I was suddenly told to follow
the Dean's verger at the head of the procession instead of bringing

up the rear. Heaven alone knows why, but as in all great ceremonials you assume a mask of composure and just keep going. I don't think that anyone really noticed and the rest went as planned. Afterwards there was a post-mortem as to why it had all gone wrong. My theory was that the times had been deliberately changed to confuse any terrorists, this being the week of the ghastly Madrid bombings.

18 MARCH

Diarmuid Gavin, Nicky Haslam and Clarissa Avon

More of London. Up to attend a gathering to celebrate my return as President of the Garden History Society and, the next evening, to introduce their lecturer, an Irish television gardener called Diarmuid Gavin, an engaging, tousled-haired man oozing sex rather than any profound horticultural knowledge, as the lecture swiftly revealed. On Thursday Hugo Vickers gave a lunch for the Cecil Beaton exhibition at Sotheby's. The show was nearly all blow-ups and, therefore, curiously old-fashioned, but there was a sprinkling of vintage prints, including some I didn't know. Lunch was for twelve, not especially notable except for the apparition of Nicky Haslam, who, I must admit, is very funny and doesn't miss a nuance. But he is a serious monument to not dressing your age – within reason. His hair is now short and spiky, dyed various shades of brown and auburn, and the rest of him encased in a bomber jacket and chinos in a shade of grey. The sight of him next to Clarissa Avon was to be seen to be believed. I said to Nicky what a memorial of times past such a grand lunch was, complete with flunkeys. It took me back twenty-five years. It can't, I said, go on in private houses any more. Nicky fished around and said that such events had now migrated to restaurants, but that Marguerite Littman, who must by now be a huge age, was still keeping the flag flying in Chester Square. I said to Clarissa, who was on a stick but tough and game, that I thought that she lived in the country. She'd gone to live in a flat in a house by Lutyens near Oxford. She said that she'd left it as she couldn't stand Lutyens. I asked her why on earth she'd moved there in the first place: 'It was cheap,' came the reply. At any rate she's now in London and has got out of Social Services taxis to take her anywhere at £1.50 a ride. And she also has a domestic to look after her, who even deals with the plumber et al. What a comment on the times.

26 MARCH

The George III exhibition opening and David Cannadine

I came up to London to be taken to a dinner at the Drapers' Company by the engaging John Patten, the hall like some belle époque casino, all glitz and mirrors. The next evening there was the opening of the George III exhibition at the Queen's Gallery. Just about everyone was there, a kind of court in waiting for the next reign and a rally for all those who can't stand New Labour and all its eternal populist dumbing down. Here was taste and splendour with no apologies. The Prince of Wales was in benign mood and Camilla seemed to be working her way discreetly around, a slightly hunched, short figure, like the wife of a public school headmaster.

There they all were: John Harris, farouche; David Starkey, a small, portly figure; boyish Marcus Binney with Anne, almost twice the size I remember her; Nico Henderson, pushing on bravely in spite of losing Mary; Fortune Grafton; Jane Abdy; Drue Heinz (who couldn't get over how marvellous I looked – was she expecting me to be ancient and doubled up? But she's a trouper and a giver); the

Carew Poles; Diane Lever; Coral Samuel; John Casey; Thomas Camoys (the budget had grim news for country house owners); Michael Heseltine, still looking pretty good; Fiona Reynolds, leaving with a suitcase; Diane Nutting; Mary Anna Marten; Geoffrey de Bellaigue; Frances Lloyd, etc.

After the private view I had dinner with David Cannadine at the Athenaeum. He seems to have gone to the right, horrified by his visit to Chequers with Linda, where the key guest was Cilla Black. He's hugely, mercurially bright, with a long face and rather starry eyes. This was a dinner about the woes of the age, on the last of the Whigs (Roy Jenkins), on the proletarianisation of everything, on the death of the universities, on the fact that even the Foreign Office was against war with Iraq, and what a mess we were in and likely to be stuck there for some time as the ghastly, messianic Blair will come back with a reduced majority. All of this was terribly depressing. I was urged to write the sequel to Noel Annan's *Our Age*; but could I? He has a point. Everyone at the top now is post-Second World War grammar school. We lamented the absence of any great people, no icons except trash, totties in dresses held on by Velcro. Where are the Kenneth Clarks, Isaiah Berlins, et al? And most of the population is now so well off that they don't care.

MAY

Retrospective

It is nearly the end of May and so much has happened but I haven't recorded any of it. Much of it is work, like the new series that I'm doing for *Country Life* on historic towns, and the other series, also for them, entitled *A Letter from The Laskett Garden*. But the nicest project of all has been the Radio 4 series, *The English Garden*. I've always loved radio and it's come back into my life, albeit that the locations and days chosen for recording the programmes turned out to be freezing cold and raining non-stop. The result was that I lost my voice and had to have a course of antibiotics. Every programme begins in The Laskett garden and then moves to another location for a conversation with the likes of Jane Brown, Anna Pavord and Jenny Uglow.

Easter came and went and, as a result of being now able to drive [I had had to learn after Julia died], I've become a cathedralist. I went to all the Holy Week liturgies in Hereford and loved it. What a joy after years of being one out of the fifteen worshippers in a village church caterwauling the hymns. How wonderful to be in a church that was full, had good ceremonial and music. Later Michael Tavinor, the Dean, came to supper and I made a new friend.

On the weekend of 16 to 18 April I went to stay with the Carew Poles at Antony House. Richard is a delightful, kind man and President of the Royal Horticultural Society. He and Mary make up a good, no-nonsense couple and, although the house is grand, live in it virtually servantless. Breakfast was in the kitchen, with them and the guests filling up the dishwasher! My bedroom seemed to be some annexe to the laundry with an ironing board and iron to hand. The house is un-done-up pre-1980s. But it was jolly, although the fact that the Heseltines didn't show because Anne was in hospital was a blow. But the Faringdons were there and also a large, engaging ex-lady-in-waiting to Princess Diana, Anne Beckwith-Smith. On Saturday the Ondaatjes arrived, I suppose Richard having his eye on them for a dollop of cash. I liked them. There was also an ex-courtier with wife number two. Oh heavens, he was one of those types who just don't relate to where we are, head over heels with courtly manners, which in fact were performed in rather a *de haut en bas* manner to people like the lady gardener, touching his check flat cap and shaking her by the hand. I could see how they would have gone down with the Royal Household, but really they both belonged to a vanished world.

The garden at Antony has a splendid fountain by William Pye and is otherwise handsome, although not so much a garden as a foreground to the surrounding landscape. On Saturday we went to the Eden Project, which is a huge whizz, very clever indeed, full of life and a very great achievement by Tim Smit. The tropical green-house was a tour de force, with imaginative touches like native huts. The Mediterranean greenhouse was less successful, lacking mystery and drifting towards kitsch.

On 1 to 2 May I had my reunion weekend: Michael Leonard, Anthony Powell and Astrid Zydower came to stay. Astrid I first met at the temporary studio she had had at Alexandra Palace, where she was doing the massive figures for the *Midsummer Night's Dream* tableau in the 1964 Shakespeare Exhibition. Now in her mid-seventies she remains quite unaltered. She should have had a great public career but, as one dealer put it, she was 'accident prone' – that is, she couldn't deliver on time. So she has never had the commissions that she should have had. Now she's kept going by Charlie Watts of the Rolling Stones, doing pieces for his gardens. But she's happy.

Michael, who drew me as an Ingres, has just had another show at Thomas Gibson's gallery with more portraits in the style of the Old Masters, all brilliant, especially Brian Sewell *en profile* as a kind of Robespierre figure, and also some nudes. Life for him now seems, like Astrid's, on an equilibrium. Perhaps we all reach this – or should by seventy?

Anthony Powell was just off to do another Polanski film and also to see his costumes for *Anything Goes*, which is being transferred to Broadway. Large and hugely bubbly, he's never tired of life with the stars, always internationally on the move, for decades propping up the likes of Katharine Hepburn or Bette Davies. I don't know how he can bear it.

So, much to their surprise, I drove in and picked them up at the station, where they stood *en tableau* like a group of refugees. There was so much excitement and chatter. In the afternoon I took them on a tour of local beauties and on Sunday we went over to David Walker's for lunch.

He too goes back a long way. He had worked with Julia and Lila de Nobili on the *Charge of the Light Brigade*. Camp and contained, we had persuaded him to come south and he's settled in Leominster, making a really wonderful house. Having spent years in the theatre he can't stand it any more, doesn't want to do it and always leaves before the first night. He'd just supervised his *Semele* back on stage at the Royal Opera House, which Michael said was a knock-out. David had Bob Ringwood staying, now resettled in England after over a decade in Hollywood. He too loved the 'stars' and he and Ant were 'off'. Ant was very funny about going to see Bette Davies, who insisted that she had to wear this wig, a monster with sausage curls and God knows what else. Ant is no fool and, instead of damning it, led her over to a mirror and said, 'Let's start with your great assets, those fabulous eyes and cheekbones. Now,' he said, sweeping a great handful of false curls to one side, 'see how they're displayed to advantage.' The old crone lit up. By the time he'd finished he'd got all he wanted. Worse than what it must be like sometimes working in Buckingham Palace. But how good old friends are – and we laughed and laughed and laughed.

Meanwhile, I trundle around flogging my literary wares. I did an *Oldie* lunch in Stratford-upon-Avon with A.N. Wilson and Jeremy Lewis. It all went swimmingly and up came Richard Pasco and Barbara Leigh-Hunt. That took me back to the National Portrait Gallery in the late Sixties! Dickie had stopped acting and Ba, having had a fall, at the moment is only playing wheelchair parts; but what a delight to see them!

A.N. Wilson entered my life again when I went to his launch for

My Name Is Legion at Random House. That was in the aftermath of a grand dinner given by the Quintons at Brooks's. I don't think I enjoyed it that much. Everyone, bar John and Louise Patten, was so old. Why can't there be a livelier mix? Instead it was the Carringtons, well on in their eighties; Clarissa Avon ditto; John Julius Norwich and Mollie, also well on the way . . . I suppose that there must have been fourteen in all. The Quintons themselves aren't in the first flush of youth either but I like him, seventy-eight, large and smiling like a Chinese god, and she dressed like all rich old American ladies, as though her physical attractions were still worth looking at. By that age they aren't and you need to do a cover-up job and avoid showing mottled scraggy and saggy flesh. This was a dinner of the old kind that I remember so well, a gathering of actors in the circle of the established stars in what was now a somewhat dated sky. And I don't want to be dragged back into that.

Well, to return to Andrew Wilson's party, which was notable as far as I was concerned for the arrival of Gerard and Rosemary Irvine like two figures from an Angus Wilson novel. Gerard had deflated since last year and lost a huge amount of weight. I kissed him on both cheeks and told him that he looked twenty years younger, which indeed he did. But he's weak on his pins and therefore sat; but Andrew is always kind enough to ask them and they love basking in the limelight. He told me that he wasn't giving me a copy of his novel because he knew that I wouldn't read it. He's right, I wouldn't.

May began with an odd week, opening with a *Country Life* gathering at Brompton Oratory, of all places, to launch Kathryn Bradley-Hole's *The Lost Gardens of England*, a terrific book reproducing all the early *Country Life* photographs, in the main by Charles Latham. The priests and brothers at the Oratory looked pure Counter Reformation and I learnt that John Cornforth used to go off with a group of them each summer, trolling around shrines in Italy hearing Latin masses. What odd sides he had.

Well, I only got back for a day when, on 8 May, up I went again to preach at St John's Wood Church on the occasion of the dedication of the new silver tabernacle doors by Rod Kelly. Preaching is a whole new dimension to my life and, coached by David Hutt, I'm getting better at it. The format is around a thousand words of double-spaced typing lasting about nine minutes, otherwise the congregation switches off. It's quite a challenge as a genre: the biblical text and how to move into it from reminiscence and then in and out of it to a conclusion. This, I think, is my number four and the best so far! It all went off with a swing with good liturgy and music. Anders Bergquist, the incumbent, has a radiant if, at times, slightly absent quality but he gets things right in a middling way, which I now prefer to the excesses of John Cornforth's requiem at Bourne Street. But *chacun à son goût*.

Monday 10 May was spent discovering Monmouth with Clive Aslet for the second in the series of towns articles for *Country Life*. Here is a jewel on the level of Ludlow, whole streets of Georgian houses, pure Rowlandson. The next day, 11 May, I drove Sarah Greenall to the HHA [Historic Houses Association] Garden of the Year Award, one of my longest drives so far. It was a gorgeous day and I dressed elegantly in a flowered shirt, open at the neck, and faded denim jacket; but all the other men were in dark grey suits and ties as though they were lunching at the Athenaeum. Johnny and Anne Chambers deserve the prize, their water garden with its tall metallic blossoms trickling water has revivified Kiftsgate for the twentieth century. The lunch was interminable and there were a lot of people there from a world that has gone.

On 15 and 16 May Hugh and Judy Johnson came to stay and I gave my gardeners lunch on a perfect day, with champagne on the terrace and the table dressed with a white tulip vase filled with cowslips arising from a tableau of eighteenth-century porcelain figures.

Which brings me to last week, when I had to come up for Patrick

Cormack's sixty-fifth birthday lunch at the Ritz. They've been so kind to me since Julia's death, but I can't stand the Ritz dining room! It was a small, very nice gathering: Richard and Rose Luce, Jamie and Sylvia Crathorne, and a violinist whose name I've forgotten. And then, on Wednesday 19 May, John Cornforth's requiem and thence back home. Jenny Uglow and Charles Quest-Ritson came on the 20th to do bits for the Radio 4 garden series, and Julian and Isobel Bannerman came to lunch and to see the garden on Friday 21 May, on which day I travelled to London to do the Sutton Valence School Speech Day on the 22nd.

The great thing to do if you get landed with a speech day is to look interesting, so I put on my Marc Jacobs pink suit. 'That'll stop the clock,' I thought, and it did. But it all went well and I travelled down and back with David Hutt. By the time I got back to Morpeth Terrace I was exhausted and fell asleep on the bed.

What is the moral of this interminable Diary entry – which doesn't record everything by any means? I don't think I have been so busy and done so much for years. Partly this is the result of saying 'yes' to things after Julia died. It is important to be active. But I do long for it to quieten down a bit so that I can get on with coronations [my next big book], which I must finish this year. Still, I am hugely stimulated. And it's the Chelsea Flower Show tomorrow!

19 MAY

The passing of John Cornforth

It was during this period that John Cornforth was whisked off to hospital, a rapidly expanding brain tumour having been diagnosed and, before one could draw a breath, he was dead. I'd had dinner with him on 26 January in his Marylebone lair, when it seemed like old bachelor times. And now, at sixty-six, he's gone. But, like Julia, it was swift.

He was a strange man, a benign balloon really. He'd written a hundred and fifty articles for *Country Life* and was greatly beloved by the chatelaines. He had a great interest in Irish art and also in interior decoration and the history of textiles and their use. All these were pioneer topics and he encouraged many.

I got to the High Mass of Requiem at St Mary's Bourne Street on 19 May. I'd never been to that church before, with its between-the-wars baroque Anglo-Catholic trumpery. The church was packed. Jennifer Jenkins, now somewhat bent, gave an address that no one could hear. The Mass itself was performed, thanks to much prompting, with an abundance of incense and the putting on and off of birettas. There was something odd about the absence of a coffin, for John had, by then, been cremated. Taking a seat at the front, I noticed what was a small box covered with a rich fabric and tied with a ribbon and a rose, looking not unlike an expensive box of chocolates. It was John's ashes. At the close of the Mass this was censed and sprinkled with holy water, rather absurd as the clerical party went round this tiny box. Afterwards the holy water stoup was left for members of the congregation to do likewise, so I gave John a triple dousing in the name of the Trinity.

All of this took me back to my youth and the Church of the Annunciation, Bryanston Street. Today all of this is more Roman than the Romans; so overcome was I with it all that, seeing the communicant next to me open his mouth to receive the sacrament, I did likewise while a silver plate was held below by a server. I'd never done it that way before. I'd no idea that John Cornforth went there but the Church of England is marvellously all-embracing. The Lennox Berkeley music was fine.

We then all traipsed along a few doors in Bourne Street to David Mlinaric's studio, where there were champagne and canapés and a rowdy get-together of the heritage mafia, decorators and art historians.

30 MAY

The Prince of Wales at Hampton Court

Two days on from the press view of the Chelsea Flower Show I went down to Hampton Court to a gathering to celebrate the replanting of the avenues either side of the Long Water. Can't think why I was asked, except that I had been always boldly in support of it. This is one of the great pieces of baroque garden design, very undervalued: a huge sheet of water now flanked with elegant rows of lime trees, beautiful, whereas before it was a mangled mix of tooth and gap.

A little tent had been erected near the Long Water, where a tree was placed with a heap of earth next to it and a shining spade for HRH to do the job. It was a gathering of Royal Palaces officials in the main and interested local amenity society officers, a lot of ghosts from my past. However, the point of putting pen to paper was HRH, who trotted on in the inevitable grey suit (I've never seen him in any other colour), his hair scraped back – or rather what's left of it. There's a dapper quality in his old-fashioned dress and movements which remind me very much of his great-uncle, the Duke of Windsor. But what struck me most were his features. When in repose this is the face of tragedy, haunted, lined and browbeaten. And then, if you make him laugh – which I always set out to do for he has his grandmother's sense of frivolity (in my case I waved an arm and suggested moving back into Hampton Court) – his face drops twenty years into the mask of comedy, impish and twinkling. But countenance-wise, for his mid-fifties he's not worn well.

LATE JUNE

Too many public performances and clearing up

Too many performances. My fault through saying 'yes'. Three in a row during the first week of the month alone: a reading I compiled entitled 'A Pergola of Poetry and Prose' on gardens in Ludlow, propping up the Elgar Society in a hotel near Ledbury; hosting and speaking at the Garden History Society's annual garden party; and performing at the Hay Literary Festival – all enjoyable but too close to each other. At the same time work began on demolishing and rebuilding the porch, as well as various other works in the garden: the stone balls forming an entrance to the new flower border and the final in Julia's recast *Nutcracker garden*.

All of this and the London flat, still awaiting the arrival of the builders, reflects my decision to put everything in order now. That links in to the weight of clearing up after Julia, who could part with nothing. What is the use of hanging on to everything? I must give careful thought and action to this. But I did, as a start, take a collection of some twenty fans I discovered to Hélène Alexander at the Fan Museum in Greenwich. Dick, her husband, had died, but she is still amazing and the little museum is a total delight. She told me what they all were and, bar one, I said do take any which might be of use to the museum. She chose two very pretty eighteenth-century Portuguese ones, shimmering with brilliants. I said that the label should read 'Given by Sir Roy Strong in memory of the Oman Family'. The rest I think I should sell, bar offering the rare Thomas Robins one of the gardens of St John's College, Oxford, as they were relaid out in the landscape style, to the college. They know it exists and expressed a wish to acquire it. If they don't want it, I'll put it into Sotheby's. Hélène put a high valuation on it, which, I thought, would pay for all the building works.

The move to this stage was prompted by the visit of my solicitor Julian Chadwick. I really must, he said, list things and where they are to go, a ghastly job. But at least I've done the fans and I'm taking all the jewellery to the V&A early in July to find out what it all is before I give pieces to Julia's cousins and friends. I'm haunted, however, by the thought that I might do the wrong thing.

3 JULY

Reflections in Bristol: decisions reached on the house

This has been a crammed few weeks. Julia's studio block I have at last come to terms with. One Saturday morning I spotted the builders' skip outside. It crossed my mind that when they went, it went too. It broke the spell. Into it went most of the fabric store, piles of paper bags, boxes, old cosmetic bottles, electrical debris – Julia couldn't part with anything. I just couldn't leave it as it was. As the 'never less than direct' Valerie Kingman said to me: 'Until you get rid of the rubbish you can't see what you have got.' But what a mammoth job! That skip was soon filled and a second even larger one came and that was filled and now there's a third. But I go through everything and pull out yet another mound for the Bristol Theatre Collection [to which I gave Julia's archive]. Two other things came together. I suddenly realised that I must create an Archive Room. That meant clearing half of the vast upper studio space, running a wall down the middle and putting up shelving. Then I could bring into it the whole of the garden archive and along with it those of the Omans, Trevelyans, James Anderson Rose [who married Emily Winter Chadwick, half-sister of Anne Oman] and myself, box it all, shelve it and leave it all in order. Only when that space was cleared could that be done, so into boxes I swept the unbelievable morass of clutter amidst which Julia worked. I was driven on by the fact that the builders were giving up in 2005. They're the best we've ever had and they're eager to get on with the job. I must move on. That achieved, I'll turn the rest of the studio block into another living area with a bedroom, sitting room and bathroom, which could be used for a guest. It could equally be used for someone to tend me when I'm decrepit. Who knows?

Yesterday I went through the Oman and Trevelyan jewellery. I took out the antique cameo rings that I could wear. God knows why she didn't give them to me long ago, but that's how it was! The rest I boxed and labelled to take to the V&A to identify. I see no point in hanging on to all this. Cousins and friends of Julia should be given pieces and the rest sold. At the back of my mind lurks the knowledge that the garden lacks some wonderful contemporary piece. That may be an honourable way of spending that money.

Meanwhile, the builders have created the new entrance porch. Stunning. It changes the whole ethos of the façade. Looking at early photographs it dawned on me that the proportions were still neoclassical Georgian. It occurred to me that I could superimpose four giant Tuscan pilasters onto the façade and, urged on by David Walker, demolish the 1920s bays and replace them with Georgian/ Regency windows with a classical pediment copied from the ones at nearby Clytha Park. The effect will be that of a Palladian doll's house. We've always said that the house wasn't interesting but it can be made interesting. I'm also reducing or taking out the yew hedge across the façade, thus throwing house and garden together. One must never stop moving on. The house would then look interesting, which it never has.

But I'm tired. I just want to get through the next fortnight, climb on to *Minerva* [to lecture for a Swan Hellenic cruise] and go to sleep. But I have crossed many bridges – as she would have wished . . .

8 JULY

Grief

I went to dinner at the German Embassy and left in the pouring rain to walk back to Morpeth Terrace. Suddenly I was seized with compulsive grief and tears en route. Still howling, I got into the flat and rested my head on a wall, clinging to it with the tears falling. Oh God, how I miss her.

II AUGUST

Home thoughts from abroad: remodelling the house

I am writing this at Masone, close to Parma, staying with Franco Maria Ricci and Laura Casalis. Distance lends perspective and I am glad of the quiet, the rest, the good company, the food, the sun – *la vita italiana*. I had left The Laskett on the eve of the painters coming to decorate the new Archive Room.

What began a few months ago as the rebuilding of the front entrance porch, which had been decided upon last year, has now escalated into a reconstitution of whole areas of the house. One decision precipitates another. The builders announcing their retirement next year triggered a keen desire to hang on to them. Also a realisation that this was a whole new phase of life, perhaps quite a long one, even if it was one's last. The Strongs and Smarts seem long-lived, so I could reckon to make eighty-eight or ninety. Father died in his ninetieth year, Mother in her eighty-ninth. It's no use hanging around. So I decided to spend quite a lot of money and do everything now.

Needless to say that, once started, this turned out to be a mush-rooming process. I couldn't leave the studio block as it was. The pile-up of things, the gloom and emotion of it all. Having cleared one side of Julia's big studio room with the idea of running a wall down one side and making a garden and Oman archive, we're now on to skip five from the studio alone: some index of just what a mountain of stuff had to be dumped. Still, when the room was emp-tied and the wall and the new door were up I realised that this was a glorious, light-filled space, quite unrecognisable from the world of Miss Havisham that Julia loved to dwell in. So I decided to 'lift' it with cornicing, two marbled pillars, a chair rail and two large bookcases with a third, an Oman Victorian one, to be added into the scheme. I purchased a handsome heavy gilt Victorian chandelier and a Victorian partner's desk. I will have the fine set of prints of George IV's coronation procession framed and banked on the walls. The result will be splendid.

Inevitably, once started it couldn't stop there. One load of indif-ferent studio furniture had already gone to the local saleroom. At least one if not two or three loads more will follow. On the ground floor I've gutted the photographic studio (I found thirty cameras!), where I'm putting in a bathroom. I may need one on the ground floor when I'm old! But a window has been punched into it looking out onto the farmland behind. That again had knock-ons, for Julia had three layers of curtains over every window and the hedge at the back of the block had grown up and cut off the light. All of that I want to reverse.

I also have the problem of her library. Most of it is in the stair-case well, piled heavenwards on both sides. I'm going through it for Oman/Trevelyan/Rose stuff and also I'll take anything that I can use myself. But the rest I am going to sell as it is of no use to me. When that has gone I can then punch a large hole in the staircase wall at the back and put in another window. It could look wonderful.

Meanwhile, in the house I've gutted her bathroom, a 1960s relic, turning it into a walk-in wardrobe. As the work progresses, more and more will need to be done. It seems important to make all these changes now and to get things in order. Much remains uninvestigated but going through the pile-up of stuff in cases must be essayed too. I want to leave everything *clear* and in *order*. Julia was a strange paradox. She was very ordered and there was a logic to everything. Order and logic, yes, but no *clarity*. Everywhere I look I now want clarity. I want to leave that house in order as a rather beautiful monument to a certain way of living at the end of the twentieth century.

Next Monday a second lot of builders go into the London flat. There's also a terrible pile-up there, with yet another accumulation of furniture and 'things' to come to The Laskett. This sort-out will go on until Christmas and beyond, but I'm determined to do it and then to draw a line.

But all these decisions and sortings-out have eaten time and my writing schedule has slipped. I've also been faced with the problem of the jewellery and the silver. What does one do? They aren't mine but there's no family any more. In the case of the jewellery, pieces have gone off to the cousins she liked, the Deanes, and to her women friends. The rest it is pointless to keep and I'm selling it. The same problem surrounds the silver. There's a range of stuff that I use or display. But silver entrée dishes, muffin dishes, caviar plates – what earthly use are they? To the sale they go.

As it is I'm putting in a safe, having had a nasty scare with the jewellery. People had been working on the house and someone nearly went off with three diamond pieces, the best. They had gone through my bedroom cupboards and drawers where the jewellery was secreted. These 'flash' pieces had been taken out of their boxes and envelopes and hidden in the bathroom linen cupboard for 'collection' later. It is a well-known ploy.

8 OCTOBER

Metz: more home thoughts from abroad

Time to draw a breath in a hotel room before I go off to yet another session of a conference on Gardens and Tourism. What new can I say about the last few months? Perhaps it is best summarised in two words: skip eighteen. Every day I get up at six to six thirty and go over to the stable block and start sorting out and throwing away. It has gone on and on and on . . . So I created the Archive Room [out of the old Studio]. I now love working there, but I couldn't have done as it stood. 'Of course, you couldn't,' said David Walker. 'It was like working in the middle of someone else's mind.'

The knock-on has been enormous and suddenly, now that I am quite far into the radical changes, energy-giving, like some inner force making me frame a new phase of life. Once that grand room emerged it affected everything else. With proceeds from the sale of the Oman silver and jewellery I'm making a fund to commission artists to paint the garden. Paul Brason for one. I want Richard Shirley Smith to compose a *capriccio* of all the garden ornaments, like a Piranesi ruin or similar. The entrance hall will have large empty walls, ideal for pictures; and no one that I know who has made a large garden has ever done this. It is really exciting.

I'm so glad to have had this surge of energy and new creativity. I want to leave something stunning for others to enjoy, and also to celebrate Julia.

12 OCTOBER

The summer: a retrospective

What happened? I went on *Minerva II*. Slept and wrote chapter eight [of the *Coronation* book], came back, went to Franco [Maria Ricci] and Laura – wonderful – came back, went to Krakov – fascinating. So much crowds in on me that I can't cope. Why there was no more writing done was because I was struggling to put together chapter eight, which I finally sent in late September. I'm now on to chapter nine, 1902 to 1953, so I'm on the homeward romp. This has been a revelatory book to write, the seemingly dull chapters turning out to be electrifying. But it has been an enormous task because of the vast pile of material and the problem of how to order it, sustain the argument and hold the reader. The end is in view . . .

Meanwhile, *The Arts in Britain*, the small paperback version of *Spirit of Britain*, appeared. I'm so pleased with it. They printed three thousand at £9.99 and 1,700 have already gone. This is how this book should be, available for all. I still think that it is a good book, a well-written, brave stab at something no one else has ever attempted. It had wonderful reviews at the time but I still don't think it had the recognition that it deserved. It was far more difficult to write than *The Story of Britain*.

25 OCTOBER

Julia's ashes laid to rest

I write this in 5 Little Cloister [Canon David Hutt's house in Westminster Abbey]. So much is crowding in, so much happening. This has been the turning of the tide, the passing of the first anniversary of Julia's death and funeral. So many things have fallen into place. I was lucky that both dates had fallen on a Sunday. The death date was when I first went to Hereford Cathedral, and I was so surprised and touched that she was remembered by name. As I left the cathedral I kissed the lady canon on both cheeks.

On 16 October David Hutt came down for the placing of the ashes. This was a winding up or down. It was odd because I was acutely aware that the mortal remains were neither here nor there. That was heightened because I carried those ashes through the garden, where her spirit was everywhere. David appeared in his canonicals and he asked me to put together a reminiscence and a reading. So I carried the ashes first to the Oman quince tree in the Small Orchard, where I read a couple of paragraphs from Julia's article on quinces. Beautiful. Next into the new Rose Garden that she had designed, where I said a prayer for the departed. Then to the Muff Monument and a recollection of cats, and then to the Elizabeth Tudor Avenue, where I recalled my proposal of marriage to her, a tearful moment of thanks to God for giving her to me. Along we went and up to the Ashton Arbour, where I read the last few paragraphs of The Laskett book; on into the Christmas Orchard and the urn. My last reading was the opening of St John's Gospel: 'In the beginning . . .' David said a few prayers, then lifted the lid and I lowered the container into it, he replacing it. I knelt on the ground and David placed both his hands on my head and blessed my new life. That meant much to me, to be sanctified in this my life's end. I hugged him tearfully and we made our way back to the house. I then took him out to a smashing lunch and I gave him a grand dinner in the evening. What I reflected upon was the fact that mortal remains seem irrelevant when the spirit of a person is everywhere.

19 DECEMBER

Pamela Harlech is seventy

Ages ago I got an invitation to a dinner at the London Aquarium for an unnumbered birthday for Pamela. It could only be seventy. When the day came I picked up Beatrix Miller and off we set. The car got to one end of the LCC building so we decanted ourselves and started the long walk round, gathering up other odd lost souls en route. We had been bidden to come attired 'like a fish out of water'. All that I could rise to was swagging an articulated silver fish on the end of a silver chain that came from Brazil across my black velvet jacket.

Eventually we found the Aquarium. This was one of those Black Hole of Calcutta experiences. Guide dogs were needed as we walked another mile downwards past living sculptures, women clad in fish-like bustles who vaguely gestured at you like some form of exotic traffic warden. And then, lo, we were there!

The noise was deafening as every surface was a hard one and the main wall of glass housed the sharks. It was so difficult to see anybody and no one had made much of an effort to be fish-like, except Derek Deane, the former dancer and a Princess Margaret walker, who came as a monkfish in monastic garb with a fish head. Pam was there with her Sixties lacquered bouffant hair. Her Ancient Egyptian make-up and dress rendered her imitation 1950s Elizabeth Taylor as Cleopatra. But she was enjoying herself. But oh, the murk! It was one long series of double-takes to recognise Elizabeth Jane Howard, Lois Sieff, Maggie Smith, Lucy Snowdon, Ant Powell, Peter Eyre, Sean Phillips, John Cox, the Rees-Moggs, Alexandra Bastedo . . .

We had been warned that there was to be a happening. A diver in fancy dress suddenly descended into the shark pool. Pam moved towards him while he held a large notepad as though about to take notes from her. Eventually we all went in to dinner at large round tables. The food was disappointing: minimalist abstracts of a bit of this and a bit of that arranged on a plate; any resemblance as to how it had started its life as a fresh ingredient was absent. I was between Gillian Rees-Mogg, fine, and Romana McEwen . . . Derek Deane was two along to the right, having discarded his cowl. I could glimpse Beatrix Miller wondering how she could escape. She achieved it when the cake arrived and everyone stood while she exited as Father Antony, formerly headmaster of Downside but now a humble parish priest in Suffolk, made the speech. That was very odd and also very worldly wise. While everyone stood, I, too, managed to sidle out.

THE END OF 2004

I am writing this where I have been living when in London, at the top of number 5 Little Cloister, David Hutt's residence and my temporary home while Morpeth Terrace is gutted and put together again. I've enjoyed living in the Abbey. I like walking through the Gothic cloisters and passages moving from dark to light, from light to dark, my feet treading underfoot a *mélange* of people, among them my favourite, the Abbey's plumber. It's been easy to go to the eight o'clock Mass in all the various side chapels and I gain much from that. And I'm grateful to get to know a little better the many faces that make up the Abbey community.

As the year ends I'm on time more or less to finish *Coronation*. Everything is in order to write the last chapter, starting tomorrow, and when I have everything in order I can scribble several thousand words in a day. This has been an extraordinary year, of grief and rediscovery, of the end of one period of my life and the beginning of another. Bewildering in a way and I keep hesitating and asking: 'Am I doing the right thing?'

I'm obsessed about putting things in order, so that when I go, whoever goes through everything knows what it is and can follow my ordering of it. There is still far to go. The Archive Room is up and running, although much remains to be sorted, identified and rehoused. So many crumbling documents! But I've got the conservation catalogues and can, by degrees, start ordering the files and folders needed. Although all the material is shelved in identifiable blocks – Oman, Chadwick, Anderson Rose and Strong – within the blocks much needs to be looked at. But I'm well pleased with how far I've got.

There remains the loft, however, which is crammed with suitcases and trunks. But I don't know what's in them. All that Julia said once was that in one of them there was the stamp collection left to her by a Victorian Fellow of All Souls. I have every intention of selling that, for I see no logic in hanging on to it. Indeed, all this sorting out has led me to decide to sell what is not central to the story. So Julian Chadwick has offered the Thomas Robins fan to St John's College, Oxford. It has the only record of their re-landscaping of the garden c.1750. It is very rare. [It is now in The Fan Museum, Blackheath.] Add to that the Noah's Ark cameo. That descended from Don Pomposo, the Mark British Consul in Malaga, and has an immaculate Spanish provenance, although I feel that it must somehow have slipped from the Spanish Royal Collection. The only other instances are in the Kunsthistorisches Museum, Vienna, and the Musée Condé. Both pieces I found were a nightmare to have in the house. Between them they ought to pay for the Morpeth building works and a fair amount of what I'm doing to The Laskett . . .

I am afraid that I've become slightly oblivious to the cost of all this. The results so far are so startling that I must go on. I see no point in stopping, and the house as well as the garden will be extraordinary.

But I'm on an even keel and going forward. Most of next year is in place. I know where I'm going and what I'm doing. Julia would probably be shocked at what I'm spending, but otherwise very happy that I've gone on. But inevitably I miss her.

2005

Kenneth Rose and others and Ramsgate and Pugin

The year opened slowly, a quiet time, one for getting things done. *Coronation* has been sent off to HarperCollins and so I'm between books. The epilogue to *Coronation* benefited from Wesley Carr's sharp observations, for which I was more than grateful, although his recommended reading in the theological field I found tough going.

I'm still billeted in the Abbey, which has made me love it even more. The builders are still in Morpeth Terrace and also at work in the country. It's all costing a fortune but I'm slightly past caring as it will be the last great spend-out in my lifetime. I love the transformation at The Laskett. It has changed the character of the house with its grand neoclassical and gothick sequence of rooms. What is also clear is that the house will be so much easier to run, and that is critical, in addition to being far more interesting to look at.

Wednesday 26 January was the evening of Robert Lacey's dinner for Kenneth Rose in the Jerusalem Chamber of the Abbey. It was quite a *galère*: William Shawcross with Olga Polizzi in tow, Andrew

Roberts with his scribbling partner, Antonia Fraser, John Julius Norwich, Hugo Vickers, Philip Ziegler, Sarah Bradford . . . Kenneth Rose looked in far better fettle than when I last saw him, loved it all and delivered a tour de force from a lectern. Hugo Vickers and William Shawcross were seated at opposite ends of the table, both having finished, or nearly so, their biographies of the Queen Mother. I sat next to Hugo, who was cutting his from 250,000 to 170,000 words, a parallel amputation to the one being done by A.N. Wilson to his twentieth-century book [*After the Victorians*]. Antonia has inherited her mother's arthritis and was on a stick, a knee operation pending. It's the first time I've seen her definitely look older, her face now lined. Harold didn't sound in that good a state but had gone off to see *King Lear*. This was a real gathering of a generation, every one of us bar the Roberts nymphet won't see sixty again, several won't see seventy. And all of us were outside the confines of academe.

Thursday brought lunch with the mercurial A.N. Wilson, who is now moving on to the reign of the present Queen and toying with a book on the Wagner family. That was followed by the College Meeting at the Abbey and the Audit Dinner. Friday found me in Ramsgate with Clive Aslet. What a surprise that place was, a late Georgian and Regency jewel awaiting rediscovery, poverty having been the great preserver. And we got into Pugin's little masterpiece, St Augustine's, a quite weird Gothic excrescence in the context of this classical town. But the church is beautiful, double aisled within, with rich and luminous glass, splendid wrought-ironwork screens, an astonishing towering font cover and a statue of Our Lady with a lamp like a silver ship suspended before it. The great man lies in a side chapel beneath a somewhat disappointing lump of alabaster. The contrast with the town could not have been sharper, all those rich colours and pattern and intricate carving. No wonder that Gothic took off after all those decades of classicism. The brother who let us in took us up and around a maze of rooms and into the vestry, opening up wide cupboards stuffed with Pugin silver vessels. What a genius he was! Next door his house was under wraps, being restored by the Landmark Trust.

Sunday brought Cambridge and a drink-sodden lunch with the unsinkable John Casey. And I delivered a sermon on the Lady Margaret Beaufort at Christ's.

LATE FEBRUARY

The weather by late February entered a cold, bleak and frosty phase. I escaped to the USA for six days, being fêted in Palm Beach and then at Winterthur, Delaware. *Coronation* was delivered and I entered that difficult in-between-books period, made worse by agreeing to give too many extraneous lectures which required original work.

The building work continues in London and in the country. It is now my sixth month in the Abbey and I rather love it, a kind of institutional framework to life. Meanwhile, in the country wonder follows wonder and this huge alteration gives me energy, a feeling of exerting the imagination, being really creative and original. I am being my own architect, making things up as I go along. And there is still so much to do. All of this has kept me going for months with not much asking for the pen to be wielded.

2 MARCH

Farewell to Angus Ogilvy

I don't want this diary to descend to the level of being a repetitious account of memorial services, except where else would one find such gatherings of *tous les grands* in their faded blacks? Still, the one for

Angus Ogilvy was special, touching and notable for a very beautifully written, perfectly pitched and delivered address by his son, James, a controlled eulogy in honour of a truly gentle man. The entire Kent clan came along, with a slightly bent Duke of Gloucester. On arrival they were herded into St George's Chapel. What triggers my pen is the contrast of the four key women: Princess Michael in her customary *Hello* magazine style; Katharine Kent a pale, distressed, Ophelia-like figure in an old jacket and skirt and trailing, with one hand by its long strap, her handbag on the floor. She recognised me and after wandering around a bit in a worrying way, was got into the chapel. Then there was Princess Alexandra, radiant, still beautiful and with a smile for everyone, just as it should be at what was a happy celebration of a special man. As we said to each other, we were lucky.

Down the line came Camilla Parker-Bowles, shorter than me, with the usual Household black kit and wearing a huge sloping hat. She had a warmth and a twinkle in her eye and she didn't give me the Diana seduction glance which had once made me blush. I reminded her that I signed a copy of *Feast* for her at the request of her son Tom as a Christmas present. I rather warmed to her but, poor thing, what a burden is about to come her way. I lined her up against the other women and it was a relief to see someone not attempting to be anything other than her own age and unashamed of her smile wrinkles. Also there's no sign of entering the fashion stakes. Who knows but that she might be just the thing?

14 MARCH

Commonwealth Observance and Santo Versace

Commonwealth Observance round again, a real Abbey jamboree but I've been to worse ones than this. The Queen was in violent fuchsia pink with her hat topped with purple. She stoops a little now. Blair skipped down the line saying how pleased he was to see us, still, in spite of disappearing hair, an amazingly boyish figure with only a light dusting of make-up. Surely it's not beyond the wit of man to throw up someone else to replace this man? I blanch at the prospect of another five years of him.

I'd been invited to my second dinner in eighteen years back to the V&A. So with Coral Samuel on my arm or me on hers, whichever, off we went. I can't think why I was asked but I never return without a torrent of contrary emotions. At any rate the great treat was to get them to open up the display of Queen Maud of Norway's dresses. Cecil Beaton would have gone crazy to have seen them. She had her mother's beauty and taste. What clothes, elegant and assured with a marvellous attention to detail and, above all, to the silhouette they cut. That saw me through the evening, for the International Arts and Crafts Exhibition, although beautifully displayed, was full of everything I could live without: hideous, uncomfortable furniture, lumpy silver and peasanty ceramics. Ugh! And it was all the routine that I began twenty-five years ago: drinks in the Cast Court followed by dinner in the Gamble Room. All of it was very well done but there were too many speeches at the start of the meal, Mark Jones giving a variant of the countless ones I used to give, followed by a lady from Heal's – adequate – and Lucy Lambton over the top, too long and unnecessary. She was curiously attired with *dérangé* spidery hair and a skirt of puffs of crumpled silk, short at the front and with a train behind. Poking out her rosette-adorned mules at me, she said that the dog had got at them. And so they looked. She was much worn about the face since I last saw her.

The great surprise, though, was Santo Versace with his pretty daughter, now grown up. I was terribly moved seeing her and he just kissed me on both cheeks as I did him. So many memories came flooding back. Now he is the front man, slimmed down and beautifully turned out, his English fluent and perfect. That was a meeting which left me with a sense of joy and a remembrance of one of my life's treasured friendships, with his incredible brother, Gianni Versace.

This gathering was about money. It inevitably must be these days. It lacked the sense of glamour which I recall, but maybe I view my own *fêtes* through rose-tinted spectacles. There was no urgency and excitement, no sense of a spectacle unfolding. I get a bit tired of being told how well I look and happy and energetic – what the hell do they expect, a withered, bent double, grief-stricken man? Needless to say, when I got back home grief hit me and for that I'm grateful – never forget.

23 APRIL

The Lady Dashwood en fête

Marcella Dashwood has style, perfect manners and elegance, a great hostess, so this time I said 'yes' to a lunch for the Sherwoods at her dower house on the Dashwood Estate. It was a long drive but I enjoyed myself, a reminder that it all still goes on. But it was very much the gathering of a certain generation, some of whom I hadn't seen for years. The Sherwoods just get larger, the ebullient James is so huge that I think that he'll go pop, but he's benevolent and exudes warmth. Shirley seemed to be wearing her collection of botanical paintings on her coat. It was twenty for lunch with three attendant domestics. Many of the women seemed to me to be in the grip of face-lifts and botox. Carla Powell was one, all shimmer and glamour but you can't do anything about withered hands. I wondered about Marcella. I don't know.

John Kasmin arrived looking like a refugee, a somewhat square figure who, in the country, lives on the Euston estate in a William Kent folly and adores Fortune Grafton. Wise man. The Belgian ambassador and wife were somewhat lumpen adornments. Sebastian Ferranti was the size of a house and, lo, there was Ned Ryan, Princess Margaret's walker. I was lucky being placed next to Victoria Getty, thin, direct, rather a star, I thought.

Sawmill House is beautiful. It straddles the waters seeming almost to float but with stunning views to West Wycombe and across the parkland. Everything is elegant, well placed and tidied, all of it on quite a small scale but I longed for some human clutter. Everyone was down about the election. Blair will get in and we'll all grind on as before.

Julian had looked after the Queen Mother when she was virtually blind with a cataract. I had always guessed that the last years were 'hidden' ones. She kept her marbles to the end and was consciously etching herself into history. As she couldn't see, Julian would support her on the arm and say one step here, three steps there. She was compos mentis to the end but life didn't go on as before. There was a 'wind-up' to epiphanies such as her hundredth. But she was a star – a great star.

EARLY JULY

The house transformed

All of this year work has gone on at The Laskett. I've become somewhat relentless. The front of the house is three-quarters done, the pilasters in place, the new front porch, the window embrasures and the armorials. The demolition of the old bay windows and the arrival of the new ones are still to come. But it all looks remarkable. The house is also being painted a different colour and looks very handsome. Inside the stable block the interior is finished, the new utility room and 'William Kent' hall awaiting repainting. I've also decided to make a French window in the large drawing room. It'll all cost a fortune but I've had huge creative satisfaction out of these works, being my own architect. For the first time the house looks interesting. Inside, many rooms have already been decorated and given new functions. Much that I've done needed doing as it was in a bad way. And now I'm at last back in the London flat, very happy in my elegant bedsit.

10 JULY

The Sixtieth Anniversary of the end of the Second World War

Up and to the 8 a.m. Mass at St Matthew's: rather touching as the few who were gathered there remembered me. To the Abbey at 10.10 a.m., which was circled by police after the horrors of Thursday's terrorist attack on the London Underground. A perfect day and, as we'd all rehearsed the event the previous evening, the service went off like clockwork. It was one of the best staged events of its kind by the Abbey, as it moved the happening around, the clergy and choir beginning outside with an antiphon and the Queen laying flowers, the Archbishop preaching from the nave pulpit and those who carried the books of remembrance of members of the civilian population who had died, walking slowly in from the two transepts led by young people as acolytes. Members of the College wore red and black and the clergy wore gold. There were a lot of banners carried by somewhat ancient and portly members of the Guild of St Edward.

Rowan Williams must be deaf in one ear as every time I talked to him, as I was to his left, he would cock his right ear towards

me. The politicos and the minor royals came down the line, Blair
with his hair another colour, Princess Michael in peachy pink and a
ludicrous hat, Princess Alexandra elegant in grey silk, perfect taste,
the Countess of Sussex rather suburban and all the princes in uniform. The Duke of York is the double of those hefty royal dukes
about 1820. Wesley Carr did his stuff well, but he's now quite a bit
bent and sometimes, I suspect, is in agonies; but he's remarkable.
Beautiful music, including a new piece by Peter Maxwell Davies
and much else by James O'Donnell. And everyone was affable in the
hustle and bustle after.

This is the kind of day where you feel you've been an extra in a
play, after which you're left with a huge blank to fill. I went home,
popped on a black T-shirt and wandered down to The Mall. This
again was thronged with more affable folk, some of them tourists
but most of them Brits of all kinds and conditions. The Palace now
knows how to put its act together, so there were huge television
screens so that we could all view the entertainment on Horse Guards.

The Queen had changed out of yellow into pale green and went
by in a carriage, to huge cheers and applause. But thanks to the television screens we were all able to see the spectacle on Horse Guards,
a predictable mix of the inevitable Simon Callow as narrator and
various people playing Churchill (well), Gracie Fields (badly),
Eisenhower (well), Flanagan and Allen (adequately), and Vera Lynn
(well). Bruce Forsyth, who usually makes me wince, was quite a
star. In the main it was music and songs with a gruesome backing
of some cavorting dancers. There was much carrying of banners et
al., all of it very moving, and the Queen was good. The Duchess of
Cornwall wore a hat seemingly six feet wide with a vast border of
fluttering feathers: not at all sensible.

The screens meant that everyone along the Mall could join in.
Vera Lynn made her inevitable appearance, not singing but stepping
from a jeep to loud acclaim at the finale. Petula Clark appeared,

large and bewigged. It all went well and then the Queen and the Duke mounted a 'Queenmobile' and slowly drove down the Mall to huge applause, followed by bands and banners. Then we all surged forward for the balcony appearances and the flyover, Spitfires, Lancasters et al., perfectly executed, and then a finale of poppies falling. The bands played 'Rule Britannia' and 'Land of Hope and Glory' and we all joined in.

12 JULY

I am seventy: Part One

It was David Hutt who said that I must mark seventy. So be it. It was sugared with the offer of staging a dinner in College Hall, a handsome medieval great hall in which Gloriana had presided in her time and now emblazoned at the high table end with large coats of arms, its walls hung with the likes of Dr Busby. So I got Richard Shirley Smith to design me an invitation card and also a menu. The card had Gothic arcading and swags of drapery, beneath which eight paws trotted along with, at one end, a feathered tail waving and, at the other, a Maine Coon's face peering around. For the menu, Richard did a trophy of books, inkwell, pen, fruits, flowers and garden tools. In the middle it read '23 August 1935' and below 'Still here'. I asked about a hundred guests and, in the end, ninety sat down to eat.

Came the day and the weather was perfect, a beautiful summer's evening with golden light. The dinner was given 'in anticipation', as everyone will be away in August. And in any case I have decided to give two, one for the London crowd and a second for '*le tout* Hereford', or as near as. On the card people were bidden to come 'Formal and/or decorative', in the hope that it would be a *mélange* and that the women would put on some good frocks and rocks.

I got to the Abbey just after 5 p.m. carrying pink flowers and lime-coloured greenery. David had got his hands on Westminster School's silver and much else, candlesticks, rose bowls, tazzas and urns, which, set on the white damask tablecloths, looked splendid. The high table we banked with more silver and flowers and on to the tablecloths I scattered small sprays of pink rosebuds. Then off I went and put on my red and black. I worried terribly about the placing but worked on the principle that the speakers should be at the centre, so Wesley and I faced each other at one table and Antonia Fraser was behind me. Then the canons and their wives were scattered, one or two at each table, taking care that everyone had someone they had something in common with on one side.

I'd cast a wide net, including my brother and sister-in-law and Julia's brother and his wife, my successors at the National Portrait Gallery and the V&A, and so many from across the years – people like Sydney Anglo and Valerie Cromwell (Kingman) from the Institute of Historical Research days; Gerard Irvine, who married us; Pamela Tudor-Craig and John Hayes from the National Portrait Gallery era; Michael Borrie, with whom I shared my first flat; and on and on and on. The trouble with these occasions is that you never have time to talk to anyone as you are more concerned about the mechanics, those who failed to show up, necessitating juggling places, and those who were late and therefore threatened the dinner. But, judging from the noise, it went well and a great number of unlikely people were thrown together, from Lord Patten to Clive Lever, who cuts my hair.

I was incredibly touched that the Dean and canons presented me with a coloured engraving of George IV's coronation procession. Antonia was very funny about me and, as she'd just finished *Love and Louis XIV*, there was much play on 'Roy' and '*roi*'. And I think that I was pretty good, ending with my credo that I was tired of hearing from friends who were downsizing, going into retirement homes or sheltered housing, saying that in my case it would be the reverse: more house, more garden, more everything!

JULY

Passions Past and Present

Passions Past and Present arrived. It's a nice little book, really in the main autobiographical. I can't think that they'd sell many but I was pleased to see a number of these transitory pieces in permanent form. There was to be no build-up around this publication. It was just being let slip into the public domain. Simultaneously *Coronation* went off to the printers. Nowadays they rush things. I was given the worst picture researcher ever. So there had been much aggro. But the designer was good and so were the editors. However, the last-minute decision to up the illustrations by 100 per cent produced most of the problems. Even then things that I wanted were never got. The book as a consequence is now swollen to 550 pages. If they sell it at £25 it ought to walk out of the shops.

But all of this and saying 'yes' to too many things and, worst of all, opening the garden thirteen times has left me exhausted and unable to get on with the next opus. I haven't yet got the balance right, but on the other hand it is good to be in demand. By nature I am more gregarious than Julia ever was. I think of her every day. She's never out of my mind and every so often I cave in again to grief. But I accept that that will be a norm of life and wouldn't wish it otherwise. Still, every day remains too full so that I barely have a moment to open a newspaper, let alone read it. By later this year I hope that a new pattern will settle.

The builders have left Morpeth Terrace and I am back living

there. David Hutt will come in August and I'm already very happy about that. I love my elegant bedsitter and tiny bathroom, all I want in London. The end is also in view at The Laskett, although I had had no idea that I would embark on such major works. But how was I to know that the roof needed repairing, that the water tanks were rotten, the soil pipe collapsed, the central heating antique, so many windows rotten, etc? So much that has been done would have had to be done anyway. I have got a huge oomph out of being my own architect. The Gothic façade and porch with its crenellations is virtually finished, a delight, and next they will demolish the bays at the front of the house. A final folly – I decided that I must introduce daylight into the room we always called Bride Hall. I kept on thinking that when I was really old I would get huge pleasure looking out onto the garden, plus the alleviation of the internal gloom. I've slightly lost track of how much all of this will cost but the sale of the Tump Lane property and the Robins fan to the Fan Museum ought to cover it all. What all of these changes have given me is a huge burst of energy and excitement. Not a bad state to be in as I enter my eighth decade.

14 AUGUST

Mirabel Osler is eighty

I drove north to Aymestrey Court, the romantic house of Jonathan and Mary Heale. This was one of those gatherings to which each guest brought a dish or some wine. I brought the first course, of red peppers with anchovies and capers in extra virgin olive oil with some crusty bread. The gathering, a small one of nine, was to celebrate Mirabel's birthday. Who wouldn't be flattered to have been included in this loving, happy gathering to celebrate a life-giver?

I don't think that Mirabel was at all pleased at being eighty and she spoke about physical things beginning to pack up. But she remains a star, dressed as usual in her highly personal Bohemian style, with swags of this and that patterned fabric and swathes of beads and bangles, looking like some gypsy princess out of an operetta by Emmerich Kálmán.

The lunch was al fresco and I was reminded of an Impressionist painting as the lively, animated faces and gestures responded to the wine and food. Daniel MacDowell produced a four-foot salmon that he'd caught and Shaun Hill, the retired restaurateur, the mayonnaise. Janet Gough, the former High Mistress of St Paul's, provided the cheese and the dessert of peaches and crème fraîche brûlée that followed. But I recall this as a magical English summer occasion, the ancient timbered house with golden light pouring into its spacious rooms, the verdant box parterre (in need of cutting!), the topiary in the making, the sense of happy clutter, the bantams strutting near us as we ate, the informality and delight of it all.

I gave a toast, very short, but recalling an exchange some years back when Mirabel had said to me: 'I wish that I'd known you earlier,' to which I replied: 'No, you were reserved for this period of my life.' And I meant it.

18 AUGUST

Meditations from Masone

Masone for me is always an oasis of calm where I sit and read and think, uninterrupted by anything or anybody. Time always seems to stand still in this extraordinary domain, although not really, for excavation work has begun on Franco's labyrinth. There is an inspired madness about Franco. I never thought it would actually happen but there they are, the JCBs scooping out the foundations of a vast maze of bamboo with a chapel in the middle. Old outbuildings seem destined to house his art collection. The Biblioteca, a neoclassical post-modernist construction, houses his library in the ruins of the ancestral villa. Franco loves it and now seems to live in it a lot of the time. He is sixty-eight, somewhat pear-shaped, effervescent as ever, original, enthusiastic, although upset that his beloved magazine *FMR* has changed hands and that this child he created has been radically changed. Laura Casalis, still dark and beautiful, continues to sparkle and preside over her polyglot guests. This is *dolce far niente*, with breakfast at 10 a.m., lunch at 2 p.m. and dinner at 9 p.m. There may or may not be an expedition. This time there was one to the Castello Torrechiara, but otherwise between meals you part and do your own thing, which in my case is to read and take notes or just read and perhaps walk, although the terrain is flat and boring.

The Laskett and England seem very distant and, as this has been an upsetting August so far, I'm glad. This is the age when illness and death come thick and fast. Joe Trapp went in for an operation, which was successful, but twenty minutes after it the blood loss was such that he was dead. He was always one of my touchstones and now he's gone, a man of huge erudition and kindly disposition. He alone in the Warburg Institute understood the path of my career and for that I'm glad. My destiny was never to be an academic, nor was I ever to scale the heights of scholarship, although I've not been bad sometimes at foraging around in the foothills.

Libby Bryan (Higgins) is now stricken with what Julia had. That hit hard and still I don't know where or when that will end. The operation was a success but chemo is to follow. When I visited her up at Vowchurch she greeted me, standing and radiant. I was both moved and touched; but whither?

I was rung last week by Morag Timbury. John Hayes had had a

massive stroke and lay paralysed in Charing Cross Hospital, inart-
iculate and in an extreme way. Oh God, I hope that they don't bring
him back and if it's that bad, he is just allowed to die. Morag was
in a terrible state, not that I'd ever worked out her relationship with
John, although I once told him forcefully to marry her. I've never
really 'known' John, although he's one of my oldest friends, dating
back to the early to mid-Sixties. I'm not alone in this. I don't think
that anyone has ever 'known' him. He's seventy-six, I think. All of
this is so very close, people just a little older than oneself departing,
familiar pillars and points of reference gone. I had a tremendous
premonition that he had died last Friday evening, but he must still
be alive and in that geriatric ward, well looked after I hear, but recognising no one. I will learn more on return.

All of this cast clouds, but we must get on with it and be stoic.
Passions Past and Present was meant to slip out as a bedside book.
No such luck as the *Telegraph*, both Saturday and Sunday, took large
areas to tear me limb from limb with hymns of hate by two people
I'd never heard of. I suppose that I ought to be pleased that hackles
still rise, but at seventy I'm not. It's about time that I was left to
'depart in peace', but no such luck. Instead I was to be berated as a
self-righteous, self-regarding clown whose person and all of whose
works should be smashed. I don't recall ever evoking such vitriolic
hate from two such people before. Everything was heaped on my
head, even though it was not me who had chosen the pieces to be
printed. To me the little book contained a few memorials to what
my life had been about. As Jörg Hensgen, who had chosen them,
said, even though the pieces covered forty years, my principles have
never really shifted, the statement remains coherent and unaltered
– Christian, patriotic, royalist, Anglican and a few other things.
Mercifully I have always schooled myself to expect nothing, but it is
undeniable that such pieces erode one's confidence, which I am sure
is precisely what the writers, who were malicious, intended to do . . .

Much still remains to be done to the house and we're on to skip forty-three or forty-four. But a letter came from the British Records Association and they will descend and go through the manuscripts. These I will let go to the various appropriate repositories. It makes such sense for them to be looked after and made accessible. So much better for me to be told what should be kept and what dumped. Obviously more recent Oman stuff I'll probably hang on to. But I'm still haunted by the fact that half the loft has yet to be explored!

27 AUGUST

I am seventy for the second time

27 August began with drizzle. David Hutt had come down and immediately that he saw the tent said that it had to have garlands at the front, so off we went to gather laurels, rosemary and branches of berried *malus*. The poles supporting the roof I decked with laurel, much of which fell off overnight in the rain and had to be tied on again. Guests were bidden for 12.30 for 1 p.m. and up they turned in dribs and drabs, some ninety of them. The drizzle was useful, as instead of the drinks being in the open they all had to go into the tent and, being pushed together, the chatter started across a discrepant group of people from the county to the builders. It was such a happy occasion. I wore an eighteenth-century waistcoat flecked with flowers over an orange shirt and pale green jeans. Dress had been billed as casual and most came that way, except for the old stiffs like Peter Walker, Peter Rees and George Williams. They, in sharp contrast, were encased in suits and ties. So many guests bore gifts that a huge heap sprang up, in the main bottles, but not all of them.

David snapped away, for the scene was a lively one with much coming and going from table to table. The latter looked delightful, with their green gingham tablecloths and posies of sweet peas. A wine lake was consumed, but who cares? I made a solitary speech, quite enough, about old age being a wind-up and not a wind-down. I also table-hopped and afterwards guests scattered to look at the garden and then invaded the house, anxious 'to view the improvements', as Miss Austen would say. The main façade had been finished, and mighty handsome it looked, and all of it was the cause of much wonder and comment.

But I loved my day. I've never had anything like it before, a birthday to make up for all the ones that weren't marked in such a spectacular way. But, as I said, it was also given in gratitude to all those who had seen me through the last two years. David made me lie down after they'd all gone. I went to my bedroom and did so and found myself remembering her and how much I missed her and cried my eyes out again. But that was as it should be. Who knows whether I will make eighty – but I'm all for it if I can.

26 SEPTEMBER

I am seventy for the third time

The National Portrait Gallery gave a seventieth birthday dinner in my honour. I was touched. It was staged in the Tudor Gallery at a long table covered in crimson damask with pretty flowers, pink roses and hydrangeas, and on each menu something from my era: Pepys, Beaton, etc. It looked beautiful. I took A.S. Byatt as my guest, an extraordinary friendship that is close, although we hardly ever meet. I said that it was 'right' because *The Virgin in the Garden* begins in the National Portrait Gallery with me, Flora Robson as Gloriana and Dame Frances Yates hovering in the distance. Antonia said that it rounded it all off. In spite of the fact that she'd been in hospital in

France having forty stones removed (I think that I heard aright), she looked thinner and better than the last time we met. But our conversation always embarks deep in and no superficialities. Her sister on her mother rankled, as did A.N. Wilson on Iris Murdoch. But, like me, she keeps going, swimming every day and reading at least a few pages of German to keep it up. She, like me too, believes that in old age the mind should still be stretched. She was into another novel.

Quite a gathering, twenty-eight in all, Flora Fraser, Gerald Scarfe, Tessa Traeger, Clive Aslet, David Bailey, Fiona Reynolds, Paul Brason, Coral Samuel, etc. David Cannadine, who is now Chairman of Trustees, kicked off by saying that I was an icon. I couldn't resist yelling: 'But icons have candles burning before them!' He said, 'Don't worry, they'll come!' Sandy Nairne, a generous, gracious man, did the perfect tribute to me and I replied by going round the table picking on this or that person and how they related to me and the National Portrait Gallery. It was a family gathering but in its embrace was history, letters, painting, photography, caricature, scholarship and much else.

The Gallery was thoughtful. They had sent a car for Oliver Millar, limping a little but wreathed in smiles and happy. He'd come to terms (as far as one ever does) with the loss of Delia. Singers from the Abbey performed Byrd and sang a Grace. It was all happiness, but at its close all I could do was think of Julia and how proud she would have been of me. Sandy saw me into a taxi but I was in tears.

SEPTEMBER

Reflections on old age and being a widower

Any habitation, however tiny, is a repository of memory, of one's life expressed through an accumulation of things, not that I'm living in a shrine. As a widower I've struck out to rearrange and redecorate the house for my life as a single man, making it work for me but, at the same time, preserving the essence which gave me over thirty years of a happy marriage.

I move from the premise that I know Julia would have wished most that I should be happy. Marriage is a compromise and when one half goes, that compromise ceases. You no longer have to preserve things as they were. I recall supping with a widow friend. We sat at a table on heavy, uncomfortable chairs, she adding cushions to hers and opining about them. Her husband, she said, had bought them. I said, 'Then why don't you go out and buy new ones?' The effect on her was electric. It had never occurred to her that she didn't need to keep everything exactly as it was when her husband was alive.

Another glorious change is that you can dress your own style and not, as in my youth, your age. As a lifelong dandy *manqué* I have no hesitation in purchasing garments that my parents' generation would have deemed not suitable at seventy – nor even at sixty or fifty, come to that. Mark you, there are boundaries. The exposure of acres of old flesh is hardly likely to excite anyone. But, with a sharp eye as to what suits and what you can get away with, you can strut as elegant mutton if not lamb. What is also a help is the attitude of young shop assistants who, instead of casting me as some weirdo, give the thumbs up or down as I try on any garment. I recall with pleasure grabbing a Nicole Farhi suit in a sale and holding it up, and catching the eye of a young girl who had helped me choose clothes on an earlier occasion. Across the sale mob she gave the suit the thumbs up!

I suppose that I'm lucky as the genes in the Strong family indicate 'falling off the perch' around the age of ninety. Who knows? Live every day as your last but recognise that you are not immortal. But take care of yourself – or why else all those vitamins at breakfast, that five-mile jog before lunch and those in the gym when I'm in London?

All I can remember of my parents' and grandparents' generations was that from sixty on they became fragile blossoms who would be snuffed out if they barely walked around the block. The message was that limbs and muscles would seize up and they should therefore be conserved and not used. I love the fact that I read recently of an over-ninety-year-old in South Africa who was still running marathons. I'm grateful that I don't feel at all out of place in a gym in which all ages mix in a hugely friendly way. And I think of all the friends I have who are all into pilates, rowing machines, line-dancing and salsa classes.

27 SEPTEMBER

A visit to John Hayes

I went to see John Hayes. I sat and waited and then this speech therapist wheeled him by. It is so difficult and also distressing to know what to make of the situation but, in the end, it was not good. This is a rerun of Cecil Beaton. I keep on thinking of what Diana Cooper said: 'Every time I see him like that I could kill him.' On the last visit John was making gestures which read 'I want to get out of here'. Those had gone. There was no sign of life in his right side at all and nothing that he said was comprehensible. His mouth was skewed down one side. One of his executors, Jeremy Love, came, a delightful man, and we both talked at John, but I was less certain how much of it, if any, that he took in. Jeremy kept on being optimistic and telling John he'd be all right again. He won't.

I concluded from the visit that that was it. He'd never be any better, a kind of living death. Really tragic. As we left, Jeremy asked what I thought should be done. I said sell the car, the cottage at Newbury and then, also, sell the Chiswick house and buy a small central London flat.

Later I rang Morag Timbury, a real saint. I said that the John we knew is no longer there. He's gone. She'd had a face-to-face with the hospital and it's not good. He'd never live on his own again. There is no way it could be done. It would have to be a nursing home. She'd got a list of nine but as the two executors had refused for weeks to set in motion getting power of attorney, she was desperate that John's assets would be seized to pay for the home. Jeremy told me that they wouldn't get power of attorney before Christmas. It is all pretty awful. Poor John Hayes. Such a very old friend, a mysterious loner but generous and affectionate; now he's all but gone.

3 OCTOBER

Coronation *is launched*

The launching of *Coronation* started last Wednesday with Libby Purves and *Midweek* on Radio 4. Libby is a large, intelligent and hugely experienced broadcaster. It was the usual gathering: an actor, a curator from the Horniman Museum and Cynthia Lennon, first wife of John, like me flogging a book. It went well.

Pause and then, on Saturday, it was the Windsor Festival. The sell-out event took place in the Guildhall in the room in which Charles and Camilla had tied the knot, the walls festooned with portraits of royal ancestors bedecked with robes and jewels. I was introduced by Hubert Chesshyre, Clarenceux King of Arms, pale-faced and hesitant. All of that went well too. And then a pause followed until today, the official date of publication. Up at 6.15 a.m. and collected to be taken to Wood Lane for *Breakfast TV*. As usual, much waiting. I was struck by how bashed the props were, which you never see on the box, and how the presenters' faces were caked in make-up, Dermot Murnaghan having his hair arranged forward to conceal its loss and Natasha Kaplinsky with a plastic tub stuffed with make-up brushes hidden under the table, which she pulled out between pieces to top up her face with yet another layer. *Coronation* got a five-minute plug, with the cover on screen and film footage of 1953. Later there were long pieces with Radios Gloucester and Northampton.

In the evening there was the launch party at the Abbey in the Jerusalem Chamber, the food done by that lovable Dickensian pair, Dick and Sheila Webb. HarperCollins weren't going to lash out on champagne but it was OK. It was a fairly small but select gathering: Antonia Fraser in her usual drapes but worried about Harold, who had been quite seriously ill, and deciding that travel by private plane was the answer to getting him to his seventy-fifth birthday *fête* in Dublin (as I said to her, 'What's money for?'); A.N. Wilson in a new black-and-white check suit, very dapper and raving about Hugo Vickers's biography of the Queen Mother; Richard Luce, avuncular and benign but worried over Rose, about to have another operation; Stephen Lamport, who is working on the next coronation (I was told that Buckingham Palace would put in for a bulk purchase of copies); Selina Hastings, very elegant in pearls and sounding stuck with Somerset Maugham, as all the interesting papers had been destroyed; the ever-expanding David Starkey, now become a warm-hearted Mr Salteena; Simon Thurley, sharp and high-cheeked, on about churches ('The Church of England doesn't care about its heritage') . . . Wesley Carr gave a warm and funny speech and I did, I hope, the same. A haze of content spread through the room and that was it. I took Felicity Bryan [my agent] out to dinner at the Garrick Club and staggered home to my bedsit.

10 OCTOBER

Memory

Knowing that I would not be at The Laskett on the second anniversary of Julia's death I retrod the path I had walked when I had
carried her ashes to their resting place. It was a beautiful day, all
blue sky and sun quickening the damp melancholy of the garden in
autumn. It was a tearful walk. Beatrix was right when she said that
the sense of loss and grief would never leave me. It never has, nor
should it. On the day itself I went to early communion at the Abbey
at St Edward's shrine (it was the week celebrating the thousandth
anniversary of his birth). How touched I was when her name was
among those of the departed for whom we prayed.

11 OCTOBER

The Duke of Kent and Lord Kelvedon are seventy

This was a *grande fête* on a scale that took me back to the late Sixties
and early Seventies. Lindsey House was ablaze, a covered canopy
leading to the entrance with batteries of cameramen watching us
arrive. Yet tragedy was at its heart. Paul Channon is in the grips of
something like Alzheimer's [later I learnt that it was]. He sat with
the Queen on his right and Henrietta Dunne on his left, like a
figurehead carved in wood from a totem pole, staring ahead. Here
was all the glitter and glamour but when dinner was finished, three
people had to support him out of the room.

This was entertainment on the grand scale. Ninety-six, I was told,
to dinner, and countless others afterwards. There was a huge royal

turn-out: Princess Alexandra, Katharine Kent, the Gloucesters, the King and Queen of Greece. The room was jammed with the cream of the 1960s, now forty or more years on. Some had worn better than others. Norman St John Stevas was bent and decrepit; Kenneth Rose had recovered and seemed positively dapper; Katharine Kent was in a weird parti-coloured dress but seemed somehow vaguely normal and teaching near Oxford. The roll-call was huge: George Christie, the young [David] Cholmondeley, Nicky Haslam, Mary Gordon Lennox, Mary Soames, Thomas Camoys, Alice Boyd, Paul Zuckerman, Patricia Rawlings, the Hornbys, Peter Carrington, Michael and Anne Heseltine, Camilla Cazalet, Christopher Gibbs, Vivien Duffield, the Dunnes, Debo Devonshire, Valerie Solti, Susan Hussey, Miranda Iveagh – the list was endless.

We all gathered in the great drawing room hung with the Guardis. There then came a moment when the crowd parted like the Red Sea and lo, the Queen appeared, white-haired and wearing glasses, in a rather hideous bespangled claret-coloured dress. The Duke of Edinburgh was in tow, an amazing eighty-three-year-old. I don't find myself inhibited by them any more and, surprisingly, found myself heading for the dining room, at which point I had a go at him. He's not my sort of man but in my research on the history of the coronation I was impressed by what he had said in 1953 about letting in something relevant to the modern world. That had made me view him in a different light.

There were countless butlers and waitresses. The tables were named after Wagner operas. I found myself at *Lohengrin* between Camilla Cazalet and Sharon Hornby. She and Simon had been on Mustique with Paul and Ingrid Channon for three weeks, and even she found sitting next to Paul a strain. In the middle of the table a crystal vase full of lilies soared ceilingwards. The Duke of Gloucester, opposite, still boyish, a kind of royal owl of the Remove. There was Georgie Channon, a pretty, nice girl, now living in Tetbury.

That bit of the family looked on the level. Someone muttered to me that the two birthday boys were somewhat more closely related than had crossed my mind. However, Chips would have revelled in this scene – all the royals and *le tout*. I've never seen so much jewellery worn – Josephine Loewenstein with three massive brooches with emeralds the size of gull's eggs. One woman wore a museum piece, a late Renaissance gold necklace, all enamel, diamonds and rubies.

Well, to return to our table, on which were also a somewhat puffed-up Donald Sinden and Drue Heinz festooned. There was no ghastly set of speeches, just a very funny short one; but I never saw who gave it because my back was turned to the giver. We all sat and drank the toast of 'Prince Eddy and Paul', and that was it.

It was quite an early event, 7.45 for 8 p.m. The dinner was over at 10.30 p.m., the Queen returning briefly to the drawing room and then going, thus avoiding the invasion of a hundred or more guests who came on from other dinners. This was a gathering which was the end of something. I shall never see the like again, a brief return to the world of Emerald Cunard.

LATE OCTOBER

On the road with Coronation

On the road with *Coronation*: Windsor, Ilkley, Wells, Brighton, Woodstock, Guildford, Southwold, Hay-on-Wye . . . and endless local radio. The audiences vary: Ilkley intelligent, Windsor rapturous, Wells somewhat stunned, Brighton surprisingly gormless . . . It's difficult to know what to make of it. Sometimes you get a meal, mostly a glass of wine and a sandwich. At Ilkley I was told that if one in ten of the audience bought a book, that was good going. Windsor was the sales highpoint, Brighton the pits. The radio pieces are all five- to fifteen-minute fill-ins between music. In the main they stick to the book but sometimes it's off down Memory Lane.

3 NOVEMBER

The Royal Warrant Holders Dinner

This turned out to be an amazing event, a thousand people in white tie and orders at Grosvenor House. I'd been twinned with Michael Portillo, which was perhaps, in retrospect, a mistake. Portillo is a charming, self-satisfied egotist, with coarse if engaging features. Having failed to get what he wanted, he abandoned politics to scatter his charms across our television screens. He's rather good at it. I last encountered him at the *Great Britons* TV competition, at which he championed Gloriana, even if everything that he said about her was wrong. So came the moment of the speeches: he grabbed the microphone and without a note did a star turn whose subject was inevitably himself, although at the close he just about managed to toss a bouquet to the Warrant Holders. The previous year I gathered poor Miles Kington sinking lower and lower in the face of a tidal wave from William Hague! I'd already drafted what I had to say – history, the Great Wardrobe, et al. – when I thought 'I'm not going to let the bugger get away with this'. Rising, I began by saying that it's very difficult to upstage a politician but listening to Michael Portillo I was reminded of a passage in my Diaries which record Julia stuck next to Edward Heath who, like all politicians, could speak only about himself. Shortly afterwards I saw Ted Heath at the Goldsmiths Company, and, on going up to him, he said, 'Page 145.' I said, 'You are too great a man to make that comment,' to which he replied, 'When are you coming next to have lunch with me in Salisbury?' I retorted, 'When you ask me.' *Touché.*

7 NOVEMBER

The Destruction of the Country House *commemorated*

To the V&A for the thirtieth anniversary of SAVE, for which I was the guest of honour. A huge, milling throng greeted me, embodying many involved in the heritage Seventies, for that was the child of *The Destruction of the Country House* exhibition. SAVE came out of it and is Marcus Binney's lasting achievement: in my speech I went out of my way to pay him a well-deserved tribute. They were just a handful of people but over the years they've campaigned for practically everything, nothing has been allowed to slip through – churches, factories, railway stations, swimming baths, parks, gardens, houses – every single building type and man-created environment. Marcus has a diffidence so he's less of a public persona. That has had its advantages but he should, by rights, have received far greater official recognition. We all dined afterwards at a restaurant which was so noisy that I couldn't hear myself speak.

8 NOVEMBER

The next Dean of Westminster

I went to 10 Downing Street to see the Appointments Secretary, William Chapman, a dapper little man who made notes of what you said in a book. The object of the visit was the appointment of a new Dean for the Abbey. I pointed out that the incoming Dean would have to deal with the coronation, the need for a more immediate common touch and for consolidation after the internal 'dramas'. Robert Willis of Canterbury came up and so did Michael Tavinor of

Hereford, who had obviously made a mark but I wondered whether or not he had the political acumen. There was a feeling that the place had to move on and be more outward reaching. I remember thinking and saying the latter, that there ought to be more interplay with other London and regional churches beyond the odd sermon and choir visit. I also pointed out the fragile financial position. He agreed with me that things like the Honorary Stewards in frock coats were, in this day and age, more off-putting than welcoming. So there is much to be done to respond to the climate of the new century.

NOVEMBER

Farewell Astrid

Astrid Zydower died in her sleep over three months ago. I would have written earlier but, no, her family wanted everything under wraps: understandable in retrospect, as on the day she died someone nicked the Gaudier-Brzeska drawing Dicky Buckle had left her, and also Astrid's maquette for the Harewood House fountain. But I'd been rung up by Astrid's sister, Anita, in many ways her double, a small, smiling, delightful East European. Would I like to choose an etching by Astrid or one of the models left in her studio? So I rang Michael Leonard and we arrived together at 32 Willes Road, Kentish Town. They'd sold the house, which had been emptied and parts of which had resembled Julia's studio block – no mean feat. But it was a happy gathering of Astrid's friends, a last day in the old house but with no regrets. I was presented with the *modello* of the Earl of Essex for the great tableau in the 1964 Shakespeare Exhibition of Queen Elizabeth watching the first night of *A Midsummer Night's Dream*. Alas, the model for Gloriana had vanished or fallen to bits [it in fact hadn't and later it was rediscovered and I had a cast of it made]. A friend offered to ferry it to Gloucester, close to a firm that could cast it. It needs a bit of repair but I really would like this bit of my past, my emancipation into the world of the living arts. Astrid's etchings were then produced. She was always very secretive about them and kept them under her bed. One of a fierce-looking cat I was told that I had to have, and a vase of flowers, but the one I could choose was a mysterious beach-marine scene of nude figures on the shore or in the water. These and the few drawings were quite unlike anything we'd ever seen her do: they were elegant, sparse line etchings reminiscent of Matisse and Marie Laurencin. Her early drawings, by contrast, had fifty lines where one would have done. The marine etching had on the back 'For LK', I assume Lincoln Kirstein, with whom she'd had a long friendship.

Astrid was a considerable artist sculptor, out of tune with the times, someone who could never produce on time and whose life was one long saga of being put upon. The house was falling apart, with a crack indicating that a wall was about to fall off. It needed a fortune spending on it. Dicky Buckle made her and ruined her. Somehow Astrid was always there but now she's gone. I took a couple of the etchings round to be framed for memory.

6 DECEMBER

Tony Snowdon at bay

The lunch had been long delayed and one never knew what sort of mood he would be in. But he was OK. We were meant to go to a restaurant nearby called Lumsden but he'd forgotten to ring early enough, so he couldn't get a table. So the luckless nymphet called Agnes was sent out to forage for lunch and returned with smoked salmon, hard avocadoes, lemons, brown bread and butter.

Tony sat below in the basement working area in benign mood. I kissed him on both cheeks and said that I was only there for the drink and the gossip. He's seventy-six, not in a good way – really terrible, in fact, when he attempted to drag himself around, and he's going deaf. So we gossiped. Jocelyn Stevens, who had left Vivien Duffield and gone off with another woman, had discovered sex at seventy-seven. Had I seen *that film*? (That film being the one on HRH [*The Queen's Sister*].) I said that I'd seen the first hour and had turned it off as it was such tripe. He had and had videoed it. David and Sarah hadn't. I told him to forget it. It was so ridiculous and really awful. Lord Mountbatten was someone else who was really awful. That didn't surprise me, a real piece of left-over upstart hierarchy. Tony seemed lonely and missing people. He missed Carl Toms and Jeremy Fry, whose memorial, wonderfully done, took place in the Theatre Royal, Bath. Lucy was 'beautiful', so the fire still burned there. I was direct about HRH. In the end I couldn't take any more of it. Life by the late Eighties and into the Nineties had moved on. But I did say that she could be marvellous and very witty. He then also recalled her best side – funny, her ability to sing, her flashes of wit. But then there was the rest of it.

Lunch was in the kitchen as usual but, as he was immobile, I had to hoick around quite a bit. This is a kitchen out of the ark. No electric kettle (I boiled the water on the gas stove, which, at least, was self-lighting), no washing-up machine, no ingredients, the whole of it tired and grubby. I told him that he ought to dump the lot. No one today would want to work in such primitive conditions. Domestically he must be hopeless. And let's face it, only someone dotty would stay in that house with all those stairs when they're crippled with polio.

I think that he feels 'out of it', but you are when you're over seventy. Accept it and be gracious. The pantheon has changed: be grateful that you were part of any pantheon at all. But, yes, the wicked old, talented thing has not come to terms with that, so he sits, glass in hand, alone in this rambling house. Sad.

29 DECEMBER

Goodbye to 2005

John Hayes died peacefully on Christmas Day, never having recovered from his terrible stroke early in August. Would that it had killed him then. As it was he was carted off to the Charing Cross Hospital but he spoke only a jumble, couldn't read or write, was doubly incontinent and would never stand again. I went to see him there several times. It was so awful, but in a way he smiled and was benign. I was never sure whether he understood what I said or not. They did what they could for him and early in December he went into a nursing home in Battersea. I went to see him on 19 December, taking a card and a box of chocolates to wish him a happy Christmas. The room was fine but there he was, slumped to one side in his chair, hardly a glimmer. He was in a bad way. As usual I talked at him, took his hand and pressed it and left. Looking back, I feel that he was sitting there, concluding, 'So, this is it': one room, a cell, and his faculties gone. I'm told that stroke victims can decide to shut down and I'm sure that this is what he did. The next day he went into hospital and one by one his vital organs ceased as he passed peacefully into a coma and died. I felt such a sense of gratitude for this. All that he was faced with was a living death. The funeral is on 6 January and there's to be a service of thanksgiving in February at St James's, Piccadilly.

While I was up on the 19th and the 20th I went to my confessor, John Gaskell, at All Saints, Margaret Street, for a robust confession.

I'm glad that that bridge has been crossed. And I had lunch with Stephen Lamport at the RAC re the next coronation. He will sound me out on ideas from time to time and that's fine. It struck me that he hadn't got that far with it and needed a good theologian-liturgist on board. But the Queen looks robust, although eighty next year. The task is a major one, as 1953 was the last of the great 'imperial' coronations. The next one, if it happens, must reflect all that has happened since 1953, a formidable challenge but filled with opportunity. I'm touched to be involved.

Now is the period of civil partnerships. So many must do it, urged on by their solicitors and accountants when they'd rather in their old age leave things as they are. At any rate, Keith Jeffery announced one with Adrian, Robin Gibson with Tom, and Christopher Goode with Michael Fraser.

I ended this year thinking, Yes, it's been a good year and people were so nice to me as I reached seventy I confess to being slightly disappointed at the reception of *Coronation*. Perhaps it's too early but neither *The Times* nor *The Sunday Times* reviewed it, which I found shocking. And we're all caught up with this down-market slide. You have to be David Beckham or Jamie Oliver to survive. It's names and celeb publishing, which accounts for my name on the cover of *Coronation* being twice the size of the title. I felt exhausted by so many appearances fighting this tide. But its time will come.

The house is almost finished. I'm more than delighted with it. I've opened up negotiations with the Vivat Trust. It would be good to get the future of all this settled before I die. I've done a huge clear-up and ordering of things. The Oman archive has gone to Bodley and they're thrilled with it. On the floor of the Archive Room now lies the only pile-up from the loft left: all my clothes since the 1960s. In January representatives from the V&A and the Museum of Costume [now The Fashion Museum] at Bath come to take their pick. All is vanity! I will then have taken things a very long way.

2006

Speculations about the Abbey

The New Year always opens quietly and also, one realises, too quickly. The farewells to Wesley Carr started to roll. Poor man he has to go to twenty-two of them and he's far from well. Natalie is wonderful, but crippling Parkinson's is no joke. He's off to the USA, which will take his mind off the Abbey. He is somebody that I have become increasingly fond of, a shy, vulnerable and often misunderstood man. Much has been sorted out at the Abbey, but whither does it go now?

It's been at a standstill for the last two years. It needs change. It calls for reaching out. It also calls for more dissolving of hierarchy. The building is both an asset and also an impediment to moving on. I wonder what will happen. Everyone is talking about change.

26 JANUARY

Princess Loewenstein is seventy-five

It was a crowded evening. I first made my way to the RIBA to 'launch' the reproduction of a manuscript about garden buildings by a mad Irishman called Samuel Chearnley. It was quite a turn-out of Irish Georgian Society members and hangers-on. The new Lord Rosse, Brendan, had none of the authority of his father but looked quite like him. He owned the manuscript and he was there to promote the sale of the facsimile. It was a mixture of the social upper end, like Miranda Iveagh and Lucy Snowdon, and the art history mafia, including the elderly, farouche John Harris and the benign and ever-larger Brian Allen.

I did my stuff, for I had to get away to catch one of the flotilla of buses leaving Eaton Square bound for Petersham Lodge. I found myself sitting behind Reresby and Penelope Sitwell, he looking crumpled and pickled and she, as usual, disagreeable. Opposite them was the tall and affable James Stourton, and next to me Leonora Lichfield buried beneath a lot of hair. I also glimpsed the shadowy, bent and decrepit figure of Norman St John Stevas climbing on to another bus.

Outside Petersham Lodge flambeaux lit up the forecourt. Rupert and Josephine stood receiving. There's something rather splendid about him, his head exactly like one of those florid princelings in German baroque portraits. Josephine, affable and with a twinkle, looked marvellous in pink with a great jewel on her bodice. There was a terrible crush of people and I struggled towards a few I knew, like Mark and Arabella Lennox-Boyd, Christopher Gibbs, Christopher Balfour, Jane Rayne and Pamela Hicks. It was *Almanach de Gotha* time, with a fair sprinkling of European highnesses and duchesses – and of our lot, Prince Michael of Kent minus his wife, and Princess Alexandra, elegant in black with a diamond choker, stunning.

Pink turned out to be the theme and a large pavilion decorated with wide pink and white stripes had been added as a banqueting hall. There were ten tables, each seating ten or twelve, with huge silver candelabra in the centre arising from a froth of pretty pink tulips and jasmine. A chandelier of pink blossoms and greenery hung from the tent's ceiling.

I found myself between Anne Somerset and someone who turned out to be a former Royal Ballet dancer and very Roman Catholic. She had on her other side Konrad Loewenstein, one of the numerous Catholic priests floating around. He belongs to an order [the Priestly Fraternity of Saint Peter] whose mission is to preserve and promote the Tridentine Mass, which he was about to lead in a church in Venice. The clerics in their robes amidst this display of grand dresses, jewels and many titles made Firbank's *Valmouth* cross my mind.

Much to my surprise, Paul Channon was there. I gave him a hug, just wanted to. He's a really nice man and what has happened to him is so truly awful. Also at my table were Michael Frayn and George Weidenfeld, blinking like an owl and missing nothing. I was told that there were a hundred and ninety in all there, and everything was done in the best style.

No sign, however, of Mick Jagger, although the statuesque Jerry Hall was there in red. But it all went like clockwork and there were no ghastly surprises. And we hopped into our buses at 11.30 p.m. and headed home.

3 FEBRUARY

Farewell to Wesley Carr

I was bidden to three of the twenty-two farewell events for Wesley
Carr: a lunch given by the Lord Mayor of Westminster; the Audit
Dinner; and Evensong followed by a huge bun fight in Church
House last Monday. It's always the same, the end of a 'reign'. The
individual concerned is a dead man standing, and voices of change
creep out of the woodwork. As Sister Elizabeth Anne said, 'We've
stood still for the last two years.' Poor Wesley, he's been kept going
by his doctors and up to forty pills a day. I have a real affection
and admiration for him. He's basically shy and finds it difficult to
show demonstrable emotion. But it's there very strongly beneath.
He's hugely intelligent and a witty speaker, erring perhaps too
much towards secularity rather than spirituality. He also lacks the
common touch, although now that he's going it has been a very
pleasant surprise to see how devoted many people are to him. He's
had a pretty wretched time wrestling with a horrendous, accelerating
disease. The Neary affair [in which the Dean decided to dismiss the
organist, Dr Martin Neary, and his wife for improper use of choir
funds, provoking adverse publicity] was also very unpleasant. But
he had inherited the Augean stables. There wasn't even a computer
in the place. The building was a tourists' Tower of Babel, which
'Reclaiming the Calm' has remedied. The statutes are almost signed
and sealed, 450 years late! So whoever comes in has a good foundation on which to build.

Who will come in? A shortlist is supposed to exist and Richard
Chartres keeps on being mentioned, a man, it is said, very high up
in royal esteem and who didn't get either Canterbury or York. But
change is in the air. The musical tradition is good but visually the

Abbey is as though the second half of the twentieth century had never happened. Not even a John Piper! The place needs to open up more. The problem is how. The building has that massive screen cutting it in two. There's not even a public loo . . .

I hope that Wesley will be OK. He loves the kudos of office. He's lucky in having Natalie, a real star for any man.

14 FEBRUARY

St Valentine's Day and the clothes clear-out

On St Valentine's Day I always saw that Julia had a card from me and the cats on the breakfast table. Alas, a phase of life gone. The garden is full of swathes of snowdrops – her flower. I need hardly write that when I stepped into her snowdrop garden grief overtook me and I howled my way round the garden. But I wouldn't have it any other way. The scattering of snowdrops garlanding the shrouded urn with her ashes says everything. RIP Dear Heart.

Today there was another step forward. For months the Oman papers lay in files and boxes across the Archive Room floor. The Bodleian Library has accepted them and told me that it was the best set of family papers they'd had for years. There were bundles of letters from Lord Curzon, A.J. Balfour, etc., etc. This archive is well placed and where it ought to be: Oxford, and accessible. Sir Charles Oman was the great figure but there's good [Eric] Maclagan, [James] Anderson Rose and Chadwick stuff too.

The papers having gone, I got down from the loft the last great 'heap'. I had kept virtually everything I had worn since about 1965, all in plastic bags and boxes, labelled. The whole lot came down and I laid it out on the floor. But today was the great descent of the V&A Fashion Department and the Museum of Costume in Bath, all very nice young people. I spread the stuff out across the upper floor of the stable block: suits with appropriate shirts, ties, hats, etc.; i.e. complete as I had worn them. It started with a pair of Vince of Carnaby Street bell-bottoms in a stretch fabric, a unique survival, I was told; lots of King's Road 1965 to early 1970s, especially from Just Men: my wedding suit by them I laid out complete. That was followed by lots of directorial gear from the V&A years, a long Tommy Nutter phase followed by Versace. Then a lot of stuff that I put in date order under hats, shirts, shoes, trousers, suits, etc. Much to my surprise, they took the lot.

Bath had really no men's clothes post my Blades suit given years ago. I think they saw my stuff as a way of solving this: one gentleman of fashion's wardrobe over thirty to forty years. They carted away enough to mount an exhibition. In their case it will be ongoing, as there's more stuff to come from here and they will need to consult the pictorial scrapbook evidence.

23 FEBRUARY

A retrospective on the transformation of the house and garden

By the time they finish it'll be two years of builders' work on The Laskett. I had no intention of doing all this. It began slowly and accelerated, firstly because certain things had to be done and then creative energy took over. The stockbroker also had a dollop of cash available. I have not, however, touched anything that is producing investment income, upon which I now draw in part. Once I started I just went on and, I guess, probably ran through a large sum. But I don't regret any of it. So much came to light that needed attention: the roof, the central heating, the wiring, the sewage, to start with. I'd no idea what a state the place was in.

I was driven on, too, by the knowledge that nearly all of those involved were on the edge of retiring and they were a spectacular team: the builders Geoff and Gerry Davis, humorous, inventive, careful with their work, always able to come up with a solution. It was Geoff who produced the Aristocast catalogue filled with historic plaster mouldings by the yard, which set me off. 'Thank goodness there's no architect,' he would keep on saying.

I've been inventing everything as we've gone along, tons of reproduction Haddonstone to transform the front of the house into a Palladian doll's house and the west front into Castle of Otranto gothick. Geoff brought in his son Greg, who was able to run up Georgian and gothick windows. Inside I began with the Archive Room and then spread outwards and downwards. Geoff and Gerry knew the 'staircase men' who built a new one for the new entrance hall. They brought in Paul Reeks and his son Chris, the painters. Paul has the best colour sense and taste ever – superb – mixing colours for every room, knowing exactly what to pick out and how much of his pot of Spanish gold to apply. Now that it is all coming to an end, we have a huge sense of achievement. The house is elegant, the spaces flowing one into another. It is grander in detail yet domestic and welcoming. I feel hugely happy in it. The drawing room sequence is beautiful, with the antechamber densely hung like a cabinet room and then the double doors leading into the light- and flower-filled drawing room we always called Bride Hall. There I solved how to conceal the awful ceiling beams and also where to put a fireplace. I put in French windows, bringing in light and also vistas to the garden. Indeed, much of the work was about bringing house and garden together as one linked composition. Into the drawing room I put all the flower pictures and marquetry furniture, the good blue and white and the Myles-Lea panorama of the garden. Sue Leyshon-James has made all the new yellow curtains. And I went into Ross for a carton of cream and came back with a large chandelier for the room. The result is Soane-ian.

Everywhere the floors have been paved with tiles. The hall has become the dining room, lovely to eat in and also to glimpse the garden. Here, as in the Archive Room, I've added columns.

I get so much pleasure now from the house. I've de-cluttered it. Much has been shed to Brightwells, the local saleroom; boxes of indifferent china and bits and pieces have gone to local charity shops. The shedding of all this has been a huge release. I felt sunk beneath the weight of it all.

Now that the builders are on their last month I MUST stop re-landscaping around the house. I've paved over fussy beds in the Howdah Court. A new gravel walk brings you face on to the façade of the house and two urns from the Jubilee Garden now frame it and the Knot Garden. The tree surgeons have thinned out the cedar and Shaun is replanting the whole area. Outside the conservatory the overgrown rosemary has been taken out of the Yew Garden and the paths are to be widened. The architecture here is clear now and open. Gate piers are arising at the bottom of the drive, onto which I'll pop the two phoney boy warriors we always called Cosmos and Damian.

It is year two of the arboriculturists, Jo and her sidekick hunk, Chris. Not only has the cedar been sorted out, but two massive conifers removed which flanked the walk to the Oman pinnacle. Jo and Chris then went on to demolish two others in the region of the Flower Garden. The result is new vistas and a new interplay between the various spaces, and light that is needed so desperately for plants to thrive. The Irish yew along Elizabeth Tudor have been reduced to four feet, thus re-establishing the huge perspective of the avenue.

My aim is to do everything now, put everything in order NOW for the rest of my life. I don't want to start doing all of this when

I'm eighty. The result is not only ravishing but also much easier to manage and run. There remain a few more 'heaps' to sort out and then I'm there! *Laus Deo.*

28 FEBRUARY

The National Portrait Gallery is a hundred and fifty

Flambeaux greeted us, and a bevy of photographers both outside and in. Antonia Fraser wore what she called her 'Stockholm' dress, the one she didn't wear as Harold never went to collect his Nobel Prize. She's amazing as ever, having had a ghastly autumn with Harold in the grips of some variety of cancer that I'd never even heard of. But he's on the mend and walking around on a stick and venturing out. She told me that she'd first met him at the National Portrait Gallery when Vivien Merchant was doing a reading in the series *People Past and Present*. He'd yelled at someone to shut up. That was her first awareness of him and then, after, there was one of those sandwich lunches and that's where it happened. Never saw myself a Cupid in that area before.

At any rate, in we plunged, the whole place quickly jammed with people in good frocks. It was less a gathering of the great and good than a rally of chequebooks. This was all about money, getting lots of it: Jane Asher, beautiful in black and white, and her gang roped in 550 people at £250 a head. The evening went like clockwork and was done in the best taste. We were in the Victorian Gallery, one table two or three hundred feet long running from one end to the other, tall candlesticks with shades, pink napery, gilt-edged glasses, handwritten place cards and so on. The table was narrow enough to talk across. I think Antonia and I were both placed to do our 'national service' for the Gallery. I had the wives, on one side one of the American Friends of the Gallery and, on the other, a Patron. There was a display of postcards, all anonymous but the work of various artists and 'eminences', including me. The surprise was to buy one, turn it over and discover who did it.

In a way it should have been a party to which all those still living whose portrait was in the NPG had been asked. That was the element that was missing. This was a party organised by the rich for the rich.

23 MARCH

Farewell John Hayes

Suddenly spring arrived after a drear winter and bitter cold and never-ending leaden skies. This was the day of John Hayes's Service of Thanksgiving at St James's, Piccadilly. It all went far better than I thought it would, although frankly, as is the case so often these days, it was essentially a secular event. I never witnessed one flicker of faith in John. I noted that so little of the words of the service were printed that when it came to the Lord's Prayer very few knew it any more. However, the centre of the church was full to the back, so that was a relief. It was a plain and unadorned occasion, a few hymns, a piece of Chopin, a little of Verdi's *Requiem*, a reading from Reynolds's *Discourses* by Brian Allen and two addresses, one by Derek Watson, former Dean of Salisbury, and the other by me.

John's estate was divided between the Courtauld Institute of Art for travelling scholarships and the Royal Opera House for a one-off ballet. It was nice and generous. And everyone was asked to a party after at Agnew's. That was a real down Memory Lane gathering, a little unnerving really. I did an interview for the BBC in which I said that John was sexually neuter. Much to my surprise, he had once had a go at Lindsay Stainton, although, she said, she rebuffed him and refused to marry him.

These gatherings are in a way ghastly, as everyone is getting older and older and more and more decrepit and unkempt. Inevitably a great number of the National Portrait Gallery staff were there, taking me back forty-seven years. Still, it all went off well, and Derek Watson's address and mine neatly dovetailed. I was lucky in being able to rewrite Gainsborough's last words aptly for John as an epitaph: 'We are all going to heaven and Gainsborough is of the party.' John, I hope, would have appreciated that. He remains, however, a person that one never really knew, an enigma, so buttoned-up, so evasive, so locked within himself. I was never asked to either of his two houses, nor, it seems, was anyone else. And yet he was thoughtful, kind and generous, and devoid of malice.

He stayed far too long at the Portrait Gallery, wickedly getting an extension to sixty-five out of Owen Chadwick, the Chairman of Trustees, between meetings. The Board was not pleased. John was also too often in America and much that happened was the work of Malcolm Rogers, now at Boston. He also made the Portrait Gallery too much like Tate Britain. But the place never went back and innovations were consolidated.

For half a century John was obsessed by Gainsborough, through whom he led a surrogate life, the painter, I suppose, being what John would have liked to have been himself. He did not take kindly to being challenged. When Adrienne Corri unearthed documents that radically changed the accepted version of Gainsborough's life, John refused to accept them. He had that academic failing of 'owning' a bit of the past, on which no one had any right to impinge.

Signs of the times

It's the end of March. I whizzed over to Jacksonville, Florida, to lecture on The Laskett garden. Eighty degrees and flowers in bloom. I write this because at home 2005 to 2006 has been an interminable winter, bitterly cold with grey leaden skies going on and on and on. Snowdrops are still out in the middle of March – unbelievable. But I plough on. What shall I record? Well, I wrote to the Vivat Trust saying that it was my wish that The Laskett should pass to them. I feel very happy about that and I know that Julia would too. I just want to settle everything and get on with life. The house is finished, the painters gone. It is beautiful. Outside the builders are winding up and there is no skip at the top of the drive. Skip seventy went last Friday.

This was a social week: lunch at Christie's hosted by the remarkable Francis Russell; an evening at the Travellers Club listening to A.N. Wilson, a star turn; lunch with the new editor of *Country Life* and one of Coral Samuel's *grandes fêtes* at the Mercers' Company. There was a lot of royal gossip as 'Fred and Gladys' were touring the Middle East. At the Travellers I sat next to Somerset Herald [David Vines White] at dinner. The heralds were keeping their heads down under this government. They were glad that I'd written up the coronation and not them. I see their point. I hadn't realised how much there was a concentration on the accession, which must be carried through quickly for it was feared that a left-wing government would demand a referendum as to whether the monarchy should continue. Food for thought there.

I do wish that Prince Charles wasn't so thoughtless. I recall the Australians who were horrified when they went to lunch at Highgrove to see him have a different place setting and food from everyone else. It won't do in this democratic age. I heard about the Prince's one-night stand with the Bacons at Raveningham. He brought not one but two valets and an entourage. The house was taken over and the hosts were exhausted. He shouldn't do it. At Christie's I sat next to Marie-Sygne Northbourne, whose great friend is the Queen of Denmark. We both went on about this and Marie-Sygne told the Queen of Denmark that she must tell him! We can't! Marie-Sygne was also at Sandringham, sitting next to Prince Philip, who suddenly pointed across the table at Prince Charles and said to her: 'What do you think of him for taking all those freebie trips on yachts?' She was horribly embarrassed and, of course, avoided replying.

This is the world upside down. The Blair government is sunk in sleaze and yet immortal. Peerages are sold off and money thrown like confetti at education and health. Both are worse than ever before. Hilary Spurling's report on the standard of literacy of those arriving at university horrified me. They were incapable of writing an essay. Many could not write a grammatically correct sentence. On my recent visit to Newnham College, Cambridge, I stayed with Onora O'Neill. She was groaning that they'd destroyed the examination system. The results were meaningless. Everything is creeping control freakery. Everything too is revised and reorganised seemingly every other month. And political correctness has stood the world on its head. Everywhere one looks it is down, down, down . . . And yet I refuse not to be an optimist.

4 MAY

I am seventy for the last time

The V&A gave a dinner for sixty in my honour, staged in the bridge gallery which straddles the two cast courts. I was quite nervous about this one but listed off everyone who had been truly helpful, from my secretary, Lindy, to the likes of Paul Williams, who had designed such wonderful exhibitions while I was Director. This was no name-dropping assembly, so no Carrington or Trustees and none of the old Keepers of Departments. They, after all, had virtually all been awful. The result was a happy evening with a special atmosphere. I went into the V&A and worked out all the details with Camilla Graham and it looked beautiful, all white and green. Twenty years have passed, so everyone looked older. John Physick is now eighty-two, but the same. Camilla kept on saying: 'But everyone said "yes".' The eulogies were humbling and what touched me most was that they didn't have to do it but they did. I felt very proud that so many of the young I'd recruited had done so well and are now at the top. Charles Saumarez Smith gave a perceptive account of my tenure and I wrote and told him to keep it for my obit. Princess Alexandra came, elegant as always, and I sat on her left: much talk of government sleaze, John Prescott and her sister-in-law's new toyboy.

11 JUNE

The Leominster Knot

I was approached about a year ago to be President of the Leominster Knot, an emblem of the town. The plan was to raise funds to plant it in front of an old house called Grange Court, which looks across a large swathe of greensward in the centre of the town. Came the day and I set off with David Hutt (we were en route to Norfolk) and arrived at the Royal Oak Hotel for lunch. No sign of anyone to meet or greet us. We escaped from the smoke-filled bar of this clapped-out hostelry and went over to the so-called restaurant. There tables greeted us, on each of which stood a narrow vase containing a trophy of two dead carnations, so dead that their stalks had folded in half. Eventually a waitress came and I consumed what seemed safe: a baked potato with some pink sludge masquerading as tuna mayonnaise. Then a man with a limp appeared who was the nuts-and-bolts guy of the Festival. Down we went to the 'ballroom', where, to my great relief, all the technical side worked. Much to my surprise, too, the hall filled. At one moment I was asked not to look round, but when I did, lo and behold a procession of Elizabethan ladies and gents in heavy velvet and ruffs swept by. Outside the temperature was over eighty. The lecture went well, mainly because I chose to talk about when was a knot a knot and when not.

Then, hey nonny no, off we went to the Knot, where the mayor and various councillors appeared in dark suits and ties. The Knot looked fine. Close to it there was a glittering swathe of fabric hiding something: a corpse maybe? Next was a performance by the costumed dancers to piped music. There were only two men and six ladies so they were a bit adrift in some of the dances where the ladies, who were somewhat long in the tooth, had to dance with each other. However, after this the large lady mayoress and various other notables spoke on the saga of the Knot, thanking everyone who'd done this, that or the other. Then came the moment of unveiling. I pulled the string and it came away in my hands leaving the fabric firmly in place, much to the hilarity of everyone. A councillor promptly rushed forward to whip off the cover revealing a small stone with an inscription attached to it recording my presence. We all then went into the house for one of those municipal teas, a cornucopia of cake, cream, strawberries, mini-pizzas and sandwiches washed down with wine or tea. And thus the Knot was launched.

26 JUNE

The Victoria Crosses, George Crosses and Lady Thatcher

The service for the 150th anniversary of the VCs and approximately the 50th of the GCs called for the full splendour of the Abbey, with the clergy in gold copes and everything well done. The Prince of Wales and Camilla appeared, she in lilac *cap à pied*, like a very tiny Mrs Tiggy-Winkle kind of lady with a sweet smile. She wore one of her vast hats, of the kind that must have a separate life of its own. Richard Chartres, enveloped in the flames of the Holy Ghost and wearing a mega mitre, knows how to do such affairs and delivered a spot-on sermon. The end was very touching, seeing all the VCs and GCs with their descendants, very ordinary people for the most part, together. I felt honoured to be in their presence.

Lady Thatcher appeared in electric fuchsia pink, of a hue that would have stopped Big Ben. But oh so sad. She was shepherded along by minders but she had completely 'gone', uttering odd phrases and grimacing and smiling with no sense whatsoever of what she was doing. Douglas Hurd said he'd never seen her in such a state. How long before we're all here again for her service, I wonder?

No news about a new Dean but the Abbey trundles on.

28 JUNE

Homage to the Pinters

The embassies, I was told, are in competition for giving tribute dinners. This one was the French honouring the Pinters, who had also provided the guest list. It was one of those 'time moves on' gatherings, people like Benjy Fraser, whom I last saw as a little boy at Eilean Aigas, was now a balding middle-aged banker with five children. Also there were the still farouche Paul Johnson with plump Marigold in tow; square Michael Pakenham telling me that Antonia kept Harold 'in the deep freeze' between epiphanies like these; saturnine Grey Gowrie and Neiti; Flora Fraser and Peter Soros; Hugh Thomas and so on – four tables of ten in all.

I made the ghastly mistake of asking Harold how he was, to be slapped down. He was seated and much thinner; indeed his legs, glimpsed through the fall of his trousers, seemed like matchsticks. The loss of weight made him look younger in one sense but he was clearly frailer than he would admit. Michael Pakenham told me how Harold wouldn't abandon his Socialist principles and, therefore, always clung to the National Health Service whereas he would get better treatment if he went private. Smoking had gone from his life but not the bottle. By midday, Michael said, the corks still popped. Who knows how long all this will go on?

I had hardly got into the room before I was told that Antonia was to do a biography of Elizabeth I. So, when I was placed next to her, her opening gambit was ruined, but she remains a marvel and Elizabeth would be a rounding-off of a writing life that had taken off with the Queen of Scots. The benign ambassador gave a charming little speech, in reply to which Harold stood and delivered an anti-Bush, anti-Blair tirade. Blair's letter of condolence to those bereaved in the Iraq war, writing of them having laid down their lives defending this country: 'I was unaware that we had been invaded,' spat out Harold.

10 TO 11 JULY

The Harewoods at Buxton

To Buxton, a delightful spa town, to perform at the Festival. I am looked after and taken to a ghastly staging of Bizet's *The Fair Maid of Perth*, which had been turned into *The Fair Maid of Las Vegas*, a monument to directorial indulgence of a kind that would have made Walter Scott turn in his grave. However, as we gathered al fresco outside the pretty Frank Matcham Opera House, who should I spot but George and Patricia Harewood? I hadn't seen them for decades but the sight of them brought back the 1960s, the Shakespeare Exhibition and Richard Buckle. Patricia is about eighty and George is eighty-four. She's still pretty, pert and bright with a pale complexion and white-streaked dark hair tied back from her face. He's thinner and looks exactly like George V, a sheepish, bearded, lugubrious look with intelligent eyes. He's now on a stick. They live at Harewood and seldom go to London; when they do, they stay at the Sloane Club. He's also deaf.

25 TO 26 JULY

The plight of rural churches and the next coronation

Simon Thurley is still dapper, although the bloom of boyish youth is beginning to fade and his hair is thinner. But he's got energy, commitment and drive, along with ambition. I hadn't seen him for quite a time but he took me to dine at the Groucho as he's now in the midst of divorcing Catherine and stays at the club when he's not whizzing around the country for English Heritage. He wants to stay put, as the agenda needs someone to hold fast. Churches are an appalling problem but he sees no quick solution, as their ownership resides with the incumbent and churchwardens. This means no overall strategy. It's going to have to be a piecemeal affair and he's rabidly against using government money, as it will start dictating the agenda as to what should happen in them, applying their litany of political correctness. Ugh! In addition the Victorian infrastructure is now rapidly crumbling, along with the nation's industrial heritage and also the country's ports and seaside resorts. We both felt rather gloomy at the end of the evening, not helped by the shocking decline in educational standards, with low literacy and no history. Also, this government hates the past.

That was Tuesday. Wednesday was Stephen Lamport and Clarence House. It's like getting into Fort Knox compared with the Faerie Queen's day. I found myself arriving at the office entrance and being ushered into a waiting room which had an inscribed copy of my *The Artist and the Garden* placed in a heap of magazines to be fingered through by anyone. That, I need hardly say, will be the last time that I ever send a book to the Prince of Wales. Lamport's a typical Household type, wearing a well-cut City suit, Jermyn Street shirt and neat, safe tie. They must clone them somewhere. But I warmed to him more this time. He'd sent me his initial dossier on the coronation and suggested that we discuss it over lunch at the club. Typical! No, I said, we need to sit down together for an hour and a half and go through it sentence by sentence. It needed it, for the dossier covered everything from a defence of Christian kingship to who should be invited. There's going to have to be a lot of invention with the next coronation, but that's nothing new. I think that its most significant failure was to take in devolution, a kind of reversal to 1603, to a series of separate kingdoms. Scotland and Wales and, I suppose, Northern Ireland. Maybe representatives of the four parts of the realm could hold the canopy poles when the monarch is anointed and not, as before, four Knights of the Garter. Out must go the hereditary peers, pure *Iolanthe* in the twenty-first century. Those who hold ancient offices, like the Duke of Norfolk and Lord Cholmondeley, should remain. There was much talk of Westminster Hall and a revival of the procession there and back, enabling many more people to see some of the event. Also we discussed how to avoid building an annexe to the Abbey; but that was not as easy as it sounds. In Westminster Hall, of course, representatives of other faiths could gather and there could be some symbolic act, like a new sceptre presented by the non-Christian faiths. There was also a need to draw in other Christian denominations in the Abbey itself, but how? Should the monarch stop at places on the backward route? But if the aim was to shorten things, this would go on forever. I said that provision for the coronation of a queen should be made now, because Camilla could well end up a much-loved one. Is the Prince interested? The answer to that was that he can't face talking about it. So, on we go. Yes, some of the robes from 1953 could go. Charles should arrive in a naval uniform and exit in George IV's coronation mantle, as his mother did. There were endless opportunities everywhere to be more inclusive, to use that ghastly word.

But he listened and we came a long way. It's all about 1902 coming round again, and Almeric FitzRoy's assertion that it should be a marriage of tradition with things invented but which appeared to be a natural evolution.

2 AND 3 SEPTEMBER

A sentimental journey

David Hutt and I share a birthday – almost – 23 and 24 August. I took him to see the three parts of *Henry VI* at Stratford, an experimental return to the Royal Shakespeare Company after a gap of decades. It was to be richly rewarded with almost fourteen hours of Shakespeare spread over two days and one of the most thrilling productions I have ever seen. We left knocked out. It was striking, as always, that you can do almost anything to the Bard and he still comes up trumps. What was noticeable was the ethnic mix of the cast, which ceased to surprise but rather, I am glad to say, seemed natural. So all of that was a joy.

I'd expressed a wish to return to Wilmcote Church, where I was married in 1971. David had contacted the priest, who asked him to say the 8 a.m. Mass. It was a stunning early autumn day. Virtually nothing was as I remembered it thirty-five years ago. Then I recall a church almost in the wilds, but here was a tiny Victorian church with village suburbia around it. The yew trees I remember because Gerard plucked a sprig of yew with which to sprinkle holy water on the gifts exchanged at the opening of the ceremony. I wore that gold enamelled sixteenth-century crucifix that Julia had given me.

On that occasion we had stood outside until David had bid us enter. That must explain why I recall so little about the interior. This time I, of course, could take it all in, a tiny Anglo-Catholic clutter of a church, rather run down really and needing a tidy. There was a shrine to Our Lady to the right of the sanctuary and the altar was up steps with a clutter of frontals and brass candlesticks. Below, to the south, there was a corner in which to hear confessions and, opposite, a prie-dieu with an image of Our Lady of Walsingham. The visit to the shrine of the latter all those years ago in 1954 had given me faith. I knelt and gave thanks for all the strength that that has always given me, and still does. Above all I gave thanks for Julia, the greatest of all gifts given, and I prayed for the repose of her soul.

The Mass was liturgically a bit of a dog's dinner but, no matter, every moment was precious to me. As David said, it was another important act of closure. What overcame me was the sense of joy I felt, almost radiance. Whatever my failings, I feel her still with me, still giving me strength and energy.

NOVEMBER

Another book completed and much else

I've finished *A Little History of the English Country Church*. The final chapter and epilogue were emailed to my editor, Jörg Hensgen, on Sunday 19 November. I set out for a five-day tour looking at medieval Rome the following day. I wanted this book to be written quickly and for it not to be over-long, to be an informative, reasonably easy read for a wide constituency. It was a follow-on from the 1977 exhibition *Change and Decay: The Future of Our Churches*, which really didn't have the consequences of either *The Destruction of the Country House* or *The Garden*, both of which truly changed things. So the *Little History* is my contribution to the problem of all those churches scattered through England that really have no or little future.

It's always a relief to finish something, although I'm aware there'll be tidying up to be done; but for some weird reason Pimlico seem to think that it will be a bestseller. I don't see that, but maybe I'm a bit cynical after *Coronation*, which HarperCollins turned into a great lump that couldn't easily be read however stunning it was to look at. But it'll have a huge rerun in the new reign, whenever that happens.

It has been an active autumn and I continue to be determined to do all the work on the house and garden now, and hope financially for the best. Everything that I've done to the garden has changed, readjusted, lifted and given new life to it. Now, after thirty years, it is chronically in need of reassessment.

Publishing is in the doldrums, so when I was asked by Graham

Stansfield, who runs an agency handling the appearance of the likes of Germaine Greer and Brian Sewell at various festivals, I said 'yes'. A thousand or so for an hour's reading from the *Diaries* and other autobiographical matter will at least bring something in and also get me around the country, hopefully building up readership.

I shall put together *Letters from The Laskett Garden* into a book [it never happened], a modest read, although as yet unfinished, with its climax in 2007 when all the great changes will have been done and all the commissions to artists delivered. Felicity Bryan tells me that I mustn't produce more than one book a year, so that's for 2008. Clive Boursnell has done a stunning photographic record of the transformation; but where will we find a publisher who can afford the plates?

And then I'll edit the *Diaries* for 1988 to 1998, although I haven't a clue as to whether anyone would be interested. The death of Versace makes a finale. I have some idea of what's there, but not that much. It's patchy, ebbing and flowing, and I'm unsure as to how much ebb there is as against flow. That could be for 2009, when I will be seventy-five – and really it's like writing one's life away [that had to wait until 2016].

Otherwise it's up and down to London with wonderful exhibitions: Velásquez, *The Renaissance at Home*, Rodin, Hockney and Holbein. And then there was my return to the ballet, a Balanchine and Tetley evening and the new *Sleeping Beauty*. At the Abbey there was a new Dean, John Hall. Remembrance Sunday this year was more poignant because events in Afghanistan have shifted what was a ritual to be got through and charged it with a searing reality. The body bags are coming back.

The Surveyor of the Fabric, John Burton, asked me to help him rearrange the Deanery at Westminster Abbey, which, I thought, should look like the Master's Lodgings of an Oxbridge college. Step one was to get the glass removed from the pictures. The dining room had been painted a good dark maroon and I arranged all the portraits of deans wearing wigs there, expurgated a horrendous cupboard and swung a sideboard into the entrance hall. The beautiful ivory crucifix in the Abbot's box was brought down, to be placed on the wall there. I also asked for the awful stair carpet to be taken off the staircase to reveal the oak boards.

Upstairs the corridor was painted a good ochre colour and a thinned-down row of early deans was hung there. Into the great drawing room we're moving the wonderful tapestry from Cheyneygates, where it's wasted, to hang on the wall opposite the window, obviating the horrible floor-level niches with medieval and Tudor windows. We'll try two or three of the Charles II chairs from the Abbot's pew in front of the tapestry as decoration and the room will be hung with portraits of twentieth-century deans, pictures that are lighter in tone. People who come here will have known many of the deans, a good talking point. The DIY shelves on either side of the chimneypiece are to be demolished and the wall lamps removed, and the collection of gifts to various deans will go to the muniments room. The ante-room is to be thick hung with images of Victorians and busts placed on the two side tables. That ought to do it. There's no money to get rid of the cheap raspberry-coloured carpet and the Dean needs furniture there which should be large and in scale with the room, so I don't know how that will be acquired. While we were engaged in this, John Hall appeared, a slim, dark-haired man with humour and steel in his eyes. He's come in from outside, not having run cathedrals before, and hopefully he'll get things moving. The Abbey's got a bit stuck.

The Dean before last, Michael Mayne, died and there was a grand funeral in Salisbury Cathedral. He had cancer of the jaw, quite awful, and in the end stopped any palliative treatment (who wouldn't?). He has left, I am told, a wonderful book reflecting on this period of his life, which is now being read by two friends who also have terminal diseases. Some people seem to be so very unlucky; who knows what fate may inflict? Meanwhile, press on, live and create while you can and be grateful.

This autumn I have become more and more involved with the cathedral in Hereford, which has become a source of joy to me in my old age. Things in my life, on the whole, have a rightness about them. So I'm going to become one of the servers. David Hutt said that I should be chief crucifer. At the moment the servers are mostly young girls who are all over the place and have never learnt to stand or sit properly.

Valerie Finnis died. I shall miss her, an early gardener encourager. 'Finnis here,' she'd bellow down the telephone when she was after me, usually to do something to flatten Simon Hornby, or 'Autumn Tints' as he was known [thanks to his dyed hair]. She was a great plantswoman who'd had this autumn romance with Sir David Scott. They were married for sixteen years. He just missed his century but they were a devoted couple, gardening side by side at Boughton like two peasants with their knee-pads tied on. Her great accolade was to dress you in the coat that stood up in its own mud. Together they occupied the Dower House which now, at last, the Buccleuchs have got back. Her plant knowledge was renowned and experts crossed the world to pay her homage. She was also a brilliant plant photographer. Her latter years were spent administering The Merlin Trust, named after David's only son, killed in the war, to encourage young horticulturalists – or her 'Merlins' as she called them. I recall her striding round The Laskett garden in its early years, exclaiming 'Has Salisbury [i.e. the Marchioness of] seen this?' She hadn't, but the comment pinpointed a kinship of approach. I last saw her at a Chelsea Flower Show, a formidable figure propelled in a wheelchair by one of her Merlins.

30 NOVEMBER TO 3 DECEMBER

London life: Wayne McGregor's Chroma, the Abbey, Antonia Fraser and a new Dean

Up in London pending the installation of John Hall as the new Dean and on the same day a service to celebrate the fifteenth anniversary of Affirming Catholicism, at which I'm to read a lesson. Yesterday I went to Covent Garden for a triple bill headed by the most extraordinary new ballet, *Chroma*, by Wayne McGregor. It was incredibly demanding on a line-up of some of the Royal Ballet's top dancers, including two 'Auroras'. It was one of those funded from John Hayes's estate, and I can't think what he'd have made of it, but his name will be associated with what is a terrific, electrifying piece. Balanchine's *The Four Temperaments* followed, fresh as a daisy sixty years on, and then a really confused new ballet by Michael Nyman, which was no good. I told the wonderful Monica Mason that the McGregor ballet was great.

Thursday was taken up by a meeting at the Abbey vis-à-vis their fellowship schemes. I wonder whether this will work? Not sure, but I made them take on the fact that we'd be having another coronation in the next ten to fifteen years and that would be the time for another appeal. America as a source for cash was doubtful. The age of the WASPs has gone and the 'special relationship' is rapidly becoming a mirage. The Commonwealth should be targeted while it exists and, when the Queen dies, it could signal the end of it. Also, Europe should be looked toward.

Off I went to meet the new rector of St Vedast, Alan McCormack, and to choose colours for his handsome rectory. But alas, there's no money to do much. In the evening to the launch of *A Glimpse of Heaven*, Christopher Martin's book on Britain's Catholic churches, beautiful and largely unknown. A motley throng was gathered in the amazing throne room of the Archbishop's house, which was covered with Bentley stencilled decoration. Many of the architectural heritage gang were in evidence: Simon Thurley, of course, Simon Jenkins, Marcus Binney, David Watkin, Sophie Andreae, Diane Nutting, et al.

And so on to dinner with Antonia Fraser at the Garrick Club. She was hotfoot from Hatchards Authors of the Year party, where she sat behind a desk to which few came up and those who did asked where Colin Thubron was! This was an amazing dinner with an amazing and vulnerable woman. Tears came on both sides. That she dreads losing Harold was the subtext; she has already, in the last few years, borne the heavy losses of both her parents and her brother Paddy. She asked me how I saw the afterlife. I said that I didn't, beyond a feeling and a hope that it would somehow be a perpetual awareness of the presence of God and, equally, of Julia. She was very funny about her mother, who believed that Frank would be waiting for her virtually with a cup of tea in his hands. Much was said about grief and loss, and I was strong on acts of closure, which I now know are so important. This was all so intense, with halting words and a touch of the hands either way as we talked of things so deep as great love and great loss. Tonight at times the beauty was still there, reminding me of one of those *seicento* pictures of the penitent Magdalene as she pushed back her hair from her forehead and her eyes were tearful.

On Friday supper was given to the key characters in Affirming Catholicism at the Morpeth Terrace flat and on Saturday morning there was a splendid Eucharist at St Mary-le-Bow. I read a lesson and Angela Tilby preached, somewhat disappointingly, I thought. We needed exhortations to move on and didn't quite get them.

Then, later, I went to the Abbey for the installation of the new Dean. The minor canons indulged in much invented tradition, John Hall being installed three times, in the choir, the sacrarium and the Lady Chapel. Four officers of the Order of the Bath wearing oyster satin mantles went off on the last but, later, Garter King of Arms complained that no one knew where they were going! It was a crowded occasion and the procession back went awry but no one noticed. I had been told to wait for a verger and the banner of St Martin but they never appeared. In the end the banners all moved off at once, in a heap. So began another era in the Abbey's history.

31 DECEMBER

Farewell 2006

Farewell 2006! A kind of nothing year but I look out of my Writing Room at the new great vista to the Kitchen Garden well on its way. The path-makers come next week. I'm trying to draw everything to an end and equally draw a breath. Next year will all be about churches. The publishers think that it's a winner. I've spent a few weeks floundering between books. I edited two years of my *Diaries* but Felicity wants me to embark on the social history of Britain. I think that she is right, as I found too much in those *Diaries* to draw blood from the living. I hope that we'll find someone who will print *Letters from The Laskett* on the garden, even if only for Clive Boursnell's beautiful pictures.

2007

21 JANUARY

A new role

I began my life as an altar server today at Hereford Cathedral. It was something that I had always wanted to do, more so as I get older and the faith becomes more intense. So, much to the congregation's surprise, on I came bearing the processional cross on high. Many of the others doing this are young things who fidget so I think that it's good that the Dean has gone along with letting a few old 'uns in to act as anchors. I've become one of what is a rota prepared to be Master of Ceremonies, crucifer or acolyte. I've done the first two but not the latter. It's all a matter of remembering movement.

24 MARCH

Dame Margaret Anstee

The Dame, who lives an hour or so away at Knill, seems to have colonised me. She is, one has to admit, really distinguished, being the first woman Under-Secretary-General of the United Nations. The problem is that she has led so much of her life out of the country that she hardly knows anyone in it. She's written a virtually unreadable autobiography but I do take my hat off to anyone who began her life, as she did, with her mother, a domestic servant, in a cottage on a Welsh hillside with no running water. Now, at eighty-one, she's still a bit of a phenomenon but finds it lonely living in an isolated house in the Welsh hills. She was clearly hot stuff when she was young, to which the photos of herself scattered through the house amplify testify, and her great love was another UN administrator, Sir Robert Jackson, or 'Jacko', as he was known.

The Dame behaves as though she's immortal and I admire the guts. Even though her clothes style is dated – post-war New Look, in a way – she looks amazing, although I suspect that her face may have had a little help. However, her taste is wholly suburban, which doesn't quite work down here, and she depends on a huge, well-meaning housekeeper called Hazel who produces lacklustre food. She's one of those socialists who can't live without servants. There is also an absence of visual taste and style, and dinner there is at best awkward. On reflection, she's also humourless.

I can never think who to have her with, as other women flee and the men don't warm to her either. I think I came to her as something of a surprise. So I find myself getting caught to escort her to some pretty ghastly things. Someone should have put her in the House of Lords as she's made for it but, alas, she's a monument to the fatality of being out of the country. As a consequence, no one has heard of her. She spends much of every year in Bolivia, where she was made an honorary citizen, and has a house there which, again judging from the photographs, could have been lifted out of Purley.

She's a passionate gardener but devoid of any real sense of design, of perspective, surprise, contrast, light and dark, etc., so it's just a collection of plants here and there with some pretty awful bedding out close to the house. But she's oblivious to such things and opens up to the public once a year under the National Gardens Scheme. The setting with the hills of the Marches as a backdrop is spectacular.

On the whole I can't but admire her. When I escorted her to some dire fundraising event at King's College, Cambridge, she appeared as an apparition wearing a couture yellow dress of an earlier era, along with emeralds that she'd once worn to open the New Year's Ball in Vienna. It was all, of course, wildly out of place in this middle-class gathering of parents supporting a grammar school. I could have told her that when I got sight of the invitation card but she doesn't want to give up.

27 MARCH

The William Wilberforce commemoration

This was the great event of the Abbey year, with the whole establishment there in full force: the Queen, the Duke of Edinburgh, the Prime Minister and Cabinet and Opposition – just about everyone. Kate Davson popped up reading one of the lessons from the nave pulpit. She was attended by a flotilla of Wilberforce descendants and looked handsome with her white hair. I recall her mother having an eye on me all those years ago! This was a beautifully planned service suddenly disrupted by a journalist erupting from the south transept screaming this and that. The Queen, who sat opposite me, buried her head in the service sheet as the heavy gang closed in on the man and edged him down the choir and out. Otherwise it all went off like clockwork.

MAY

Turning point

There was a moment this year when I decided not to write a diary, but it seems a shame not to record something. Somehow at the moment I can't get my bearings. Not quite true, for I'd reached the end of a phase and I'm taking stock of where I've got to. Skip ninety-four left the house. Bar painting and a few pieces of carpentry to The Folly in the garden, everything is finished. It all looks stunning.

The changes in the garden are beginning to give intense pleasure. The new great vista from the west front is a knock-out already. And the decision to go on and re-lay out the Kitchen Garden was right. It continues the vista right through it and, in practical terms, makes the running of the Kitchen Garden so much easier, now just four large beds divided by gravel paths so that there's no grass to cut, and with the blue arches that were once at the centre resited to add to the long perspective. Already the vegetable seeds are germinating and by August it will be awash with produce. The statue of a gardener which is to act as its focal point from Haddonstone I'll have polychromed. Reg Boulton has produced lovely plaques with 'RS' and 'JTO' for the entrance piers, and another with the date for the pedestal of the statue.

I've been bold enough to fell all the leylandii behind the Shakespeare Urn, replacing them with laurel to repeat the laurel exedra at the opposite end of the avenue. But it'll look pretty awful for a few years. The other great change is the Serpentine Walk. This is virtually a new garden, a quite thrilling surprise, a winding pathway through drifts of hardy perennials and grasses in the new manner, from which topiary arises. The crowning of the *Cornus mas* and the decimation of the conifers here too has revolutionised the area. Everyone who has seen it just gasps.

5 MAY

I go on stage

The curtain went up in the Trinity Theatre, Tonbridge Wells. I'd realised that I could do this after I'd seen a young actor, Timothy Ackroyd, do a 'performance' in the drawing room at Wilbury, Miranda Iveagh's house, last year. I thought, 'I can do that', and did a trial run on a Hebridean cruise. The script I compiled is good, a *mélange* of National Portrait Gallery days, people, events, cats, gardens, happiness – it moved from laughter to tears with, from time to time, pieces for reflection. I said 'yes' to too many venues so it was Tonbridge, Poole, Newbury, Beaumaris, Chelsea, Stamford – but I did learn a lot.

Marc Miller came to see me in Chipping Norton, a nice little theatre with seating for 300, of which 294 were filled. He rehearsed me in to how to make an entrance; always to pause and let the audience 'take one in'; never to sit on a bar stool again (my right hand apparently wandered up and down my thigh!); only to move deliberately, without hesitation; and to exercise my voice half an hour a day.

Most of that I did and it made a lot of difference, and the voice exercise meant that I'd almost got the script off by heart so that I was free to look at the audience. As Patricia Routledge said to me: 'It's showing off.' And, I suppose, she's right! But it is another string to my bow and I've been so touched by the audiences. It's usually a two-part performance, opening with a fifty-minute 'act', then an interval followed by a second half given over to questions, pretty intelligent ones too, from the audience. But it was interesting to learn how to get into the swing of it and knowing the punchlines.

The venues are incredibly varied. There are apparently some six hundred of them scattered through the UK. They vary from theatres to Arts Centres to multi-purpose buildings. So my routine is always as follows: go expecting nothing, arrive early, rearrange things, check the lighting, sound, etc. The dressing rooms, if they exist at all, are awful, run down and scruffy. Think yourself lucky if you get a tuna sandwich and a glass of wine. But I can't deny the fascination.

6 MAY

Westminster Abbey

I've promised to help the Dean over vestments and paid for a handsome dalmatic to match his best set. There was a grand Eucharist with a full orchestra on 6 May and I was the first to wear it as MC. David Hutt was there and said that it looked at times like a con-celebration!

16 MAY

A visit to the Fashion Museum, Bath

A droll day in Bath. Much to my amusement, the Fashion Museum is planning an exhibition of my shirts. It was so astonishing to see the stuff all carefully folded away, wrapped in tissue paper. My task was to choose the right ties for the right shirts but, in spite of the fact that I'd given so many away to the V&A and other museums, I managed it! What is so striking is that they're already history: the huge collars and very narrow shirts of the late 1960s with 'kipper' ties, the narrow-collared mid-1970s shirts with thin ties, and the expansion of the 1980s. Also the changes in colour and pattern: the art nouveau revival of the late Sixties and the early Art Deco one in the mid-Seventies.

I told them that there was a lot more to collect: the clothes from the late Eighties to 2000 ought to go. Also, we ought next time to rummage through the knitteds, scarves, handkerchiefs, belts, etc.

17 MAY

Dinner at Lambeth Palace

I found a voicemail on my phone last Friday, on my return from the Lake District, asking me to ring Lambeth Palace. I did. Much to my surprise, I was asked to a dinner by the Archbishop of Canterbury to which the Queen and the Duke of Edinburgh were coming. I can't think why, so I had to rejig the day as the English Gardening School was bringing a group to see the garden. It was a long day, as I got up at 6.30 a.m. to go to Ascension Day Mass at the cathedral. But then it's not every day in one's life that begins in the Lady Chapel of Hereford Cathedral and ends with dinner in Lambeth Palace in the presence of the Archbishop and the Queen.

I haven't been in and out of Lambeth that much but it looks pretty good these days and the garden, which Lindy Runcie did, looks marvellous from the windows. There was Rowan Williams in black and purple, standing on the steps with Jane in one of those dresses with a looped drape across the front which are said to be flattering to the fuller figure. It was in fact a summer frock and, although I was bidden to come in black tie, the dress was low-key, which set the tone for what was, I thought, a rather unpretentious, domestic evening.

I can't imagine how they arrived at the guest list. There were sixteen of us. There was quite a contingent from the Household: Ginnie Airlie as lady-in-waiting (killingly funny as she'd gone to the United States with the Queen and described to me the state of those now ancient crones at the White House dinner, Lee Annenberg, Betsy Bloomingdale and Nancy Reagan, all about ninety and pretty ga-ga); Tom and Elizabeth Camoys (he the former Lord Chamberlain); Robin Janvrin, the Queen's Private Secretary (he asked me to send him what I'd written for the *Mail* about the Annie Leibovitz photo of the Queen but which was never printed); Salley Vickers, a novelist who was staying with the Williams; and the Smiths (he was the Archbishop's Chief of Staff). Onto these were grafted the former chairman of the Canterbury Festival, Peter Williams, and wife; Neil MacGregor of the British Museum; and an amazing lady called Camila Batmanghelidjh, who is Director of something called Kids Company. She looked as though she had arrived from somewhere like Martinique, her head swathed in bandeaux and her capacious person parading a beguiling patchwork of exotic fabrics.

The low-key formula was rather agreeable, as it had an un-wound-up quality, whereas usually these occasions tense people up. What was odd was to find two glasses on the table already filled with red and white wine and the food just put before you on a plate. But I warmed to the fact that this was how things were done here on a slender budget. And, in any case, I don't think that the Queen notices food very much.

She was dressed in a pale emerald green frock with a lot of bead embroidery. The belt had been put on slightly askew and I think that she must have done her own make-up, for her face was a mass of pink powder put on in a way that I recall that my mother did in the 1950s. But, as usual, she did her stuff both before and after dinner with us all. She came to me and set the conversation going by saying what about that incident of the man protesting at the Wilberforce service. At any rate I was able to express my sadness at the death of Oliver Millar: 'Begun under Blunt, you know,' she said. And then I expressed my pleasure that the Royal Collection had bought Annigoni's study of her head for the 1970 portrait. She was enthusiastic about that, so I recalled the lunch at the Palace decades ago and how I'd been dragooned to ask her to sit for her portrait and how she had said that she had just sat for her portrait for Scotland in which she looked like a pygmy, and how, when she came to the National Portrait Gallery, she had paused in front of the Annigoni picture and delivered the line: 'It looks very different with a frame.' It was all very easy and both she and the Duke of Edinburgh looked fine. He'll be eighty-six this year and he'll hit ninety easily.

30 MAY

The Gresham Lecture

The Annual Gresham Special Lecture was delivered under the auspices of Gresham College by someone deemed to be a leading figure in British academic or public life. It took place in the crypt of St Paul's Cathedral. On this occasion it attracted a lot of attention and paved the way for the publication of the Little History.

Came the great day. I'd done *Start the Week* on Monday with Andrew Marr, which went well, although one of the guests said, 'Great idea, make the church over to the teenagers but make sure that the vestry's stocked with condoms!' The actual lecture took place in the Crypt Chapel of St Paul's, rather an awkward space with transepts from which no one can see the lecturer. It seated 350, all of which seats had long gone, so, much to my astonishment, 150 more turned up and had to stand.

This was a state occasion and I'd reworked my Council for the Care of Churches oration to far greater effect and retitled it 'The Beauty of Holiness and its Perils: Or How to Save Ten Thousand Churches'. It had a terrific reception and there was a dinner afterwards with the Bishop of London two along from me so we couldn't speak, which was a shame as he's pretty good on this topic. I feel that I had hit on the right subject at a crucial moment. This will run and run.

4 JULY

A visit to the Bodleian Library

I drove to Oxford and nearly drove out the other side. It has a nightmare one-way system and before I could turn I found myself heading for Abingdon. However, I did manage to turn round and hit the Old Bank Hotel in the High. I had lunch at the Bodleian with Chris Fletcher, a delightful, owlish young man. Afterwards we went back and found his colleagues working on the Oman Papers, much to my surprise on Carola Oman's travel diaries, many of which, to my horror, I'd ditched. But I'd kept three, including one to Russia in 1928, which, I thought, could be interesting. Sadly I hadn't taken in that this was a woman of her period's travel diaries and, as such, of great interest from the feminist point of view. They were, however, so pleased and excited about what they had got. I said that they had better come and scoop up what else was relevant. I found all this incredibly moving. I'd done the right thing and honoured the family. The tears came as I left.

Later it made me think that Julia's negatives should go to the Bristol Theatre Collection. I rang Jo Elsworth and she'll collect them. Meanwhile, I'm sending odd notes to Julian Chadwick as to where various other things should go.

12 JULY

Hide and seek in the National Portrait Gallery

I took a handful of 'retiring' Abbey choristers and Jonathan Milton, Headmaster of the Choir School, round the National Portrait Gallery. I'm rarely exposed to the very young, most of these having been born about 1995, some sixty years after me. Their whole time in terms of lifespan is yet to come. But I'd thought of a way of getting around this, having done a recce the day before. We pursued portraits of composers and music-making, which took us all the way from Henry VIII's 'Pastime with Good Company' to Peter Maxwell Davies.

Sometimes I would stand in the middle of a gallery and say 'Find him' and around they would reel. It was Purcell or Elgar or whoever, and up the cry would go, and they were then asked to remember which of their works they had sung. But it was a means that took them all through the Gallery. They were, I think, fascinated. I told them not to miss the computer area, where they could dial up on screen anyone they wanted. But it was rather fascinating finding them look at a portrait of Paul McCartney as someone 'old'.

16 JULY

Farewell to Joan Griffiths

Joan Griffiths was a country friend who lived not far away, in Wellbrook Manor in Peterchurch. She was a distinguished restorer whose principal

work had been the cleaning and restoration of Mantegna's cartoons, The
Triumph of Caesar, *at Hampton Court. We had mutual friends like
the critic Brian Sewell and the painter Frances Stainton, and she was a
good gardener.*

The weather was mercifully fine. I drove over to Wellbrook Manor
but was too early, so I went to the church to find Michael Fraser
and Christopher Goode arranging things. This is not the prettiest of
churches, being devoid of anyone with an eye or any taste. In fact,
everything was in the wrong place, untidy, unkempt and scuffed. At
the back there was a ghastly cheap carpet; the one running the length
of the nave was soiled; there were chairs where they shouldn't be, a
piano plonked beneath the pulpit and strips of carpet on the choir
stall seats. We couldn't move the piano but managed with flowers
to pull the whole thing together to make some kind of tableau. No
wonder, I thought, that the Church of England is in the mess that
it's in. Who'd want to come to this dump?

However, back to Wellbrook Manor where the closer circle fore-
gathered: Irish cousins; Lorna Mary, Joan's 'adopted' next of kin; and
Brian Sewell with Dominic in tow. Brian is such a contradiction,
always playing the hermit and yet he's never off radio, television or
being on the road doing his 'Adventures of an Art Critic'. His face is
now a pale babyish pink, his white hair immaculate. I always find it
difficult to make conversation with him. It wanders along haltingly
as though there was something unsaid meaning that a bridge was
there which could never be crossed.

The church was fairly full. The organist was good and a singer
performed Faure's 'Pie Jesu' well. It was all pretty good, although not
that memorable. I gave the address, taking my cue from the name of
a shop near where I lived in London called 'The Delightful Muddle'.
It made them laugh, for Joan was both a muddle and a delight. Then
we went to the churchyard where Gerald, her husband, lay buried
and that was curiously moving, a shady English scene with the

immemorial words said, the earth scattered on the lowered coffin, bestowing a touching finality. Everyone there was a bit awkward but I felt with this it was all very complete.

Afterwards there was tea at Wellbrook with champagne to toast 'Gerald and Joan' on the lawn in front of the house. As we raised our glasses there was a clap of thunder and the rain fell in a manner that was curiously apt.

This was the end of a saga which had gone on since last autumn, when Joan was diagnosed with pancreatic cancer like Julia. She had come out of a ten-hour operation clear, came to me for Christmas and then began chemotherapy in late January. That had precipitated a stroke, so in to Cheltenham General Hospital she went. Awful. She hadn't even made a living testament. I wished that they had let her die almost at once instead of the ghastly six months that followed, with all the tubes and two hospital infections. We all did our best to go and cheer her but it was a long way to travel.

When I went on the 9th I knew that it would be the last time I would see her. I entered the ward bearing a single rose and exclaiming 'Rosenkavalier'. She died thirty-six hours later. A pretty and really sweet woman married to a very boring man. She leaves as her monument the restoration of the Mantegna Cartoons.

19 JULY

Farewell Souci

Souci has been trying to escape for a couple of months [all our Maine Coons are house cats with access to a large outdoor pen]. This, I know, means only one thing: that the end of life is near. Every time he sees an open door he heads for it but I deny it to him.

In size he's a third of what he was and now weighs so little that he's nothing but bones in a fur bag. But there is some life. He has wanted to be brushed in the dressing room and when I've picked him up he has purred with happiness. But this week there's been a sharp downturn. He's finding it difficult to move round and I just sensed, as I did with Julia, that this would be the week.

Today I caught him dragging himself across from my writing room to the dressing room with something that I'd not seen before: his head not held up but down. This was a tragic creature. I rang the vet and described all the signs. Yes, this was it. She said that she would come now and I steeled myself. I held him in my arms and he was painlessly put to sleep. I was grief-stricken. His body was laid on a piece of Julia's patchwork. It seemed so right. Lettice was got to see that he had gone. She sniffed the corpse and wandered off. They know. Then Souci was carefully wrapped in the patchwork and placed in a box and carried out towards the orchard to be buried as we'd agreed so long ago, next to his half-brother, Larkin. Shaun dug the grave.

Later I came down to the kitchen to find that my houseman, Dane, had left a rose on the floor where Souci's body had lain. I picked it up and went into the garden through the rain and picked more, carrying them to the grave and laid them on the stone slab that Shaun had placed there.

Next day I found that Dane had put a little vase of flowers on the conservatory windowsill where Souci had sat. It made me feel guilty that I had taken a creature's life. But there was little of it left. I was haunted by Joan Griffiths with all those tubes in Cheltenham Hospital being kept alive when, yes, she should have been allowed, or even helped a little, to pass away.

21 JULY

The Great Flood

The rains came: the Great Flood on Friday, pouring down like some passage from the Apocalypse brought to reality. Down and down and down it came. My hoped-for guests couldn't get out of Bristol. The city was cut off. Nothing like this had been seen for sixty years. Tewkesbury was cut off, Evesham was under water and Gloucester and Oxford are threatened. There is dislocation and misery in all directions. The Laskett garden is a wreck.

This is the worst summer I can ever remember, more and more rain and cold and little if any sun. It's the world upside down – or rather, Climate Change. Last year it was drought. What can be said in its favour is that all the new planting flourishes and burgeons.

22 JULY

The Little History

The final proofs of *A Little History of the English Country Church* have gone and the finished book, I am told, will arrive mid-August. It starts its public life at a little gathering in Church House Book-shop on 18 September. Then I go on the road to various cathedrals: Durham, hopefully York, Hereford, Exeter and, I think, Norwich. The Church of England in the person of Alexander Nicoll from their Communications Committee was extraordinarily helpful. I feel strongly about the message I bring: change and move on or go under. A lot won't like that but I don't really mind.

II SEPTEMBER

Reflections made in Graz, Austria

This, so far, has been a nothing year, another in-between year, nothing but clearing up and deciding which way to go. It has been the end of a domestic phase. Dane Jacobsen, the Norwegian New Zealander who came here as a butler/houseman from Greycoat Placements in January 2004, went back to New Zealand on 5 September. He was a delightful man, loyal and affectionate but not exactly a ball of fire. His exit marks the end of a phase which began with Julia's death. Dane lived through the reconstruction of the house and the establishment of a new pattern of life, but he cost too much and, frankly, I didn't need that kind of service any more.

The Vivat Trust, to which house and garden go [that was to change] was more than helpful and coped with finding a part-time housekeeper, Sharron Lane, from nearby Peterstow. So there is a reapportioning as to how to run the house and garden. Sharron comes three days a week and also pops in when I am absent. Jo Fishly comes on Mondays and Fridays. The most important figure in this scenario is Philip Teague, the new extra gardener, who moves in to Little Laskett in mid-October. He is a delightful and responsible man; his wife, Fiona, is a carer. He will do four days a week on the garden but also keep an eye on security and look after the car. Shaun will go on as before. All of these new people are fifteen to twenty years younger than me so it looks as though I am well set up and it is all much less costly . . . All of this takes up so much time! I can't seem to get on with anything. What has appalled me is the state of the three dependent properties. They have had to be put in order on account of rotting woodwork and the need to repaint the exteriors. We are coming to the close of that. Otherwise all I think is will it all ever end? So The Folly inside was remodelled, the outside changed from pink to honey-cream and caramel, and Laskett Lodge painted.

Workwise it's been the close of a period. Felicity Bryan was brilliant at landing a two-book deal with HarperCollins. They got *Coronation* and I'm due to start on a second magnum opus for them [it never happened]. I produced a scheme for a social history of England working through a succession of families. They loved the idea and I began work on it (the Pastons) but I then realised that I'd be seventy-seven or eight by the time that I'd finished it, if indeed I did! It seems to me to be stupid to embark on large tomes in one's seventies, far better to write shorter ones on a variety of subjects [I was wrong about this!]. At the moment we are trying to sort all of that out.

A Little History is launched next week. Cape tell me that I've written a winner and I will be all over the place doing it. My instincts tell me a little book on the English village could also be a winner: what is it, where did it come from, does it still exist, what is its future? But it's a mistake to go from churches to villages directly. Bearing in mind my age, it seems the moment to return to another volume of Diaries. I have begun typing these up to obtain the block of marble to begin sculpting it into some shape. Inevitably they can't be like those covering 1967 to 1987, which had the sustaining thread of two great national institutions to bind them together. These, in contrast, are jottings of a self-employed writer observing a scene in which one is no longer a central figure. As far as I've got it is clear that this volume has to be distanced from the earlier one, fulfilling more the title I give to my stage performances, *Pages from a Life*. Like Beaton's diaries, they don't need an introduction to each chapter or indeed chapter titles, as was the case with the previous volume. They should just be a straight read with minimum annotation identifying the people mentioned. As a phase of life they should end with Julia's death, although that at the moment I can't even trespass into. But it is a period, 1988 to 2003, which has a coherence. A new phase, a final one, begins late in 2003. I think that with judicious editing I can have the Queen Mother's funeral as a finale.

So far I've typed 1995 to 2001 inclusive, about 150 pages of A4, so it doesn't look that long a book. The urge to write ebbed and flowed but there are some wonderful setpieces. At the moment I'm typing up what I wrote, well aware that much of it will have to be toned down! I suppose it will appear in 2008, five years on from the last year it will cover. I think that that can be done without ruffling too many feathers. [They were not to appear until 2016, after a somewhat tortuous history.]

It has been, as can be seen, a bitty year, not helped by miserable, rain-sodden weather. However, 23 August, the date of my seventy-second birthday, I marked by giving an al fresco lunch on one of the few glorious sunny days. It was hugely happy, with five tables laid up overall with silver, glass and flowers.

Yesterday, Monday 10 September, would have been our thirty-sixth wedding anniversary. She is always with me. On Sunday I tucked myself into a church here, catching the odds and ends of two Masses, giving thanks for her and petitioning God for those now among my friends in the grips of cancer. A candle was lit.

9 OCTOBER

Retrospective

I am on the *Hebridean Spirit* on a cruise along the Cote d'Azure and on to Barcelona. I am grateful for the rest after a busy period with masses of coming and going and no tranquillity. August was full of visitors coming to stay or for a meal – Patricia Routledge, David

Hutt, Pamela Wedgwood and Bob Lockyer, Gordon and Marilyn Darling. Then there's been travel: to Franco and Laura at the beginning of August, to Stratford for the plays and a tour based on Graz. Everything seemed one long disruption.

One sadness was putting little Souci, Julia's cat, to sleep. This gave me a terrible sense of guilt that I should have waited longer but to watch a final spiral downwards would have been awful to go through. I searched on the Internet to find out where I could get a new Maine Coon cat. Dane said that I should not do that at once, as, he said, the Royals never do! But in September I contacted a breeder who had just had a litter of six, which I went to see. I wanted a little boy cat. There were two to choose from and I chose the one with the white ankle socks. He is brown and white and is going to be called Perkins. I will collect him on 19 December.

On 20 September *A Little History of the English Country Church* was published. I am well pleased with this book. It reads smoothly, is a delight to handle and gives out its message well. In terms of the media I had great luck with both the 'Sunday' programme on Radio 4 and Breakfast TV. And there were terrific reviews in *The Times*, the *Daily Mail*, the *Telegraph* and the *Sunday Telegraph*, with only Simon Jenkins damning it with faint praise in *The Sunday Times*. Well he would, wouldn't he? There were huge pieces too in the *Church Times* and in the *Church of England Newspaper*. There was, of course, a mass of local radio and there is a gruelling schedule of appearances all through next year: Hereford, Durham, Lincoln, York, Exeter, Cheltenham, Guildford, Bridport, the V&A, Ely, and so it goes on and on. But it has stirred things up and it could move a dire situation on.

2 NOVEMBER

The Perils of touring: Bath

I went to Bath to do a performance for the *Little History* in Robert Topping's excellent bookshop. As the audience gathered a lady came up with a photograph of me she had taken when I was doing the Fox Talbot film in 1987, I think – I was all in Versace white. Would I mind if her daughter sketched me as I talked? No.

Came the moment. The daughter I thought looked odd, her head shaven and wearing a bowler hat with a scarf tied round it. As I was about to begin she got up, turned round, bent down and raised her skirts to display to me her un-knickered bottom. She then sat down. I didn't bat an eyelid but muttered something like 'I've had some very strange beginnings to my lectures in my time . . .' and sailed on. Afterwards she edged ever close to me as I was signing books but I dodged her and bade the bookstore manager to keep her away from me. I later gathered that this was called 'mooning'.

19 NOVEMBER

The Queen's Diamond Wedding

The rain fell for most of the day. Having mislaid my entrance ticket, I wondered whether I'd get in to the Abbey due to the small army of police surrounding it, but the Director of Communications recognised me and I was in. The place was lit to a brilliance by television arc lamps and swooping camera beams. The gathering was of the Royal Household and the Queen's friends. What was so striking was that everyone as they came through the Great West Door was smiling. This was a happy occasion, a pretty grand one but not five-star.

But it had a certain splendour due to the presence of the Yeomen of the Guard and the Gentlemen-at-Arms. And, of course, the various processions.

The minor royals arrived in a gaggle, a disparate lot. Princess Alexandra, beautiful as always, was impeccably attired in dark green velvet and diamonds. The Princess Royal, shorter than I remember her, with her usual businesslike movements, was very well turned out in oatmeal. So was Lady Gabriella Windsor, a tall, beautiful girl with a stunning hat worn with great aplomb. I said to her at the end: 'Great hat.'

Others, like Princesses Eugenie and Beatrice and, unusually, the Duchess of Cornwall, fell short, the latter in brown and with a small hat with a large cream flower clamped onto it. The Queen, however, looked marvellous in off-white shot through with a subtle glinting metallic thread. She was really striking, wearing, of course, a large diamond brooch and a feather in her hat, also spangled so that it shimmered as she moved. She looked really happy and was clearly touched by the service, the climax of which was the Archbishop of Canterbury, in a handsome new cope, descending from the sacrarium and blessing the couple. Judi Dench read Andrew Motion's 'Diamond' poem from the nave pulpit.

Everything went according to plan, although I heard later that there had been some cock-ups between the Abbey and the Palace. It was a good imaginative touch to have asked other couples who were also celebrating their Diamond weddings. The Queen did her stuff with them, as did the Princess Royal and the Archbishop when he could. There were some two thousand or so present. I haven't seen the official listing but I didn't spot Tony Snowdon, although he took the rather lacklustre official photographs of the couple for the occasion, monuments to Beaton's dictum 'If you get stuck, go for a column'.

23 NOVEMBER

Fundraising in Birmingham

The fundraising for arthritis evening was in Birmingham. I was
picked up at 3.45 p.m. for a two-and-a-half-hour nightmare journey to the King Edward VI Grammar School. This was their major
fundraising event of the year, with no fewer than 250 for dinner
in the school refectory and me as the cabaret after. As so often
happens, I'm the last person to find out what kind of evening they
wanted and it was only after a call on the Wednesday that I realised that I must go for entertainment, so it was an edited version
of my road show *Images from a Life*. These were good people out
for a good time for a good cause. The head lady, Sue, was crippled
by the disease, hands permanently clenched, but what radiance
she had! She alone made the journey worthwhile. It was a simple
meal, the tables festooned with balloons and cyclamen. I knew
that I had to let the adrenaline run. So into the large hall I went;
someone asked me: 'Were you ever a stand-up comic?' There's
hope yet.

27 NOVEMBER

Book signing and Balanchine's Jewels

A day largely spent signing copies of the *Little History*, first another
two hundred at Hatchards and then, later, three hundred at Random
House. It was Balanchine's *Jewels* at the Royal Opera House in the
evening, dazzling except for the hideous sets. But what a genius he
was.

28 NOVEMBER

Struggling with the Diaries

Paul Greer of the BBC came to interview me for the *Today* programme vis-à-vis the churches book. They are going to do a piece.
Otherwise I am struggling with the 1988 to 2003 Diaries. Mercifully
Julia MacRae has agreed to read them. She came back to me after
the final batch of text and said: 'You're holding back.' Where was
the garden, for a start? I sat down and went all through 1993 again,
transcribing a mass more of it. I have emailed this and await her
reaction. These Diaries are so very different from those covering
1967 to 1987 and I'm only now beginning to find a way of dealing
with them.

2 DECEMBER

The struggle ends in defeat

Julia MacRae rang. She voiced the queries which in my heart of
hearts I knew about the Diaries. A volume two, she said, wouldn't
work. In the case of volume one there was a structure and a passion
framing the running of two great national institutions which gave
it a beginning and an end. As she read it struck her as abrupt and
scattered and, indeed, I'd been myself progressively unhappy as I did
the transcripts. As she said, the world has changed so dramatically
that the whole cast list belongs to an age that has gone. We talked
it through and I emailed to her the transcript from 1994 to 2001 to
see if she thought that there was anything that could be salvaged
(there wasn't). I still think that there is a book in there, with a title
like *Pages from a Life*.

Volume two eventually did appear in 2017, to some acclaim, but it needed the distance of a decade to be seen in perspective.

6 DECEMBER

Funeral of Billy Talon, the Page of the Back Stair

This took place in the Queen's Chapel at St James's Palace, the interior of which I had only glimpsed once before, under the aegis of Sir Oliver Millar, who opened the door for a quick glimpse and promptly shut it again. It is beautiful with superb Inigo Jones proportions, really elegant. Having been told to bring one's passport and to remember a number, 157, I was greeted with 'Hello, Roy' and ushered in. The service sheet opened to reveal a photo of Billy walking the Queen Mother's corgis and closed with one of him with Reg, his partner and Page of the Presence, with beneath: 'Together at last'. They'd been together for forty-two years.

It was heartening to see this recognised in such a setting. As funerals go it was a good one, with Bill Scott, Sub-Dean of the Chapel Royal, setting the style. Patricia Routledge read a poem and so did Derek Jacobi, a hilarious portrait of Billy by Leonard Whiting which opened: 'Have another one.' 'No, I couldn't.' 'Go on, 'ave another one . . .' As one knows, they ran on alcohol (Clarence House did) and Billy died of sclerosis of the liver. The service closed with 'I'll see you again' (Noël Coward) and a reading of Sondheim's 'Bring on the Clowns'. I took Patricia to lunch at the Garrick. She and Billy had an ongoing friendship and every telephone call began with Billy saying 'Woof, woof' and whenever he saw her he did a full curtsy.

10 DECEMBER

Into 2008

After a very heavy and depressing few weeks searching for what to do next, I suddenly hit on the English family. It is a topic about which everyone will want to know, as the family as we have known it for so long has been dismembered. After Christmas I go into a ridiculous six-part television series, *The Best Diet in History*, with me as a cross between Professor Higgins and Sherlock Holmes.

11 DECEMBER

Nutcracker *returns*

To London to see Julia's *Nutcracker*, as beautiful as ever. It gave such delight to the packed Royal Opera House. I felt very proud of her.

12 DECEMBER

A London Day

I had lunch with Brian Allen and dinner with Ken Howard, one old and one new friend. I've always admired Ken as a painter, like me a product of grammar schools, and a talent from a background down the line even from me, but in the North. But he always wanted to be a painter. Three wives though; number two was his first love and he married her after he'd divorced number one. His present wife is Italian, twenty-five years younger, and from the Veneto. We had such a good, warm and happy time together.

There was also a long meeting with the television company Silver River vis-à-vis *The Best Diet in History*, one of those meetings where new faces seem to come and go, but I liked them. The amazing Peter Radford arrived, older than me but once an Olympic athlete and in stunning condition at seventy-six, I think. His role is to supervise the historic exercise for our nine luckless dieters. I was recently cheered by my gym trainer that I was the fittest over-sixty-year-old he'd ever trained. So there's hope!

13 DECEMBER

A tipple with A.N. Wilson

I took A.N. Wilson to lunch for our usual jolly tipple. He's writing volume three of his British panorama, taking it from 1953 to the present. We had the usual lamentation on the times so there will be no happy end to that book. He's so prolific. I can't keep up with it. He's finishing this five hundred-page book by March!

Hélène Alexander sweetly took me to the Fan Makers' Company dinner at the Mansion House. I so admire her for creating the Fan Museum, but heavens the dinner was interminable, with dull speeches.

POST-CHRISTMAS

Christmas came and went agreeably. David Hutt came to stay, and there was much coming and going to various parties and lunches. David Walker and Bob Ringwood came to lunch on Boxing Day. Indeed, there was so much social activity that I felt tired at the end of it and relieved on 29 December to be left largely on my own.

This is always a period in which to get things done, so I compiled a two-volume inventory of everything on the walls. I can then annotate this with where everything will go on my demise. I also had Norman Blackburn, the print dealer, to lunch and let him take away all those Victorian scrapbooks and solander boxes full of prints. He will work out what to do and sell them all. There's no point at all in hanging on to them.

I am on the last lap of sorting out everything since Julia died. A fence is going up in front of The Folly, there's a new gate for Shaun, whose house is to be painted inside, as also is my dressing room, and the draperies for my four-poster bed are to be made. *And that's it.* This has been a long and unrelenting haul to make everything work, to sort everything out. I thought that it would never end. But it has. There are only scraps left to deal with now. No one will ever have to go through all I've gone through. I'll leave everything in order, with clear directions.

And now, at last, I can get on with life!!

Off I go tomorrow, 12 January [when I wrote this], to film *The Best Diet in History*. It'll be a change and if I bring it off, another lease on life. I had a wonderful time at Cosprop and I know that I can wear period dress as though born in it. I can immodestly say that I really looked good, like a late 1880s middle-aged dandy, really elegant. The clothes tell you how to stand and move, as indeed they should. I'm going to go for this one – it's different – and, as Sue Ayton, my lovely performing agent, said: 'The last thing I want to see is you waving your arms around in front of an old building.'

2008

7 JANUARY

Preparing for the television series The Diets That Time Forgot

I went to London for a script meeting with Silver River followed by a
visit to Cosprop, which is on the Holloway Road, to be fitted for my
costumes. Julia always had a huge admiration for John Bright, who
runs it; he appeared and so, together with the Silver River designer,
my wardrobe for the series was put together. The date was 1890s.
Everything sat on me as though I was meant to wear it: country suits
and hats, cut-away jackets, evening dress, a coat to the ground and
a top hat.

8 JANUARY

A dialogue with the Dean of St Paul's

This was a debate at St Mary-le-Bow between me and the Dean of
St Paul's on the future for churches. Alas, I found him a bit of a

disappointment, somewhat dull in fact. Patricia Routledge was in the audience, bless her, along with Stephen Lamport, the Prince of Wales's former secretary. No clue as to what brought them. I had a little exchange with the latter, saying that the topic of the coronation was to be reactivated. There was a gathering of both the members of the Grocers' and the Mercers' Companies to hear me and I remembered to give a plug for the latter, which had produced the money for the adaptation of churches competition run by *Country Life*. After this there was a grand lunch at Grocers' Hall for eight of us with the *soigné* George Bush, the cleric in attendance.

In the evening I took Sarah Greenall to the ballet to see *Patineurs* and *The Tales of Beatrix Potter*. It was a packed house and I'd forgotten that *Patineurs* was so good. In the Thirties Fred Ashton was the Noël Coward of dance, bright, acerbic and witty. *Tales* was delightful but not a classic. There was no long shelf-life there and the dancers must have had a horrible time in those animal heads, not knowing where they were going.

9 JANUARY

St Botolph's

This must be my ecclesiastical week. I launched Alan McCormack's website at St Botolph's after a perfectly mad Epiphany service with lots of processions and two censers in overdrive. There were three men in copes as the Magi, one of course black, all bearing gifts of gold, the gold being wrapping paper around sweets! Alan is a brilliant if zany Irishman. In the evening there was a dinner arranged around me, which was done really well. I talked to Simon Callow about the Theatre Museum and how the V&A had got away with shutting it. It is really appalling that all its treasures are now in store. I suggested that he press the V&A for a major exhibition in Olympic year on British Theatre in the second half of the twentieth century.

JANUARY

Joy: Mr Perkins arrives

All through this period much joy was had from the new Maine Coon kitten, Mr Perkins.

12 JANUARY

The series gets under way

To be involved in a television series is like entering another world populated by people you will probably never meet again. I only escaped twice from this five-week internment, the narrative of which speaks for itself.

I was picked up and driven to Sennowe Park in Norfolk, a pretentious late Victorian/Edwardian mansion built by the heir of Thomas Cook, the travel agent. The house figures in Clive Aslet's book *The Last Country Houses*. The architect was one Thomas Skipper, who, in the main, designed hotels in Cromer. The owner had commissioned from him this house, promptly gone abroad and came back asking 'Where's the ballroom?', which accounts for the Winter Garden! It is a horizontal house built to look larger than it in fact is, for it is one room thick, the rooms stretching in a long line on an eminence. What a mixture of styles! Wren, Bernini and Beaux-Arts. Inside it is gloom all the way, with heavy dark-stained wood panelling and all sorts of features cobbled together from pattern and picture books, with chimneypieces derived from baroque altars. There is not a decent picture in the house but instead bad watercolours by someone who travelled a lot, and expensive furniture from Maples. Outside the baroque statues on the pediment are a bit of a surprise.

This is the house hired by the production company Silver River as the setting for the six-part Channel 4 series with the working title *The Best Diet in History*. It is a cross between a history programme and reality TV, in which nine overweight souls are to be cut off from the outside world for twenty-four days and made to relive the diet and exercise regime of William Banting from the 1860s, the 'chew-chew' one by Horace Fletcher from the 1900s and the 1920s calorie counting one of Dr Lulu Hunt Peters. It is quite a clever idea and the house features in it as an Institute of Physical Culture, of which I am the Director, with Jane DeVille-Almond as Matron (she is a member of the National Obesity Forum), Lady Davenport (a former Mary Quant model) as the movement and dance instructor, and Peter Radford (twice Olympic champion and holder of the world sprint record) as the Professor of Physical Culture. We were dressed, more or less, in 1890s costume.

Matron is a North Country lass who knows her nursing and diet stuff. Peter Radford has the looks and figure of a matinee idol, a modest and agreeable man who works from the premise of encouragement. Lady Davenport is all over the place, sixty and divorced, but her partner died some years back. Oh and I forgot to mention Hugh Edgar, the butler, who is a Scottish architect with a sideline of being the perfect butler. He was in the series Silver River made at Manderston called *The Edwardian Country House*. A slight figure, with the creases of his face arranged in deference, he preserves a perfect indifference as to what he sees going on all around him.

Attached to this project is a small army of sound and cameramen, props and costume people, lighting men, producers, and writers of the series. I've never seen so many before, although the budget is very tight indeed and we have to shoot a complete episode every four days. The last series they did had twelve days allotted for each episode. So it is exhausting and concentrated, the days long, getting up at 6.30 a.m. and collapsing into bed at 9.30 p.m.

The participants are two women and one man for each group – Victorians, Edwardians, Twenties. These form a very discrepant lot, with ages ranging from the thirties to the late fifties. They are walking monuments to 'where we've got to'. Not only are they wreathed in bands of fat but they have no sense of correct posture nor how to make clothes enhance their appearance. Their gait is slovenly and what they wear has been flung on.

What has not crossed their minds is that losing pounds is not enough. They will have to change themselves and gain control of their own bodies and appearance. Proper posture and movement immediately change people: they appear thinner, have presence and are in command of how they present themselves. Dress can equally contribute to that. For at least two generations none of this has been taught. Even those who educated them didn't know about it. Two of the participants had never sat at a table to eat a meal before. Virtually none of them had any idea of table manners, which are not just etiquette but the basis for community. Most didn't know how to hold a knife and fork. One woman even blew her nose on her napkin. Another shouted. Several just shovelled any food into their mouths.

On day one we had to take a firm line with them as one man swore at the butler and another struck up a rock song in the bedroom. So I gave them a tough talking-to on the cruelty of being rude to those who had no right of reply and also on consideration for others. All of that was important, otherwise the whole situation would have got out of control.

Sometimes tears were shed. The greatest shock for them came when they were told their metabolic age. One woman, who's fifty-eight or fifty-nine, found that hers was seventy-four and was duly shattered. They all were. It was odd how out of this simple experiment so many wider issues arose. Deference, of course, should go, but not along with it things like good manners and courtesy.

23 JANUARY

The show goes on

By now I'd hoped to have left for London and done a star performance at Leighton House to raise money for Westminster Cathedral, returned to The Laskett, coped with twenty voicemails and thirty-seven emails and put twenty-five envelopes ready to post. I left for Sennowe Park at 7 a.m. on Sunday 20th, arriving back there to cope with a crisis. Mr A of the 'Edwardians' wanted 'out'. Revolution and revolt were in the air. First others and then all of them wanted to chuck it in. The whole 'experiment' was about to collapse.

So up I went, minus cameraman, and sat on the bed opposite Mr A to try and sort it out. However, I couldn't persuade him otherwise. His main thrust was that he'd got into something he realised that he should not have. But I persuaded him that he would say to camera what he had learnt so far. That evening he made his exit from Sennowe with me, Lady Davenport and Matron lined up to bid him farewell. He said his piece to camera so that at least it would be reasonably wound up. But the group was better without him as he had upset the women with his sense of humour and this drama pulled this chaotic show together. It was no wonder that they revolted, because no one told them what they were doing and there was too much hanging around. So a blackboard went up in the entrance hall listing off what was to happen each day.

As I write on the 23rd we're now all back on an even keel. I've also melted a bit. A lot was achieved when I joined in the Scottish dancing and gradually they've realised that I've got a twinkle in my eye. But I have to hold on to my authority over them, which, I feel, is now held by respect.

24–26 JANUARY

Filming continues

Yesterday knocked me out. It began well with the opening to programme three, which was set outside the front door of the house with a desk on the grass and me sweeping in wearing a tweed suit, hat and gloves and carrying a cane, saying that this episode was dedicated to 'The Great Outdoors'. But then, at lunch, two of them were late: Miss C a little but with an apology; Miss B querulous, noisy and complaining. I immediately asked for an apology, in reply to which she said that she'd think about it. Then, after much havering, grudgingly gave me one and promptly decided that she was ill and left. I ended the meal by saying that punctuality was not only a courtesy to me but to all of them and that I'd been extremely distressed by the incident, and swept out.

Later Miss C came and apologised to me but she's so loquacious and undisciplined. So that was fine, although Caroline [Ross-Pirie, the producer] was screaming because I'd seen Miss C minus a camera's presence. But I felt that I ought to: all my instincts told me that. At any rate, we then did an interview with her that encompassed that, so all was back on an even keel again.

It's easier because they are now outside. Yesterday afternoon it was go-kart racing with much hilarity and today they're off to the seaside with a trip to Cromer. After eight days they've collectively lost four and half stone. The Banting diet won, followed by the 1920s Lulu one. But they all already look so different. Inch by inch they've learnt to eat properly and to hold themselves. They look taller, have presence and, thanks to fresh air, bloom. In a way they are rediscovering themselves, having had time to reflect, and realising that this is just not all about diet but a whole way of life, one that incorporates restraint, discipline, courtesy to others and exercise.

I was eventually weighed. Apparently I am the ideal weight although I have an index of nine for visceral fat. Ten, I learnt, was no good, and thirteen a disaster. I need to get my mine down to six and remove flab from my abdomen. But my metabolic age at the age of seventy-five is fifty-seven. That was amazing and such a tribute to chugging on with being restrained in what I eat and persevering with exercise.

I've now discovered that there are forty-two involved in this production. It is, as I've already written, chaotic behind the scenes. It's also cash-starved and there's no money for anything.

The day by the sea, although good television, saw virtually all of the participants throw away what they'd learnt so far as they headed for the nearest pub, where they consumed alcohol and pork scratchings. They came back elated and at dinner I asked about their day, and wasn't at all pleased with what they told me. Matron had also been buried in the sand! Lady Davenport read out the number of calories they had consumed and indicated that this lapse would have to be worked off. It would have been different if I'd gone with them, a case of 'while the cat's away' . . .

As part of their discovery of 'The Great Outdoors' there was pony-carting and bicycling. These again were the causes of more hilarity. Then Richard Hobday arrived, an architect who had studied sunlight and its effects on health. Sunlight is vital for the body as a source of Vitamin D. Florence Nightingale knew that. Sunlight through the windows destroys bacteria, a fact that used to condition hospital design in a way that included patients being wheeled out in their beds into the sunlight. Modern hospitals have no provision for fresh air or sunlight. They are air-conditioned and no window is ever opened, hence germs like MRSA and *C. difficile* circulate. The Victorians, Edwardians and Twenties knew this and acted upon it, particularly in relation to people and the young in the inner cities, with the result that tuberculosis and rickets vanished. They are now returning because of this lack of exposure to Vitamin D-sunlight.

Friday was the end of programme three weigh-in. Hallelujah! We're halfway through. Bigwigs suddenly arrive from the production company, Silver River, and Channel 4 and everyone is suddenly excited. Money is to be sloshed around to film me as a kind of megastar in Holkham Hall [the Norfolk ancestral home of the Earls of Leicester]. More, I hear, will be spent on that than I'm being paid for doing the whole series. [The filming at Holkham never happened!]

Saturday 26th and it's programme four, a progression from 'The Great Outside' to 'The Great Inside' – everyone's insides. In other words, you are what you eat and the theme is junk food and its consequences for the digestive system. Weight and the glow of health, the inmates learnt, were not only about fresh air but also about consuming the right things within. So they were all told that it was no use spending a fortune on creams and unguents to plaster on themselves if the food they were eating not only made them fat but eroded a healthy exterior.

So the inmates were all sent off to Fakenham market to buy fresh food to cook. While in Fakenham, Matron got out of hand and bought a beefburger and ate it. The participants shopped well, with £5 a head to spend, and in the evening the chef cooked what they had purchased. All went well until biscuits and cheese were brought in for Mr D. This was divided equally but Mrs E left a piece and offered it to Mr C and, although we tried to stop him, he wolfed it down.

Then the eminent gastroenterologist Dr Preston arrived and laid out a pig's innards on the billiard table. This they were all summoned to see: the stomach, intestines, etc., punctured and the digestive system explained. Dr Preston told me that normally someone fainted but that didn't happen. None the less there was much horror at all of this, although some intelligent questions were asked. It was all a bit eerie.

27 JANUARY

Norwich and after

Sunday for the inmates was full of treatments like colonic irrigation and other consultations. I was taken to Norwich and went to the cathedral Eucharist, which was very well done with good liturgy and music. I had a lovely time looking at old Norwich and the quite wonderful Cathedral Close. After the Eucharist I poked my head into the church nearby – St Michael's, I think – and found an altercation going on and I was recognised. It was all about taking out the pews! I encouraged them to do so.

There was, however, much drama when I got back to Sennowe. I was told not to appear at any meal as Mr C had admitted to going for a walk and having two pints of beer at the local pub. Much drama ensued around this.

28 JANUARY

A reprimand

This morning [Monday] the inmates all petitioned for a reprimand for Mr C before they went off to see a working farm. I had them all lined up in a row on the gravel outside the front door, swept out and gave it to them hard on a sense of betrayal not only of me but themselves, the breaking of a trust. I asked for a pledge that henceforth they would stick to the rules as given. Mr C was told that the farm trip for him was off and I swept inside again.

Later that morning I saw him. He's forty-nine, his metabolic age is sixty-four and his visceral fat is twenty! Thirteen signals danger; ideally it should be between two and six. Matron said that he was at risk from type 2 diabetes. Later in the morning I confronted him with all of this.

31 JANUARY

Respite

Thank God it's Thursday and I go home for thirty-six hours. This is a madhouse and I need to return to the real world, but that's how the media is. Today a sergeant arrived and the inmates were blasted out of their beds and forced to do drill. It was *Dad's Army* gone crazy. There was a great setpiece with me emerging to do a grand slam at them, which really worked.

At last I've learnt how to do television!!

ENVOI

At this point my Diary stops, not even going on to finish the narrative of the filming. There is just a plaintive note, which reads:

I gave up here. I'd put together a book drawing on the Diaries 1988 on but no one wanted it. I'm afraid that the will to keep a Diary evaporated. It might return [it did!] but I doubt it. I made three attempts in all to put something together but nothing worked and the result sits on my shelves in typescript labelled *The History Boy.*

The television series I of course completed. It went out as *The Diets That Time Forgot,* not exactly a masterpiece but it was honest gainful employment in a year that witnessed the world financial crisis, which hit me and everyone else hard. It was also the year in which *A Little History of the Country Church* was published. This was inspired by the need to write a book giving to a wide public the history of these buildings, icons of our identity through the countryside, their use in times past as well as the huge changes that they had undergone. I was haunted by the failure of the V&A exhibition *Change & Decay: The Future of Our Churches* in 1977, whereas the two others, one on the country house and the other on the garden, achieved their objective.

The one thing my tiny appointments diary records is the places to which I went to speak with passion on this topic and awaken communities to the fate to which a high percentage of these build-ings was heading. Here is the list, as far as I can reconstitute it: Farnham, Lough, Bridport, Exeter, Poole, Oxford, Tring, Malmes-bury, Hay-on-Wye, Hereford, Leominster, Lowdham and Knole. For two years the Mercers' Company sponsored a competition for church adaptation, which in addition involved going the length and breadth of the country to inspect those on the shortlist. The net result was that I collapsed and was carried off, just in time, to Hereford General Hospital with pneumonia. It was a near miss but a terrible warning that I had to slow down.

Complete silence, however, did not entirely fall and this year can be accounted for by an email to a very old friend, Professor Jules Prown, who had been the first Director of the Yale Center for British Art at New Haven. This letter is a reversion to the type that I had previously written to Jan van Dorsten. Again they were motivated by the fact that making international phone calls was expensive. It also marks the beginning of the realisation that as the email had replaced the letter, I must from time to time print off what I wrote. This one was written on 31 December 2008 and summarises the year:

Your letter and enclosure arrived on this New Year's Eve. It is bitterly cold here with 9 degrees of frost and the garden is spangled and wonderful to look at through the enveloping mist!

I was so pleased to hear from you as you have often been in my mind. You must be the only friend I have who doesn't write of financial collapse and the credit crunch. In my case this has been a mixed year. I returned to television in an absurd series of six fifty-minute programmes in which reality television met social history. Wearing full late Victorian costume, I assumed the role of a Director of an Institute of Physical Culture to which nine hapless people were assigned to relive the diets and exercise regimes of the late Victorian and Edwardian eras and 1920s. We attracted a consistent 1.2 to 1.8 million viewers over six weeks. I agreed to do it for little because I wanted at last to conquer television and I did [untrue!]. The result is that Channel 4 can't wait to get me back on the screen [they didn't]. In any case it was such a change from writing yet another book and I loved the crew of forty-three lovely young people. So there are two companies framing ideas around me. One is a fun series in which I 'educate' someone. That started with the idea that I should relive the Grand Tour with Russell Brand. Mercifully that never happened but it's an idea still running with Channel 4 if they can discover the right person.

That is just *fol de rols* but more important is the series with

Lion Productions who've done landmark ones on the history of Britain. I said that the social history of Britain since 1945 has never been done. So *The New Elizabethans* has been born, a seven-part series, thematic on the changes in ordinary people's lives from 1952 to 2012, the year of the Queen's Diamond Jubilee. It has jumped every hurdle with Channel 4 so far and they've produced 'seed money' for two days' pilot filming in the second week in January. It would be a wonderful project, a three-year one for it is a huge commitment and would not hit the screens until the fall of 2011. It is to be about ordinary people, with titles like 'Shameless', 'Where did the dining room table go?', etc. I also broke a mould in *The Diets That Time Forgot* in that, unlike David Starkey, Simon Schama, et al., I became an acting part in the series and wouldn't do what they always do, which is to walk on and lecture the viewer. So one minute I'd be helping a bride choose her wedding dress and the next walking in the Gay Pride march, etc. There would also be highly original restagings of social events and manners from earlier decades and a great use of home movies and of film. The awful thing is I'd be seventy-six when it comes out! [The series never happened.]

The last year has been nothing but the fate of the rural church, to which I said that I would give a year (i.e. 2008). It has been a huge success. The *Country Life* competition for church adaptation is being run for a second year (I raised the money for that). This year I've been all over England on the topic, kick-starting the debate, which is an urgent one, also attacking the conservation and preservation societies who wield power without responsibility. They were a positive force in the twentieth century but now they're in danger of becoming a negative one. You cannot keep a building going without a use and it can only gain a use through change. I now want to bow out of this and will only carry on a little through 2009. *A Little History of the English Country Church* has been a bestseller for what it is – just under 16,000 in hardback and over 15,000 in paperback since late September, when it was published. However, financially this has been a disastrous year. Publishing here is in free-fall. I was used to getting six-figure advances and now you're lucky to get five, and low at that. When I went into Random House I learnt that no member of staff was to take a taxi, take an author out to lunch, no launch parties, and all books were to be printed on only two sorts of paper. I wrote a second volume of autobiography. No one wants it. I then began work on *The King Returns* about Charles II. No one wants that. And I'm an established author with a large following! Cape want only one thing from me, a book on England, so that's what I'm writing. It is the most difficult book I've ever agreed to write. It is needed as the island falls apart and Scotland drifts off. What is England, who are we, what holds us together, why are we different . . .? So it will be thematic, with chapters like 'The Island', 'Visionaries', 'Icons', 'Legends', etc.

The news here is nothing but disaster, shops that have been here for decades closing. Worse is to come in the New Year. The rhetoric used by government is that used in the Second World War. There's going to be a series of cataclysmic bankruptcies through the first half of 2009. My income has collapsed – the share portfolio has dropped by a third. The lovely guest cottage in the grounds, The Folly, I am letting the Vivat Trust take over and give over to holiday lets to raise money to pay the second gardener. The garden is a famous one. It gets better but to keep two gardeners four days a week eats up £40,000 p.a. in wages, plus houses for each of them and their council tax. The only remission is that I can claim 50 per cent of that in tax. So after a golden decade it's batten down the hatches.

So it's been a gloomy end to 2008. Harold Pinter died on Christmas Eve and I'm taking Antonia out to dinner next Monday. She's devastated. Another old friend of ours, David Walker, the theatre designer whom I saw three times in Christmas week, had a massive stroke and died instantly. Now I'm involved in the funeral. Another close couple have the husband dying of cancer and the wife, who props him up, succumbing to Parkinson's.

But life goes on. Apart from that, everything works well. David Hutt, who has most of my London flat, is hugely supportive and companionable. We're a bit like Sherlock Holmes and Dr Watson! The house here is beautiful, even if I can't afford to put the heating on most of the time. I have two wonderful cats, the Maine Coon ones, Lettice, who behaves like a dowager duchess, and young Perkins, a bouncy baby. I have a lot to do with the cathedral in Hereford and paid for the restored shrine of St Thomas Cantilupe, a great event in the local year. Everyone is incredibly nice to me, treating me like a revered minor national monument. The *Tatler* has just done a huge profile of me, with the photographer being flown in from New York for the pictures! So I should not complain. And I can have as many free holidays as I like if I am the canary, which explains why I'm mugging up on South African horticulture at the moment.

This letter records the sad loss of David Walker, the designer, who entered my life on my marriage and belonged to our inner circle of friends. He had worked with Lila de Nobili and my wife on the film *The Charge of the Light Brigade*. His presence enlivened any social occasion and he had an uncanny ability to read palms with a devastating accuracy. I always smile when I recall him telling me how Julia said that she would never marry anyone as she couldn't cook, to which his reply was: 'Don't worry, darling, you'll marry a cook.' And she did.

2009–2010

A NEW BEGINNING

The Diary begins suddenly again in 2009 with these words.

I wrote two years ago that I would not continue to write a Diary. At my seventy-fifth birthday party John Swannell, who had recently photographed me as an Elizabethan, ruff and all, was horrified to learn that I had stopped. 'But, Roy, you're the Mr Pepys of our time!' he said. 'Well,' I replied, 'I'm not, and God knows who would want to read what I write.' But John was the reason that I began again.

Inevitably picking up my life story here calls for at least etching in the whole of 2009 and part of 2010. These were far from easy years. First the price of oil shot up and then came the credit crunch and the collapse of the investment market. Until then I had been pretty comfortably off but, all of a sudden, I felt threatened. This was further aggravated by the contraction of publishing and journalism. The opening decade of the new century had seen me able to command large book advances. Then came the crisis and my brilliant literary agent just about extracted a quarter of what up until then had been the norm from Jonathan Cape for *A Little History of the English Country Church* – which, thank God, was a bestseller in non-fiction terms, with sales of over 30,000 copies as I write.

But then Jörg Hensgen, my wonderful editor, bluntly said to me: 'There's not a market for what you write any more.' That was a terrible shock. 'There's only one book we want you to write and that is on England,' along the lines of *The Little History*. I can see the need for such a publication, as devolution was progressively dismantling the island, posing the question 'What is England?' There's some wonderful academic stuff on the topic, unread outside academe, so there's space for something for everyman.

But I found such a book difficult to structure and I also felt that it had to be written quickly, a kind of essay based on a lifetime's commitment to the unique nature of the country, and it had to be quite personal too. When I'd finished it I knew that the contents were fine but the structure didn't work for the reader. Somehow or other it had to be made chronological and it called for a fresh mind to take a pair of scissors and rearrange the text. I finished the book last year, 2009, and Jörg is wielding his scissors now as I write. It'll come out in the spring or summer. I'm not sure that I will write another. Financially it isn't worth it and, after pneumonia last year – a huge marker – I don't want to expose myself to any form of stress.

Journalism has equally shrivelled up as newspapers have gone down the plughole and now, in the main, use only in-house authors. Also I now feel at seventy-five that I don't want to get embroiled publicly in controversy.

Television rediscovered me in the absurd *The Diets That Time Forgot* series, and that must have led to Channel 4 choosing me as one of the presenters in their *The Genius of British Art* series this year, along with Janet Street-Porter, David Starkey, Jon Snow and two others. I did one on landscape and I know that it is the best programme that I have ever done, in spite of it pouring with rain during early March when we were shooting it. But no one interfered with my theme that English identity is rooted in the land, hence Turner, Constable, Palmer and all the literature, etc. It goes out this autumn on 24 October. Channel 4 loves the programme.

But that may or may not lead somewhere. The real turning point has been the decision to open the garden. So I was into flyers, websites, bookings, a shop, parking, building a loo, merchandise – cards, guide, notelets, shoppers, book bag, etc. My young painter friend Jonathan Myles-Lea has been a huge help. He drew the plan of the garden, which is gorgeous, and he also designed the guide. Someone called Fiona Fyshe, who started here looking after The Folly lettings, has now become my PA and I can't believe my luck. She sold country houses for Savills. She's county and Barbour, a powerhouse of energy, affectionate and funny and just gets on with everyone. So she now has a little office in the house and deals with all the online bookings for the garden.

We opened post-Easter, in April, two days a week (Tuesdays and Thursdays) and closed on 15 July; we reopened by popular demand for two weeks late September. It has been a great success. To finance it I sold Little Laskett to Philip Teague, another wonder and my second gardener. Frankly it's a relief to shed one of the properties. By the time we close next week I'll have taken over £18,000 overall. To that must be added income from letting The Folly.

The latter got off to a slow start but now word is getting around that this is one of the best of Vivat Trust properties. [Headed by Frances Lloyd, The Vivat Trust was to become the recipient of The Laskett and its gardens at this juncture, until it became clear to me after she had left that they were unqualified to run a major garden. The National Trust, first mentioned in 1999, then came back on the agenda.] Opening the garden has been a joy. Shaun and Philip love it and the visitors are stunned by the garden. There have been no complaints, although it has inevitably led to more labelling of plants, and a greater consideration of planting sequence and flowering times.

My life, according to Beatrix Miller, goes in seven-year cycles and this is the beginning of another. The signs are good. But I don't want strain and stress. I am also decentralising as much as I can. Now I go to the gym in Fownhope and have given myself a personal trainer for my seventy-fifth birthday. James Dickson seems about thirty, a gentle soul with a shaved head and owl-like glasses. But I love having new goals to conquer, and also the return to free weights and away from machines.

Ultimate Travel has 'discovered' me, so there are trips abroad. The groups are usually of people I know or friends of friends, select and small. Tanya Illingworth is the guiding star of these expeditions. In September 2009 there was a German tour and a second the following September. I also arranged a stunning Herefordshire weekend for them.

Something I now find a need for is sun in winter, so I went to Burma, or as it is now called, Myanmar with the company as an ordinary punter. It was wonderful to go to somewhere about which I knew absolutely nothing. The winter of 2009–10 was a hard one and I was snowed in at The Laskett for a fortnight.

Inevitably as I withdraw from London I get more and more caught up locally, especially with Hereford Cathedral. I gave them a lovely Gothic silver censer and also a few vestments, together with the feretory for the shrine of St Thomas Cantilupe. David Hutt suggested that at the hidden end next to the wall Peter Murphy, the icon painter, should create one of me and Julia presenting the shrine. He's done it and although it's not much like us, that doesn't matter. There we kneel, presenting the shrine to an enthroned Christ in Majesty flanked by the Bishop and the Dean and representatives of the county. I'm sure Julia would have been horrified by the idea of it! But it's touching and it's tucked away.

This summer Marcus and Anne Binney came through en route to the Blains at Monaughty. It is difficult to predict what the consequences of their visit will be. Marcus was stunned by the house and the garden and wrote afterwards of both, saying that the National Trust should seriously look at it all. He wrote that he knew of no other house that opened such a window into the arts of the period. Bearing in mind the wishes of Julia [she had always wanted the Trust, reflecting her strong opinion that The Laskett needed the backing of a major institution], I felt that I had to do something in this direction [reactivating what went back to Martin Drury's visit here in 1999], so I wrote to Fiona Reynolds. In August a delegation came, consisting of Simon Murray, Fiona's number two; Mike Calnan, head of gardens; and Dominic Cole, chair of their gardens committee. Simon grasped it in one and said that the Trust would need both, as house and garden were interconnected and that themes in the one were re-echoed in the other. So off they went.

Meanwhile, *Country Life* came to 'do' the house, rather fortuitous really. John Goodall and Jeremy Musson got what I'd done to the place: 'Oliver Messel, Cecil Beaton and John Fowler.' The piece appeared in the 1 September issue and looked stunning. I now await the second National Trust delegation. I do want to settle what is to happen. I can't leave it any longer, so I made it clear that I must know by Christmas, or by next March at the latest. I did sit Simon Murray down and said that with it came a substantial endowment.

So that's where I've got to.

But I did keep a travel diary from a visit to Myanmar in February 2010:

8 TO 20 FEBRUARY 2010

Trip to Myanmar

As I wasn't the tour leader, there was much time to write lengthy diary accounts, which disrupt the flow of this Diary. Rather than abridging each entry, I include here a handful of them. These give a flavour of a trip that was not to be my favourite travel experience.

8 FEBRUARY

We take off

Stuart, my taxi driver, picked me up at 6.20 a.m. in order to be at Heathrow at 8.50 a.m. 'Don't worry,' he said. 'We'll be there by 8.20.' We arrived at 9.30 a.m., thanks to the massive road works around Reading. The usual group of well-heeled retired couples and widows from the professional classes gathered with our tour leader, Marie-Therese Hill, thirteen of us in all. Heathrow Terminal 3 looked like the airport of a third-world African state. The flight by Thai Airways was eventless and I travelled economy, really rather spacious. We arrived at Bangkok Airport at 6.10 a.m. and transferred to the flight for Yangon (the old Rangoon). Bangkok Airport was spectacular.

9 FEBRUARY

Yangon

Yangon came as something of a shock. It was pretty tacky and run down. This had once been a seat of government but the present regime decided to build a new capital close to Mandalay. The consequence has been rows of empty, boarded up and decaying Victorian and 1920s government buildings and ambassadorial residences. The university, a lively centre of political agitation, had been removed to a site an hour away. So again, huge stretches of abandoned buildings and open spaces.

At 12.30 p.m. we went off to have a good lunch at the Monsoon Restaurant, and then began our sightseeing tour. First on the list was a giant reclining Buddha circa 1960, a gargantuan hideosity about two hundred feet long and covered by a huge metal shed. This was not a good beginning. With this, too, we entered our barefoot phase, in the main leaving shoes and socks on the bus and doing a mega scrub-down at the end of each day. Back to the bus and from there to the floating royal barge. By then I was so zonked that I fell at once into a deep sleep, from which the decision was taken not to awaken me. I suddenly awoke to find the bus, much to my horror, empty, and peeled off to find everyone looking across the Kandangyi Lake at a vast royal barge that had been constructed out of concrete in 1972 as a restaurant. We were all getting more and more tired. Our last port of call was Shwedagon Paya, a vast temple which was, I must admit, a knock-out. But what is so curious is how much of it was so very recent. The impact on coming out of the lift was akin to finding oneself on the stage of a Hollywood Far Eastern movie set, gold everywhere and a forest of towers and shrines. By then we realised that our benign guide's knowledge was limited and that this was the only thing worth seeing in the place.

10 FEBRUARY

Bagan

Everyone up and punctual, if dazed. We touched down in Bagan at 7.50 a.m. At this point we all realised that, apart from the hotels and restaurants, the plan of the tour as printed had been totally jettisoned. No rest but straight into sightseeing. Up until now I had seen nothing that I would have missed seeing. But all of that changed as we drove into this vast archaeological park, twenty miles square and dotted with some two thousand temples. I would not have missed seeing this, a haunting landscape of dusty scrubland punctuated with temples as large as St Paul's and as small as a dog kennel, all in a rose-coloured terracotta brick rendered with decorative work. This was a surreal experience. God knows which temples we went to, as our list had long been discarded. We've been promised a list of what we've seen each day. What they call 'restoration' was on the go everywhere. For restoration read rebuilding. It was the overall visual experience that was so extraordinary. The workmanship was in fact very coarse and the painting crude, although it could also be incredibly refined. Lunch was at the Beach Restaurant, a pavilion overlooking the Irrawaddy River. The food was indifferent but the location wonderful. We were booked into the Thiripyitsaya Sakra Hotel, quite stunning: a series of pretty bungalows scattered across gardens, again by the riverside. The rooms are pretty good, each with its own terrace. We were by then exhausted and were given the afternoon off. I collapsed asleep for three hours and then slept a further nine at night.

12 FEBRUARY

The Irawaddy River

After a late start at 11.15 a.m. we boarded a boat, extremely well appointed, with spacious cabins and everything maintained to a very high standard. The Irrawaddy River is not beautiful but wide, shallow and muddy. At 3.30 p.m. we disembarked for an expedition to a village and then up to a Buddhist shrine on a mountain top. I don't like visiting native villages and looking at people living their lives as exhibits, which feels condescending and demeaning for them. The wooden architecture was interesting but we were soon put into jeeps for a hair-raising thirty-minute ride upwards. We were all clinging on like blazes as we were flung around. For this we were handed out 'yashmaks' so that we didn't inhale the dust. At the top there was an astounding view and the usual gilded stupa, white elephant, temple bells, etc. Down we came again and back to the boat for cocktails. A somewhat indifferent dinner was followed by a puppet show.

13 FEBRUARY

En route to Mandalay

We set sail for Mandalay. There was a stop at about 9 a.m. at a village. This was like stepping back into the Middle Ages. Water was fetched from the river with milkmaids' double pails. The village itself was immaculate, a working, farming one. Everything was in shades of beige into brown: the earth, the houses of bamboo, the roofs of dried palm leaves, the utensils, even the animals. The only colour was in clothes and in the odd poster pinned to a wall. They had one decades-old television, which was placed in a communal 'cinema' and around which they gathered to see long Korean films. The tended fields all around were green but the view from the boat most of the time was of flat landscape, hard mud and plains beyond, with little activity visible on either the land or the river. Still, it was gloriously restful and quiet, and sleep forever overcame me, for which I was unashamedly grateful. No signs of any tensions in the group. If any appear it is usually on day eight. I share friends or experiences with most of the people, so there's much common ground. There are three couples and the rest are widows; there's only one I don't warm to. The set of her teeth tells me that she's probably an awful mother-in-law.

14 FEBRUARY

Mandalay

We left the ship at 8 a.m. for a really bumpy two-hour journey to Mandalay, where we were plunged at once into sightseeing. Everything here is mid-Victorian or later: the city was also flattened in the Second World War. It is on a grid plan but pretty primitive, motorcycles jostled by bullock carts. First stop was a rare survival, the 1860s Shwelabia Monastery, all the upper level in teak smothered in carving and with a stunning Buddha Hall, beautiful and very high. There are thousands of monks in Mandalay. Here was an oasis of quiet, with tiny cats stretching themselves. It was an enormous contrast to the Matiarum's Pagoda, which we'd stopped to see on the way, a horror of shimmering mirror glass, gold leaf and flashing coloured lights. This was a big Buddhist site destroyed by fire in 1884. But what you see looks 1950s. The Buddha image is hugely venerated and the head and face are about all that's left of it, the remainder sunk beneath sheets of gold leaf. Underneath there lurks a sixth-century bronze image.

Another awful meal, with the usual array of dishes: butter fish, cauliflower and carrot, etc., and a horrendous semolina cake. On to Shwenandaw Monastery, which was not operating and was under government cultural auspices. Again this is a rare wooden survival, quite amazing: carved panels and gilding everywhere. Part of it had started its life as a royal palace but was adapted to a monastery in 1880. On to Kuthodaw Pagoda, begun in 1887, with its 729 inscribed marble slabs, each with its own white stupa.

This was our LBT (Last Bloody Temple) for the day and the last time we all took our shoes and socks off, which we'd now done endlessly for a week. Each time we got back on the bus we were handed a moist wipe to remove what we could from the soles of our feet.

16 FEBRUARY

Heho

The market at Heho was enormous, much like a souk but temporary, jammed with people and a plenitude of everything. Quite fascinating.

We then arrived at the boat to take us to our hotel, beautifully situated on an eminence, with huge rooms with mega electric fans, draperies to avert mosquitoes, and capacious balconies with panoramic views overlooking the lake. A splendid lunch was produced, after which I took the decision not to go on the boat trips. So I finished 850 pages of Tolstoy's *Anna Karenina* and felt a better man. These mega novels are exhausting, call for time and concentration and surrender to another world. Dinner exceeded lunch: eight courses, quite tiny, each one arranged like a minute still life with attention to stylistic detail as exact as in Japan. We all called for the chef and gave him a round of applause.

The Diary proper for 2010 starts again on 15 September. And here begins the tortuous saga with the National Trust which, far from being settled by the spring of 2011, was to drag on until the summer of 2015 and beyond.

15 SEPTEMBER

A 'works outing' to Highgrove

Once a year Fiona, my two gardeners, Shaun Cadman and Philip Teague, and I have an outing to another garden.

I hadn't been to Highgrove since 2000, so I was curious as to where it had got. It still remains fragmentary and unresolved, and I recall Rosemary Verey trying, as she said, to 'pull it together'. So did I, and so did the Bannermans. But it remains confused and lacking cohesion, going off at tangents all over the place. It is now very large and with eight gardeners, I think too large. Some 34,000 people a year go through it so, in view of the Prince's charitable enterprises, there's a need to generate income: now it's £15 ahead to visit it.

It ebbs and flows as a garden. My hedges and topiary have reached maturity and, I think, look splendid and the designs have been closely followed. The Prince has fine young topiarists doing a splendid job. The golden yews are wonderfully clipped but really ought, as Rosemary and I agreed, to be taken out. A lot of the problems besetting the garden at Highgrove go back to not being ruthless enough at the outset, so large trees which muck up the structure have been left standing. Some have since died but others still muck it up! The great cedar near the house has gone and something akin to a Buddhist stupa has arisen out of its remains, looking wildly eccentric. The Prince wants creeping plants all over the house, although it's sad to conceal the eighteenth-century architecture.

The heroine of the saga is the Canadian head gardener, Debs Goodenough, who really is a star. She also copes with the Castle of Mey, Birkhall, Clarence House and the new Welsh property, all of which have ever-expanding gardens. I was relieved to find that, contrary to a report in the *Telegraph*, there was no head of me in the Azalea Walk; but there were those of Debo Devonshire, Miriam Rothschild, etc. What was sad was the Kitchen Garden, which was once so glorious but is now tired and all over the place. As Debs said, it was due for rejuvenation – and you can say that again. They too have the dreaded box blight.

I still love the Bannermans' stumpery, although a shrine to the Queen Mother has sprung up, a huge mound with a head of her in a hat with rays exploding out of it like a baroque Madonna. Rather unsettling, I thought.

The Oriental Garden is exactly as it was at the Chelsea Flower Show, hell to maintain but not devoid of delight. But it does look like a show garden, which indeed it is. Of course the public loves it.

Our works outing, just the four of us, was good fun and Debs couldn't have been nicer. But I don't envy her that job.

17 SEPTEMBER

The Pope at Westminster Abbey

This was the day when the Pope went to the Abbey. Living in Morpeth Terrace didn't help, as streets were cordoned off and I had to have a passport and an invoice addressed to me to move in and out of the area at all. The Abbey service was a long haul. Everyone had to be seated by 5 p.m. I arrived at 4.15 p.m. and didn't get out until 7.45 p.m. Douglas Hurd and I, in red and black, sat in our stalls on the south side of the choir. Everything ran twenty minutes late but the television screens installed in the Abbey meant that we heard the Pope's address in Westminster Hall. It was a good one on faith, reason and conscience in a secular state. It was an attempt to push back from where New Labour wanted to sideline any faith group, now cast as oddities who somehow had to be accommodated but no longer relevant to where we were.

In that sense the Pope and Rowan Williams could sing from the same hymn sheet. The service was a kind of truncated Evensong, at which were gathered representatives of all the different Christian denominations in the UK. The service lacked any sense of the momentous until both Pope and Archbishop left the sacrarium, at which point the congregation spontaneously burst into applause [I later gathered, that this been 'arranged']. There seemed to be a real rapport between the Pope and the Archbishop. Both would have appreciated the other's mind. There was a touching moment when both kissed the Gospels of St Augustine, and also when they embraced.

But it does seem odd when the Pope doesn't even recognise the validity of Anglican orders. The Pope himself is quite diminutive, a cuddly old grandfather type rather than a dictator. In that sense one responded to his vibes, which were of humility. What the Pope made of it all I know not, for it was a very Catholic event, with the Dean censing the altar and *les grands*, and the Pope and the Archbishop praying at the shrine of St Edward.

18 SEPTEMBER

Gounod's Faust, *the Pope and Frances Yates*

The Pope came to celebrate Mass at Westminster Cathedral, so I gathered myself up and retreated to the London Library in order to ginger up my introduction to a new edition of Nancy Mitford's *Sun King*. Later I went to a new production of Gounod's *Faust* at ENO. I love the opera and there was some fine singing but the gulf between the text and the staging was vast, another case of director's indulgence. There was no sense of period. All of it was done in a tubular structure with walkways and spiral staircases to the flies. I know not why. Trolleys and hospital beds were wheeled on and off, bombs lowered, choruses came and went dressed as laboratory assistants in white . . . However, I was lucky to get there as I had decided to walk, unaware of the Pope's progress along Horse Guards, The Mall, etc., to Hyde Park. The result was that I got stuck in St James's Park and couldn't get out. The Pope went by in his mobile fish bowl looking exhausted. I was forced to rush down to Birdcage Walk and then virtually ran up Whitehall. At the close of *Faust* a bright young woman from Channel 4 bounced up to me and said how she loved *Visions of England*. I was very touched.

I was put on to a biography, a bad one (was one necessary at all?) of Frances Yates by an American. This was a poor book, full of literal mistakes. But I didn't know that so many papers survived. In the end Frances Yates and I didn't have an easy relationship, however keenly I felt my debt to her. There was a period in the twenties when she didn't keep a journal and something, I guess – what? – must have happened that made her into the complex figure she was. I find Hugh Trevor-Roper's cult of her creepy. She could be 'adored', as it were, as she didn't impinge on him, although his letters could reveal him to be quite critical of her.

19 SEPTEMBER

The Battle of Britain, Camille Silvy and Beatrix Miller

I went to the 8 a.m. Mass at St Matthew's. There was a tiny congregation but a few asked about Gerard Irvine [the former vicar]
so I must find out. The Battle of Britain service at the Abbey was
immaculate and moving but let down by a B+ sermon by the RAF
Chief Chaplain. Down the line came the Prince of Wales, now sixty-
plus, Camilla with a lot of make-up but easy and with a twinkle:
'How are you?' 'Still here,' I replied, and we giggled. Prince William,
a tall, handsome young man very like his mother, fresh and open of
countenance. After the service there was a march and fly past and
then it was all over.

In the afternoon I went to the Camille Silvy exhibition at the
National Portrait Gallery, which had been done by Mark Haworth-
Booth. It is a little jewel of a show, the *carte-de-visite* photographs
sometimes having the jewel-like quality of Elizabethan miniatures.
When I started at the Gallery in September 1959 the cupboard
behind my desk contained the Silvy collection. I recall looking at
them and thinking them beautiful but the Gallery had a rule that
no photographs should be exhibited except the one of Mrs Beeton!
How things have changed. It was a great thrill to see the gallery filled
with people. If I'm just remembered for recognising photography
there, I'll be happy.

In the evening I went to have dinner with Beatrix Miller. She is
now very old, mid-eighties, quite bent and heavily rouged. The flat,
which is mercifully ground-floor, is falling apart and she has no or
little money. She will sell the country house by the end of next year.
I have no idea what she does all day beyond shuffling around in this
shadowed limbo. She's completely domestically hopeless and studied

how I scrambled eggs to go with the inevitable smoked salmon. She goes on about the amount she's spent on the place but the moment that she dies it'll be gutted. I hate her drifting into extreme old age in this gloomy cavern amidst a shambles of papers and tottering piles of books.

20 SEPTEMBER

The Diaghilev Exhibition at the V&A

A coalition government, Conservative and Lib-Dem, had been voted in and a new era of austerity inaugurated.

Coral Samuel asked me to accompany her to the V&A. This was a dud of a show, lovely things but dead: costumes in low-light-level cases that obliterated any glamour they may have once had. There was no sense of excitement, movement or spectacle, no magic – all missing. I remembered going to the Forbes House exhibition in 1954 with its unforgettable theatricality, as arranged by Dickie Buckle. At the V&A there was one moment only that thrilled: the great Goncharova drop curtain for *Firebird*. Stunning. And there was music.

But I did enjoy myself. Mark Jones is benign and I warm to him and, after twenty-three years, the time had come to return. And it was full of people I was happy to see: Peter Wright, Monica Mason, Beryl Grey, Anya Sainsbury, etc., etc. There was a large dinner after and I sat between Jill Ritblat and a Mrs Stephen (Anne) Durrant, who'd never heard of me. She described herself as a 'corporate wife' and all I'd add would be: 'Yes, of the most boring variety, loaded with cash and houses and knowledge and interest in nothing.' Jill was beefing on about the V&A reneging on their agreement to accept all her clothes in tranches and I don't blame her. God knows how the V&A will cope with 25 per cent cuts. I closed the service to the regions and my successors have shed Apsley, Ham and Osterley. It'll be interesting to watch.

25 SEPTEMBER

The garden and local fundraising

Charlie Smith and the tree surgeons came and we decided what had to be cut down: the remnants of the holm oak at the bottom of the drive, the oak on the opposite side that was ailing [it's still there], various conifers along Elizabeth R Walk and the one large conifer left in the Silver Jubilee Garden.

There was a fundraising lunch at Whitfield held in their barn after a clay pigeon shoot. It was a wonderful, golden autumn day and the usual gathering of tweeds and Barbours. All very well done and Audley Twiston-Davies of The Mynde paid £1,000 for lunch for eight at The Laskett, together with a garden tour, in the spring. Alice Boyd was there and she came over to see The Laskett garden. Her husband, Simon, had had a stroke, which was not good news.

27–28 SEPTEMBER

We enter the apple-juice market

Simon Abbiss and his juicer arrived and worked all day pressing apples for juice. Rather exciting. The next day Simon delivered 1,800 bottles of apple juice. It's so good that he's putting it in for a prize in the Three Counties Show next year. The reason why it was so good was because it crushed together so many local old apple varieties.

28 SEPTEMBER TO 2 OCTOBER

Germany

A second German tour, again with Tania Illingworth and Wilfred Rogasch, following on the one of last year for which I did not keep a journal. It was the usual well-heeled group of elderly – if not to say old – English upper classes, including friends like Marian Brudenell, along with a countess, a viscount and viscountess, one knight and three honourables. But it was a heavy tour full of stuff.

Wilfrid is a whizz at seeing that everyone is lined up for us in the way of guides and museum people. It began with a visit to Schwetzingen on a perfect golden day, the restored garden quite ravishing. Heidelberg Castle was in the same mess as always. There were visits to huge baroque palaces: Bruchsal (totally rebuilt and therefore fell slightly short), Schloss Rastatt (better) and, exceeding all, Schloss Favorite, a porcelain trianon for the Margravine Sybilla Augusta, all intact, along with a creepy hermitage with life-size wax models of New Testament scenes, all of it quite worrying and very un-Church of England! (It included a case with the Margravine's whips and chains.) Maulbronn Abbey I found slightly disappointing, being too much a nineteenth-century make-over. Karl Eugen's Schloss Solitude was an extraordinary version of Sanssouci with a wonderful shifting of styles from rococo to neoclassical Louis XVI. On to both the old and new palaces, including the Landesmuseum, which had the Württemberg Schatzkammer contents. Baden-Baden had elegance and a concert performance of *Otello* lifted the spirits. Architectural jewels like Solitude on the edges of Stuttgart awoke me to the beauty of German Louis XVI into neoclassicism. And there was a splendid performance of Cranko's *Romeo and Juliet*. The palace at Ludwigsburg was the finale. It went on forever, miles of it, but again the empire-style king's apartments were both ravishing and elegant. The pavilion in the park, called the Favorite, evoked Pavlosk.

5 OCTOBER

Evgeny Lebedev becomes a British citizen

The day of the Russian oligarch Evgeny Lebedev's dinner to celebrate him gaining British citizenship. The location was extraordinary, the Royal Courts of Justice in the Strand. There was security screening and then I was ushered through huge black curtains into the main hall to the astonishing sight of a table stretching seemingly to infinity beneath the cavernous Gothic ceiling. It was a dazzling spectacle of great taste and style and great expense. Everything was dark – chairs, tablecloth and flower containers – the napkins and china white, along with the flowers. And what flowers! Great urns filled with immaculate explosions of white stocks, some as much as eight feet high, raised on blocks along the table. Between them ran other containers filled with snowberries, bunches of sage, globe artichokes, etc. Outside a Buckingham Palace state banquet, I've never seen anything quite like this. It turned out to be what I dreaded. The invitation said seven for seven thirty but we never sat down until eight thirty. I got home at midnight.

It was an odd mixture of guests, ranging from the respectable to the raffish to trash. There were some eighty of us in all. Evgeny Lebedev himself has the perfect elegance of a Regency dandy, slim and immaculately attired with, of course, a white flower in his jacket buttonhole. Bearded and with dark, expressive eyes, he had the appearance of a figure out of Tolstoy or Proust, perhaps a bit of both. Elton John I've always thought benign, although he's saddled with features that aren't that good and now he's in his sixties he's showing it a bit. But I reminded him of the garden I did for him, gave him a peck on the cheek and we talked of how much we missed Gianni Versace.

God knows who everyone else was. I was introduced to Elizabeth Hurley, a tall, once beautiful woman with too much make-up around her eyes. Nicky Haslam looks quite ravaged these days but he's very affectionate and funny. It was certainly not worth having his face lifted. There was Nick Serota of the glinting predatory eyes, who'd attacked the government in the *Guardian* today and whose era I would have thought is drawing to its close. Janet Street-Porter was furious about the portrait group of us for *The Genius of British Art*. There were the two Davids – Linley and Cholmondeley – so I sent my love to Snowdon, although really he doesn't deserve it. Norman Rosenthal, flaccid, untidy and leaning in every direction, was clearly hating not having a national power base any more. Then there was the Duke of Marlborough, a ducal caricature with his receding face line and a living reminder that those we used to read about in P.G. Wodehouse actually exist. On and on it went. J.K. Rowling I thought was a delightful, rather beautiful woman, with her husband in full Scottish array. I told her that I hadn't read a thing she'd written. The unsinkable Richard Rogers and Ruth, her face now heavily lined and her dyed hair falling straight down, styled as though she was a woman of eighteen. Then Peter Mandelson – I hope a fallen idol – with those dead-looking eyes set into a face that was still in good condition but which only sprang to life at the mention of anything political, God help us . . .

The dinner was excellent but interminable, working through caviar, a thimble of soup, lamb and a still-life pudding, all of it laced with good white and red wine constantly interspersed with shots of vodka. I was placed between a beautiful young actress, Rosamund Pike, and her partner, which was OK but rather boring. They probably thought the same of me. There were speeches, very short ones, from time to time, the best by Boris Johnson, who was hugely witty and ebullient. By 10.30 p.m. people began to drift away from this Wagnerian event, the cost of which must have been around £100,000. I made a point of going up to Evgeny, kissing him on both cheeks and saying 'Best taste, best style' – which indeed it was.

7 OCTOBER

A visit to Penshurst Place

I travelled down to Penshurst on a beautiful autumn day. Isobel De L'Isle is a sensible, four-square type of woman. I was there to launch their church appeal, although I wondered why I had agreed to do this when it took so much time. But I'd not been to Penshurst for decades and it somehow purged the memory of how awful her father-in-law had been to me when I was the young Director of the National Portrait Gallery. So ghosts were laid. Bill De L'Isle must have brought in or made a lot of money, as the place was done up and the huge gardens, as we now see them, created. But we're half a century on and by now it all looks a trifle worn and faded. Standards in country houses have gone up since then and this house belongs very much still to the post-war hardboard era. The carpets are worn and the splendid great drawing room, late Victorian, desperately needed a make-over.

But they're welcoming and I really wanted to see the garden, which was also a bit tired and post-war. The box needed replanting, the great parterre beds lacked verticals, there were too many pink roses and too much grass – miles of it. Like the house, it needs to be rejuvenated.

Then off we went to John and Anthea Warde at Squerryes, a

handsome, late seventeenth- into eighteenth-century house in a wonderful verdant setting. I had no idea that there were so many good pictures there, in the main Dutch. Anthea is sweet, always hesitant, as though put upon when young, but she has a real feeling for gardens. John is the archetypal English country gentleman in tweed jacket with not that much to say. After lunch we toured the house and garden and then returned to Penshurst. I then went round the public part with Isobel, which works very well, although nearly all the pictures need cleaning.

Penshurst fascinated me as a time warp of a particular period, the 1950s, which must have been the last time the interior was done over. So it was all rather DIY with lots of boxing-in with hardboard, all very 'make do and mend', the kitchen and the nearby offices out of the ark, everywhere threadbare, worn carpets, candlewick bedspreads (remember them?), post-war boxed-in sinks in the bathrooms. In my bedroom the pattern of the floorboards showed through the carpet and the bathroom had a Casa Puppo rug (remember those too, from the early 1960s?). Little if any attempt had been made since to update, so it's a time capsule of a great house attempting to re-establish itself in the post-war period after 1945.

The event in the evening went off well. The 'Save Penshurst Church' group were early middle-aged and enterprising, headed by a whirlwind of energy and organisation, David Lough. The Barons' Hall had ironwork torchères ablaze with candles and there was a fire in the centre. The room was crammed with some 170 people, who had each paid £25 a head to come to the launch and hear me. It was all very well done. The speeches, including mine, went well – short, passionate and funny. They'll get the money but I urged them to be more radical and reorder the church, and warned them that they'd come up against the Victorian Society if they attempted to get rid of the choir screen.

10 OCTOBER

Remembrance Day

The seventh anniversary of Julia's death, a golden, lyrical day so very right for her as grief ebbed and flowed. I had asked to be MC at the ten o'clock Eucharist at the Cathedral. The icon [which I had given] had arrived for the opposite end of the shrine of St Thomas Cantilupe, so it could be dedicated. Everything seemed right. So it was the Bishop, the Dean and I who gathered at the shrine at 8.45 a.m. Anthony Priddis appeared in a cassock and stole, holding a wooden crozier. The prayers were all extempore but they forcefully brought home to me that the feretory had helped transform the north transept into a holy place of prayer. Julia would have liked that, although she wouldn't have liked the shrine and the relic! But I'm sure that she would forgive me. The icon by Peter Murphy was simple and touching: Christ in Majesty with his arms extended in an embrace, Julia and I kneeling below, holding up the shrine (me in my High Bailiff robes). Behind us, to the left, stands the Bishop and, to the right, the Dean along with figures bearing baskets of apples and hops. It was a golden day and I harvested quinces from the tree near her urn in the Orchard: moments of grief, of course, but so much for which to thank God.

12 OCTOBER

Government cuts and Canaletto

I took the early train to London in order to lunch with Sandy Nairne. Inevitably there was much talk of the government cuts. I advised transparency about funds so as to carry the public with you. It was, of course, somewhat parallel to the university fee-paying reform, working from the principle of letting those who benefit pay. I said introduce something like a diagram of what is wanted and fill it in as the money is raised or given. Sandy took me into the Lawrence exhibition that was going up. What glamour – and what a painter!

In the evening I took Sarah Greenall to the Canaletto private view [*Canaletto and his Rivals* at the National Gallery] and came out raving about Guardi. Canaletto is at his best in his smaller, more muted pictures. But it was a rare opportunity to study how a succession of painters essayed the same view or ceremony juxtaposed.

13 OCTOBER

The Wrap Party for The Genius of British Art

The evening was the wrap party for *The Genius of British Art* [the television series for which I did one programme]. It was held in the Clerkenwell Kitchen, of all places, for me the outreaches and one of those DIY restaurants that were all old bits of furniture and general murk. We all queued up at a trestle table where the food was dolloped out. Mercifully it turned out to be rather good. There was no placing, so you just grabbed a table. I sat down with Janet Street-Porter and her current man, who turned out to be a good talk as he dealt with schoolboy fall-outs whom he sorted out and set again on their way. Janet is unsinkable and quite endearing in a way, which quite surprised me. Starkey came over, the same as ever, until his chauffeur swept him away. He's not that much to look at these days and somewhat running to seed. They all rounded on Neil Mac-Gregor and his *History of the World in 100 Objects* [on Radio 4]. But what we all agreed was that age was back in favour with the media.

Did I enjoy all this? Not that much. It was good to see the

balloon-like Marisa [Erftemeijer] from Oxford Films and the delightful, smiling, Lucy Swingler, who was the director of my programme. Nick Kent, the head of Oxford Films, was there when I arrived; he almost immediately made a short speech and promptly left, which seemed to me to be incredibly rude.

I'd not seen Starkey's film but my agent, Sue Ayton, said that we'd heard it all before. Gus's on Hogarth was wonderful to look at, with stunning details juxtaposed against ones of today. It worked, however, from the premise that Hogarth was British – what the evidence was for that I know not: he signed his self-portrait 'Pictor Anglus' and he can't have loved the Scots who invaded England in 1745. [On the following Sunday I saw Howard Jacobson's programme on *British Art and Sex*. All we got was an hour of William Etty, again and again and again.]

14 OCTOBER

Hidcote revisited

I was picked up at 7.30 a.m. to go to Hidcote to do an interview on the garden. I first saw that garden in January 1974 and it had a huge and acknowledged impact on the design of The Laskett as a series of rooms, and on the fundamental importance of structure. I'd returned several times since but now they were doing a one-hour programme on the garden and on Lawrence Johnston for BBC4, to be shown on BBC2.

I'd never seriously had to analyse that garden before or taken in that the house is planted out, obscured by the garden. There must, I thought, be a reason for this. Johnston's mother looks a ghastly crone and it was she who in the end ring-fenced the capital so that he couldn't spend it. Was the garden with all its many rooms laid out as an escape from her? He was incredibly rich, being American banking on both sides.

A long exploratory interview prompted a number of other thoughts. Johnston converted to Catholicism in the 1920s and that must have caused a huge family rift: it invariably did at that period. Also one noticed that the few pictures of him that exist always show him with dogs, and those who find the expression of human affection difficult often find it in their pets. Perhaps he did. Heaven knows whether he was gay or not, but we do know that he longed to be an English gent with a coat of arms. And so we rambled on . . .

After lunch we walked through the gardens with me making comments on what has become a sacred icon of horticulture. It's the orchestration of space which I admire most, those alluring vistas through one of the garden pavilions. But on the other hand, I'd get rid of the red borders, really awful. Arrived home exhausted and went to bed.

16 OCTOBER

American visitors

Mirabel Osler had wished on to me two Californian women, Molly Chappellet and her sister. Molly, who was the chatelaine of a vinery in the Napa Valley and wrote gardening books, promptly presenting me with two great lumps of vanity publishing, all pictures with a trickle of text. They had driven down from the Connaught and Mirabel had made her way by train and taxi from Ludlow. From my point of view this was a wasted day, but I do love Mirabel, now eighty-five, who arrived ashen and crippled with sciatica. But she had gone to California and visited Molly, and this was the payback.

Mirabel said that you never know, they may ask you. I *don't* want to go. But I did my act. Molly was bright and sharp but her sister was rich and dim. I wanted to sink through the floor when she produced the latest mobile screen and I had to sit through photographs of her family and utterly awful garden.

20 OCTOBER

Just Friends

I travelled up to carry out a quid pro quo for Brian Sewell last year, for so kindly stepping in and replacing me at the St Albans Festival when I had pneumonia. The 'quid' was to talk to a club of gay and transsexual men called Just Friends. I hadn't a clue as to what I was in for but took with me my current screed on England and put on a suit and tie. I began by going to the organiser's house in Molyneux Street near Paddington Station, a pretty terrace of small Regency houses. I wish I hadn't, but I've always had an aversion to domestic chaos. This was a one-room ground floor with furniture that had just been put there rather than placed. The floor was engulfed in swathes of books and papers. I've also never known anyone disappear for so long to produce a cup of tea. My host was an amiable writer and journalist, tallish, wearing a short-sleeved shirt and tie that should never have gone together, and his feet were in over-sized slippers. Most of the time was passed in him asking me my opinion of his proposed three volumes of new aphorisms. I was honest and said that that I couldn't think of any publisher who would touch it but it would make a good, witty small book of the type that booksellers pile up near the cash till at Christmas as stocking fillers.

Into a taxi we then went to a house in a delightful square in

Canonbury. Bit by bit I was able to disentangle precisely what Just Friends was. It was founded for men of this orientation aged over forty left 'widowed' by the loss of their partner. They were 'alone' and, within that age bracket, very isolated. They would often have lived the life of a gay partnership during a period when it had to be 'dressed up' as something else or, if open, would mean being socially ostracised. As they arrived one by one, I got the scene. Whereas in the upper classes there was not really a problem because people accepted it within a code of behaviour, these men were socially lower down the scale, educated and intelligent, yes, but doing middle-range professional jobs and coming from middle- and lower middle-class backgrounds which would have cut them off. They were patently hard up. You could see that as they shuffled in wearing worn, nondescript clothes, nothing smart. The club was of seventy men and they paid £3 for each event and brought a bottle of plonk.

The host house this time was occupied by a pair, both of whom had been quite high-powered professionals. The event had been a sell-out: forty chairs, seats of varying kinds, were crammed into the first-floor drawing room. I gathered that there was an event every week and, in addition, expeditions. It was clear that for many of them this was the lifeline that had rescued them from loneliness. I twigged that what they most wanted me to talk about was myself and my career. The idea of doing that for an hour horrified me, so England they got, which I laced with asides, but it only took off after I'd finished and we embarked on a dialogue. That was fun and ranged over everything you could think of. This was a generous and caring private initiative and, when asked in the taxi home whether I'd be a patron, I said 'yes'.

21 OCTOBER

Salvator Rosa, Lawrence and Girls with Pearls

The golden autumn weather continues and, a rare thing, a day to fill. So down to West Dulwich I went to see the Salvator Rosa exhibition [at Dulwich Picture Gallery]. He is an artist who is always popping up in the literature about the Grand Tour and I've never quite taken him in. There were very few people in the exhibition but it was excellent. Back to central London and to another fine, small, considered exhibition at the Courtauld in Somerset House on Cézanne's *Card Players*. And, finally, to the National Portrait Gallery's Lawrence exhibition. Oh what glamour! The Cecil Beaton of the Regency. From the age of twenty on he was a painter of genius, the paint handled in such a succulent way you could cry over it. Everyone was made to look ravishing, and boy did Lawrence love red as a colour – although perhaps not always. The portrait of Eliza Farren I have always coveted. Who wouldn't? The elegance and beauty of this picture is almost unrivalled, with its cool colour, wonderful rendering of the fur and muff and that seductive glance towards us.

In the evening to the Girls with Pearls *Country Life* party at Christie's. Most people there were under forty, leaving Nicky Haslam, dressed in a boiler suit, and myself as the two 'ancients of days'. But it was full of one's *Country Life* friends. I've lived through two if not three generations of them, having first written for the magazine in 1966. The walls had an array of the women who had appeared in that slot over a century. What a comment on social change! But I always love the pre-1914 ones, romantic, elegant, a froth of fabrics, presenting women as unattainable goddesses. Mark Hedges has proved an imaginative editor and the magazine sails on, just tacking a little hither and thither to reflect all the changes taking place around us.

22 OCTOBER

The Genius of British Art *again*

I was stuck in London, as indeed were all the other contributors to *The Genius of British Art*, to do a performance at the National Gallery. A very good audience, clips of the programme and then me doing my England thing, followed by questions and answers, during which I wound up a Scottish lady who was furious to be told her identity was ethnic and tartan. As someone sharply observed in the audience, the symbols of English identity were never ethnically based, hence the monarchy and the rural idyll.

23 OCTOBER

Trafalgar Day in Worcester

This was the evening of the Trafalgar Day Dinner in the Guildhall at Worcester. I fell for it as a guest, believing that it was an event that stretched back to 1805; but what rubbish that proved to be! It was only invented some five years ago. Tim Ackroyd landed me with doing the Loyal Toast. This was an evening of Wagnerian length which began at 6.30 p.m. We were all bidden to come in black tie and orders. There were drinks before dinner and a roll-call of the victims in the Iraq–Afghanistan war with appropriate silences observed. A regimental ram was then paraded and there was much saluting.

Eventually we went upstairs to dine in what was a quite magnificent room that had been lit under the aegis of the municipality like some brothel. However, I found myself next to the man who was organising the Paralympics, who was certainly interesting, and on the other side, by an affable Nelson descendant, Viscount Bridport. The indifferent meal went on seemingly forever and, according to the schedule, toasts and entertainment were due to start at 9.30 p.m. By then I was a bit dazed but got up and quickly did the Loyal Toast, although others proposing toasts for this or that went on a bit. At 10.30 p.m. the show began, which signalled a call to dim the lights and in the ensuing darkness I made my exit. I later heard that the evening then descended into farce, with someone singing sea shanties that no one had ever heard of and Tim Ackroyd being urged to recite John of Gaunt's speech, which he had already delivered earlier!

WEEK OF 25 OCTOBER

A visitation by the National Trust

The great event was the National Trust delegation headed by Simon Jenkins with Mark Jones, Giles Waterfield, Sarah Staniforth and Sally Villiers. Penny Johnstone did the lunch and Kevin acted as butler so that I could concentrate on the group. I saw that all the lights in the house were turned on and took them round and then out into the garden. There was much amazement by all. Everything seemed very upbeat, but who knows? Simon Jenkins in benign mood now, at sixty-seven, wrinkled but much enjoying the debate over the Trust houses as to whether or not they were being Disneyfied. Seeing that everything was in order for the visitation had called for a massive adrenaline rush as it was such a wind-up. After they'd gone I broke into tears and Fiona gave me a hug. All I could think of was Julia and what she had wanted.

The week was enlivened by an entrancing production of *The Rivals* by Peter Hall at the theatre in Malvern en route for the Haymarket, with Penelope Keith as Mrs Malaprop and Peter Bowles as Sir Anthony Absolute. Memorable.

All through these weeks I've been going to the gym twice a week and following James Dickson's programme. I'm making, I think, good progress and I told him that I wanted my 32-inch waist back without giving up drink. There were many emails, cards and phone calls from those who loved my Channel 4 programme, which went out on the 24th.

Life, too, is wonderful since I cancelled *The Times*. I now only buy a newspaper when I travel. I'm sick of the mounds of print which I never had time to read and I'm more than stuffed with news by Radio 4. Newspapers in the old sense seem a doomed genre.

3 NOVEMBER

Rosemary Verey anatomised

I came up to London on Tuesday, All Souls Day, and took the mercurial Alan McCormack to dinner at the Garrick Club. On Wednesday I had lunch with Charles Saumarez Smith, a hugely benign and happy man so that you almost forget that his wife, Romilly, has MS and is now wheelchair-bound. It makes me realise how lucky, if even I can use that word, I was with Julia. There was much talk about the government cutbacks but the nationals seem to be OK.

Then came the Rosemary Verey evening at the Garden Museum. Christopher Woodward, its Director, is in his early forties, bright, enterprising and sharp. He has transformed the place into the land of the living. Considering that the Underground was on strike, there was a full house for La Verey, although much to my consternation a phalanx of Verey children appeared: Charles, Davina, Denzil and more, whom I'd forgotten. It made me quite nervous and I warned them that I had a shock surprise. Charles promptly moved from the front row to the back!

Mollie Salisbury was there, looking like the Woman in White, so were Felicity Bryan, my and Rosemary's literary agent; Jerry Harpur, the photographer; Erica Hunningher, who put together both Rosemary's and Penelope Hobhouse's books; and a horde of other genteel folk.

The American lady who was writing a book on Rosemary and spoke first was anodyne. She didn't say anything or analyse anything or have an inkling about the sociological setting into which Rosemary's work fitted. Delightful Andrew Lawson showed his Barnsley through the year photographs, revealing that Rosemary was a brilliant plantswoman with extraordinary layerings of bloom and juxtaposition of flower and leaf, both colour and shape.

Then I got up and led up to the fact that Rosemary was hot stuff in her day and was not received in several Gloucestershire houses. Did she, I ask, have a lover from whom she learnt a lot about gardening design and history? The answer was David Vicary. John Harris had found her letters to him in a shoebox while clearing up his house. The Bannermans, I was told, have them now. Vicary was an intriguing, wretched, feckless character but endowed with faultless taste and huge gardening and plant knowledge. He was one of a gang, along with Christopher Gibbs and Robert Kime, who were obsessed by the English country house. In 1972 Vicary had designed the new garden at Wilton, a historicising one and much in what became the Verey manner. He must have been a tremendous influence on her. But I find it all quite difficult to exactly pin down. Candida Lycett Green thought that some of the famous innovatory features at Barnsley owed their origin to him, and they were certainly created in the later Sixties and early Seventies, when all of that was going on. Mercifully the Verey offspring were not in the least thrown and Vicary, or 'Madame Vicaire' as he was called, was around a lot and went off on tours with Rosemary. Was he gay, bisexual? I really couldn't work it out at all.

Afterwards James Aldridge came up to me, unrecognisable at first. He had been one of the two gardeners at Highgrove, along with David, who displayed his torso whenever he could. Aldridge, an upper-class lad, was now running his own garden design firm. He'd ended up hating his last years at Highgrove as it became like slave labour. David Howard, the previous head gardener, had also been worked to death.

4 NOVEMBER

Farewell to Peter Walker

Peter Walker's service of thanksgiving was to have been at St Margaret's but the lighting system blew up and so it was moved at the last moment to the Abbey. Funny that, in a way! The children did their stuff and Lord Hunt gave a passable address. I learnt that to all intents and purposes Peter had 'died' in about 1990. He was a hugely ambitious man and really not all that easy. Apparently he had been ill for up to five years but refused to go to a doctor and, when he did, he was found to have cancer of the intestines and it was too late to do anything.

I was in the front, next to David Brewer and his wife, along with Geoffrey Howe and the Heseltines behind. It was a very full but dull occasion, with the same old hymns and the usual line-up at the end. Tessa looked strangely out of place, with her hair almost to her waist and no hat. Her whole life had been him and those five children. I wonder whether she'll have the guts to strike out, or will she end up being 'mother' again, carting around the grandchildren? Robin was Julia's godchild but somehow we'd drifted apart.

5 TO 7 NOVEMBER

Old friends come to stay

Michael and Gillian Borrie came to stay. Michael and I shared a flat, 14 Lancaster Gate, between 1964 and 1968. He rose to be Keeper of Manuscripts in the British Library, a benign, diffident man, not handsome of feature and a little rotund of body. But he embodies old-fashioned decency, as does his tall wife, Gillian, in a marriage of a Catholic and a Dissenter that ended in the Church of England. Michael is a year older than me and two years ago was hit by cancer of the jaw and a thirteen-hour operation. A year later it hit the other side and there was another thirteen-hour operation.

This end of life can be cruel but he has come through it all, arriving at The Laskett toothless and with the left side of his face swollen and bulbous, held up by strips of elastoplast. Still, this was their first outing of this kind for a year and my aim was to lift their spirits, and hopefully I did. He's conscious of what he looks like and worries about food and is easily embarrassed, but I did my best with soft pasta dishes, risotto and home-made soups. At any rate, we toured the garden, went to Ledbury for lunch, watched *Strictly Come Dancing* and laughed, ventured to The Loughpool [restaurant] for supper and went to the cathedral on Sunday. But I'm left haunted by his comment on leaving. Standing by the car, he looked towards the great topiary walk to the Kitchen Garden and paused. Gillian said, 'What are you doing?' 'I'm looking for the last time.' [It was to be so.]

19 NOVEMBER

A busy fortnight

This was a crammed fortnight, which began with me on the 9th travelling down to Street in Somerset for a performance in its theatre. There was a huge audience, which amazed me. I spent the night in a B&B in Glastonbury and was then driven to Harley Lodge in Bristol to see my old friends the Kingmans. Valerie [who had suffered a stroke] is a tough North Country lass and has improved enormously since I last saw her. She could walk and now even go upstairs. John was extraordinary, reminding her to move this or that limb. How far she will regain total control of her left side it is difficult to predict, but the signs are good.

Thursday was the Herefordshire Craft Fair at The Courtyard in Hereford, which I opened for the third time. The quality was up and I bought a stone shaft inscribed 'N. S. E. W.' [by Caitriona Cartwright] for which I'll find a home in the garden. Friday was the Croome Court National Trust fundraising dinner. The food was no good but the room gave a sense of spectacle to the occasion. I had a Mrs Morgan on my left, an actress wearing Lanvin – 'That's a good frock you've got on,' I said – and the wife of the deputy chairman, Sir Laurie Magnus, on my right, peaches and cream with brains. He's Caroline Magnus's brother and so has part-inherited Stokesay. I got up and did a star turn, so I hope that it helps them.

On Saturday Shan Egerton [a painter friend] came to lunch and later I was inveigled into supporting a charity quiz in Hereford Shire Hall. It lacked a good presenter to give it pace and wit and so it just dragged on and on and on.

Monday the 15th was the occasion of the National Trust dinner vis-à-vis their houses at 32 Queen Anne's Gate, although there was no sign of either Fiona Reynolds or Simon Murray. Others included Laurie Magnus (again), Merlin Waterson, John Harris, John Goodall, Sarah Staniforth . . . There was no wild dissent but most went along with the policy of giving the houses a bit more spark, albeit with reservations.

On Tuesday 16th I went to Abbott and Holder to collect the Oliver Messel costume design for Constanza in the *Seraglio*. To have a Messel design filled an aesthetic gap on my walls. I'd always wanted one. Messel was my earliest memory of magic in the theatre.

On Friday 19th it was lunch with Margaret Anstee at The Walled Garden. I loathe that house. It is so 1950s suburban, without one decent room in it and everywhere painted pink. But you can't help admiring the old girl, who is eighty-three and won't give up running around the world. Why, I thought, can't she give it up and just be old and gracious? But no. Now she has a lung condition and her face, sunk beneath make-up, looked bruised. Lawrence and Elizabeth Banks were there, Lawrence looking better although still in the grips of a disease which is akin to having gout all over. The melancholy effect is that social gatherings now are rapidly becoming assemblies of the ailing. The food, as usual, was awful, the kind of roast pork lunch of half a century ago. Out host was overpowered by her guests – and anyway a little of her goes a long way as she's devoid of humour.

20 NOVEMBER

Huw Wheldon recalled

I drove to Ludlow via Leominster and Brightwells saleroom, where I left a bid for a pair of rococo Chelsea anchor figures. I took Mirabel

Osler out to lunch. Now eighty-five and afflicted with angina, she was in sparkling form, embowered as usual in an encircling array of patterned scarves. She let a rare glimpse of her past slip over lunch in the restaurant. She had been one of Huw Wheldon's mistresses, recalling how he would recite Gerard Manley Hopkins in Welsh when they were in bed.

On return the flu-cold I'd been dreading gripped me and so I watched *Strictly Come Dancing* and fell into bed. I went to church on Sunday but afterwards stayed in, feeling both exhausted and ill, and went to bed again.

22 NOVEMBER

Adriana Lecouvreur *at Covent Garden*

I came up to London to go to *Adriana Lecouvreur* with Antonia Fraser, she, as usual, in unsinkable mode. She had done eight major cities in Canada and the USA, including the West Coast, in ten days. Everywhere she was greeted like visiting royalty. Although her face is now lined, the beauty is still there, with marvellous eyes in particular which, every so often, she hides behind enormous glasses.

I thought that we might be in for an archaeological exhumation, which would be a mistake, but no, it was all done with such passion and commitment and mounted in the lush manner of Zeffirelli. Gheorghiu carried the role of Adriana as only a great actress can.

23 NOVEMBER

The inauguration of General Synod and a book launch

At the inaugural Eucharist at the Abbey for General Synod the dioceses, together with various other limbs of the Church of England, trundled on in procession, each section holding a placard aloft labelled 'Oxford', 'London', the 'Religious Communities', etc., forming a disparate, ragged lot which just went on and on. Roly-poly Kenneth Clarke arrived as Lord Chancellor and Secretary of State for Justice. I'd met him before. 'Didn't know that you were here,' he said, to which I replied, 'I wear a number of hats.' The Queen arrived, wearing a pale orange coat and hat, together with the Duke, who was amazingly sprightly. 'Where's your ?' gesturing his hand to his neck in allusion to the fact that I wasn't wearing my grander robes with a ruff frill. 'Oh, I'm not allowed to wear it any more,' I sighed. To my left was Rowan Williams, whose beard had been tidied up at last, and he looked magnificent in a crimson and gold cope and mitre. York was to his left but I never met him.

So up the nave we all processed. This time I was placed on the south side, about eight feet away from the Duke of Edinburgh. An altar had been erected at the crossing, dressed with cloths and a frontal, which looked fine. It was an uneventful Eucharist with uneventful music and hymns, all rather run-of-the-mill really. The sermon by Dame Mary Tanner was a plea for a coming together and an understanding of other people's viewpoints based on the Council of Jerusalem. She was educated, coherent and spoke well but lacked a commanding presence, so that I felt that she was pleading a lost cause.

John Hall loves it all. I suggested to him that a plaque should commemorate the Pope and the Archbishop of Canterbury kneeling at prayer together. He loved that idea. But today they had announced that the royal wedding would be in the Abbey, so he's set up more than any Dean within memory with a royal wedding, a Diamond Jubilee and probably a royal funeral and a coronation. What more could he ask for?

In the evening there was a launch party for Vanessa Remington's catalogue of the Victorian miniatures in the Royal Collection, a great achievement. Coral Samuel had picked up part of the bill. There were lots of young people there, the new crowd making me realise how old I was!

This is where the 2010 Diary stops. Early in 2011 I wrote as follows, giving the reason.

The gap in the Diary is explained by a horrendous flu-cold, which literally 'knocked me out'. In addition, Arctic weather arrived. The whole country was locked into sub-zero conditions along with ice and snow. I was meant to travel up to London to take part in the carol service in aid of Hereford Cathedral, but I never went. Temperatures day in and day out sunk to being two to five degrees below freezing. I've never worn so many layers of clothing. When eventually I went to London, I put on 'long johns' beneath my corduroy jeans.

I began work on my autobiography 1935 to 1967 and discovered how fascinating all that was. The letters I'd written to Jan van Dorsten, once the academic contents in them were discarded, were mines of information. Also the Internet threw up masses of obituaries of people who figure in the story, along with places and schools. From 1956, the year I began postgraduate work, there's a mass of material, for that was when Jan van Dorsten entered my life and my letters to him [returned to me years later by his wife] took off as a memoir. I'm not sure yet how I'll cope with the pre-1956 years, but there are so many people after that date whose works inspired me whom I later came to know. So when they pop up I will be able to take the story on.

David Hutt arrived on 23 December for Christmas. It was a few days of in and out of the cathedral, which was freezing cold. Christopher Goode and Michael Fraser came on Boxing Day and I cooked partridge with all the trimmings and dressed the table with all the silver. The day after I took David to dinner at the Castle House Hotel and, as I left, I said, 'You don't happen to do Christmas Dinner do you?' 'Yes,' came the reply. 'Can you book me in for 2011?' I said. I just don't want to do Christmas any more. The cold left me utterly exhausted and most evenings I went to bed at 9.30 p.m., singing the Allelluias of he who invented the electric blanket, with Lettice 'tucking me up' and staring into my eyes.

I used to write a reflection on what a year had been like. 2010 was a good year. The opening of the garden was a huge success, giving joy to everyone who came and also to us, Fiona, Shaun and Philip. That and the accountant telling me that another, final annuity had matured, which would yield me an annual amount until I died. I must be careful but the ghastly financial crisis of 2008 and 2009 has been resolved. Add to that the landscape television programme, of which I was so very proud. And I'm so lucky with the people that surround and love me.

2011

Trouble with a book

I'm afraid that my intention to keep this Diary fell to pieces as a result of the onslaught of the coldest December for a century. The last proper entry is 23 November and this one is being written two months later. I have been under enormous pressure to recast for the last time what is now called *Visions of England*. Jörg Hensgen, my beloved editor, sent me his reordered version of the book labelled here and there with notes like 'more of this'. I sat day in and day out in front of the computer screen working on this. Chapter 3 never came back so I assumed that it was fine but, oh no, he had sent it and it had vanished into cyberspace. I'll have one last phenomenal effort to get this book right. God knows why this tiny publication should have given me such trouble! It's written for a wide audience. It has to be personal, historically unanswerable and it must flow. I have never before had to toil over a text of mine so much – on and on and on . . .

I am beginning the Diary again, trying to catch up. January is always a working-time month. In the main it has been spent at The Laskett and filled with the domestic cycle, to which I add visits for teeth implants and a resolution to go twice a week to the gym, where I am carrying out programmes laid down for me by the slightly chaotic but amiable and owl-like James Dickson.

11 JANUARY

Sir Thomas Lawrence

I came up yesterday evening and met Antonia Fraser at the National Portrait Gallery at 11.30 a.m. prompt in order to see the Lawrence exhibition. Antonia appeared wearing her usual dark glasses and a copy of a Jean Muir dress. The exhibition's subtitle is *Regency, Power and Brilliance* but it was more truly *Power and Glamour*. The presentation of the exhibition was a bit dull but the gilt of the frames and Lawrence's use of crimson more than made up for it. Antonia is now well into her Reform Bill book with all those Whig ladies. Lawrence was an astounding painter already by the age of twenty-two. It was worth coming to the exhibition yet again, if only to see how he'd painted Eliza Farren's fur muff with its delectable pale blue bow. Antonia, needless to say, got the sexual innuendo of such an item of clothing dangled before the spectator.

Although her face in movement has lines, Antonia was terribly pretty today, with lovely blue eyes. We lunched in the NPG restaurant with Jon Snow at the next table. She must have listened to me a bit as she's begun to change things around: you must, I'd told her [Harold had died on 24 December 2008]. My autobiography, she said, ought to be called *Young Strong*.

In the evening I took myself to see ENB's *Romeo and Juliet*, which I last saw in 1977. The Frigerio sets and costumes still hold up but, oh dear, Nureyev wrecked every classic he laid his hands on [in retrospect not true].

12 JANUARY

Lunch with Brian Sewell and dinner with Deborah Swallow

I took Brian Sewell to lunch round the corner in Rochester Row, at Le Due Amici. He entered bundle-like and on a crutch. Brian is not a cheerful soul these days, although, I have to admit, his health woes are legion; but optimism, fun and cheerfulness of spirit have largely evaporated in favour of *O tempora! O mores!* He will be eighty this year and really had little to say in favour of anything. Instead it was a long litany of everything having gone to the dogs: the Courtauld Institute, which now only did the twentieth century, the newspapers, education, the government . . . Oh dear, I must never get like this.

In the evening I took Deborah Swallow to dinner at the Garrick Club. She had problems, yes, but not woe-laden: instead a radiant smile and a sense of joy, in spite of the misery of money and cuts. I loved seeing her and both of us, I think, sparkled. Time flies by and I said was she in the running for the V&A [the directorship had come up yet again]? I thought that she might at the most be fifty-five but no, she was sixty-two. Good grief, how time flies . . .

16 JANUARY

The Dowager Marchioness of Bute comes and goes

The doorbell rings. I open it to find Jennifer, Dowager Marchioness of Bute, hung with tweeds, standing there gesticulating wildly! She had asked herself to lunch yonks ago and I'd got it ready but I'd not heard a word from her since. It was all one long drama. She had left or lost her handbag at her last port of call so I provided her with £100 in notes. The dog needed exercising and water, so off they went around the garden while I rustled up a four-course lunch. Most of the conversation at lunch was about how awful she felt Timothy Clifford was. Clifford, she said, now tours the States lecturing for 'millions' and has a large country house not so far from London.

19 JANUARY

The third National Trust delegation

Thanks to the exchange with the National Trust rekindled by Marcus Binney's excitement about The Laskett house and garden, serious negotiations were opened up as to whether or not, endowed, the Trust would take it on my demise.

The third National Trust delegation came. They were the hands-on group: the manager of the Midlands area, a money person and a marketing one. They were all a delight and were entranced by the place, its domesticity, scale and atmosphere. This was a nuts-and-bolts visit but, yes, there were ways of opening the house. The garden presented no problems. Parking did. The Laskett is surrounded on all four sides by land owned by the same farmer and, as usual in Herefordshire, relationships in these circumstances can from time to time be testy. The field opposite, about two acres, is the only piece of land he owns on that side of the road [it had once been part of The Laskett]. It is needed by the National Trust for parking and a shop. What can I do? Little. I said to Ben Shipston that it would be up to the National Trust to deal with this. They must, I said, have had similar instances. I'd buy the land but not if the farmer was after blood money claiming that it was open for development and building. Is it? So they said that they were going to look into it and whether it's listed or not. But, yes, they were entranced and I so want it to happen.

20 JANUARY

A London party

Coral Samuel's party in her London flat was, as usual, impeccably done by Mustard the caterers, with a rare glimpse of Glyn Woodin, their head man, which took me back to all those occasions we did with him at the V&A. Tables were arranged around two rooms and I sat on Coral's left and Hugh Roberts on her right; there was Neil MacGregor down at the opposite end, his hair still a uniform shade of brown even though he's into his mid-sixties. There was no gossip of any consequence, although Stephen Lamport wanted to tell the Queen that she ought to see *The King's Speech*, but I heard later that someone who sat next to her at Balmoral dared to ask, to which she replied: 'No, they were my parents and that's how I wish to remember them.'

27 JANUARY

RIP Fr Gerard Irvine

St Michael's is my sort of church, a vast Victorian Gothic Anglo-Catholic pile filled with mystery, images and the whiff of incense. As I entered half an hour before the Mass I was confronted by a huge congregation jammed into the chairs. Rosemary Irvine was at the front, large, encased in fur and looking lively yet shattered. She had never known what it was like not to have Gerard, who was two years ahead of her. In the centre aisle lay the coffin, upon which rested a crucifix, a stole and a biretta with a red pompom on the top. This was the overture to a two-hour service presided over by a bishop assisted by twenty clergy, all in white and gold chasubles. Gerard had specified everything that he wanted, so it was a kind of joyful High Mass of Requiem using the new Common Worship rite but with bits added. Relics, we were told, were on the High Altar, one of St Gerard, St Thomas à Becket and the Curé d'Ars. A choir sang splendidly in the west gallery and the whole event must have been well rehearsed as it went off without any visible hitch, although at the close the procession didn't go far enough to allow all the priests, one by one, to sprinkle holy water on the coffin, so they had to shuffle.

There were three addresses (one too many), by a priest, by A.N. Wilson and by Imogen Lycett Green, Betjeman's granddaughter. I sat next to Donald Buttress, who had redone St Matthew's after the fire and, on the other side, I had a Betjeman Society delegation. Andrew's eulogy spoke directly to Gerard as though he was there. He is very good at these addresses. I loved the story of the bishop who asked Gerard which church he'd most like to work in. 'St Cuthbert's, Philbeach Gardens,' he replied. 'That', the bishop replied, 'is the Church of England at its most effete. Why on earth would you want to go there?' 'That's why I want to go there,' was the reply. Imogen recalled a wedding where Gerard had more lace on than the bride! But this was a true priest. He knew all the Peabody Buildings people, the owners of the market stalls as well as his celebrity cast of everyone from Iris Murdoch to Osbert Lancaster and Tom Driberg. He married me, God bless him, and for several years – 1968-ish to 1987 – was my confessor. It was to him I turned when affairs with my brother Brian became heated and I needed help. He put me on to solicitor John Underwood. Imogen's address went on too long but was stuffed with stories of Gerard's Christian dottiness. Once he helped a down-and-out who stole from him and everyone else. He dossed in St Matthew's. The man was sent to gaol on the Isle of Wight. Down Gerard went to visit him and, when he was released, Gerard took him in again. I don't think that priests like that exist any more. He loved the Church of England and never left for Rome.

Afterwards Andrew and I went back to Gerard's house in Montpelier Road. It was being dismantled and so the Matthew Smiths and John Pipers had gone. There was a shuffling gathering of people. We did our bit and left. Rosemary is going into a retirement home in Ditchling. She's eighty-seven and I wonder how long, brave soul, she'll last. This was the living world of Barbara Pym and Rose Macaulay. Dearest Gerard, God rest you.

30 JANUARY

First impressions of India: a fact-finding tour

Ultimate Travel, an upmarket travel agency, had asked me to take a tour to India but I'd never been. Julia's family on both sides had connections with the Raj: the Omans had been tea planters in Bengal and the Trevelyans served the Raj for two hundred years. Taking that connection as my theme, I began exploring in my mid-seventies a whole new world, with which I was to fall in love. I read frantically and rapidly and a whole section of library was built up; it was incredibly stimulating.

I left for India for a recce with Joanna Worsley [with whom Ultimate had paired me and who handled the practicalities of the tour]. We touched down at Bangalore, where we were met, as indeed we were met everywhere else, by a driver and a guide. We drove straight to the Lalitha Mahal Hotel in Mysore, a palace erected by the Nawab for his guests, a Valhalla of a place. This was my first experience of India and of anything that comes under the aegis of its government. It was wonderful to stay in as a curiosity but the gulf between it and the private sector was mind-blowing. At its worst, anything to do with government was filthy, falling to pieces and a sea of petty bureaucracy. It was heartbreaking to see magnificent late Victorian buildings let go to rack and ruin, literally falling apart, sunk beneath dirt and litter. I could have wept over the Chepauk Palace and also the Ripon Building in Madras. The Indians have no sentiment or feeling for these buildings. We arrived in Madras (Chennai) anxious among other things to see the old Madras Club and Old Government House, huge, handsome classical Regency buildings. But they'd already gone, bulldozed without a tear shed! John Goldingham's great Banquet Hall could only be glimpsed from afar. No one was allowed near it. At Seringapatam it was also heart-breaking to see the neglect of the British side and the restoration and apotheosis of anything to do with Tipu Sultan. It was a struggle to find the British monuments at all, although an English woman had paid for the restoration of the graves. In the fort at Madras new, ugly, ramshackle buildings had sprung up, ruining the classical parade-ground square.

But the size and the magnificence of these old buildings were amazing. St George's Cathedral in Madras had three great pediment-ed classical porticoes. In Madras the area around the Connemara Library resembled Victorian South Kensington, with vast public galleries. The Law Courts were as large as the Natural History Museum. The building was a labyrinthine compilation of corridors and courts and staircases, with armies of legal people in British-type robes, bands, waistcoats and gowns, milling around. But so much of old Mysore had gone or was going.

Oh God, I worked so hard on this tour. I had to do Calcutta on my own, checking hotels, food, loos! There was a splendid woman who took me around everything, on one day for as much as eleven hours. You couldn't invent Calcutta if you tried. It was the most extraordinary place, where even the traffic jams have a fascination. Calcutta is the city as car crash, bewildering and beautiful. Everywhere there is the juxtaposition of hotels, the acme of taste, elegance, cleanliness and service, while outside is squalor, rubbish, chaos, on a scale that left me bewildered. They have no idea of preservation or conservation. The Flagstaff House at Barrackpore was wonderfully presented but nearby the old Viceroy's house was a wreck. I could have wept.

The whole place is weird and pulsating. There's energy to it and excitement, and everywhere you look there's life jostling at you. But my job was to put this bit of the tour together. I've done it and it could be wonderful, with visits to the flower market, to the street of the idol-makers and entry gained to the Marble Hall and Ballroom of old Government House. I'm seduced by this country!

I'm writing this stuck for a few hours in a hotel like a stage set near Delhi Airport, where I had a drink and dinner with the head of Quo Vadis (the Indian end of Ultimate Travel), a reticent and thoughtful man. Is this the end of tours as we know them, I asked him. He was so fascinating on the imminent 'death' of the cultural tour and how, as no one knew any history any more, now came the *Hello* magazine generation. Americans wanted to respond to the impact of 9/11. As a result there was social concern of a sort but tours now focused on dealing with modern stress and anything to avert the effects of ageing. All of it now is about surfaces, how you looked and felt with no desire any more to learn or know anything.

11 FEBRUARY

Return to The Laskett

Back from India and a hundred emails to cope with and a mound of post. But the great joy is the garden, the snowdrops at their height, drifts of dappled, snowy flowers along Julia's snowdrop walk and garlands of them around the apple trees in her orchard, not to mention the display in her Snowdrop Garden. It's a poignant time of year, as she loved them so much. Suddenly the weather has changed and we've had the occasional day of blue sky and sunshine to lift the spirits. The green tips of bulbs are pushing up and even the perennials are stirring, but there's much lamentation over what had gone, the pieris, bays and salvias. So many other plants, too, bear trophies of blackened leaves. The rosemary hedge leading to the Kitchen Garden has been killed off for the second time, so we've decided to plant yew accents with borders of the hostas we had removed from the Silver Jubilee Garden. Shaun says that they ought to do well there.

Jörg sent through the final text of *Visions of England*. It's been such a saga but it's a terrific read. I felt very proud of having written it. It supplies something missing from the current debate: historical context. And the book keeps firmly out of the political arena. There, explained in simple and direct English, is what the country cherished at its heart. The end is open, leaving the reader to go in whatever direction he wishes.

15 FEBRUARY

Farewell to Joan Sutherland

All I seem to do is write about services: this was a celebration of
Joan Sutherland. John Tooley gave the address, which was OK but
not inspired. The Prince of Wales came: 'Oh, the beard. You look
like a Van Dyck!' 'It's what's called a good look for a senior citizen,'
I replied. Recordings of Dame Joan were integrated into the service,
a bit of Handel and Bellini's *Casta Diva*. It all went like clockwork
and there was a reception in the Jerusalem Chamber afterwards
with lots of figures from one's past: Valerie Solti, Beryl Grey, Jeremy
Isaacs . . . I learnt that Julia's sets and costumes for *Die Fledermaus*
no longer exist but her *Bohème* still sells and the Opera House will
hang on to it as long as John Copley is prepared to do revivals – and
then it'll all go if it hasn't fallen to bits by then. It was good to go
and remember Joan Sutherland's kindness to me all those years ago,
when she sang *Messiah* in the Albert Hall to aid the appeal to save
Thomas Hudson's portrait of the composer.

17 FEBRUARY

I begin my early autobiography

*All through this period the National Trust saga dragged on although, at
last, I found out that the recommendation to the Trustees was to accept
The Laskett. They meet on 16 March.*

I've begun to write *Young Strong* [later to be retitled *Self-Portrait
as a Young Man*], or, at least, I've done chapter one, 'Hard Times'. It
kind of wrote itself, not that it was that long, seventeen pages of A4
describing 23 Colne Road, the family history on both sides and life

during the war, together with character studies of both parents. That gets me to the age of ten and the grammar school whose archivist I contacted and I'm going to see what she's got. Fortunately the phases in my early life neatly tailor into the changes in the educational system: the 1944 Butler Act opened the door and the following year I went to Edmonton County Grammar School. Chapter two will run from 1946 to 1953, a more complicated period with my interest in theatre, costume, history and art emerging.

22 FEBRUARY

The television programme on the grammar schools

The television company that was making two one-hour programmes for Channel 4 on grammar schools came. They'd been filming people like Denis Healey. But I had got out all my school stuff, designs for plays at Edmonton County Grammar School, piles of other artwork and drawings, my letters to Joan Henderson and the *faux* Elizabethan miniatures that I used to send her at Christmas. It turned out to be quite a traumatic interview, which ended in me breaking down with emotion as I described my last visit to her, just hours before she died in St Mary's, Paddington. I apologised but Steve the producer said, 'You've just paid her the greatest tribute that you ever could.' It's strange that all this happened as I have been starting to write about it but perhaps it was meant to be.

25 FEBRUARY

Another National Trust visitation

Lisa White, chair of the National Trust Art Panel, came. She'd worked at the V&A in the 1970s and recalls it as a hugely innovative period. She loved both the house and the garden but was worried about what the Trust managers would do to it. Indeed, the National Trust is all about money these days, encouraging vast numbers of visitors, obsessed with shop and cafeteria takings and money-spinning events. A hundred thousand through The Laskett would ruin it.

28 FEBRUARY

Guida Crowley

To London. The weather was leaden and it was freezing cold. And I was still knocked out by a root canal operation last week. However, David Hutt was there, in good mood but sad that Guida Crowley had died just a few years short of her century. But she had hung on for him to return from Agadir so that he could give her the last rites. She was secretary to A.J. Ayer for a time, an exceptionally bright woman, and, latterly, the assistant editor of some academic magazine [*Journal of Ethnic and Migration Studies*], which she only relinquished when she was ninety-two. She worshipped David and was devout, having come to the faith quite late in life, in her early eighties. Guida was deaf but wouldn't wear her hearing aid, which was so infuriating, but there was a joyous quality about her, like a bird on the wing. I took David to a rather drink-sodden dinner at the Garrick.

1 MARCH

Lunch with A.N. Wilson

Ghastly cold weather and I was still feeling 'done in', but nonetheless I had lunch with Andrew Wilson in the Valhalla of the Travellers Club. Andrew never ceases to amaze me. His book on Dante is about to come out and he's finished his Elizabethan book and is about to embark on a novel about the Wedgwoods. There is always something vaguely rustic about the way he dresses but he was, as usual, up to the mark on things, very pleased about Alan Moses's article on the ordinariate in the All Saints, Margaret Street magazine, of which David Hutt had sent me a copy. I must say that reading Diarmaid MacCulloch's history of Christianity has put quite a lot of people off Rome. We were both unhappy about the introduction of university tuition fees. If they had existed in 1953 would I have ever gone?

2 MARCH

St Benedict and a curious memorial meeting

The day began in Westminster Abbey, where a multi-costumed array of clerics took part in a service to light a torch that was to be carried to Monte Cassino in time for the feast of St Benedict. John Hall in his new cloth of gold cope presided and there were many RC clerics and abbots, all in black and red with lots of tassels. The Abbey did the works, including incense and censing the shrine of St Edward. There was a rather bad address by the Bishop of Wakefield and a far better one by the Abbot of Monte Cassino. The flame was carried out with representatives of the various localities in renaissance costumes, a handsome sight.

The memorial meeting for Julian Thompson at Sotheby's was a weird event, a gathering of the world of art, the saleroom and the collector. I had known Julian since the late Sixties. Even then he had a fatal effect on women. His appearance was that of an amiable owl, both reserved and charming, but God knows what was going on beneath the surface. It was decades later, at another Sotheby's bash, that I was told about his Chinese family, a wife and three children. Did Jacky and the English family know? I've no idea. He then billeted one of the Chinese children on her for weekends from Cheltenham Ladies College, which she attended. That was when the break-up of the marriage started. I was told that he'd spent all Jacky's money and had gone off with another Chinese woman who was in her early twenties and had yet another child. James Stourton told me that it didn't end there. There were apparently about ten children of his roaming around. The last Chinese wife and child were present in the front row of what were a series of tribute recollections of the man chaired by Grey Gowrie. Jacky, however, looked stunning in an Issey Miyake jacket. This was inevitably a highly edited version of the life of the man who was the world's expert on Chinese ceramics but also it seems more than wayward when it came to women.

8 TO 12 MARCH

Florence

I'd rented a flat near Santa Maria Novella and took David Hutt. Fifty-nine stairs up was a bit much but the flat was adequate and we could walk everywhere. This was the first time I'd been back since Julia died and I'm glad that I took the plunge. There was bright blue sky and sun but it was cold in the shade, a wonderful four days before the mobs came. What a joy to see San Lorenzo again, now so well presented, the grand-ducal tombs, the Fra Angelicos in San Marco, the Laurenziana, the Duomo, Santa Croce, the Pazzi Chapel, the *mercato centrale* with its cornucopia of food – so much, so beautiful – the shops and elegant window dressing – the Pitti Palace and its gardens – I adore the Isolotto and, *mirabile dictu*, the costume museum was actually open! I had never got into it before. So much everywhere the eye fell.

16 MARCH

The National Trust turns down The Laskett Gardens

This was the day when I was rung by Simon Murray and told that the National Trust had turned down The Laskett. I was shattered. 'Simon Jenkins will be writing to you [he didn't] and Fiona wants to see you.' 'Why?' I said. 'She's just slammed the door in my face. It's a waste of her time and mine.' Later an email came from her, clearly upset and saying how dreadfully sorry she was that this had happened.

20 MARCH

Patrick Reyntiens stays

Patrick Reyntiens came through and stayed the night. There was much bemoaning of the times and of the tide of ignorance, and also much consumption of alcohol. He brought his perfectly awful piece on Barbara Cartland, which *The Oldie* had refused to print. I was not surprised! But he's now in his mid-eighties, spry, mentally active, still circling the globe and as switched on as ever on everything.

30 MARCH

Plugging Visions of England *in Southend*

I travelled up to London on the 9.15 a.m. train via Newport. This was the day of a dry run on *Visions of England* at Southend-on-Sea. I set off on that drear line from Liverpool Street, to be met at the other end by an affable, lanky youth with an earring, called Daniel. The library was 'modern' and rather successful, with a perky head called Suzy Chaplin. I arrived as they were taking down the fluorescent tubes so that my Powerpoint images could be seen. There was much coming and going as my laptop images failed to marry with the projector, so it was over to theirs with my disk. I was part of their somewhat truncated Literary Festival. The leaflet on that made me cringe. Writers were presented on the level of the stick of Southend-on-Sea rock I was given at the close. It was as though there was no difference between Dame Edna Everage and Tolstoy. No matter, I retired behind the scenes and a sandwich and platter were produced, and then out I trotted. It was a good, if dishevelled audience, no one younger than fifty and all looking as though they ought to be sent to the dry cleaners. Life, I felt, had not treated them that well but there they were, some 140 of them who'd paid to hear me. So off I went after the usual hiccup over the sound. I made them laugh and I made them think. They hadn't done that for a long time but they sat up when I talked of the dissolution of the island. There was no lack of questions after, in the main off the point. One man went on and on, saying that England to most people was the football team, and then there was the lady who wanted me to express an opinion about the refusal of a church group to allow their twelfth-century building to be moved elsewhere to make room for a runway. But they were happy, had glasses of wine and home-made eats and bought masses of books. In fact we ran out.

31 MARCH

A London day

I'd got out my morning suit and found that there was no way, even if I breathed in very hard, that I could get into it. Oh God, I'm such a lump, but have had the suit for thirty years at least. With Robin Walker's and the Royal Wedding coming up I rushed to Favourbrook in Jermyn Street to order a new one. It'll be my last, rather fetching in a light pale grey fabric which I'll jolly up with an embroidered waistcoat and stock. Thence to the Royal Academy for a hugely enjoyable hour and a half of Watteau drawings. These were quite marvellous. What a facility that man had! Beautiful.

Lunch with John Goodall, the owl-like architectural editor of *Country Life*, at L'Avenue. He presented me with his castle book. I was very touched. John is almost Pickwickian, a bubbly, bright, sunny person. My 'Soul of England' series had been a great success, so it was the usual cut and thrust of new ideas. We came up with two series. The first was what we don't do or have any more – smoking, hereditary titles, servants, walks, etc., quite a list. The second was what makes a village: shop, pub, pond, church, graveyard, etc. [neither happened].

In the evening I went to the University of Worcester dinner in the House of Lords, which was very well done. I thought I'd know no one but there they all were: Antony and Kathy Priddis, he the Bishop of Hereford; Sue Darnley, the Lord Lieutenant; the Dunnes; Bill Wiggin; Howard Flight; John de la Cour, etc. I sat between Judith Elkin, an expert on children's literature and also a fundraiser, and Chris Robertson (I think), an educationalist. I warmed to both of them. Although they were younger, they'd both had to work hard to get where they'd got. Worcester has been remarkably successful but I see the future for it as being more and more based on the area, county loyalty and giving instead of government handouts. 'Big Society' stuff. What was good was the turn-out from Hereford as the two counties had hated their now ended shotgun marriage. Richard of Gloucester as Chancellor said a few fair words, and that was it.

1 APRIL

Ida Kar, Hoppe and Fidelio

I took Gillian Wagner out to lunch feeling glum, but she's such a star that I picked up. The purpose was to start the ball rolling to get Pamela Tudor-Craig an Honour. I said that I'd do the write-round [sadly we failed]. Afterwards I went to the Ida Kar and Hoppe exhibitions at the National Portrait Gallery, both OK but not thrilling, being too like each other.

In the evening to *Fidelio* with Antonia Fraser at the ROH, she, as usual, in full flight, being just back from doing *Must You Go* in Sweden. She was supposed to have only one glass of wine a day but alas that went to the wall as we went through two glasses of champagne followed by wine with supper after! *Fidelio* was an expensive and perverse production, devoid of magic or any power of emotion. By mutual consent we left in the interval for a hugely talkative aftermath at the Garrick Club.

2 APRIL

A fundraising concert

Shan Egerton drove over and we went to Kentchurch for a song recital in aid of St Bridget's, Skenfrith. It was oddly enjoyable, although peppered with the usual old and somewhat tottery locals. But it is always beautiful, listening to music in a country house drawing room. Jan Lucas-Scudamore was skivvying in the kitchen over the inexpensive but passable supper of rice, chilli con carne and salad. Afterwards we grabbed a table in a corner of the dining room with Christopher Goode, with beard again, Michael Fraser, very thin, and Christopher's brother. Nothing of consequence was said but we departed happy.

4 APRIL

The National Trust saga continues

All of this should have been written earlier but it has been all I can do to keep going. This goes back to the morning of 16 March, when Simon Murray rang and told me that the National Trust had rejected the offer of The Laskett. No reason was given for its rejection. I emailed Fiona Reynolds and said was it money? No reply. I then, aided by Beatrix Miller, concocted an email that *had* to be answered. I had to know why, or else I could not make any other arrangements. Her reply was that there had been disagreement on the Board as to its merit. The Laskett was also in an Area of Outstanding Natural Beauty and therefore it would be difficult to make a car park. She had earlier emailed me saying how dreadfully, dreadfully sorry she was. I was left stunned and deeply depressed. If this was to happen, why had they let everything go so far? People I had to tell were stunned and couldn't believe it. They also thought that I had been treated disgracefully. Fiona begged to see me and so she's coming here on 19 April.

Simon Jenkins was godparent to Felicity Bryan's daughter so today, via her, I got more as to what had gone on. I gather that out of the twelve trustees, ten had voted for and two against. I don't know who those two were. Fiona was apparently in tears and Simon Jenkins was also dreadfully upset. This was the first time that they had rejected such an offer. But it was the Art Panel all right.

They must have enjoyed wielding their axe against me. Now I'm left with what to do next. The National Trust has made a horribly wrong decision based on the malice and envy of a few.

6 APRIL

The Kingmans and Doug

All this week I have been at The Laskett. The garden becomes more and more beautiful. The Flower Bedroom, as I call it, was finished when the canopy over the bed was put into position. I'm glad that I have done this. Who knows but that I might need such a downstairs room in old age?

Valerie and John Kingman came to lunch on Wednesday, she hugely improved, more upright than I've seen her for two years. The physio has done her good and I think that she will go further, but not all the way. She has been told that she will never drive again. John is marvellous with her; however, her problem is not only physical but mental. She has nothing with which to fill her time. Valerie has never written and therefore never had a life away from academically running something. So she now emails all her friends constantly, so I find that an awful lot of my time is taken by giving her chatty updates on this and that.

All through this period I have observed what I call 'Doug Rules' after my trainer [a new one], so one glass of wine a day, red meat twice a week, avoid bread, pasta, etc., and drink lots of water. I go twice a week to the gym and on other days do my five-mile circuit jog and stretches. I've lost six pounds and feel tons better for it.

9 APRIL

Julia's godson marries

Robin, son of Peter Walker, was Julia's godson and this was his marriage at St Margaret's, Westminster, as he's just been elected MP for Worcester. Julia would have been proud of this bright, well-mannered young man. His bride, Charlotte, had been president of the Oxford Union and is beautiful. There was no undercurrent at this wedding. It was joy all the way.

Andrew Tremlett married them. The congregation was in early middle age, very successful city types, public school, Oxbridge and international. What was striking was the ethnic range – and a clue to the future. They were a group. The last time I was here for a wedding was for David Linley's, all Freddie Fox hats like coal-scuttles, short skirts and thin legs. This time it was the Kate Middleton look, silk dresses and fascinators. I always watch carefully as to who knows the words of the Lord's Prayer. Not a lot of them, really.

Over we went to the Houses of Parliament. There were drinks on the terrace with the cutting of the cake, followed by lunch for 140 in one of the dining rooms. It was beautifully done, really pretty with six-foot-high floral arrangements arising from the tables, an eruption of greenery into pink and white roses, and then candles. Then we saw them off. Down the grand steps in Westminster Hall we went, where we were photographed *en tableau*. Then we all lined up as they left, climbing into a white chauffeur-driven vintage car. I feel that this is going to be a very good marriage. Tessa brought all five of these children up very well. It's just sad that Peter never achieved what he patently wanted, the premiership, and became prematurely old.

A golden evening

All this week I was at The Laskett, reflecting a resolution to spend far more time here, a good decision. Andrew Piper came to supper and we walked through the garden on a magical golden evening of rare beauty.

At the moment I plough on with chapter two of the autobiography when I can ever get to it. So many interruptions, so much going on now that the garden is open and groups come.

Mucknell Abbey with the Dean of Hereford

This was the day that I drove with Michael Tavinor to Mucknell, the new home of the Burford Community. The setting is marvellous, clear countryside in every direction but treeless, so young saplings have been planted everywhere. But oh, the lack of water this year, so that unsurprisingly our first glimpse of Brother Thomas was of him watering them. The initial impact of the new monastery is not beautiful but time and planting will soften it, a ruined farm building adapted to form a courtyard in which there is a chapel. Everything is functional and driven by Health and Safety and Fire regulations, all of them the death of architecture and atmosphere. The inner courtyard was bleak and bare, not even any grass, although we were told that tubs and flowers were on their way. But we had a wonderful welcome by these holy people and their beloved Abbot Stuart. It was confession time, Michael with the abbot and me with Michael in an act of symmetry. And then came Mass in the new chapel, a handsome, cavernous space yet to gain patina and atmosphere. None of the furniture was fixed as they were experimenting with its placing and they await the large icon to go behind the altar, which will begin to pull it together. But it was a privilege to be there, silent amidst such spiritual intensity. Although I'm an administrant and handle the chalice at the cathedral, I'd never administered the Host before. So, much to my surprise, each of us administered both as we formed a large circle in a manner akin to the loving cup ceremony at a City dinner. We lunched with them afterwards off Lenten bread and cheese, dried fruit and apples and water. And they were pleased with my gift of a dozen bottles of white burgundy for feast days!

18 APRIL

Sky TV comes

Gym and then Sky TV took over the place, filming my various writing rooms and the gardens for the Sky Arts programme. This went on from 2 to 6 p.m., all for only about four minutes of screen time. But they were intelligent and well behaved. The PR for the book was a powerhouse of energy and I'll be interested to see what she brings off. Publication date is 7 July but we'll have copies by 20 May for the V&A Friends 25th Anniversary performance.

19 APRIL

Fiona Reynolds makes a visit

Fiona Reynolds came. Now in her early fifties, still eager, charming and canny, I've always liked her a lot. Yes, she admitted, the ghastly wrong decision had been made. She'd read The Laskett book and she wanted the place for the National Trust. We went around the garden on one of those spring days that are unforgettable for their utter beauty of light and shade, colour and freshness. We did the house. She took it all in. Here was something utterly unique. She wanted the archive to stay here and then came how could the decision be reversed. We must let the dust settle, she said. Behind the scenes I should receive advice from the Midlands National Trust officer as to how to jack up the numbers and how to display the place. I made it clear that I had reached a decision. There was to be no question of a separate trust because I wouldn't do it. If the National Trust came back to me in my lifetime I would re-offer it as before, land, houses, contents and a substantial endowment. Otherwise it could be offered on my death but minus the endowment. She got the message. I couldn't get out of her which of the Art Panel had mucked this up. I suspect it's going to be a waiting game but I'm putting my decision on paper for The Laskett's three trustees and Julian Chadwick, just in case. None of this should have happened. She was clearly devastated by it.

Later a letter arrived from Fiona Reynolds, which was very appreciative and supportive and saying that she would get the local National Trust in the interim to offer me all the help that they could. That was later to prove a vital helpline.

20 APRIL

Wedding fever

London is stuffed with tourists for the Royal Wedding, to which I am going. Just as well that I got the new morning suit! That sea of unkempt humanity pushing and jostling is really awful. But the spectacle of the wedding will cheer everyone up in a gloomy time billed as one of austerity. But I remember austerity from 1945 to 1955 and we're nowhere near that. People still can't accept the fact that we're one off being broke. There is no money. Living standards and just about everything must be reduced, and for a long time. There's a weird belief that after a couple of years the good times will roll again. They won't. This is one of those periods that will define the century. We are a minor power and God knows what we're doing in Libya – oil, I suppose.

21 APRIL

Two Maundys

This was the day of two Maundys, the royal one at Westminster Abbey in the morning and the second in the evening at Hereford Cathedral. The Abbey one was I would have thought the last one that the Queen would do there, as she'll be ninety-five next time. It was different from the previous occasion, when I appeared in full robes, was presented to the Queen and received Maundy money. This time we all wore red and black and I trotted in with the Abbey officers a quarter of an hour before it all began. I didn't even get my stall. So I wondered why all this had changed. But there was a splendid procession, the Dean in his now much-worn cloth of gold cope. The Queen was in a horrendous brilliant turquoise outfit with a diamond brooch on her hat and another one on her coat, top left. The Duke looked frail but read the lesson.

Back I went to Hereford and was MC at what was a truer ceremony, with the feet washing, the stripping of the altars, the dimming of lights and the carrying of the Sacrament to the Altar of Repose. And there were more people there than the previous year.

22 APRIL

Good Friday at Hereford Cathedral

This was an extraordinary event. It was the most spiritually charged ritual that I have seen at the cathedral so far. Once again a huge turn-out and the queue to venerate the cross was seemingly endless. The clergy were totally overcome by it. But it was the simple devotion of the people, each spontaneous in their response to this great wooden cross, which was so deeply moving. The intensity of it was almost tangible. There was nothing cold or false about it, each person responding as he or she wished.

24 APRIL

A country lunch

Lunch at Aymestrey Court with Jonathan and Mary Heale, Sarah Steer and Janet Gough, and two other people whose names I've forgotten and who didn't quite fit in! However, the house is a splendid seventeenth-century one and it was in addition a wonderful day, the orchard an explosion of blossom, the parterre filled with tulips and tiny black sheep bouncing around.

Jonathan had quite a funny story from a friend of his who had to stay with the Prince of Wales in Scotland. The phone rang. It was Wills. Said person offered to withdraw. 'No, no.' Receiver eventually put down and all the Prince said was: 'They don't read books any more.'

26 APRIL

Garden changes

All day spent sorting out a mountain of papers for the accountant. I loathe this annual penance but at least it's between books and I was relieved to have the house to myself again (a guest had gone). The incredible weather continues. Clive Boursnell came and the bust of Diana was moved to the mount near the Jubilee Garden. It looks fine and we gravelled around it and added some evergreens. We decided that the grasses in the Yew Garden had been killed off by the frost and removed them, keeping the stachys but adding box on the corners and rosemary either side of the amelanchiers. I had also bought some incredibly pretty multi-coloured Shasta daisies for the containers in the parterre. Still no rain.

All this week the media went on and on and on about the wedding.

28 APRIL

Signs of the times

I took Stephen Vakil to dinner at the Garrick. Much talk of the direction in which we were going. How much more of Europe will we take before we opt out? What has happened to education since the abolition of grammar schools paved the path for a lumpen proletariat and an educated upper group? Can stability be maintained with such a structure? I wrote along these lines as long ago as 1988.

I walked across St James's Park to the Club. The Mall was festooned with Union Jacks and there were camera vantage points everywhere. People were camping along the route, many with canvas igloos in which to sleep. I walked home down Whitehall and then attempted to walk along Victoria Street past the Abbey, but it was hopeless. It was jammed with people and more igloos. But the mood was good-hearted, cheerful and celebratory. So I turned back and made my way home the other side via Birdcage Walk.

29 APRIL

The Royal Wedding

I'd taken in the lack of loos at the Abbey and that anyway they would all shut at 10 a.m., so I got up at 4 a.m. to have my daily pills in a few tablespoonfuls of water, went back to bed and up again at 6 a.m. Drink of any kind was off the menu. Morpeth Terrace is only ten minutes' walk from the Abbey but I suspected that it wasn't going to be easy to get there. I was right. Admittance was through the Great North Door at 8.45 a.m., so I set out at 8 a.m. The taxi rank at Victoria Station had vanished. So I decided to walk towards the West Front. Armies of the nicest policemen couldn't have been more helpful and I was escorted by a policewoman all the way round to the Millbank side and went through security. And thence to the North Door, where there were batteries of cameras, and got in. The Head of Protocol said to me, 'I've given you a good seat.' He had. I had the last seat in the front row next to the arch through the choir screen, so one way I could look down the red carpet to the Great West Door and then, peering the other way, up to the High Altar.

The flowers were pretty good, great trees along the nave that should have been in flower but thanks to the warm weather had leaves on instead. I loved the trailing green and white above the High Altar and along the triforium. I was sitting with a group of Abbey functionaries. Next to me were Douglas Hurd and Richard Luce, and opposite were the Archbishop of York and his wife, together with three cardinals in black edged with scarlet and, beyond the people behind them, a television screen on which we could see what was going on at the east end.

I'd got in at about 8.50 a.m. and then there followed a lot of hanging around, as nothing happened until 10.15 a.m. I couldn't see what went on in the transepts but the nave became like a cocktail party minus the drinks and canapés, everyone moving around and chatting. Although I noticed how the media after the event seem to feature pictures of the likes of Elton John and Tara Palmer-Tomkinson, they formed the rare exception in a gathering that, from where I was, consisted of those who served the Crown in one way or another. The men were virtually all in morning suits. In the case of the women there were an awful lot of pink dresses, with jackets for the most part, and flying-saucer hats skewered on at various angles. Some were pretty awful. Jewels were thin on the ground, apart from the odd diamond brooch from the bank vault. A maharajah from Rajasthan had the most, with a huge diamond sunburst on his hat and a two-inch-wide solid diamond necklace, while his wife was hung with the equivalent of Asprey's jewellery department. The prize for the most inappropriately dressed woman from where I was sitting went to Mrs Bercow, whose plunging neckline suggested that she'd mistaken the occasion.

Long gone are the days when the likes of Norman Hartnell or

Hardy Amies would design the clothes of all the leading royal personages, ensuring that they composed a harmonious tableau. In the last decades this has been replaced by fashion chaos, with too many of them competing for attention. The width of the otherwise stylish Princess Michael's hat was such that it suggested that she would have to navigate some doorways sideways. The Duke of York's two amiable daughters are desperately in need of fashion counselling. The Duchess of Gloucester and Princess Alexandra displayed both taste and restraint; and there was the superbly low-key Sarah Armstrong-Jones, beautiful in immaculately cut grey with just a sprinkling of diamonds. As they all walked up the aisle I was amazed at how many members there were of the Royal Family in its extended capacity, less these days a family than a tribe.

The two princes ambled by in such a way that one hardly noticed, Harry with shoulders the width of a baseball player. But it was a reminder that the real fashion stars of the day were the men in uniform, dark blue or scarlet with a mass of gold frogging and superb posture and bearing. The clergy too were in their cloth of gold period, which added to the shimmer.

Reading between the lines, what both bride and groom would have liked would have been a quiet country wedding but there was no way out of this. There was a persistent thread of understatement and a desire for modesty running at the heart of these nuptials. The Middletons caught that, Mrs Middleton elegant in pale blue with no attempt to draw attention to herself. Her daughter's dress was equally seemly, simple, exquisite in its detailing but never screaming 'look at me!'. The bride had a natural, unaffected poise. The diamond tiara had almost to be looked for tucked under the veil. With care the new Duchess of Cambridge might avoid becoming that fatal role for a royal, a fashion icon. We've had that, and the Queen is a monument to believing that that is not a role she has ever aspired to occupy.

The music under the aegis of James O'Donnell was faultlessly performed. I've never heard Parry's 'Blest Pair of Sirens' better rendered. But some of the hymns sounded a bit odd, particularly the Welsh rugby anthem 'Guide me, O thou great Redeemer', which had been sung at Diana's funeral, and that stalwart of the Last Night of the Proms, Blake's 'Jerusalem'. But no doubt that's what they wanted.

Everything went like clockwork. What couldn't be heard in the Abbey was the bride and groom's responses; but they were heard by the relay to the crowds lining the route, as we gathered from the cheers outside. The only snare-up happened at the end, when half the crowned heads of Europe and heads of the Commonwealth stopped dead in their tracks on the red carpet. There they stood and stood! The coaches, I assume, hadn't turned up to take them to the Palace.

So much pageantry and splendour can make what follows a real comedown. But the Dean had arranged for us Abbey folk to raise a glass to the newlyweds in a garden off Little Cloister. There we were able to compare notes, congratulate the canons, members of the choir and others who had worked so hard for so long to make all this work.

It was easy leaving by about 1.30 p.m. The crowds had vanished. I was hungry and, still in full fig, popped in to Pret à Manger for a sandwich. The counter staff looked a trifle amazed at this apparition. But, yes, it had been a very good day: a good day not only for the bride and groom and for me, but for the entire country. I had been present at hope.

4 MAY

Garden visitors

Isobel De L'Isle of Penshurst and Anthea Warde of Squerryes came to lunch and to see the garden. I was ticked off for letting visitors in on 'closed' days at the same price as open days. I was told to charge 50 per cent more, which I will do. All through this period the opening of the garden has been a huge success. We're fully booked for May, June, July and most of September. The garden itself has never looked lovelier. Visitors heap praise on it, saying again and again, 'Better than Highgrove.'

7 MAY

The Monnow Valley Arts Centre

I drove up to the Monnow Valley Arts Centre to open their exhibition on John Piper and Graham Sutherland. The setting is wonderful, with its panorama of lush Welsh hillsides, but it is very, very remote. It was a happy occasion, which included also a show of Reg Boulton's work. He was there, a jolly, benign eighty-seven-year-old. I sense that the government's cut to the arts budget will hit Rupert Otten, who runs the Centre, hard.

11 MAY

The fate of the garden

Chris Young of *The Garden* magazine came and stayed the night. He's matured and over dinner we took the discussion over the future of the Laskett garden to its logical conclusion, which was the National Trust or nothing at all. At the moment, thanks to the Trust's decision, I am left in limbo. But it is clear that running a garden is beyond the capacity of The Vivat Trust. The trouble is that since involving them things have moved on. The house has now become increasingly interesting to people. House and garden are intertwined. If one goes, both should. None of this is easy. Also the garden, now opened, is hugely loved.

13 MAY

Michael Leonard stays

Michael Leonard arrived for the weekend and presented me with his portrait of me as a Clouet. It is brilliant and there's a wonderfully quizzical look in my eye. It was so good to see him and on Saturday we had such a happy day driving up to Leominster to look at a Brightwells sale and on to Ludlow for a wander and lunch at The Courtyard. We went into the Silk Hat Gallery and I bought a lovely little painting by Simon Dorrell of an open window – very Biedermeier. Back we came, and then to dinner at the Green Man at Fownhope.

15 MAY

The travails of training

During these weeks I have been stuck with my trainer's sheets of instruction. I'm into phase two for mobility, weight loss and strengthening. I try to go to the gym at Fownhope three times a week and jog and stretch on the other days. I am making progress, measured by my ability to do squats with one hand on a pole, but I'm finding the need for the pole lessening. I can in fact see it being discarded quite soon. But I'm sure that this targeted exercise is a good thing at my age. It is very difficult to lose weight at seventy-five but I know that I'm fitter and I still have no aches and pains. Instructions include one glass of wine a day and the importance of keeping one's metabolism going, so a handful of dried fruits every four hours or so, red meat only twice a week and lots and lots of water, and eight to eight and a half hours' sleep. When I'm in the country, which I am now a lot, I cheerfully go up to bed at 9.30 p.m. and I'm asleep by 10 p.m. But I get up at 6.30 a.m.

5 JUNE

The Hay Literary Festival

Up at 6 a.m. and Mass at 8 a.m. in the Lady Chapel at Hereford Cathedral. The car arrives at 10.20 a.m. to take me to Hay. The Festival is now vast, stretching in all directions, but better organised than I remember it, a young person being attached to me. The green room was awash with both familiar and unknown faces. James Naughtie said 'Hello' and Simon Jenkins bounded across the room and said, 'Don't worry, we're going to do something' [i.e. about

The Laskett and the National Trust; they didn't], to which I replied that first the dust must settle. At 11.30 a.m. I was on stage with the novelist Howard Jacobson and a 'solitary' about the bits of the Bible we'd chosen to read [it was the four hundredth anniversary of the Authorised Version]. I didn't enjoy this much but I was landed with it. I had a buffet lunch at Penymaes with Shan Egerton and her guests, and wisely grabbed a bedroom there and went to sleep until 5 p.m., when I was collected for a 5.30 p.m. performance. This was in the Oxfam auditorium, which, much to my surprise, was two thirds full. On all my previous occasions at Hay I was a sell-out but, I learnt later, virtually all the events this year were down in numbers. I pulled out the stops and got a rapturous reception and then signed twenty or so of the books [*Visions of England*] afterwards. Clara, the public relations officer, told me that 120 copies had gone that week. A short break and then back on stage again, three of us reading the Book of Revelation in the King James Version. And that was it.

8 JUNE

A Norfolk tour

Off I go with Jamie and Tania Illingworth to Norfolk to stay at Sennowe Park, now the home of Charlie and Virginia Temple-Richards. Much has changed since 2008, when I was immured here for five weeks filming *The Diets That Time Forgot*. What a nightmare to take on as it's an awful house really, an architectural mish-mash of Wrenaissance, the various bits and quotations never quite cohering. But they've begun the mountainous task of lightening it room by room. The kitchen, which was a building site when I was there, is up and running, and most bedrooms painted and curtained. But how can you make a go of a house like this? It's not worth opening, so there are just the odd location fees and then a group like this one coming for four extravagant days. This is last year's Herefordshire jaunt rerun in a different county, a small group of over-seventy-year-olds, about fifteen in all. There was dinner for twenty-two each evening, with Tania juggling the *placement*.

9 JUNE

Holkham

We sailed off at 9.25 a.m. with the weather swinging between cloud, cold and rain and blue sky and warm sun. Being the egg-head lecturer, I sat at the front of the bus. Holkham was our first port of call so I told them about Palladianism, Kent, Holkham and how awful its builder was. The house is amazing and I was struck by the Kentian severity of much of it: spare with much use made of paint, classical mouldings, gilding and statuary. Then there are the great rooms with their crimson wall-hangings and pictures, everything rich and gilded.

We emerged out of that to go to the Model Farm for lunch given by Eddy and Sarah Leicester, he four-square, direct and sensible, she petite, charming and with an eye. A delicious lunch arrived with three domestics doing their stuff: cold chicken or warm crab in a shell with melon, green and tomato and mozzarella salads followed by vanilla ice cream and deep-fried elderflowers. *Perfetto*. Then out into the garden, where too much had been done for immediate effect, with yews already six feet high and box a foot high. There are a parterre rose garden, a small orchard, a small grotto and a narrow pond and rill, all by George Carter. It'll be fine but nothing unusual.

In the afternoon we visited two stunning Norfolk churches, Salle and Cawston. I'd been to them before and both are amazing, but Cawston I like best, spacious but contained, Salle almost absurdly oversized. Then on to the village of Heydon, which has belonged to the Bulwer-Longs forever. Here was the village green and an assemblage made for a television location for a Jane Austen novel. Beautiful. Tim Bulwer-Long appeared and narrated the ghastly story of the family's recent history, with too many deaths, too many daughters and too much inheritance tax.

On Friday we visited Houghton and Raynham but for some reason I never wrote it down!

18 JUNE

Sculpture at Quenington

I drove to David and Lucy Abel Smith's house at Quenington for their sculpture exhibition. The house is a beautiful old rectory with a stream running close to it and with large lawns sweeping away, upon which to display such hideosities so totally at variance with the realm of Nature. But Lucy, with her long, pale face and hair, has style and brio. There was a marquee for lunch and various people were mustered: John Julius Norwich and Mollie, gargantuan James Miller and Mary, Nick Spencer and Kai, Victor and Annamaria Edelstein . . . And there was Lucy Lambton, diving around in what registered as an assortment of rags, who grabbed me, screaming about how awful the stuff was. She was right. It was awful but it was nice to see the folks.

21 JUNE

A celebration of the London Charterhouse

Lunch with Fred Hohler at Boodles, he feeling edged out of the
Public Catalogue Foundation. I advised him to accept that and
concentrate on being chair of St Paul's School, otherwise time is
wasted on squabbles and there is less time when one is older. This
was the evening of the drinks party to commemorate the foundation of the London Charterhouse. James Wilkinson had asked me
to give the speech. It all went well and the Lord Mayor came. It
was a lovely speech to make, largely off the cuff, about the year
1611 – Shakespeare, Jonson and Raleigh were alive. The founder of
the Charterhouse made his fortune out of money lending and kept
the gold in a chest so heavy that it was in danger of falling through
the floor. But in his will he made provision for the education of the
young and the care of the old, establishing a great City tradition.
There was a dinner afterwards in a not very good Italian trattoria,
with only one bottle of wine between the four of us!

23 JUNE

More life with a trainer

I went to the gym to be given a new schedule by my trainer, Doug.
I rather love all this. He asked me to do a press-up with my knees
on the ground and, seeing that this presented no problems, to do
a proper one with my knees up. I did four. 'Do you realise that it's
very rare for a man of your age to be able to do that?' I felt pleased.
So I was given the aim of three sets of twelve [a note states 'Achieved
in July']. I like exercise with a programme attached to it and this

new one will take me into September. I resolve to go three times a week and to lay off too much wine!

24 TO 25 JUNE

Compton Verney and Stratford

I drove to Stratford to stay at the Arden Hotel for two nights. But today it was for me to open two exhibitions at Compton Verney, one organised by Timothy Mowl on 'Capability' Brown and the other of garden paintings by Stanley Spencer. I like Steven Parissien, an ebullient academic who was deputy at the London Paul Mellon Centre. I love the atmosphere of the place, which is hugely lively. So it was the usual tour around, then a reception with me buttering up potential sponsors and then a public opening with a speech by me. Afterwards there was a dinner. Sir Peter Moores, the founder of all this, appeared, a large, elderly gay man with a friend in tow. It is not a happy set-up as he's withdrawn his financial support.

I stayed on an extra night so that I could go to the new RSC theatre. I love it. It was a great success. I went to a matinee performance of *Macbeth* with the witches played as children (so no bubble, bubble), a good Macbeth and a poor Lady Macbeth. There is such a lack of great younger generation actresses – no sign of another Judi Dench, Peggy Ashcroft, etc. They're really feeble. In the evening I went to *Merchant*, a brilliant and wildly perverse production, a comedy, which it is, but set in today's Las Vegas.

27 JUNE

The Abbey, this and that

In the morning I went to an Abbey fundraising meeting. We were told of a New Development Committee with Robert Salisbury and Lord Harris, who promptly gave a million. The need is for the triforium project, the repair of the Cosmati pavement around the shrine, etc. From their minutes it seems that they want to hone in on the non-doms, Russians like Evgeny Lebedev and the Brazilians.

I took A.N. Wilson to lunch at the Garrick. Much anger about how Rowan Williams had treated the gay community. I gave him a copy of *Visions of England* (he later wrote a postcard, having read it – in places with tears in his eyes – and said that it was one of my most marvellous books).

I took Sue Ayton to The Ivy for an early dinner. We both agreed that I should not endlessly be 'used' by TV companies to give an interview that was then used throughout a complete programme.

28 JUNE

Getting it 'in the bag'

Two ITV interviews on the Queen in the Oxford and Cambridge Club in the afternoon. One was for her Diamond Jubilee and the other for when she's dead! It was the same questions for both. Rather surreal – and both to be presented by Alan Titchmarsh, of all people.

29 JUNE

The book hits the Today *programme*

A very long day. Up at 6 a.m. and off by car to Goudhurst with Justin Webb of the *Today* programme team. It is always a great coup to get a book on this. We did the piece on the roof of the church tower, looking over an amazing panorama of 'this England'. Webb is in his fifties, tall and thin and wearing jeans, a check shirt and slip-ons. Three of the *Today* presenters wanted to do the book: a good sign.

Lunch at Tate Britain with the *Bodley Head* people [publishers of Visions of England]. We all seemed optimistic. After that came a very long Abbey event, Petertide. It began with a meeting in which we were divided into groups to discuss this or that. My group discussed the formation of Friends and were anti, but pro Overseas Supporters and an annual nave dinner at £15,000 a table. Then followed a sung Eucharist and after that the Petertide Dinner. I took Jocelyn Burton in black and jewels and sat next to one of the new canons. I ended up with the minor canons on a terrace drinking too much, leaving rather a hazy memory of it all . . .

1 JULY

Gardeners' World *hits The Laskett*

The whole place was taken over by *Gardeners' World*. The presenter was a woman called Rachel de Thame, beautiful with balletic features, and indeed she had been in the Royal Ballet School when Fred [Ashton] was doing *Month in the Country*. So we were friends at once but she was in awe of me! And she had so many of my books.

It was a long and very tiring day with the need for all those repeat shots from every angle. I went to bed at 9.15 p.m.

Eddie Smith of Westminster School pointed out to me that an Elizabethan portrait was in a local saleroom at Pontrilas. It was of a lady dated 1603, the year Elizabeth I died. I left a bid of £5,000 and got it for £4,260. Amazing!

7 JULY

Tim Richardson visits

Tim Richardson came and stayed overnight. He's a delightful, off-beat character who really knows about theatre and gardens. I told him the National Trust saga and he said don't worry: as long as he and Dominic Cole are around The Laskett Gardens will never go. He warned me not to let flowers seep out of the centre of the garden elsewhere and I realised that he was right. Alterations will be made this winter.

Shaun pointed out to me that the Silver Jubilee Garden was still not right. It needs a parterre! So I will design one. Also it needs verticals in the surrounding beds, so I need four or, ideally, eight wooden pyramids up which to train roses. I must get a costing.

11 JULY

The reception of Visions of England

The radio piece on *Visions* was meant to go out on 27 June but Rupert Murdoch and the phone-hacking scandal blew the scene apart, so the *Visions* piece didn't run. Nor did it run, as promised, on Friday 8 July. Mercifully it didn't run on the Saturday, the dead slot, but it did, by a stroke of luck, at 7.55 pm on Monday 11 July.

The reviews so far are odd. It's as though no one had actually read the book, which is very straightforward – perhaps for the reviewers too much so. No one faulted my historical accuracy but although it was spelt out up front that this is about the *imagination*, they wrote as though it wasn't, which was very, very odd. But the reviews were all huge for so small a book. The *Guardian* review was by a raving Marxist on about the ground-down poor, *The Sunday Times* reviewer went off on a tangent about Colonel Gaddaffi and Queen Elizabeth (*sic*), and the *New Statesman* lumped it together with a series of essays on the Olympic village as offering two views of England: utterly weird.

20 JULY

Just Friends comes to The Laskett

This was the Just Friends gay contingent day but it was a shame that it was so overcast. Seventy-five events a year are arranged for members and you have to be elected. Thanks to Brian Sewell, I was landed with being one of their patrons. But it's a benign institution that really cares for a lot of 'widowed' gay men. We all went on to Jan Lucas-Scudamore at Kentchurch, who really did her stuff, and I was landed with a speech when I didn't want to give one and couldn't think what to say!

23 JULY

Robin Lane Fox

The day of Robin Lane Fox's review of *Visions* in the *Financial Times*. I saw it at Sarah Steer's and was much moved by it. Already friends had rung me about it. Robin Lane Fox had read the book and, like Andrew Wilson, was touched by it and understood what I was trying to say. It had every quote a publisher would ever want for the paperback edition. Later I wrote a postcard to Robin Lane Fox, something that I have never done to a reviewer, to say how touched I had been and what respect I had for him.

The handwritten Diary stops suddenly on 1 August, when I ceased to write it from time to time in longhand and I went over to using a laptop. The effect of this was that I wrote much more and shorter pieces. I was later to realise how the discipline of the handwritten was best for diary-keeping, the result being fewer and more descriptive and observed pieces, and, in the end, I was to revert to the pen.

10 SEPTEMBER

Jonathan Myles-Lea takes The Folly

Jonathan Myles-Lea has taken The Folly for a year. I'm very pleased about this. He moved in and the place came together very quickly into an elegant home. He should soon start painting. I hope he realises that he's in his forties and no longer young, and should settle. He's so mercurial but everyone likes him and he fits in exactly with the madhouse of The Laskett Gardens.

13 SEPTEMBER

A newspaper interview

A reporter called Nick Curtis from the *Evening Standard* came to interview me for a major profile for the paper at the request of the editor, Geordie Grieg. The result was a double-page spread. God knows what people thought, if they even saw it, but I'm still here even though the V&A is now twenty-five years ago. There was a lead-up to the jugular: 'The subtext of all your interviews is that you are gay and was the marriage a lavender one?' I'd already been coping with this in the autobiography, where I was as honest as I could be in what is an era so changed in attitude. But I did fall in love at thirty-five with Julia and to me our marriage was sacred and fulfilled in every sense. I can write with truth that I have never been to bed with a man but, yes, I have with a woman. But sex was never the driving force of that marriage, although it was certainly part of it.

16 TO 17 SEPTEMBER

Buddleigh Salterton

I went down to Buddleigh Salterton for their literary festival. I had no idea that I would be put up in a private house – and I wish that I had known so that I could have dodged it. My hosts were delightful but this means that one is on stage the whole time. At 6 p.m. I had to be at the launch party in the parish hall, which was one long give-out. At 7.30 p.m. – I couldn't escape – I had to sit through one and half hours of Carol Ann Duffy and the Welsh national poetess. Duffy was good, the other second rate. I got back to the house exhausted and hungry and munched smoked salmon canapés for an hour. Duffy and co., and along with them Tim Ackroyd, appeared and we eventually sat down to dinner at 10 p.m. They'd done their bit, mine was on the morrow but I had to shine for another hour or more. At last I got to bed but I was done in. I got up early so as to avoid having breakfast with anyone.

I performed in the local church to a packed audience. John de la Cour turned up and I said that I was amazed at my warm reception, to which he replied: 'You say what everyone is thinking but dare not articulate.' I longed to go home but, oh no, a woman who claimed to know me at the V&A had fixed me for lunch, from which again there was no escape. That meant another performance. I could have cried. And even the driver both ways was local and had to be spoken to. I could have done without all of this.

1 OCTOBER

Gerard Irvine memorialised

The final requiem for Gerard Irvine was at his church, St Matthew's, Westminster, over which Rowan Williams presided very well. Everything had been laid down by Gerard. The packed congregation included Donald Buttress (who had designed the wall plaque in Gerard's memory, which was unveiled); P.D. James, rather diminutive at ninety-two, I think, but a marvel; A.N. Wilson; and Frank Field. It was a proper requiem Mass with a good address – one only, something we owed to Frank, who had laid down the law to Gerard's sister, Rosemary (who will be ninety next year). Afterwards there was the usual parish finger lunch of home-made bits and pieces. Alas, by the time I had got back to Hereford the fireworks to celebrate the opening of the new Cathedral Close had come and gone.

2 OCTOBER

Hereford Cathedral Close celebrated

It is unbelievably warm for this time of year: more like July. In the afternoon was the service to open the Cathedral Close. It had been scripted by the Dean, Michael Tavinor, and at times teetered close to something out of E.F. Benson's Riseholme, with Puritan soldiers hustling an Anglican divine from the altar and Elgar riding up the nave aisle on his bicycle. It was provincial but good-humoured – but it did go on and on. Then we all went out to the West Front and the Bishop blessed the Close, striding across the mosaic of a Hereford-shire apple tree. We were meant to go back in and party but I was churched out.

4 OCTOBER

Help from the National Trust

Ben Shipston of the National Trust and his colleague Helen came to lunch. They were so helpful: one loo or two? Two, one of which should be for the disabled. Tom and the builders are here busy on that and on smoothing out where we can in the garden for access for the disabled, including a ramp to the shop. All good but costly work. But this relationship with the National Trust I am most grateful for. I'm starting to think that I can't keep on like this but must tie things up so that I don't have to think about them again.

7 OCTOBER

The educational gulf

I went to Dauntsey's School near Devizes for what turned out to be quite a marathon: tea with the sixth form, then drinks, then dinner, then *Visions* and then questions. I gathered later that I was quite a culture shock. Good. But I was left meditating on the gulf between this well-taught, articulate lot and where the state system had got, in effect re-establishing a different 'us and them' system. I realised how lucky I was to catch the brief flowering of the grammar school before it was wiped out.

I'm taking the gym seriously, although passed from hand to hand. At last I came to rest with Ady Watts, with three mandatory visits a week plus exercises at home. I realise the importance of keeping fully toned at this period of my life. I like setting goals for myself. But every time you get a new trainer it's back to square one again so it'll be weeks of stretching – oh God, it's tough! But I told him that my goal was to be the fittest eighty-year-old he'd ever had [I am!].

10 OCTOBER

Julia's day

I went to the 8 a.m. Mass at the cathedral with Bishop Anthony celebrating. I was much moved that Julia was commemorated and me prayed for as still grieving. I am. I also prayed for Harold Pinter. I didn't know that it was his birthday. Antonia told me.

12 OCTOBER

Scam victim

This was the ghastly week when I was the victim of a scam. It left me gutted. Someone had stolen a friend's address book and there came this email saying that they had been held up at gunpoint in Madrid and needed money, £1,500, to get air tickets. It all sounded very convincing. I rang her but could get no answer so it seemed OK. I had a dreadful time getting the money and sending it to her via some company. Next day there was another agonising call asking for a further £2,000 for the hotel bill. I sprang to again. I was exhausted. Fiona came and looked at the emails and immediately said 'It's a scam' but I was too late to stop the money. More emails arrived, written in a manner which the victim would never use. The nervous exhaustion of it nearly wiped me out. It was a terrible lesson. The victim reimbursed me with the money and I said that I'd pass it on to the cathedral for the vestments I was giving.

17 OCTOBER

Problems with Mr Perkins

I've had a lot of trouble with Perkins [my cat] who has started peeing on the curtains, etc. However, someone who went round the gardens called Diana Stewart – or the Cat Lady – had seen Perkins reclining on the table in the conservatory and snapped him. She saw that he was upset, so she called him and they 'had a conversation' (*sic*). He said that he was lonely. I rang her and we had a good conversation, resulting in me purchasing cat toys and playing with him. She also advised me to reduce the area of the house open to him when I was in London.

23 OCTOBER

A gift to the cathedral

I was MC at the 10 a.m. Eucharist at the cathedral, which was preceded by mc presenting and the Dean blessing the black and gold vestments for use at All Souls and on Remembrance Sunday. They are magnificent, although I'm afraid they make some of the other vestments look rather cheap.

26 OCTOBER

The gap widens

Richard and Susie Walduck arranged a dinner for me to meet Jeffrey John, Dean of St Alban's, and his partner, Fr Grant. The former lived up to expectations, a benign, clever, wonderful if frustrated man who should have been made a bishop. It was a wildly extravagant dinner at Gordon Ramsay's. That restaurant is a sell-out. All through this period, when we are in economic crisis with massive numbers of unemployed and no money, the very rich seem to be richer than ever. Antonia Fraser told me later that she wanted to have tea with a friend at either Claridges or the Ritz but both were booked up for months and so they had to 'make do' with the Connaught! Every time that I come to London I notice the gulf.

27 OCTOBER

John Swannell and David Montgomery

This was the day of my dialogue with John Swannell at the National Portrait Gallery. Sandy Nairne was welcoming and it was a happy occasion with a very good audience. John Swannell is a very good performer. In the audience was the photographer David Montgomery, whom I hadn't seen for years. I reminded him of the brilliant photograph that he'd taken of me at the V&A when the baroque galleries were being redone and the objects were surreally swathed in vast sheets of polythene behind me. I was told later that he had at one stage burnt his negatives, a disastrous thing to have done.

29 OCTOBER

The garden attacked

I went back to Hereford as usual on the 8.22 a.m. train from Paddington. I went to buy a copy of *The Spectator* and saw to my horror on its front the byline 'The Emperor's New Weeds'. I couldn't believe it. Within there were two columns of malicious and envious rubbish which was very hurtful. It was by someone called Anne Wareham who, I later learnt, has a garden somewhere in Wales. I then recalled that she must have been one of the group of gardening folk that I welcomed on a closed day, let into the house, gave coffee to and showed the garden archive, also giving them the map and booklet on the garden. I received no note of thanks but instead I was stabbed in the back. I tried to stop anyone writing but I couldn't stop Andrew Lawson, who wrote, I am told, a good letter.

2 NOVEMBER

Valedictory thoughts

The All Souls Mass, at which I was MC. For the first time, the vestments I had given were worn for a requiem using Faure's music. I decided that I would request this for my own funeral. Apparently it was deeply impressive.

19 AND 20 NOVEMBER

The survival of the aristocracy

I went to Oakly Park for a dinner which turned out to be a lively celebration, both chaotic and affable, of Ivor Windsor's sixtieth birthday. God knows who they all were. I sat next to Caroline and said that someone ought to say something and, needless to say, that fell to me. Apparently everyone was much moved by my oration, for I did say that people like Ivor were living arguments for aristocracy with his generosity and interest in everything and all sorts and conditions of people. And the role of the great house as a mecca – it was beautiful, filled with people celebrating, the tables laid with silver, the great log fire and the informality with which things were done.

I stayed there but got up at 6.30 a.m. and left at 7.10 a.m. to drive back. The dashboard had ominous lit-up signs, which meant nothing to me but indicated that something must be wrong. But the vehicle went and I drove off hoping that I'd get home. No such luck. It conked out on a nasty bend on Dinmore Hill. That was awful, but a Good Samaritan appeared in the form of a sturdy lady gardener who stopped her car and told me what to do. The AA man appeared and eventually the car was got to a garage and left at their gates to repair. He then took me home but I felt gutted and stayed in doing letters and went to bed early.

21 NOVEMBER

A disastrous event

I was given a lift to the cathedral for their big charity viewing of a film called *Resistance*. It was crammed with people. The film was based on a book about a Welsh valley in 1945 and what would have happened there if the Germans had taken over. It was to be the big fundraising event for the cathedral's trust and both the director and the producer were there. I did ask, knowing how chancy these things can be, whether they'd run it through. The answer to that was 'yes'. So we were all seated by 7 p.m. with earphones on. The film started well but, lo, after ten minutes or so it packed up. It couldn't be got going again and the event was reduced to a fiasco.

29 NOVEMBER

Hereford in London

This was the day of the Hereford Cathedral Choir Advent Service in the Guard's Chapel. I travelled up early and went to Dr Vogt, my eye specialist, and was told that my eyes were OK. Then to Clive at Michaeljohn's in Albemarle Street to have my hair and beard put in order, and thence to the Chapel. I didn't warm to it but I suppose that God was in there somewhere: the atmosphere suggested that His presence was an intrusion onto this festival of militaria. I was to be an acolyte in an alb cassock and the crucifer had to be this man in military uniform who carried the cross in, plonked it down and then stalked off into the vestry, where he just walked around or lolled until he popped back in again to carry it for the exit. I didn't enjoy any of it but I was told that front of house it was OK as it was a gathering of the county: Dunnes, Arbuthnots, etc. Princess Alexandra came with Henrietta Dunne in tow. She was sweet as always and dived across the official reception line to greet me. Later, at the reception, I told Henrietta to bring her over to see the garden next time.

30 NOVEMBER

The day of the transport strike

I walked to the National Gallery to meet up with Antonia Fraser to see the Leonardo exhibition. I got straight in thanks to the piece I'd written for the *Telegraph*. It was an amazing exhibition, beautifully hung and visually argued. We had coffee afterwards when Roger Katz, formerly of Hatchards, subjected us to a non-stop tirade, after which I went on to Hatchards to buy the new biography of Georgette Heyer as it had a lot in it about Julia's aunt, Carola Oman.

Afterwards I took A.N. Wilson to the Garrick for a somewhat bibulous lunch. We always start with dry martinis! I told him that he'd be the speaker at my service of thanksgiving in the Abbey: 'You'll get me in one and you'll make them laugh.' Much talk about everything but in the main about the doom and gloom which will go on for years and years. He feels the financial pinch as he has a daughter to educate.

The whole of this period has the feeling of being on a cliff edge of something ghastly and, of course, one feels helpless. The outlook is unrelentingly grim. The EU is like some juggernaut with no one at the wheel.

5 DECEMBER

Tim Ackroyd, Julia's Nutcracker *and Ptolemy Dean*

An Abbey Foundation meeting in the morning: very optimistic, which was weird in the present climate, but the Abbey has luck on its side with the goodwill engendered by the Royal Wedding and Diamond Jubilee next year. The fundraising committee looks formidable, with the Prince of Wales as patron calling for the millions needed to carry through the triforium project.

I gave lunch to Tim Ackroyd, a delightful, raffish baronet who's stuck with finishing Beryl Bainbridge's play in which he is to play the lead. This is to happen at the Yvonne Arnaud Theatre in Guildford, where Julia's *Hay Fever* died a death at the hands of Glynis Johns. He is so effervescent and funny that I always get carried away with laughter. He wants me to do something in Macclesfield, of all places, where he runs a festival.

In the evening I took John Hall to Julia's *Nutcracker*, which still holds the stage and looks radiant, with supper at the Garrick after. I learnt that Ptolemy Dean is to be the Abbey's new Surveyor of the Fabric, which will work very well with the Prince of Wales. He's a delight and not a modernist and knows a lot about churches and, with his sharp and delightful visual sense, is just the chap who would respond to what needs to be done for the rituals of state, as a funeral and a coronation are on the *tapis* in the next few years.

6 DECEMBER

The National Portrait Gallery, an Elizabethan portrait and a Goldsmiths' Livery Dinner

Lunch with Sandy Nairne, which was incredibly thoughtful and caring of him – but he does now have a Maine Coon cat called Augustus! I told him to buy the Jane Seymour portrait which Mark Weiss has, a perfectly good Cast Shadow workshop piece [he didn't]. I was surprised to find that he didn't even know of Susan Martin's PhD on the National Portrait Gallery. But he's a buoyant soul and the National Portrait Gallery has almost hit two million visitors a year. Wonderful. It looks as though the East Wing ceded by Charles Saumarez Smith to the National Gallery will in the long run be retained.

I went with Mark Weiss to see the portrait of the Countess of Nottingham from Cowdray Park at the restorer Katherine Ara's. Next to images of the Queen this is the most spectacular late Elizabethan costume piece I have ever seen. Apart from the background, it is in the most fantastic condition and certainly from the workshop of Robert Peake.

In the evening I took Joanna Worsley to the Goldsmiths' Company Livery Dinner. She sat next to Christopher Lennox-Boyd, who came in late, huge and flaccid and propped up on two sticks, saying that he had a heart condition and should he marry his Chinese carer. Indeed, he asked Joanna whether she was my carer and would she be taking me back to Herefordshire! There always was an inspired madness about him but he seemed pretty far gone to me.

10 DECEMBER

The Queen sits for John Swannell, my godchild and the social divide

I went to the National Portrait Gallery to be photographed in front of John Swannell's image of me as an Elizabethan in a ruff. John is such an unusual and agreeable man. He told me that he had been asked to photograph the Queen for the Diamond Jubilee and had been granted an unprecedented two hours. He had worked out what he wanted but she wouldn't sit on Queen Victoria's throne but on another one. Also he had wanted her near a window but that was ruled out as once she had gone near a window and someone saw her from the Mall and crashed the car. I posed, including reclining on a banquette like a tomb effigy, and he was happy.

In the evening I took my godchild Charlie Aslet to *The Sleeping Beauty* at Covent Garden. It was an awful evening for demonstrations and Whitehall was closed, so it was a nightmare journey costing a fortune and in the end I got out of the taxi and walked. But the production was interesting, as they had reinstated the original Oliver Messel costumes and it made a huge difference. It was as I remembered it, the sets pale and wispy, the costumes with very strong colour. Sadly Carabosse remained a woman (it used to be a man) in a Peter Farmer cocktail dress.

We got back to the Aslet household in Tachbrook Street and I had a long chat with Clive until almost 1 a.m. Much was on the fact of the present financial divide between rich and poor on a scale unknown since Edwardian England. Someone like Clive was caught. Those with masses of money spent fortunes on private tutors for their offspring to get them up to what was needed, even, in one instance that he knew, taking the tutor out with them to the Bahamas. Clive has three fine boys to provide for and it's a nightmare. Basically he would like to withdraw from the metropolis and work from Cambridge. My own view is that in the period we are going in to it would be wise to get out of the cities as there could be much unrest and violence.

All of this gloomy conversation was in the aftermath of Cameron's use of the veto in Brussels. The EU is wildly unpopular and if they had a referendum the country would overwhelmingly opt out. All through this period there has been a great concern about the economic crisis. It's been like looking at a slow-motion train crash. What concerns me is what we haven't been told. Mervyn King's message of doom was bad enough, but it conceals as much as it says. God knows what the consequences are.

16 TO 17 DECEMBER

Oxford and Self-Portrait

I took the 8.49 a.m. train to Oxford and went straight to the Clarendon Building to meet Samuel Fanous of the Bodleian Library Press, his assistant, Janet, and my editor for the early autobiography, Johanna Stephenson. The rapport between us was instant, which was wonderful. She's a mature woman, in her late forties or early fifties I would guess, who had worked at the National Portrait Gallery and the V&A. It was a very exciting meeting and we decided that the book should appear in 2013. Good points were made about it and so that afternoon I went back to the Old Bank Hotel and drafted a prologue.

The 17th was the day of the Dragon School great charity sale. There were a lot of authors this time, including the likes of Jeremy Paxman and Jeremy Clarkson. However, I had a hundred copies of *Visions* and all went.

21 DECEMBER

Mucknell Abbey

Michael Tavinor collected me for our pre-Christmas visit to Mucknell Abbey, where we had the warmest of welcomes from Fr Abbot Stuart. I took them a dozen bottles of claret for Christmas. The place still seems very bleak and unsettled. So Michael made his confession to Fr Abbot and I to Michael, who has an extraordinary understanding of humankind. The Bishop of Worcester was there, a good Catholic priest who had been spending his sabbatical on and off in the hermitage. In the chapel was the moving ceremony of a youth being christened and then confirmed. Afterwards we assembled in a little sitting room and various bottles of fizz were produced and we had a celebration! Lunch in silence of bread, cheese, dates and an apple while Brother Thomas read from William Hague's biography of Samuel Wilberforce, which was rather dull.

23 DECEMBER

Raine Spencer comes to lunch

To help Henry and Cressida Legge out I had Raine Spencer to lunch and lined up Ivor Windsor, her godchild, and Caroline. I got Penny Johnstone to do the whole lunch, with Kevin as factotum and butler. Poor things, the Legges have Raine for Christmas. She arrived looking larger than I remember her, in a purple tweed two-piece with the perennial good jewel pinned top right in the manner of ladies-in-waiting. But she stuck to wearing her large fur hat all through lunch, an aberration abandoned years ago – very 1950s and earlier! She was still hooked up to Harrods, has a house in Devon, another in Chelsea and a third near Chichester. Utterly unsinkable.

DECEMBER

New Year's Eve reflection

Have I had a good year? I don't really know. I do know that I want to be in the country far more. I'm less stressed and healthier. It's been a year when so many I know have died or who have been unwell or still are. I was shocked to get a card from Chippy Irvine saying that Keith had died in May. How awful. They were some of Julia's oldest friends from Royal College of Art days. He'd worked for John Fowler and then went to America, where he had a fabulously successful career as a decorator, with a clientele that included Drue Heinz and most of the Kennedys. He was eighty-two. Beatrix Miller rang me telling me that she'd fallen over and broken her ankle, which added to her ulcerated leg and rendered her bedridden in Mulberry Walk. I didn't know what quite to say, for I love her dearly but honestly she never quite remade her life after leaving *Vogue* all those decades ago . . . I really wish to come out of London, and place my flat in the hands of an agent to do up and let.

The upside of the year has been the almost three thousand visitors to the garden, which is much loved, to which can be added its appearance on *Gardeners' World*. I don't know what to feel over *Visions of England*. Over six thousand copies were sold but it ought to have done better; it was blighted by the *Daily Mail* buying an exclusive and then ditching it. It said something that needed to be said. Maybe the paperback will be a greater success. It signals the end of my long association with Jörg Hensgen and Random House. Perhaps the best news is the affectionate roots I have put down in the county, both through the cathedral and the opening of the garden. Fiona has been a huge bonus, creating a sense of 'family' among those who look after both me and the garden.

2012

David Hockney and Dickens

I started early with a walk across St James's Park to the Royal Academy and met Antonia Fraser, looking good in fur, Charles Saumarez Smith then letting us in early to the David Hockney exhibition. It was a wonderful privilege to see it without anyone else there, room after room of happiness and joy, a sunshine quality with those radiant landscapes of East Yorkshire and the Dales. There were all sorts of influences evident: Monet, Van Gogh, Samuel Palmer, etc. One wonderful room had about six views of the same formation of trees through the seasons from the same viewpoint – pure magic. I preferred the softer ones without violent colour. Strange how close Hockney comes to kitsch but just somehow misses it.

Then we moved on to the Abbey for the Dickens commemoration. It was a huge turn-out for a rather splendid and moving occasion. The Prince of Wales appeared, with his usual smiling if slightly agonised look, along with Camilla, who's terribly easy: 'How are you?' 'I'm fine. How are you?' Then she told me how they'd been to the Dickens Museum and how I ought to go. He asked, 'How's the garden?' I said 'Stunning, but you've never seen it.' The Archbishop was there, glad to have escaped Synod for an hour or two (women bishops). I think that he's been done over a bit as his hair and beard were in order. Off we all traipsed to the south transept and then followed what was a really touching occasion. Rowan Williams gave an amazing oration without a note in sight and Ralph Fiennes read the death of Jo from *Bleak House* with perfect balance, which brought tears to my eyes. The Prince laid a wreath of white flowers and two Dickens descendants laid posies (there was a lunch for 150 of them: they must have bred like rabbits). It was all perfect. Claire Tomalin then did her stuff and we all ended up in the party afterwards. There was P.D. James, a real love of a woman, on a stick over ninety but amazing. I spoke to Ed Vaizey, saying that I hadn't seen him since he read at his father's memorial service all those years ago.

I whisked Antonia off to Le Due Amici in Rochester Row, where we saw Kathryn Bradley-Hole of *Country Life*. I always have such a good time and giggle with Antonia. She made me promise that I'd wear one of my Indian bridegroom's costumes to her eightieth dinner.

8 FEBRUARY

The coronation, Freud and the Opera House

I did an interview on the coronation for a ninety-minute programme for BBC 4. It was interesting to learn how much unused film footage exists of meetings and rehearsals, including Archbishop Fisher 'crowning' Lavinia Norfolk. In the afternoon I went to a private viewing of the Lucien Freud exhibition at the National Portrait

Gallery. It was a stunning show but it was difficult to enjoy so much unattractive human flesh and it made me wonder what constituted a portrait nowadays. But what a painter of a private world he was.

On to the London Library, then the Weiss Gallery to see the wonderful Elizabethan full-lengths from Cowdray and finally to Favourbrook, which hadn't noted the fabric that I had chosen so couldn't start on my suit. In the evening I went to the Opera House for *The Dream* and shed a tear for David Walker [the designer] and also Macmillan's *Song of the Earth* but I was so tired that I kept nodding off. As I went in I saw David Hockney, the first time I'd seen him for years. I reminded him (he's deaf) of who I was and told him of the happiness his exhibition had given me and how English he'd been, which he knew. 'We're both of an age,' I said. 'I'll be seventy-five this year,' he said. 'I'll be seventy-seven,' I said. 'You'll never catch up with me.' He remains on my rather short list of originals.

6 MARCH

The suit again

I went to Favourbrook about my suit and chose lovely buttons for the waistcoat. I'm larger than I was but at seventy-six I don't feel like starving myself. The fabric is a lovely shade of blue and the trouser legs narrow with a fifteen-inch bottom. Inevitably on to the London Library and then the V&A for the Beaton exhibition, all of which I knew. It was elegantly done although nothing new was said.

In the evening there was a vastly expensive dinner at the Weiss Gallery hung with the Cowdray Elizabethan full-lengths. They looked quite wonderful. Much kissing on both cheeks by Jasper Conran, who is now, I suppose, in his forties, a puckish man but with a latent sadness about him. I never knew that my work had had such an impact on him, but it had. He fell in love with Elizabeth I at the age of seven while staying at Woburn.

10 MARCH

A gardeners' quiz

A heavenly day, warm with blue skies and the garden a paradise of spring flowers, snowdrops almost over but the daffodils about to come. This was the day of the *Gardeners' Question Time* quiz in aid of Herefordshire Growing Point [horticultural therapy charity] to be held at the RNC [Royal National College for the Blind, Hereford]. This is a lovely charity, a very modest one, which aims to get people out of care homes to tend a plot at Holme Lacy, where they can sow and harvest on a small scale. There was a great turn-out of about 120 to 150, all of whom had paid £15, for which they also got nibbles and wine. I was the chairman and the panel consisted of Stephen Anderton, the court jester of gardening, larky and fun; Nick Dunn, a lovely guy on trees; and Robert Myers, the garden and landscape designer who did the Duke of York's Square and Hereford Cathedral Close. The great thing was to be warm and funny and to the point, which we were. I always feel nervous when I start but the atmosphere was great and it took off.

12 MARCH

Commonwealth Observance and a photographic project

I went up for Commonwealth Observance at the Abbey. As with the Diamond Jubilee, there was a big turn-out and the clergy wore their

1937 coronation blue copes. There were a lot of royals, including Sophie Wessex in the most absurd hat like a flying saucer skewered on to her head with an explosion of feathers; the Prince of Wales in his usual blue suit; Camilla chatty in purple; the Queen in plum and happy; and the Duke as usual, although he suddenly looked at me astounded and asked whether I dyed my hair! I said that I was in my Van Dyck period.

It was pretty good as these services go and went off without a hitch on the Queen's principle of 'a bit of something for every-body'. There were prayers by the various faith leaders; a reflection; a Commonwealth song; a message from the Queen, which really said nothing except that what linked us was that we were all human beings; there was African dancing of a kind but someone should have stopped them wearing black as they were invisible; and a few hymns. It all went off like clockwork. Richard Luce came, looking frail and propped up on a stick, but he got there and back . . .

Later I had dinner with John and Marianne Swannell at Odins in Devonshire Street. He produced the snaps of me in front of the one he took of me in Elizabethan costume at the NPG. There were some very good pictures. I told him about the man in Calcutta who told me that I had the face of a maharajah and that all that was needed was to darken my skin. I had looked at maharajahs' portraits, especially those produced by the Lafayette Studios, and yes, he was right. I'd bought the clothes in India – everything, that is, except a turban. To do the photograph we'd need to get some phoney jewels as these maharajah portraits are an extraordinary genre, rather exotic and romantic, with turbans hung with jewels and pearls and swags of necklaces worn in profusion. John wanted to do the picture in Leighton House and also wanted to take a Victorian one of me, for which I suggested 18 Stafford Terrace [Linley Sambourne House] as the location, if we could get in.

19 MARCH

The Freud exhibition revisited

I met Antonia to go to the Freud for a second time. She lived just
around the corner from him and he had painted Harold but the portrait was never finished. So off we went round the exhibition where
virtually none of the portraits were identified, just a man or a woman,
but there was Elizabeth Cavendish, Andrew and Debo Devonshire,
Jane Willoughby, Bindy Lambton, Andrew Parker-Bowles, etc. On
reflection there's something disturbing about Freud's work, all that
acreage of naked flesh, flabby or emaciated, and all those downcast
eyes. There's a kind of cruelty about stripping people who are not
beautiful but ugly. They are men and women as meat. Everyone
is contained into a closed world that never opens out, just a large,
filthy, airless studio with a sink and rags and an old iron bedstead.
The women in particular seem humiliated in their nudity and then
there's the odd, creepy feature like part of a body protruding from
under a bed. Only in the Watteauesque group is there a hint of
lyrical happiness. All the sitters look like troubled souls in anguish.
The texture of the flesh is dry and in no way luscious, as it would be
in the case of a Titian. I'd been saying that I'd never met Freud but
then I recalled him at Ann Fleming's gatherings in the Sixties and
Seventies. He moved in a quite rarefied world of the upper classes.

30 APRIL

La Bohème *revived and John Copley's fiftieth*

This was the evening of a revival of Julia's *Bohème* at Covent Garden,
to which I took Antonia. It still holds the stage and the *Barrière*

d'Enfer scene I hold as one of her best. This was also John Copley's fiftieth anniversary of directing at the Opera House and at the close a cake was wheeled on and speeches made and then we discovered that the Prince of Wales was there. John was very funny about the last time there was an occasion like this foisted on him. Then a Union Jack had been lowered and a male stripper appeared, and one of the women on stage passed out when he removed his jockstrap. Antonia went off but I penetrated backstage and wished John the best. He said that he was here now most of the time as his partner, the other John [Chadwyck-Healey], was ninety, bedridden and unable to move. It was very touching.

I MAY

The Prayer Book and Leonardo exhibitions

Over to Lambeth Palace for the opening of the 1662 Prayer Book exhibition by the Prince of Wales, where I found myself among those chosen to be presented, even although I protested that I hadn't done anything towards the exhibition. It was a small gathering with money much in view, with the likes of Guy Weston, Robert Salisbury and the representative of the Wolfson Foundation. Robert was already on to Saudi Arabia for the Abbey and I couldn't help thinking that it is really awful that we are reduced to this, John Hall, the Dean and another group having just left for the United States also with money in view. At any rate we all peered at the showcases with their tasteful arrangement of books and manuscripts in that magnificent room. The Prince arrived and went round the exhibition looking quite lively and wearing the usual blue suit but with a patterned pocket handkerchief, all very 1950s. I said that I hoped that he'd enjoyed *La Bohème*, which surprised him, but I reminded him that Julia had designed it. He chuckled when I referred to John Copley as Coppers. He'd been to Knole the day before, where there's another fundraising job as I learnt later that day, for the old Lord Sackville wouldn't allow the National Trust into his part of the house and now he's gone the roof is practically falling in. We went upstairs to join the awaiting throng and the Archbishop did his stuff, followed by the Prince, who referred to his Dickens address, as well he might.

Afterwards I slipped into the Garden Museum to see their somewhat disappointing exhibition on garden opening, later to the London Library, then to Favourbrook to collect my beautiful new suit and, finally, to the opening of the Leonardo exhibition at the Queen's Gallery. It was stunning but quite cerebral for Joe Public; but every drawing is a graphic miracle. The world and his wife were there, jostling and not really looking, but it gave me pleasure to see Sarah Greenall and Paul Zuckerman, Fiona Reynolds, Jill Ritblat, Diane Lever, John and Valerie Guinness, etc.

27 MAY

Cataclysms ahead

I went to lunch with Mark and Gillian Archer at Colwall in their beautiful Voysey house, which has really settled in. Noel Malcolm and the *Financial Times* Arts editor were staying, so there was much good conversation. Noel agreed with me that all the news is bad and that we're moving towards a series of cataclysms. Things can't go on like this. Here we are, all bread and circuses, while the EU is falling apart in front of us. This is going to be a long haul and we're only at the start of it.

30 MAY

A visit to Bath: the Fashion Museum, Paul Brason and Alexander Sturgis

I went with Jonathan Myles-Lea to Bath, a city I have always loved – I've even toyed with buying a flat there, although that would be a stupid thing to do, but it has scale and style and I always feel happy there. First we went to see Rosemary Harden at the Fashion Museum in the Assembly Rooms. Rosemary is a short but definite person, grateful for all my stuff, and didn't mince her words as to why museums couldn't get enough fashion these days. It all, she said, went back to me at the V&A, which cheered me up as it had been such a struggle with the Textile Department, which, in Donald King's day, hated dress. We then went on a tour of the stores, beginning with boxes of my ties all beautifully wound around with tissue paper. The ones we pulled out were mega kipper ties, very late Sixties, hugely wide. I was struck by how interesting they were, even more time having elapsed. And then we saw a whole mass of my stuff hung on racks, which was rather impressive. It had all grown in status since I had donated it. I told her that really they ought to go through the scrapbooks and copy the pictures in which I was wearing these pieces. I uttered a sigh of regret on seeing so many of Gianni Versace's garments.

Then off we went to Beechen Cliff to Paul Brason. I'd never been to his house, which has that clean-cut quality in its arrangement and hanging of things which his pictures have, very precise but not cold. It was a wonderful summer's day and we had a salad lunch outside. Jonathan was anxious to see Paul's studio, which was not in the least like what we imagine an artist's studio to be like. It is very tidy, with everything in order. In fact you would have to look twice to establish that it was a studio at all, except that it had glorious north-facing windows. Paul is busy painting the Duke of Edinburgh and, after much coming and going with the Engineers' Company and the Palace courtiers, it is to be a triple image. It will be three heads and Paul has drawn four. I told him which one to drop. The Duke is sitting with an open-necked shirt, which he wants to keep but he knows that the Company will insist that he wear their ghastly tie. This was a wonderfully happy visit and there on the mantelpiece was yet another portrait of me, a head labelled 'Roy III', if I recall rightly. Jonathan took lots of snaps.

On we went to look at the Holburne Menstrie Museum to see its new extension. I asked whether it was possible to see the Director, Alexander Sturgis, and, lo, he walked out of the new restaurant towards us. He'd done a stunning job: a beautiful glass box added to a late Georgian building, which was just perfect. He had also hung and arranged things perfectly. Oddly enough, I was struck by how lacklustre and sloshed out so many of the Gainsboroughs were!

3 JUNE

The Diamond Jubilee water pageant

This was the day of the Diamond Jubilee water pageant. Months ago Martin Owen, the dealer, had asked me to his flat at Chelsea Bridge to see it. It was not, I thought, to be missed. James O'Donnell and his partner Noura picked me up at 11.30 a.m. and we walked there, all the roads being blocked off. It was, however, a bitter day for June, the weather having gone in sharp reverse. That worsened through the day as it got colder and colder. Martin lives in a modern apartment block with a huge balcony to which a steady stream of relatives and friends made their way. There was Buck's Fizz and much loitering on the commodious balcony, from which could be observed the never-ending queue of those going into Battersea Park – some ninety thousand of them – who were also thronging their way across Chelsea Bridge. There was much chatter and then followed lunch and, at last, about 3 p.m. the pageant began.

There was no lack of vessels but they looked thin and scattered over the Thames, except for balletic groups such as that representing the Commonwealth. There was a desperate need for large punctuation marks – proper larger ships like the *Golden Hind* or the *Victory* to hold it together. What we couldn't see was made up for on television, where the Queen stood stalwart to the end, attired in white; but she was certainly cold. As a spectacle it was a failure, being too scattered and too thin, and then there was the weather: icy cold followed, by the time they reached the Royal Barge at Tower Bridge, by torrential rain. None the less, the public didn't shift from their places, enduring everything to pay her homage. Afterwards I walked back home to Westminster through the pouring rain. It was sad as so many people wanted to party but couldn't because the weather was so awful. I got home soaked and thoroughly chilled through. I took my wet garments off and decided that I just couldn't face going out again, so at 8 p.m. put on my pyjamas and climbed into bed, and slept ten hours.

4 JUNE

A Jubilee Party in Hereford

I got up early in order to catch the 8.22 a.m. train back as usual. Pam Row, one of the minor canons, had asked me to her Jubilee Party: after 4.30 p.m., she said, so bearing a bottle in a bag, off I went to a house in an alley off the Cathedral Close. Pam is a smiling, down-to-earth lady who is sometimes deacon at the Sunday Eucharist. This was a lovely medley of all sorts of people from the Dean to a gay pair whom she once met out walking the dogs. We had drinks and crisps and nibbles and then we walked over to what must be the staff canteen of the Choir School, where we found tables set up with Union Jack napkins and bunting festooned around the room, along with a table laden with supper: cold salmon and salads, the inevitable coronation chicken, warm rolls and quiches followed by strawberries, a square of brownie, chocolate sauce and ice cream.

I sat at a table with Michael's partner, Tim, with a gay couple, one of whom was a Green Party councillor, an interesting man doing much to prevent the county being wrecked by central government, who don't know the place. Afterwards there was a quiz about the Royal Family and earlier we had all toasted the Queen with champagne. This in its way made up for yesterday. Here was a piece of Old England still going on, a mixed gathering of young and old, high and low, but with a common bond.

I got back home and found the house so cold that I lit the fire and caught the second half of the pop concert in front of the Palace, a splendid spectacle showing a brilliant deployment of the area in front as theatre. The use of lights and projections was quite incredible and made yesterday's water pageant amateur and feeble by comparison. The finale went into a short but exuberant firework display. The crowds were immense, stretching the whole way to Admiralty Arch. Quite astonishing. We also learnt that the Duke of Edinburgh was in hospital but OK.

What was so striking after the event was that there was no analysis of what actually had happened. Euphoria was poured over it in torrents. In reality it was not in any sense a multicultural event at all. There were no street parties in Bradford for a start. Also in Scotland there was little sign of universal celebration. The hold, as Lord Luce remarked to me at the wedding, was thin north of the border.

5 JUNE

Diamond Jubilee finale

I saw the service from St Paul's Cathedral on television, an impressive spectacle with a superb sermon by the Archbishop. The Queen, dressed in ice blue with odd gauze panels down the back, was clearly much moved by it in parts. St Paul's looked like a painting by Panini and all the old pageantry worked, including a stunning tableau of the heralds outside the cathedral. I then went off for a tough training session with Ady at the gym and returned in time for the carriage procession, the Queen travelling with the Prince of Wales and Camilla. As usual it looked beautiful. Then, after a gap, came the balcony tableau, which struck me as significant: the Queen was flanked to her right by Charles and Camilla and, to her left, by William and Kate. What it seemed to say to me was that the future of the monarchy depended on the women, as indeed it had done through the twentieth century.

12 JUNE

Dressing the part

Jonathan picked me up at 9 a.m. and we drove to the costumiers Angels and spent three hours sorting out the two changes of dress for the 10 July photo shoot with John Swannell at 18 Stafford Terrace and Leighton House. The Tissot-Sargent man in full 1890s evening dress worked a treat and I looked perfect in it with cane and topper, stiff shirt and high collar. The maharajah was more complicated, offering two options, one a crimson and gold robe and the other much lighter and in cream and gold. One must always keep an eye open against slipping into fancy dress, so it ended with a 'less is more' solution, always referring back to the Lafayette Studio photographs. To complete the picture we took swags of pearls and a couple of turban jewels, along with an upright feather. The turban presented them with a problem but in the end they produced about nine metres of muslin with which to tie it. I'd seen someone do it on YouTube and realised how complex it was, but Jonathan rang up his friend Krishna, who will come and do it for me on the day. It takes seven metres of fabric and must cover my ears, I was told.

23 TO 24 JUNE

A visit to Brighton

I took the 4.06 p.m. train to Brighton, where I was met and delivered to Pauline, a nice widowed lady who was to put me up for the night in her large house in Clifton Road. It was then up to St Michael's Church, in my role as patron of their appeal, for a dinner of some 120 placed at round tables in the nave. It all looked good but the food was cold by the time we got it and the gaps between courses were interminable. In spite of this the festive air never vanished. Everyone had paid £30 towards the restoration of the church's famous Pre-Raphaelite windows in the part of the church by Bodley. I got up and did my stuff with a joke or two and ended with telling them to go home and rewrite their wills! Lots of figures from my Brighton past loomed up but I'm so bad at remembering names. It all went tremendously well, although it was too long, starting at 7.30 p.m. and not finishing until midnight.

Next day I felt very tired but the show had to go on. In the morning I walked around Brighton and took a sentimental look at John and Valerie Kingman's old house in Montpelier Terrace and then on to where I had lived, Wykeham Terrace. I pressed my face against the railings and then heard a voice calling: 'Roy!' It was Michael Ginesi, who was still living at number nine. His partner was long since dead but they had been such good neighbours, so I stepped in and had a cup of coffee with him. I still have such a sentiment for that period of my life and for my first house. I gather that whoever has it now has ripped out the pretty gothick bookcases and put in a jukebox instead. Then I walked on through the Lanes and brought a stunning striped jacket at Pretty Green, and so back to base.

Then on to lunch given by another supporter of the church two or three along the road. There, inevitably, was Rosemary Irvine, sharp as a needle at eighty-nine and asking why I hadn't been to see her. I pointed out that it did involve a six-hour journey! But she nailed me for her ninetieth birthday on 20 October, when I'll hopefully persuade Andrew Wilson to come down with me. It was a good three-course lunch, which I could have done without. And then back to St Michael's for the dialogue with Charles Saumarez Smith. There was Romilly, still beautiful, in her complex wheelchair, along with an audience of just over a hundred. Charles and I went on and did our stuff to great applause, with a lot about me but that was why I was there. Charles revealed that the senior staff of the V&A used to meet in the basement of the Daquise restaurant near South Kensington Station to plot my downfall. I knew that they met regularly – monthly, I think – but never knew where. What a hell-hole that place was! Then tea and more give-out to more people and then I took the train back to Victoria.

27 TO 28 JUNE

Oxford and the Bodleian Library

As it was never announced that to get to Oxford I had to take the train to Birmingham and change at Newport, I missed it. In panic I rang Mick Davies, who drove me to Oxford at vast expense. The railway system from Hereford is ghastly. This was for the opening of the Dickens exhibition at the Bodleian Library, followed by a dinner after in the Sheldonian Theatre, which I'd never seen. But it started with having lunch at Cherwell Boathouse with Chris Fletcher. There's an engaging boyishness and sweetness to him and we found ourselves rewriting late twentieth-century English culture as a continuation of native romanticism, a discussion that arose out of him going through Gerard Irvine's papers. It was how the network was continued among those who adhered to it – and indeed much of the conversation was about that network and how he cast me as a key figure in this transmission. It was so pleasant sitting outside above the water with its reflections and feeling of dappled light, all rather like being in an Impressionist painting.

I had tea with the Bodleian Library Press team, headed by the ever-smiling Samuel Fanous, and learnt that *Self-Portrait* was trundling its way on and is to be published in March. There was a demand for quotes on the book (I've never had that before) and then they were on about the literary festivals. The only way that they would work is with a dialogue between me and someone of a younger generation like Dominic Sandbrook. So there it was left to wend slowly on its way.

I then wandered over to the opening party for the Dickens exhibition, which took place in the Divinity School. Claire Tomalin kissed me on both cheeks. What an incredible biographer she has been;

but even she was longing to move on from Dickens. Then I spotted a smile across the room. It was Marina Warner, still beautiful: that took me back a decade or two and there she is, still scribbling away in Kentish Town. Then Claire opened the exhibition but went on and on too long, all of it good but really unnecessary. The woman who was to design the cover of *Self-Portrait* whispered in my ear, 'Joyce Grenfell,' to which I whispered back, 'No, an Alan Bennett talking head.'

The dinner in the Sheldonian Theatre was a novelty and I saw the Robert Streeter ceiling just restored, although it was not exactly Veronese! The table I was at was quite agreeable, on my left a Lady Roberts, diplomat wife of the head of Trinity College, and on my right a woman whose husband opposite ran a television company. Sarah Thomas, Bodley's Librarian, sprang up for a second time and spoke in her new guise, having slimmed down and exercised and hence was almost quite unrecognisable. But she's a star and a real driving force.

2 JULY

Princes and Poets: *A poetry reading at Eastnor Castle*

I was picked up at 2.20 p.m. to go to Eastnor by Joy, whose husband had died a couple of years back. There was a long conversation in the car as to how we both coped, in her case more of a problem as she had time on her hands and there were empty days to fill. I don't have empty days. In my case it's always been a matter of how to get through the mounds of paper. So we arrived at Eastnor, which I've never liked: a great, threatening hulk of a Regency castle glowering over the surrounding countryside. In we went to find Mary Constable, a sweet, bubbly lady who will direct stage movement, and Gareth Rees-Roberts, our guitarist. He's a splendid, big-built Welshman with a magnificent head of white hair, with beard and moustache to match, and beautiful eyes. So we all heaved-to and set the scene. The stage was there and the next thing was to find a carpet. Done. Next two good chairs, so we raided the next room and returned with a pair of Pugin ones upholstered in crimson velvet and adorned with tattered gold fringing and brass knobs. The setting began to look good.

We then established ourselves in a nearby bedroom with a huge four-poster bed to await the arrival of Siân Phillips. At last she came, tall and thin with an angular face betokening that once she had been very beautiful but still looked marvellous, and endowed with a voice and articulation that were both distinctive and stunning. So together we did a read-through, with Gareth popping in the music, after which adjustments were made. As Siân had only put in one contact lens, she had difficulty reading the script!

Then out we went and rehearsed it again on stage but the light was so bad that we couldn't see our scripts, so in the end clip-on lights arrived. There then followed a lull while Siân went into Ledbury to change and I returned to the bedroom and put on my performance clothes. The audience, which was a sell-out, was meant to arrive at 7 p.m. for a glass of wine but the place was besieged by 6.30 p.m. and the doors had to be opened. The pressure was such that, although we were scheduled to perform at 7.45 p.m., we had to pull it back, so off we went. Mary had loved my script *Princes and Poets* and I do think that it was a good one, with lovely contrasts of light and shade, poignancy and humour. The performance went off without a hitch. A third of the way in there was a real rapport between the two of us and Gareth's bridging music was just perfect. There was a storm of applause at the end and we were presented with the usual ghastly craft pot that seems obligatory at such festivals these days. I'd done my deep sub-Gielgud voice for items like lines from *The Faerie*

Queene. As I left, Siân said that she'd love to do it with me again [she did in 2015 in Dore Abbey for the Hereford Three Choirs]. I left happy.

10 JULY

The great shoot with John Swannell

We all converged on Linley Sambourne House, 18 Stafford Terrace. The last time I'd been there was decades ago, for a lunch that Michael and Anne Rosse gave for the Queen Mother. Later I recognised it as one of the locations in a Merchant Ivory film. On the first floor is the most marvellous late Victorian, slightly Aesthetic Movement, drawing room that I know. It is an amazing clutter of blue and white, of photographs jammed on the walls, the frames edge to edge, along with an obstacle race of chairs and little tables scattered with lamps and bibelots, heavy fringed velvet curtains, bookcases and mirrored overmantels.

This was a major shoot, unlike the Elizabethan one, which just took off. Now it was the whole works, with huge boxes of equipment arriving: cameras, tripods and lighting. As it was me, the facility fees for this and also the Leighton House shoot were generously waived. Several girls bustled around and then John arrived with Robert and a further dogsbody. Jonathan Myles-Lea was in attendance on me, plus a make-up girl called Wendy. John Swannell is amiable, enthusiastic and had clearly done his location homework as he knew precisely where he wanted me to pose. This was Costume One: me as a kind of aristocrat out of an Oscar Wilde play. Downstairs I put on full evening dress with a killer of a high stiff collar, stiff-fronted shirt, white gloves, top hat and cane, not to mention what from a distance passed as a white gardenia in my buttonhole. Wendy painted out any deficiencies on my face and my hair was parted in the middle and smarmed down. Up we went and John knew precisely where he wanted me to stand and how he wanted me to look – grand and haughty – and he snapped away. I was positioned with my face slightly to the right for some, with one hand resting on the cane, but for most the hand holding hat and gloves was behind me. John got very excited and said that the pictures were great and he'd got what he wanted in the bag.

It was then time to decamp to Leighton House, that exotic tiled and marbled tribute to the late Victorian fascination for the Middle East. This was the setting for Costume Two. Again John had done his homework and knew exactly what he wanted. In the boot of the car was a silver-plated armchair throne, much to my surprise, which was carried in and set up with a wall of tiles and marble pillars behind. Downstairs I began to be made up by Wendy, with my face darkened and touches of eyeliner added. On went the clothes in gold and crimson, and eventually Jonathan's brilliant Indian friend Krishna arrived to tie on the turban of scarlet silk. That had to be done twice as it was better when my ears were beneath its folds. Krishna brought his father's sword with him, which I tied round with a crimson and gold-fringed scarf. A jewel and an egret feather were pinned on to the turban – never in the centre, he said, but always a little to one side. That and a couple of pearl necklaces and I was ready, if unrecognisable! Up we went and I sat enthroned while once more the maestro clicked away and then said: 'That's it – I've got it.'

Then we all scattered. I took Jonathan Myles-Lea out to lunch and then he carried the costumes back to Angels and took himself back to Hereford as he was photographing the Queen's visit the next day. I was quite exhausted, as posing is very tiring and demanding in terms of concentration. But John had asked me to dinner that evening with Andrew Logan and his partner and Susie Howard, who was head of PR for the Crown Commissioners in the St James's area of London. John is working on a book for her. Marianne was as beautiful as ever, warm and welcoming and spontaneous. It was a terrific evening. Logan was dressed in an orange suit with a couple of his mega jewels, a benign, funny and intelligent presence. John produced some immediate prints of the morning's sittings. They were extraordinary and he wants to do more. I'll have to look for ideas as to what we could do as they must ring true. A beard and moustache rather knocks out the eighteenth century [in the long term it didn't, as I shaved them off!] but I could be an ancient cavalier. It all went on far too late and I didn't get to sleep until 12.30 p.m., knowing that I had to get up early. But it had been a wonderful and exhilarating day.

25 JULY

A Three Choirs Festival cameo encounter

I was the guest of John de la Cour of the Elmley Foundation, who had laid on drinks in the Deanery garden in the main for members of their board. The concert was Dyson's *Canterbury Pilgrims*, which I'd not heard before and don't think that I ever wish to hear again as it was so difficult to catch the words, which should have been on the television screens scattered around Hereford Cathedral. There was supper in the Deanery afterwards, to which I took Jonathan Myles-Lea, who was very funny, putting one of the board members in her place. Lady: 'What do you do?' Jonathan: 'I'm an artist.' Lady: 'You mean that you can make a living?' Jonathan: 'Yes.' Lady: 'But the artists we deal with need grants to exist.' Jonathan: 'Perhaps they aren't any good.' End of exchange.

27 JULY

The launch of the Olympics

This was the day on which the Olympics began and I had fled London to avoid them. When I was last up I had attempted to walk across St James's Park and couldn't, as areas both within the park and along The Mall too had been fenced off. The dislocation to London, it was clear, would be total.

In the evening Jonathan came up from The Folly to have dinner with his composer friend Simon Whalley, Fellow of Keble College, Oxford. We planned to watch the opening spectacle on my large television screen together afterwards. Simon was a nice man, thin and rather lanky with a boyish face that slightly belied his age, which must be late thirties. Jonathan had decided that he was to compose 'The Laskett Gardens Suite' or some such. At any rate, Simon was hugely intelligent and funny.

We missed the opening sequence of pastoral England with sheep and cricket and entered at the eruption from below of towering factory chimneys and hordes of workers marching everywhere. The technical feats were amazing and the deployment of armies of voluntary actors, hundreds and hundreds of them, was dazzling. So out of this industrial chaos the rings of the Olympic symbol were forged and floated aloft. And then, suddenly, hundreds of hospital beds with patients in them propelled by nurses filled the arena. This apotheosis of the National Health Service went on far too long and I lost the plot (if it had any), which culminated in the Queen giving an assignment to 007, in the form of Daniel Craig. He escorted Her Majesty, who next turned up seemingly lowered from a helicopter and, tight-lipped, opened the Games. As she now looks like her grandmother Queen Mary come round again, this was surreal, plus the fact that it was a stunt that reduced the Queen to the level of Daniel Craig.

However, we ploughed on and on and on with the ghastly parade of the nations, which went on until midnight. This was tedious and then the royal barge, the *Gloriana*, was caught coming up the Thames. David Beckham, stunning to look at as usual, appeared bearing the torch and delivering it. There then followed a mime sequence in which a veteran group of Olympic heroes gave not one but several torches, all lit from the main one, to seven young athletes, who then careered off. They formed a circle and lit little beacons of light, which suddenly all soared aloft and came together to form the sacred flame.

I can't think what people globally thought of all this. Much cannot have meant anything to them at all and I can't think what it was saying to Britain. But its debt to the iconography of pop concerts and the Lloyd-Webber musicals was more than evident. It also had the virtue of being unlike Beijing and also of being quirky, although it lacked any coherence or statement – which was probably just as well.

26 JULY

Princess Alexandra comes to see the garden

The Dunnes were due at about 2.30 p.m., bringing Princess Alex-andra and a couple of their in-laws. All of this had been arranged months ago when I'd offered lunch or tea but, no, Henrietta said, the Princess doesn't eat either (which statement I related to her son, James Ogilvy, when he passed through). Perhaps she just starved. But then Henrietta relented and said, yes, she wanted tea. So I recruited Jonathan Myles-Lea, as he'd hit it off with the Dunnes when the Queen visited Hereford, and it was helpful not to be left carrying it all out on my own.

The Dunnes announced that they had been south in order to go to Baileys, the architectural salvage store near Ross. This struck me as a bit odd, but later it transpired that they had visited to see what the Prince of Wales was up to at Harewood End (that remains a mystery). At about three o'clock, in swooped two cars and the group disgorged itself, dressed in the usual conventional 'county' look, although Thomas was, somewhat unexpectedly for him, wearing jeans with his tweed jacket.

The Princess was shorter than I remembered her, always shy and sweet, her hair falling down all over the place, which it always does unless gathered up under one of those hats. She was wearing a long, light embroidered coat, her face now lined but still beautiful, with lovely eyes. Henrietta stated that they must see everything, so I thought, yes, you will, although she hadn't taken in what they were in for. They were duly amazed by the garden, having not appreciated the scale of it.

James had told them that they must see the house, so we did the whole tour of that too, which also knocked them sideways. Tea and biscuits were served on the terrace and it all went with a swing, the Laskett visit having clearly made their day. Jonathan had done his stuff and they also went through The Folly, hugely fascinated by his skill as a topographical draughtsman.

31 JULY

Italian interlude: Masone, near Parma

I love being here. I'm perfectly happy reading all day, and during these three days have read all 650 pages of Lawrence James's history of the Raj. Also I sleep well, so a big catch-up and no emails and no post and no phone ringing. The big event of the day is the visit to the Labyrinth at 6 p.m., by which time all the workmen have gone. I walked across with Laura [Casalis] to join Franco [Maria Ricci], who is there talking to the fire regulations people. I have seen this project arise for several years but nothing had prepared me for the sheer scale and detailing of it – *la Fortezza di Franco*! It is on the scale of a renaissance monastery, all in brick with exquisite detailing. I daren't think what it is costing. It is still a building site. There's a courtyard with a gallery-museum above for Franco's art collection and library, housed in large, spacious galleries, both airy and elegant, while at ground level there are a shop, a restaurant, etc. Out of it a walk flanked with plantings of bamboo leads towards what looks like a triumphal arch, the entrance to a second large cloister quadrangle: beautiful, with handsome brick columns forming an open pergola acting as a frame to the enclosed space. On the far side at the centre there is a chapel that in shape resembles the famous Canova pyramid. This is a performance space available for hire for events like weddings and concerts. I find it difficult to grasp how all of this will work as a financial proposition, but the utter madness of it appeals to me. I've never seen anything quite like it, with this magnificent built structure sitting at the centre of a vast bamboo maze – which again puzzles me in terms of practical maintenance.

7 AUGUST

A London day and the photographic project takes off

I came up to London to give my 'England' lecture at the New London Media Centre in Glasshouse Street off Regent Street. London was curiously empty. I went to have my hair cut by Clive and found the salon in South Audley Street empty. So was Bond Street. Everyone who could avoid London during the Olympics had done so. On from there to see Catharine MacLeod at the National Portrait Gallery and discover what she had for the Prince Henry exhibition: in fact many really interesting things that I didn't know about. And then to the Royal Academy to see the [Sterling and Francine] Clark paintings, which reminded me what a lousy painter Renoir was: so many smudgy messes. I also walked through the Summer Exhibition, quite the worst I've ever seen. I then, at last, went to the New London Media Centre and gave 'England' to a gathering of some fifteen. I did my best but it was difficult to gauge whether they took it in or not.

Afterwards I joined up with John and Marianne Swannell at Scotts in Mount Street. John is very keen on these historic photographs of me and sees an exhibition and a book out of them. I said that we could quietly accumulate them until my eightieth birthday in 2015. He wants about fifteen of them, so there's a way to go. But he loves the El Greco cardinal and the Frans Hals cavalier [both my ideas]. Others came to mind like one based on Julia Margaret Cameron's portrait of Tennyson. John wants one of me at Lord's as W.G. Grace at the wicket. I said that Edwardian shooting dress would work a treat – like Edward VII [neither of these ever happened].

II AUGUST

I am seventy-seven

The day of my birthday lunch as I am away on the 23rd. It was perfect weather and I staged it in the Topiary Garden, behind the fountain. I was dressed in my best Indian robes of cream encrusted with crimson and gold with matching slippers. I looked very good,

I thought, and so did everyone else. About thirty-five came for what is called a canapé lunch, which means that there is no sit-down – which is when everyone gets stuck – but guests can instead wander around. These days I am obsessed by the superfluity of ancient people and those with something wrong with them, which makes me feel quite guilty.

15 AUGUST

Mucknell Abbey comes to The Laskett

The Feast of the Assumption and the day of the Mucknell Abbey annual outing. There was Mass at 12.15 p.m. in Hereford Cathedral at the shrine of St Thomas Cantilupe, with the cauldron incense burner used and me as server. Suddenly, as I was in the south transept, there was Abbot Stuart pushing an ancient sister in a wheelchair. Our mutual delight was immediate. It was a joy to see those familiar faces gathered around the shrine together with a few like-minded Anglo-Catholic members of the cathedral congregation. Michael Tavinor was celebrant and my role was to look after him and keep the incense burner stoked. This gathering of the faithful in the north transept was curiously moving.

I then rushed back to The Laskett through pouring rain, groaning about the weather. It was still pouring when the Mucknell Abbey group arrived, so they were gathered into the shop where I gave them the background to the garden. By the time I'd finished my talk the rain had stopped and off they went with their maps to explore it. I set up tea for the dozen all told in the conservatory, for which I'd bought a large coffee cake at the local farm shop, which vanished rather fast. The garden of course amazed them but it was also a help to them, for they were starting one in their new quarters at

Mucknell with a *tabula rasa*. And then I showed them some of the house, a monument to worldly goods! This was their sole outing of the year so I was deeply touched that they had asked to come here. Somehow their presence sanctified the place. And as tea drew to a close, the sun shone.

17 TO 25 AUGUST

Le Marche: staying with the Kyles in a rented villa

I had known Francis and Christine Kyle for some years. Francis had a brilliant gallery in Maddox Street, straddling Regent Street and Bond Street. He had an original eye and eschewed fashionable quirks, assembling a bevy of painters, each with a distinctive style. We became very good travelling companions.

17 AUGUST

The journey begins

Stuart picked me up at 9 a.m. and off we sailed to the airport. I knew that I wouldn't see the Kyles virtually until the plane took off. Christine had done a good deal and we flew business class. At Bologna we picked up a car and then Francis drove for hours south into Le Marche. This is an area of Italy which I don't know, so the reality of the terrain came as quite a surprise. The country is hilly to mountainous, beautiful in fact but not easy to get around without masses of tearing round hairpin bends. This is an area of villages and little towns on top of hills. Eventually we found our way to Santa Vittoria in Matenano, a one-street town superbly situated with views on every side to hills and wooded areas, with little if any sign of life or other buildings. The house Christine had found was just out of the little town and down a steep road but it had been stunningly put together. From the word go I took over the catering, knowing that if I didn't it would be desultory and disorganised as the Kyles don't live with set mealtimes and proper cooking. And also it's enjoyable if the ingredients are amazing: wonderful real flavoursome tomatoes, huge red and yellow peppers, lovely *fagiolini*, local mozzarellas, etc. What quickly emerged is the extent of Le Marche and the difficulty of getting around it, so that many of the places I had researched and hoped to have visited had to be abandoned.

18 AUGUST

Rest

Sunday. A quiet day after all that driving. I was glad of it. We shop in Santa Vittoria. I cook rather well! I sleep like a log. Wonderful.

19 AUGUST

Ascoli Piceno

We went to Ascoli Piceno, seemingly a local drive but the route is sinuous and once in the town it's difficult to get out of it and find the right road back. Everything starts late so that by the time that we arrived it was fifteen minutes to closing time, but we caught the Diocesan Museum, small but well done. Carlo Crivelli is the local star painter. The *pinacoteca* is closed on Mondays so that was that. But we got inside the cathedral just in time, a large, cool space with a side chapel with a splendid Crivelli altarpiece. Next to it is the Romanesque baptistery, austere and partly a former pagan temple. Then everything of course shut at lunchtime.

It's a gracious town, beautifully kept, so we wandered around looking at the exteriors of closed churches and shops. In the Piazza del Popolo there's a marvellous 1907 art nouveau café, just perfect in every detail, and there we sat and had coffee and tea and ate tiny cakes. Lunch was found in a modest hostelry behind the theatre. I had a plate of excellent San Daniele ham and melon followed by some home-made ravioli topped by vegetables from their garden. We then spent an awful time trying to find the right road home! We got back at 8 p.m. and I produced a pretty good dinner: a plate of red and yellow peppers stuffed with chopped tomatoes and anchovies, followed by a *zucchini frittata* with *fagiolini* dressed in oil and lemon. Applause all round.

20 AUGUST

An abortive expedition

Life begins here slowly but then it's good to slow down, so a quiet morning. As in any gathering like this, much chatter about this or that person, institution or situation back home . . . Christine makes a suggestion that a good expedition would be to Montepaone, where they make straw hats seemingly for the whole world, and then on and up to Massa Fermana. So I put together a pretty al fresco lunch of cold meats, the remains of the *frittata*, cold peppers, a tomato salad, etc. Then off we set.

What no guidebook ever tells you is about *la fermata*, 15 August, the Feast of the Assumption, on and after which everything closes down for a fortnight. So we start on this journey hopeful of buying a hat and of coffee and ice cream in a café, etc. Although Montepaone was famous for its straw hats, no luck as this was a journey to a city of the dead. Both places were entirely shut up, deserted, with windows shuttered and doors firmly locked. There was not even a café open.

Eventually in Massa we found the lady caretaker of the church, which she opened up. Its interior was unattractive nineteenth century with a large tapestry portrait of Pope John XXIII, a sizeable Madonna dressed in fabric with a sword hilt poking out and an altar set with a jumble of items for the Mass. In the side chapel, however, were two good pictures, one by Vittore and the other by Carlo Crivelli. We thanked her and wandered off past the closed hat museum, which we glimpsed through a window and, en route, encountered a handsome elderly man repairing old bicycles. He turned out to be the sole creator of Massa's bicycle museum, which was housed in two different subterranean spaces beneath the city walls and therefore inside the hillside. As the bicycle caught on as an inexpensive means of transport, it became a vehicle for every kind of mobile function anyone could think of, and here they all were – the dentist, the priest, the carpenter, the tailor, the haberdasher, the letter reader and writer, etc. This went on from the late nineteenth century right down to the 1950s and only died with everyman's car or van. Our friend had been a racing driver, as was his son. There were therefore banks of silver trophies. His wife, now in her seventies, eventually appeared, large and smiling with her hair upended punk style and partly tinted pink into mauve. They must, when young I thought, have been hot stuff as a couple. All of that somehow redeemed Massa and so home we went where I made a chilled soup, prawn risotto, salad and fruit salad. And so to bed and out like a light.

22 AUGUST

Fermo

After yesterday we decided to head for Fermo in hopes. But we went after lunch, so a leisurely morning was more than welcome. This is another city of the dead, although the *duomo* was open and we were able to see the great Crivelli altarpiece in the Chapel of the Blessed Sacrament, paid for by selling jewels from a cope given by Thomas à Becket. The latter we failed to see. Terrible heat and much walking. In the end, as often happens with the Kyles, everything got later and later and I pointed out what time we would eat if I cooked. So we opted for eating out at Servigliano at a ghastly hotel and ate a dreadful meal, making me realise what a good cook I am! What I haven't referred to, and which we passed through twice, was a small town rebuilt by the pope in the late eighteenth century – untouched, a rectangle with three entrances and a grid system with a piazza, a great church, *palazzo*, etc. – everything in order and identical. Most extraordinary.

23 AUGUST

My seventy-seventh birthday: Loreto and Recanati

I am seventy-seven and not that pleased about it! But this was to be the day of the mega expedition, first to Loreto and then to Recanati and hopefully also to Macerata. The temperature was 39 degrees Celsius (100 Fahrenheit) and today I began to feel it knock me out – but I did long to see Loreto. Off we set and, as we took the coastal *autostrada*, we were there in an hour and a half. Loreto is a stunning vision with its *duomo* soaring against the blue sky. It is not a place easy to imagine and it is extraordinary to think that stones from what by the time of the Crusades was regarded as the Holy House in Nazareth eventually made their way here, an early instance of moving rooms or buildings! I've never known such heat, but onwards and upwards we toiled. The main piazza frames the church with an arcade, never finished, grand and anticipatory of all the splendour within.

We started with the art gallery in what was the Palazzo Apostolico, up above the lower arcades, room after room leading on and on, up and over, the roof timbers taking us to galleries filled with maiolica pots and a collection of religious folk art. But the Lotto paintings are the thing, although in a way they disappoint. One thing caught my eye in a gallery of metalwork and that was a small figure of a kneeling mid-Tudor woman with her hands clasped in prayer – English, it said, and certainly the dress was Mary I or early Elizabeth – what was it and why was it there? And how did it get there? We then moved on to the cathedral, a vast Gothic space culminating, where there would normally have been a high altar, in a huge enclosure of white marble by the best sculptors, enclosing the 'house'. There were thirteen side chapels surrounding this, including a stunning one with a ceiling by Melozzo da Forlì. I walked into the Holy House and said a prayer about being seventy-seven, giving thanks for the gift of faith. The building reminded me of Walsingham, a dark, rough space lit by a few guttering candles and above the altar a candle-blackened image of the Virgin swagged with diamonds. But it was a busy place of pilgrimage, with monks and nurses and sick visitors in wheelchairs. After this we went in search of lunch and I found the perfect place overlooking a vast landscape panorama, packed with Italians; the *spaghetti vongole* was the best ever.

I was flagging but we pressed on to Recanati, another handsome hilltop town, and attempted to find the *pinacoteca*. This was quite a performance as no one seemed to know, but eventually we were told

Four Directors of the National Portrait Gallery from 1967 to 2015: Sir Charles Saumarez Smith, Dr John Hayes, Sandy Nairne and me

Standing in my stall at Westminster Abbey as their High Bailiff and Searcher of the Sanctuary, 2005

In front of the display at the
National Portrait Gallery to
mark my 80th birthday, 2015

On my beloved trike, 2014

and off we set in the heat across town. First we visited the *duomo* with its Venetian compartmented roof, and then on to the gallery. It was worth it. There was the celebrated Lotto painting of the Annunciation with the startled cat and Madonna and, even more astounding, the altarpiece, without a doubt the best picture I've seen on this jaunt. Wonderful. We made our way back to the main square, with its impressive tower, and had ices and coffee. By then I was done in, but not Francis, who set off for the Leopardi house. I could have cried but there was nothing to be done. We got home at 9 p.m. and I then cooked a *parmigiana* followed by escalopes of chicken *al limone* with potatoes with rosemary and *zucchini fritti*.

24 AUGUST

Exhaustion

I woke in the night my pyjamas wringing wet with perspiration. I felt awful. It had all been too much and I didn't get up till gone eleven. This was a much-needed quiet day but I was able to cook for a last lunch on the terrace. In the evening, much to our surprise, we found a good restaurant in Santa Vittoria.

25 AUGUST

Homeward

Today was a journey home out of hell. We set off, minus break-fast, by 8.30 a.m. and the drive to Pesaro was fine, although we did encounter hold-ups. But we got to the Kyles' beach hotel, a monu-ment to kitsch in white but hugely comfortable. Francis came with me to the station, which was really kind. The train to Bologna was over an hour late and jammed. Mercifully I had a first-class reserved seat. The BA plane had been replaced by one from Titan airways, which was meant to leave at 6.40 p.m. but was delayed until past 8 p.m. All we got was a roll in a paper bag. I arrived home eventually at 1 a.m. and got to sleep at 2 a.m. I was absolutely 'dug up'.

30 AUGUST

Antonia Fraser is eighty

This was the evening of Flora Fraser's dinner in honour of her mother Antonia's eightieth birthday, one of a series of *fêtes*, I gather. I'd promised that I'd appear in my Indian guise and arrived early to do a quick change and make a somewhat surprising entry into the drawing room. The house in Kensington Park Gardens is large, expensively interior decorated and therefore characterless. Antonia was presiding on a sofa and I presented her with Jonathan's minia-ture of her as Mary Queen of Scots, asking her to open it so that I could take a snap of her holding it. Her surprise and delight were palpable. She was dressed in an ivory-patterned silk caftan and looked pretty good, I thought. But she's weak on her legs and when we went upstairs after dinner, she took the lift. In the guests poured, including a great number of grandchildren and married-ins, Flora's ex-husband, Peter Soros, Tom Stoppard, Anthony Cheetham, an academic from Bradford writing on Napoleon, a distinguished pianist, who midway through dinner bashed out 'Happy Birthday' while two appalling flat cakes made by the children were carried in. There must have been twenty of us in all. Between courses we were all encouraged to make little speeches. I was on Flora's right and Antonia on my right, so that was a compliment. It is easy to forget the enormous, sprawling nature of the Pakenham family, now three generations and all containing people of real talent, not to mention the married-ins. After dinner I talked to Flora, still fiddling with her biography of the George and Martha Washington marriage. At fifty-two she has just got rid of the last child and can now function on her own. The party broke up at about 11.30 p.m. and off we all went.

31 AUGUST

Kensington Palace revisited

A rare blank London day, so I decided to go and see what had been done to Kensington Palace. The weather was idyllic. The tidying up of the Palace exterior is a huge improvement, including the creation of a garden and vista from it to the Round Pond with the statue of the young Victoria acting as a focal point set against the façade. It is a simple formal garden but it gives the Palace presence. Inside it is greatly improved, a potpourri of five loops – the King's apartments, the Queen's apartments, Princess Diana, the 1897 Diamond Jubilee and Queen Victoria generally. There is a strong emphasis on accessibility and making the place come alive, very anti-academic and a pell-mell mix of real exhibits, commissioned pieces and props. It took me back to the 1964 Shakespeare Exhibition and Julia's Pepys exhibition at the NPG. I would think it unlikely that those who did this were aware of its antecedents. I could see what they were doing but it needed editing.

I TO 3 SEPTEMBER

A visit to Alnwick

I took the train to Alnwick from King's Cross to Berwick-on-Tweed, a confused and poor town but also charming in its way. Here was a divided and equally confused community very much feeling that within a few miles people got healthcare and provision for their old age and education of a kind denied the luckless English, who were no doubt paying for it. I was met by the large but benign figure of Matthew Rooke, the local arts factotum, with a companion called Sebastian who seemed to know all the great houses. Off we went to their arts centre, the usual cheap build but with a very good restaurant. This was small-time but about fifty turned up, which was pretty good. Alas the publishers had sent no books so I felt quite cross about that. I was then handed on to Claire Byers, the Duchess of Northumberland's appointment to bring life into the Alnwick Garden. She was a nice but tired person and I think she's got a post minus the resources to fulfil the mandate. So off we set at about 6 p.m. for Alnwick, where the head gardener took us around. It was the tenth anniversary and I was to do a dialogue with the Duchess the next day.

Well, it is a spectacle, like a set for a Busby Berkeley musical, rather wonderful in its way but once you've seen it, that's it. At the top of the great ascent there's a garden divided into squares but it's nothing like as good as the new garden at Houghton, which is of the same kind. Jane Northumberland had attracted the knives from Mary Keen, Robin Lane Fox, et al., but the mistake she had made was to bill it as a garden. It's the modern equivalent of Vauxhall or Ranelagh, pleasure grounds in which things happen. That is the only way to keep it all going, but to fulfil this function it has a great drawback: there's no auditorium. Next day I told her how important that was, and of the need for a green theatre. How can poor Claire stage anything without a venue? There's some lovely landscaping but not enough flowers for Mr Average. There's also a very up-to-date pavilion by Michael Hopkins, which is at complete variance with the garden. Jane hates it but she commissioned it and now she wants to demolish it. What a mess.

On Sunday I went to church and there was a well-done communion service. Afterwards I went back to Alnwick Castle to meet the Duchess, who is a striking, energetic, intelligent, opinionated woman, a monument to the old dictum that the future of any great house depends on daughters-in-law. The Duke is a shy countryman and doesn't want to know about the garden. There seemed to be no lack of money, as apart from the multimillions spent on the garden, the castle had been done over at fantastic expense with its magnificent, lush, high Victorian State Rooms. They had, the Duchess said, just started on Syon, which rather amazed me. We had lunch in the restaurant at the theme-park end of the garden, which is, of course, a huge success. Then we went on stage and talked about garden opening and what we set out to achieve from our own perspective and then threw it open to the audience. It went well. So, with kisses all round, that was that. But this is a depressed area and mining has gone under and so has fishing, so the Alnwick project aims to help in its way. I travelled home on the Monday.

5 SEPTEMBER

A works outing

We went by train and taxi to Wollerton Old Hall to John and Lesley Jenkins. They and the garden are so special and it was an incredibly happy day in perfect weather. I did my lecture while Fiona, Shaun and Philip went round the garden with Andrew, the head gardener. A splendid lunch was laid on. It's a garden of rooms but some not quite big enough or, rather they were not of contrasting sizes, although since my last visit they had thrown two together, which was a huge improvement. What they had, which set me thinking, was a room in the garden where people could assemble.

6 SEPTEMBER

The Colonnade is born

Inevitably the trip to Wollerton Old Hall Garden had a knock-on effect. It seemed to me that my Kitchen Garden wasn't actually needed. It was labour-intensive and not needed to feed one person. I then thought that what we required was an orangery providing an area in which people could shelter. I therefore began to do research on orangeries and rapidly realised that £150,000 could be gone through very quickly. Also, although a tax claim could be made for supplying water, electricity and fitting, the actual building was not tax claimable. So, on reflection, I came up with the idea of a colonnade. I measured it out – forty feet across with columns twelve feet high – an entrance at one end through a classical doorway and an *œil-de-bœuf* at the other, looking over the landscape – busts of emperors on plinths within. I rang up Gary Grimmitt of Haddonstone and talked to him. He said that I should send him one of my drawings and he'd give me a costing for the reconstituted stonework. The rest would be Tom and his men. The idea also would be to tack on the back a place for the gardeners.

7 SEPTEMBER

A Visit to Oxford

I took the 1.14 p.m. train to Oxford. This was to give a lecture on English identity to the British Irish Association meeting. I'd been dragged in to give this by Margaret Anstee's friend Onora O'Neill. I'd never been to Magdalen College before and I'm always overcome by these hidden worlds of history, greenery and architecture. But there it was with me in the disabled suite, for an unexplained reason, which did make me realise why the shaving mirror was at knee height!

In we went and I spoke on England, which was apparently a huge hit. Dinner was in Hall with all those portraits of Wolsey, Prince Henry, Prince Rupert, et al. I sat between Thomas Pakenham and Onora and took to her this time, for she was less austere and cerebral than before. She was grateful that the Lords had thrown out Clegg's idea of reform, which would have meant the Lib Dems forever.

I asked Thomas what he was writing but he hadn't recovered from when I said to him that what he was doing was a spin-off from the last book. He remembered how Harold Nicolson and Vita Sackville-West had once dined with his parents at Bernhurst but never again! He'd also known Lanning Roper a bit.

10 SEPTEMBER

An unusual garden

An expedition with Stephen Anderton to see an extraordinary formal garden in the middle of Swansea. Stephen lives up on a hillside near Llanthony in a stone-built farmhouse surrounded by twenty acres of land, which sweeps downhill away from the house, at times precipitously, to a rivulet. I would find it too remote and too much to maintain but he loves it there. After bread and cheese and a handful of grapes and coffee, off we set to see Tony Ridler's garden. It was such a surprise to find this relatively small private enclosure in the middle of prosperous middle-class new housing in Swansea. It was nearly all yew enclosures, often quite narrow, but intriguing and very restrained and elegant. I'd never seen anything like it on such a small scale. Everything was clipped and in order for my arrival. It was so exciting as a garden and a deployment of space.

A huge amount of time during this week and last was spent setting up to film what is called a 'taster' for a BBC4 profile of me. This was by What Larks Productions, whose Managing Director is Claire Whalley, wife of Tim Richardson. All they need is six minutes but by the time I'd put together what they asked for they must have had twenty minutes of edited film, I would think. So I've set up for them a photo shoot of me as a Frans Hals cavalier at Ham House (fees waived), ditto at the NPG, and in addition they are interviewing Brian Sewell, Antonia Fraser and Sandy Nairne, covering both house and garden and making use of earlier TV film material. We start on Sunday 23rd with me as MC in Hereford Cathedral. [It never happened.]

20 SEPTEMBER

The Colonnade is to be built

I have decided to go ahead with the Colonnade. I have reduced it to thirty feet and four twelve-foot Ionic columns. Overall it will be fifteen feet high. Tom the builder came and said he would proceed with it at the same time as he did the drive – so if the weather holds it will go up through October–November. Tom advised that we should set it back further and he was right; he also suggested reusing the dismantled tools and equipment garage hidden away at the back. He also made me realise that thought must be given to the Colonnade's forecourt. Both water and electricity are up in that area, so fountains are possible. All sorts of possibilities open up with this large covered space.

21 SEPTEMBER

Farewell to Rowan Williams

To London for the Abbey's farewell dinner for Rowan Williams. This was held in the Jerusalem Chamber at one long table and the guests were the Dean and canons and their wives and a few others, but basically 'family', if one can call it that. Michael Macey, sharp-eyed and bright, is now busy on the service to mark the sixtieth anniversary of the coronation. I told him that he needed to get St Edward's Crown and have it carried up and placed on the high altar, or at least just be on it. He's already on to that but he wants to see me; already he sees, which I thought interesting, a way in which that service could anticipate the direction of the next coronation. Andrew Tremlett, next to whom I sat, thought along the same lines, a kind of extension of the Commonwealth Observance formula. Probably the times are right for this to happen. At any rate it would be interesting to see how the public would react to such a move.

Rowan Williams sat opposite me. He is such an extraordinary man: I almost felt that I just wanted to look at him! He's a holy man of extraordinary unconscious charisma. I'd noticed that his facial hair had been tidied up – it used to be all over the place, untamed and with too much eyebrow. We had a benign and jolly conversation about Gerard Irvine, A.N. Wilson, Fr Philip North, how much one could learn from the young and their ability to stir one's intellect, the importance of moving on before you have to . . . He hopes now to be able to find time to read and particularly to write poetry. John Hall paid him a delightful tribute, recalling in particular his sermons and addresses here – in my recollection they were all memorable, particularly that on Dickens. We all recognise his profound brilliance but what he exudes through his presence is a touching humanity. He is on my list of those I consider an honour to have met and talked to, even if only a little. He must be an incredible confessor.

24 SEPTEMBER

Dressing a cavalier

I was driven by Jonathan to the RSC Costume Store at Stratford, far better than Angel's, everything neatly hung or boxed under period, etc. It was a ghastly day with rain pelting down but once inside the warehouse Katrina Lindsay and her colleagues couldn't have been more helpful. This photograph by John Swannell is based on a full-length by Frans Hals of a cavalier type who looks my double. I was snapped by Jonathan thumbing my way through the racks, pulling out what was possible. Marvellous. It soon came together and we found a large, many-layered ruff, just like the portrait. When I put it all on it was perfect for about 1630, except for the hat, which had feathers that tipped it in the wrong direction so they were taken off. I looked as though I'd walked out of the picture.

26 SEPTEMBER

I become patron of the Elgar Chorale

In the evening I drove to Elgar's birthplace and there the Elgar Chorale sang for me, welcoming me as their new patron in succession to Janet Baker, who has done it for thirty years. This is a good local voluntary choir and I like the atmosphere very much. Didn't enjoy driving back in the dark!

27 SEPTEMBER

A London party

Travelled up to London for Coral Samuel's party at the Soane Museum, which looked wonderful with many rooms candlelit. Tim Knox has done a great job here. I love Coral but I find these gatherings of the art world less than inspiring as I get older. It made me so glad that I'd left it and enjoyed a successful life without it. But perhaps this entry, written ten days later, is affected by what at last I discovered. The saga of The Laskett Garden and the National Trust was not a happy one – piece by piece I've put together what happened. Fiona Reynolds was in tears at the meeting. My offer had had the support of the NT staff. It also had the support of Simon Jenkins and his deputy, Laurie Magnus, and of the Gardens Advisory Panel headed by Dominic Cole. Who stopped it happening? It could only be members of the Arts Advisory Panel. It had taken me ages to discover who was on that panel and I now know. Lisa White, who was chair of it, came and loved The Laskett, but it must have been the other members – 'friends' – who rejected it. This was an act by envious people and it has left me with a very bitter taste.

2 OCTOBER

The shoot at Ham House

The day of the shoot at Ham House. Jonathan picked me up and off we went to Petersham. Ham is a magical house with a wonderful quality of light through ancient windows. The hall looked extraordinary, with its black and white chequered floor and its early Caroline staircase leading off and up. Dapper John Swannell was there, along with his right-hand man, Robert. John always knows precisely what he wants, so the camera was already positioned for the first take. Claire and the TV gang hovered around. I told them that I was taking no notice of them and giving my whole attention to John. The RSC costume looked perfect and they'd washed the ruff and dry-cleaned the hat. Then we awaited the arrival of the sword, which Jonathan had got from a young curator called Toby at the Wallace Collection. On arrival it turned out to be a splendid early seventeenth-century English one four feet long. And so at last the shoot began, with much positioning and instruction on the placing of hands, fingers, shoulders, etc. The pose was completely unnatural and the placing of the feet almost made one keel over. Then followed a second session at the foot of the staircase, and then Jonathan wanted some snaps of me higher up, descending, which made John realise what a terrific picture that would make. Huge canvases, copies of Titian originals, adorned the walls and a mysterious light fell on me through the old glass. And then it was over. John showed me the results – the best yet, quite extraordinary.

8 OCTOBER

St Albans and Jeffrey John

To London and thence on to St Albans to give the annual Friends' Lecture in the cathedral's Lady Chapel. I was met by the ebullient Jeffrey John, a large, bright, easy, stocky Welshman. He should have been Bishop of Reading, but Rowan Williams was bullied by the evangelicals and gave in. Jeffrey is gay and has a partner, Fr Grant. None of this seems to bother the good citizens of St Albans and the main Sunday Eucharist attracts a congregation of a thousand. The problem, he says, is not the lack of local spiritual commitment but of money. They are mean with it, still living in an age which assumes that the Church has some, and that any shortfall will be picked up by the local aristocracy and gentry, who don't really exist any more. He's been there nine years and I felt that he's more than bored with it all, in a place where as late as the 1950s the Dean had six live-in servants.

So we went over and set things up and rehearsed and then retreated for tea and a somewhat hesitant conversation in what was once the Deanery and is now offices. It's all very suburban Anglican, with no taste. At 5 p.m. we returned to the cathedral for Evensong, for which a whole flock of black-clad canons of every variety, including RC, surfaced. And then off we trotted to the north aisle for a glass of sherry and, as usual, I did my stuff. Thence to the 'Abbot's Kitchen' for a horrendous meal with a pheasant breast that called for a hammer and chisel. The Bishop of St Albans sat on my right, a sharp, bald-headed man who'd been suffragan at Shrewsbury so he knew my area a bit. But he was quite interesting about the media and the Church – always on about redundant churches but never mentioning the new ones which opened on housing estates, multi-purpose buildings that no longer look like churches as people conceive them. Jeffrey and Grant want to end up in Ludlow. He's a good man who needs a change of job soon.

10 OCTOBER

Julia remembered, ballgowns at the V&A and A.N. Wilson

To the early Mass at the Abbey. Andrew Tremlett remembered Julia. It's the ninth anniversary of her death. I was a little tearful. How could I not be otherwise? And so I enter year ten as a widower.

I went to the V&A, busy and bustling, to see the misnamed *Ballgowns* exhibition in the old Costume Court. It was really dresses for grand occasions, for who has a ball any more with women in floor-length dresses? That kind of frock would only be seen today at a State Banquet at Buckingham Palace or for posing on the red carpet at an awards ceremony. It was only of British designers with a time-span of 1950 on. So many of these items had entered the collection in the period of my directorship and it was full of Hardy Amies and Norman Hartnell.

A.N. Wilson had lunch with me at the Garrick and my non-alcohol resolution collapsed in the face of a dry martini and a bottle of burgundy. Andrew is now in love with television, explaining how easy it is. Like me he has discovered that it no longer has the problems of twenty years ago. His programme is on Josiah Wedgwood but by the same firm that's doing the trailer for me at the moment. Much clerical talk. He'd discovered some Anglican nuns in Kent, so they seem to be his new spiritual fix. Much gloom about the state of the country and that things will get worse. Andrew had been to the Shakespeare exhibition at the BM twice and said I ought to go. I did. The installation was better than yesterday's exhibition

– much – but Shakespeare the man was missing. It was done with the RSC so it was all global and obsessed with political correctness. The arrangement was thematic but there was no section on women, which was odd, and none on hierarchy or much else.

Patrick Gale

Back to The Laskett. In the evening the novelist Patrick Gale came to talk in College Hall in the cathedral. The Dean has a fixation on him. He gave me a novel of his to read when I had pneumonia. Gale is a man in his late forties, I would guess, who lives at the tip of Cornwall and makes a living from writing, which nowadays is unusual. Middling in height and rather dapper, but engaging. I liked the man. He knew Raleigh Trevelyan. Afterwards there was a cold collation in the gothick chapter room.

Prince Henry revisited

To the NPG for the Mark Weiss dinner to mark the opening of the Prince Henry exhibition. The exhibition is fine and classic and OK, but it added nothing that I could see to what I had published in 1986. It lacks excitement and oomph. This was a brief foray back into the world I left twenty-seven years ago, a foray that makes me glad I left it. It is so inward-looking, the same old people, the same old chatter, the same old backbiting. But the dinner looked splendid in the Tudor Gallery, with deep crimson damask tablecloths and

candles. I sat next to a nice woman who was doing the Lely catalogue with Catharine MacLeod, which Oliver Millar never finished.
Karen Hearn, redunded from Tate Britain, where virtually all British art has been wiped out by the incoming director, has a job in
University College literary department. Nice lady. The Lely lady on
my left told me how shocked she'd been when the organisers of the
Mellon conference on sixteenth-century English art had deliberately
set out to exclude me. That sums up that world in the same way as
my encounter with Christopher Brown, director of Ashmole, did.
I congratulated him on the pleasure the refurbished museum had
given me. He asked me what I was doing. I said that I'd just finished
a volume of early autobiography: 'Better get the lawyers onto that.'
'It's not that sort of book,' I frostily replied.

Sandy Nairne is always a delight and incredibly nice to me.
There's a Bailey exhibition in the pipeline, so that's good, and, not
so exciting, one on Virginia Woolf and yet another Sargent exhibition. I said that what needed doing was a reassessment of 1920s and
1930s academic portrait painting. Sandy agreed but it's not on the
schedule. I've been to worse evenings and it was all well so meant;
but I'm so glad that I'm out of it!

16 OCTOBER

Planning the Diamond Jubilee of the Coronation

In the afternoon I went to the Abbey to discuss with Michael
Macey the service for the Diamond Jubilee of the Coronation. I
was surprised at how little he knew and he certainly hadn't read my
book – which, frankly, he should have done – but he's bright and
quick. I said that the service should remind the wider public what a
coronation was and also throw up markers indicating that the next

one would be very different in many ways because society had so dramatically changed. I said that the central act was the anointing and that the ampulla and anointing spoon should be borrowed. The idea would be that it would be carried up the aisle in procession by children, a microcosm of where we are now, and presented to the Archbishop of Canterbury and placed on the altar. The State Crown would be there on the altar already, as a symbol of royal secular power, and could perhaps be carried in procession at the end; but all sorts of hurdles needed to be crossed, including security. There would be a poem by the Poet Laureate read beside the Coronation Chair at the West End, and prayers from both Christian and other faith communities scattered around the Abbey along the nave. The Queen liked 'Zadok', so that was in. 'I Was Glad' was recently used, so that was out, and the exit would be to whichever of Walton's marches hadn't been used of late. I think it was 'Orb and Sceptre' for the wedding [of Prince William and Catherine Middleton]. The Abbey had asked for a carriage procession. I said that greater prominence should be given to the line of descent: they're considering new chairs which could set the Prince of Wales, Camilla, William and Kate aside. At the moment it looks odds-on that the Queen will have lunch in College Hall.

17 OCTOBER

The Opening of the Cellarium by the Duke of Edinburgh

Every time the Duke of Edinburgh appears he must be aware that everyone is studying him as to his state of health. Well, he's amazingly nimble for ninety, although his face and skin are pretty far gone, but he did his stuff up and down the motley assembled company and unveiled a plaque. The Cellarium means that the Abbey is beginning to catch up with what other great churches had thirty years ago – a restaurant. It has been constructed in an awkward site and the food, I'm told, is expensive. But it's a step in the right direction. This was one of those long hang-around occasions. Andrew Tremlett said vis-à-vis the Diamond Jubilee service that the crown, if it came, ought not to be on the altar but worn or carried before the Queen. Interesting. Ptolemy Dean showed me the drawing for the lift up to the triforium. He said everything had been passed by the interested parties and it was to go ahead. Another step forward at last.

18 OCTOBER

The Diamond Jubilee Coronation service again

At 5 p.m. I went to see Stephen Lamport at the Abbey with a list of things he wanted to discuss. The Dean liked the double portrait of the Princes in the NPG – what did I think of the artist [Nicky Philipps] as the painter of his portrait? Fine. It's a good picture. That enormous portrait of the Queen by an Australian painter [Ralph Heimans] might come the Abbey's way – something like nine by eleven feet! – I said that the critics would hate it but the public love it. She is standing on the Cosmati pavement on which she was crowned. They can get it up into the triforium. It seems OK to me but don't let the donor make a condition that it always has to be on display.

Then much talk about the Diamond Coronation service and how to handle it as a commemoration of 1953 and not a re-enactment. The ampulla idea goes down well but the crown throws up all sorts of problems which can be sorted out. Then there is to be an Abbey lecture on 1953. Of course I'd do it if I had to but it would be far better done by Ian Bradley of St Andrews because he is head man when it comes to the theological/constitutional side to the rite, whereas my focus is on the wider cultural, political and social framing of 1953. It would also be a good thing to bring in someone from Scotland.

19 OCTOBER

Dress Studies come of age

In the evening I helped officially launch the School of Histor-ical Dress at the Society of Antiquaries under the aegis of Jenny Tiramani. All very well done but where's the several million they need to buy the London property coming from in these hard times? I spoke and so did Vivienne Westwood, rather raddled these days with her ginger hair growing out and her lined face etched over with make-up. Global warming is her thing and she spoke more about that than about the poor school. The spur was the fact that those involved were all getting older and older and they couldn't go on. They have all Janet Arnold's archive but it would have made so much more sense if it had been attached to somewhere like the V&A.

But it was a joy to see some familiar old faces. John Bright of Cosprop was one and the elusive Ant Powell another. Ant is huge, a kind of ball with a head on the top; we've known each other since the mid-1960s. It's difficult to predict which way this will go but the work is a step change in the study of dress – very impressive.

20 OCTOBER

Rosemary Irvine is ninety

It was off to Ditchling with A.N. Wilson for Rosemary Irvine's nine-tieth in the canteen of her superior care home. This is a compound with blocks of flats looked after by RC nuns and with a church for Mass in the middle. The whole event was lifted out of Barbara Pym, full of genteel long-in-the-tooth ladies and gents, among them Pamela Wedgwood at eighty-four, her hip operation transparently having gone wrong, but on she battles. Most of the old ladies were widows, their hair done for the occasion. There was a nice cleric who'd been one of Gerard's long-suffering curates but who now lives in retirement in a flat in Bermondsey. He boxes and coxes, assisting three churches, and has found himself landed with all the sermons. There was a teacher from Lancing College who'd been there thirty years and lives in Worthing but still goes on teaching things like Pinter's *The Homecoming*.

In all there were about thirty or so of us: plum paper tablecloths and napkins, coronation chicken, salmon, cucumber, tomatoes – the usual – followed by a lemon mousse or cheese and a ghastly dry chocolate cake, at whose entrance we all sang 'Happy Birthday'. There's nothing frail about Rosemary. Although she's not so good on her feet, I can see us coming to her hundredth. She remains rectangular and sharp as ever. This was apparently her third ninetieth bash. St Michael's had given her one and there was a second in Brighton. We seem to have been relegated to the B list!

25 OCTOBER

Welsh wall paintings discovered

Jim Murrell's widow, Ann Ballantyne, picked me up to take me to the remote Welsh church where she and her colleague were uncovering an incredible series of late-fifteenth-century wall paintings. I hadn't seen Ann for over twenty years and there she was, larger and with white hair piled on her head, a delight. The area consists of one large wall at the west end of what was a double-naved church. One painting was a huge St George and the Dragon about fifty feet high. To the west of it, bit by bit, they were uncovering the Seven Deadly Sins, with many a devil doing this and that. But it's a slow process lifting off the overpaint with a scalpel. They come for two sessions of eight weeks a year and they've been doing it for four years already. It was all painted in great haste in red, black and ochre, but there's nothing of this size elsewhere so it's quite a major find.

26 OCTOBER

The Cavalier and the Colonnade

John Swannell's photos of me in seventeenth-century clothes at Ham arrived. They are the best yet, somewhat haunting and mysterious. He sent with them a list of ideas from me being everything from a matador to Genghis Khan! We spoke on the phone and I can see a logic to experimenting in another direction. Our friend Toby who produced the sword was anxious to get me into armour, so perhaps we ought to pursue that too. So John and I saw a kind of Sir Galahad picture set in a castle with me *en profile* bathed in an aureole. I thought I could do Tsar Nicholas II and Augustus John; and then I love the idea of being a matador because the balletic arrangement of the body would be so very different from what we'd done up until now. But I'm bit past it really! At any rate it's a lark but the key is to get the right clothes (not easy), setting and props.

At last the Colonnade has begun to go up. It will be astounding, by far the largest building in the garden. Its construction has been dogged by bad weather but by the close of this week the Ionic columns are up, giving a sense of the scale of it. That I'd got right; but then, as usual, the rest must be done by eye. So I've decided that the statue of the gardener stays put and that the two busts of emperors shouldn't go in the Colonnade but be deployed without – I can't decide where. The idea of surrounding it with water now seems a bad one. Tom the builder has a good eye, much to my surprise, and they are thrilled to be putting up such a structure. The layout of the paving can't be decided until the building is up.

28 OCTOBER TO 10 NOVEMBER

An Indian recce

January 2013 would see my third Indian tour with Ultimate Travel. Each one called for a recce with Joanna Worsley, an adventure in itself, both in terms of looking at accommodation and in working out the logistics of moving around, the need for variety and contrasts of experience not only of hotels and restaurants but in terms of a tour that laid as much emphasis on visits to spice and fruit markets as historical buildings. Joanna and I were en rapport *on what made a tour special. At the Indian end there was the remarkable Harpreet of Quo Vadis, who was able to solve any crisis or problem in response to a call on his mobile. The following diary entries are a selection from an exhausting but fascinating two-week trip.*

28 OCTOBER

Mumbai and an honoured guest

I was picked up at 4 p.m. and driven to Heathrow Terminal 5 for the great Indian recce. Joanna arrived, organised and, as usual, a delight. The flight was uneventful, except that I must have sat on my

Kindle and broken it and I was so enjoying Dominic Sandbrook's *Seasons in the Sun*. We arrived in Bombay and were met by the Quo Vadis representative Harpreet and driven to the Taj Mahal hotel. The weather was settled: clear blue sky, hot and humid. I have a room on the nineteenth floor overlooking the magical Gateway to India, around which people ebb and flow and little boats bob in and out. Mumbai, as it has been relabelled, has none of the instant mystery of Kolkata. Odd that. The Marine Drive is an Art Deco paradise but all the time the cityscape is dominated by the towering mini-skyscrapers of money.

In the early evening we met our Indian guide, who was charming, and off we set for the opening of the new sculpture gallery in what was once the Prince of Wales Museum. This is a vast Indo-Saracenic building, striking in its way, at the beginning of a series of major public buildings along what is now Mahatma Gandhi Street, through which we will walk tomorrow. This was a grand occasion, so my instincts to put on a white suit, patterned shirt and tie were right. I was treated as an honoured guest and, of course, they lit up at the mention of Robert Skelton or Deborah Swallow [distinguished former members of the V&A's Indian Department]. This is the world of museum academe at its best.

There were soft drinks and snacks and then we all sat down in the entrance hall beneath the V&A-type cupola for endless speeches thanking everyone. The chair of trustees was a lady in her seventies, gracious in a manner that evoked the Distressed Gentlefolk syndrome. There were endless bunches of flowers presented and books unwrapped, and finally the gallery was declared open. At its entrance there was an Indian Hindu torchère; one by one the key people involved lit a candle and, much to my surprise, I was asked to light one too. This was so moving and I said that I did it in recognition of the long friendship between my Indian Department colleagues at the V&A and this museum. And then in we all went.

It wasn't an expensive installation but a placing of fine sculptures well lit, which also had Braille labels so that the blind could 'see' and touch. There were also video projections and maps showing the sources of the different types of stone and where everything came from. There was much hustle and bustle and then came Indian dance by a beautiful young woman. Unfortunately I missed most of it, being behind a large statue of Buddha.

1 NOVEMBER

Hyderabad: ruins and wrecks

All Saints, one of my favourite feast days and the hymn resonated through my head. We started off at 8.30 a.m., a huge mistake as nothing much moves before 10 a.m. Worse, the rain began to fall and went on unremittingly all day. The nice new guide, Hassan, kept on switching to autopilot and trotting out this or that set-piece, so it is difficult not to say that I wasn't enchanted by Hyderabad, a mess where seemingly no single area had been cared for, cleaned or put in order. There was clutter, filth and litter everywhere. The fact that nothing moved before 10 a.m. was a blow, which took some time for our guide to respond to. He showed us the inevitable British clock tower, 1892, in an area close to the Charminar, which led on to what was a new part of the city once full of the palaces of the Pariargh family, the Nizams of Hyderabad. Two of these palaces survived in parlous state, one modelled on the British Residency, a vast neoclassical building. It was heartbreaking to see it in its present state, uncared for, falling down, its windows shattered, its ceilings collapsed, a school occupying one room on the ground floor, along with some goats, which were also on the magnificent double staircase. What is so fascinating is that such buildings were late nineteenth or early twentieth century and were up and running until 1947.

Hassan had been scathing about what had happened after Independence, which had been followed by the systematic confiscation of the princely estates and their possessions. It had thrown a large section of the population into unemployment, plus the fact that skills which the rich alone could afford vanished. He was also critical of Mrs Gandhi and the poor boys she subjected to vasectomy, together with a rule that no one should own more than a thousand square yards of land. Hassan and his family lost everything. It was take, take, take and spend, spend, spend but when everything had been taken and spent they had to find a way of raising taxes from everyone. 1947 and its aftermath was the end of a civilisation.

After this we went on to one of the Nizam's numerous former palaces, Chowmahalla, which was huge and well kept, a good hour's worth for a tour. On and on the rain went. Then we walked along the street filled with jewellery and bangles and looked at the quite extraordinary Charminar and at the gates glimpsed in each direction and at the nearby mosque. But virtually everything around had been wrecked. So off we went to another palace where a museum on the last ruling Nizam presented endless rooms filled with silver gifts to him but of which the jewel was the walk-in wardrobe, a hundred yards long and with a gallery above it, which had housed his vast collection of clothes.

And so we staggered on, driving past the High Court by the British architect Vincent J. Esch, to the British Residency. This was a major revelation. The scale is enormous: a vast Palladian mansion with wings spreading either side, the central portion of which followed the pattern of town halls in being in effect a suite of assembly rooms. There was a huge ballroom, the chandeliers still there, together with vast gilt-framed mirrors, a musicians' gallery at the upper level to one side, and also galleries looking down from the upper floor. Everything was in the grandest Palladian style, with Corinthian pillars, but the ceiling was Mogul in pattern. This was most extraordinary, although in keeping with its creator, James Achilles Kirkpatrick, the man we know as the White Mogul. The whole place was abandoned, filthy and dilapidated. There was a wonderful Adam-style double staircase but again in a sad state.

Outside we went in search of the model of the house in the so-called grounds. I had photographs of it from the 1980s and one from 2002. Struggling through the undergrowth, we found it but virtually none of it was left except one upstairs window [it was being rebuilt when we returned in 2015]. Nearby there was a British burial ground, also a tangled, abandoned mess of decaying graves with trees thrusting up through them. How tragic all of this was.

3 NOVEMBER

Delhi: the Mutiny and I order a sherwani

At 8.30 a.m. we set off with our new guide, an intelligent and organised lady this time. We began in the Old City with the Jama Masjid, a mid-seventeenth-century mosque in red sandstone, magnificent with its vast prayer courtyard and surrounded by bazaar-like shops. We've decided that this will open our itinerary. Then with Hari, our driver, we went on to the Red Fort, again magnificent and on a far larger scale than I had anticipated. There was no rain but on arriving in Delhi we were in what amounted to a thick pea-soup fog. The Red Fort has suffered from fearful depredation, the loss of gold, jewels, paint and fabrics, all reducing it to a pathetic shell. It was once in effect a series of sumptuous marble pavilions, now all crying out for restoration, the marble filthy, the paint having long since gone. We saw where George V and

Queen Mary stood on the occasion of their Durbar in 1911.

The rest of the day was consumed by Mutiny sites: the Kashmiri Gate, St James's Church, the Telegraph Tower, the Mutiny Monument, the Magazines and the cemetery with John Nicolson's grave. After lunch we dashed in pursuit of a tailor who was going to charge me too much but sent us to a fabric shop where I chose a length of purple and gold silk from which to make a *sherwani* and a length of cream silk for the leggings. We went on to another tailor, where I was measured up for a *sherwani* that was to be 'royal' in length – that is to below the knee. It was of the kind that I had seen in the Lafayette photographs of maharajahs. We would return on Thursday for a fitting. Joanna was as usual incredibly buoyant all day.

4 NOVEMBER

William Dalrymple

The journey to William Dalrymple's so-called 'farm' went on forever, but at last we got there. The gates swung wide, leading on to an untidy stretch of bare earth on which bantams scratched and a patch of vegetables was cultivated. The house was ugly and untidy and not too clean. Everything was everywhere but I know the type, all bristling brilliance and little visual taste or sense at all, and only a vague and tenuous hold on life's practicalities. This, however, is not to belittle a larger than life character in his early fifties, smiling, benign and with a twinkle, but with little hair left and a figure that indicated scant care for personal appearance. But he was quick-fire fun as we darted to and fro on the scene that we both knew so well. Only massive blockbusters on hot and very large topics can command large advances now. Everything else has gone to the wall. He was toying with doing an Orlando Figes *Natasha's Dance* book on

India or one on the break-up of the Turkish Empire in the light of what was going on at present. He'd just finished one on the Afghan wars [*Return of a King*], which will be out soon, but he felt that he'd missed the boat. And anyway as his three children have reached a certain age he felt a need to return to England. His wife, Olivia, was in England having just had a hugely successful exhibition of her work in a gallery in Cork Street. But they'll miss having servants, I feel. This releases them both for creative work, whereas so much time would otherwise go on keeping the household wheels turning.

William had asked a couple of guests, one of whom was an art history professor who revealed the horrors of government legislation which laid down that he had to have 50 per cent of PhD students from the deprived and unqualified classes. The result was that in seven years he'd only had one student who was any good. All of this social engineering is just dreadful, leading to a wholesale lowering of standards. I felt for him. He, of course, knew all the members of my ex-Indian department colleagues: Robert Skelton and Deborah Swallow. He so much respected the Warburg Institute.

William had a film deal in the making of his book *White Mughals*. Ralph Fiennes had bought it up and was busy putting it together. Lucky man. I agreed that I'd have a bash about the appalling state of the British Residency in Hyderabad via James Hervey-Bathurst, now Chairman of the World Monuments Fund. Dalrymple is well connected in every direction.

6 NOVEMBER

Imperial Shimla

The weather is splendid, blue sky and a nip in the air but not cold. Shimla cascades down steep hillsides, a city, we were told, of some six million (*sic*) and very different in size from its Victorian imperial ancestor. Surprisingly there is an awareness of preserving the old heart of the city, and restoration instead of demolition is the name of the game. The architecture is quite idiosyncratic, a hybrid with more than a touch of Olde Tudor England mixed with a hint of an Austrian Alpine resort. The result is unique. At its heart there is The Mall, a long, pedestrianised walk with an open space in front of Christ Church. What holds all of this together is the roof level of the shops, whose scale is that of those of an English market town.

We set off at 9.30 a.m. for a non-stop walking day. Our first port of call was the Ripon Hospital by Henry Irwin (1885), an exercise in wooden half-timbering with open circular turret staircases at the corners like those on a French renaissance *château*. It was all picked out in white and blue. Inside a long narrow corridor wound around, in which there was a brown plaque listing all those, both English and Indian, who paid for it.

Onward and upward we went to a 1938 house, now a faded hotel with the princely family still living upstairs. In the 1930s this had been a state-of-the-art house but all of that has long since departed. A television crew was there so everything was a bit chaotic. It is noticeable that in all these properties still in use by the diminished princely families, photographs of the old viceroys and of the British royal family remain firmly on the walls.

We had an appointment to see Barnes Court, now the official residence of the region's governor. We stood or sat in the guard-room as papers were shifted around and endless telephone calls were made. Eventually we were let in. This is a very large house in the half-timbered manner but with a lot wrong with it – although well worth a visit. It used to be the British Lieutenant-Governor's house. It was the usual assemblage of bits and pieces from pattern books of this and that. The rooms were huge. There was an enormous drawing room with two fireplaces and an even larger Durbar hall. As is common, running around the house was a conservatory-type corridor. The ceilings were Jacobean-Elizabethan plasterwork derived, I think, from Blickling but I could be wrong, and there was a grand Elizabethan-style staircase with prominent newel posts. The billiard-snooker room survived intact and there was a 'baronial' dining room seating, I would have thought, up to fifty. God knows whether we'll ever get the group access, but we'll try [we did].

So we left and walked to The Mall, the historic part of Shimla. Christ Church (1844) is a cream-painted stucco building with some quite good stained-glass windows and lots of brass memorials on the walls. It was well kept. Next to it was the library, another bit of half-timbered Merrie England, and what was once the bandstand but now, in-filled, a restaurant. This is a large place of parade crammed with Indians and a few beggars and children. All of it was again well kept. Indeed, what was so striking about Shimla was the absence of refuse anywhere.

This led on to a long walk with shops, hugely enjoyable, punctuated by public buildings. We visited the Gaiety Theatre, again by Irwin (1887), not long ago on the point of collapse but now totally restored. It is a little gem of a late Victorian theatre used in the summer months for amateur theatricals. Upstairs there was an excellent display on the restoration and a stunning series of photographs of the productions, very up to date, with Wilde's plays performed quite soon after their debut in London.

After lunch we went in pursuit of another house, about 1910 in date I think, and now a holiday home for medics. Again the architecture was very interesting, a hybrid style all of its own. This had been the home of Gandhi from the late 1930s to 1940s. And finally up to Chapslee, a house originally belonging to the British military attaché but since the 1930s the home of the family of the Raja of Kapurthala. And there he was, Reggie the raja, ready to greet us, an intelligent, smiling man, slightly corpulent and in his sixties. There was a huge, comfortable drawing room with sofas and chairs and photographs of him and his family and their connections in all their bejewelled splendour. And, of course, photographs of George V and Queen Mary. Tea was produced, over which Joanna was bidden to preside: good china, a tea cosy, a silver muffin dish with scones, butter and cream. We could have been in a tearoom in Rye. Reggie now takes a few selective paying guests. We met a retired QC from Winchester and his wife and a couple of Australians. We toured the house, which was perfect for the finale dinner of our 2014 tour. The usual exchange of cards took place and off we went, very tired, to the Cecil Hotel, a drink, a light dinner and blessed repose.

7 NOVEMBER

The Viceregal Lodge

A sparkling day: beautiful. We set off at 10 a.m. to board the one-track train for three stations, to be picked up by car and brought back at the other end. The train was a bit tin-pot but full of people going to Kolkata, a five-hour journey at a snail's pace. But the views across the green wooded landscape were delightful and we talked en route to a travel photographer who was on his way to the camel fair. Our group would love that.

On we went up to the Viceregal Lodge, an astonishing neo-Elizabethan fairy palace in granite and sandstone, its features drawing on the country houses of England. We were thrilled with this. And then, once again, everything vis-à-vis our guide hit the rocks. We said that we might be late for the time we had been given for our visit. 'No trouble.' How often I've heard that one! We were meant to go in at 12.30 p.m. and finally got in at 1.45 p.m. The man that the guide dealt with was off for the day. Then outside we asked if we could walk around the building: 'Yes', was the reply. Well in fact you can't, as it's a sheer drop on one side. This was the culmination of a litany of misinformation and boobs on a scale that we simply couldn't have if we brought the group.

The man who eventually got us inside didn't know a thing either – or, at least, only what had happened post-1947. His information on all the rooms was wrong. The scale of the house is huge and in its heyday it must have been magnificent, serviced by six hundred servants. What our guide did do was take us down to the lower two service floors. The kitchen was still intact, with its ovens, lift, tables, sinks, etc. So was the boiler room supplying the house, leading on one side to the laundry, which had two rectangular marble washing enclosures with scrubbing 'lecterns' at one end that were supplied with hot water. Everywhere we looked there were mountains of old broken furniture, rooms full of it. In other words, much that would be needed to restore the lodge was still there. Upstairs the entrance led on to a vast hall/guard room running the full height of the house, with galleries around it. A huge staircase swept up on the right. The lodge was now a university for advanced studies so the state rooms had been converted into book stacks. There was the state drawing room, which led on to the ballroom, and off that the state dining room. Going in the opposite direction there was a second series of public rooms. The fireplaces and chandeliers were all still there and the walls bore faded photographs of the viceroys and their consorts. Now the rooms were shown as the site of the signing of the partition treaty. One room did have a display of photographs with some from the viceregal era but there was a far better display in a room behind the souvenir shop. Upstairs, where the family lived, had been chopped up into rooms for students. From the photographs one got a clear impression that the great entrance hall had been decorated like a guard room, but often new viceroys changed it, hanging it with splendid carpets or full-length portraits. The photographs captured the upstairs drawing rooms, the vicereine's bedroom, the school room, the viceroy's study, the state dining room laid up and dressed overall, etc. But oh so sad! There's a wonderful book to write on all of this.

8 NOVEMBER

Back to Delhi

Up at 6.30 a.m., breakfast at 7 a.m. and off at 7.45 a.m. for the three-hour drive to Chandigarh Airport. The landscape with its mantle of greenery was breathtaking. We then took the flight to Delhi on a tiny plane, were met and given our driver, and off we set. This was our only so-called free time, so first to the tailor for a fitting for my *sherwani*. The baggy honey-coloured leggings looked great. The coat will also but it needed a lot of adjustments – it needed pockets, a waist, the sleeves narrowed and the length shortened. Buttons. They offered ghastly ones for a gent's suit but, going through drawers, they discovered a box of metal ones; some of muted silver highlighted with gold were chosen, seven down the front and three on each sleeve. It should look stunning.

9 NOVEMBER

Lucknow

Up at 5 a.m. and off to Lucknow, where we were met by the best guide of the tour so far: well turned out, with good English, educated and enthusiastic, charming and funny. We went first to La Martinière, now a kind of Sandhurst, founded by Claude Martin

(1845), a Frenchman and wheeler-dealer who went over to the East India Company, made a fortune and built this amazing and mad house. He left it to become a boys' school. As we arrived there they were in the open, eight- to fifteen-year-olds, doing their physical jerks. As we continued up the path to the house a contingent playing the bagpipes met us. Weird. The house is also weird, like an inverted footstool at the centre but with vast, columned curved wings on either side. We could only see the ground floor with its elaborate, pretty painted plaster decoration. One area had been made into a chapel where they were rehearsing Christmas carols. Beyond that lay a small rotunda with a bust of Martin on a plinth, marking his burial place. Memorable and surreal.

Then we went to Dilkusha, the ruins of a hunting and pleasure lodge of the Nawab. Unlike so much elsewhere in India, everything here was cared for and preserved. It therefore came as quite a shock. This had been damaged in the Mutiny in 1857 but the walls and much else were still there, the Nawab having built an English Palladian-style complex. We then drove on through an Indian army area, the new cantonment laid out after 1857, and on through the new British post-Mutiny townscape, a bustling 1890s arcaded shopping area and circus – all wide streets and very spacious – and then on to the old cantonment, a magnificently presented ruin of the 1857 siege. What was so extraordinary was that all of it was presented and paid for by the Nawab. The buildings, now shells, were grand Palladian in style: the doctor's house, the banqueting hall and the residence were huge structures. All of this covered the original grant of fifty-three acres. Of course the Gothic church had been reduced to three feet and around it there was a forest of tombs from the ghastly siege. It all had a very powerful atmosphere, so unexpected and so utterly unlike anything else we had seen.

Much time was spent looking at restaurants and also deciding that we needed three nights here and not one. The Imambara was utterly amazing, followed by a second mourning mosque which we reached by means of a silver-plated donkey cart. Everything was beautifully kept and tended, the gardens fresh and green with banks of flowers in pots. We wandered through the Chowk and saw men printing embroidery patterns onto cotton and muslin. Joanna bought a dress and I spotted a shop with men's things. In we went and I found myself looking again at bridegroom's clothes. I found an outfit in cream and gold for about £75, the price of a shirt in London. It looked marvellous on me. The shop assistants all looked and said 'Maharajah'! So I bought it and off we went happy to the airport. I loved Lucknow.

10 NOVEMBER

Finale: Delhi and Lutyens

We began watching the Changing of the Guard at the President's Palace in New Delhi, which only happens once a week. I was stunned by the Lutyens/Baker scenography, the architectural orchestration of space, like a baroque stage set with projecting departmental government buildings with forests of columns as wings leading to the iron gates of the entrance with its piers and elephants. And then there was the rhythm and precision of the Indian soldiers, a group on horseback holding spears wearing incredible turbans, and the infantry in dark green, again with extraordinary detailing on their turbans and waistbands. And then there was the band. This was so English, so like our Changing of the Guard and Trooping the Colour. The precision was faultless and balletic. I was entranced. This was a glimpse of the India that had gone, although this had somehow survived.

The garrison church of St Martin's by A.G. Shoosmith was quite astonishing. It was undergoing restoration, as part of the roof had fallen in, mercifully missing the congregation. It was here that our buttoned-up guide opened up and I began to take to her. Her great-grandparents had suffered horribly, with parents dying when they were infants. So they were sent to an orphanage and there they were marooned. They had twenty-three children (*sic*), only seven of them surviving. Her grandfather had converted to Christianity. Her father and mother, in contrast, decided to have only two children and to educate them properly, which they did. Her mother had died earlier this year and now she looks after her ninety-year-old father. Her brother is in the United States. Life is tough. Guides are not well paid and, like everyone in certain professions, you work like blazes for six months and then, with the arrival of the monsoons, there is no work as no one comes. I was moved.

And so back to the hotel where I packed. Ramesh the tailor arrived with my purple and gold coat – stunning! We all purr at his achievement and he is so proud of it and I try it on in my room. I am touched that I have the face to go with it!

At 9 p.m. I arrive at the flat of Joanna's friends Vikram and his wife Jundy for a gathering in my honour. As usual there were too many people and too many names, but this was an intelligent and rich lot, concerned with the workings of the mind and not just with appearances. My host and hostess were benign and moved me around. There was a magnificent, large lady swathed in a sari in a variety of shades of red plum, and her thin husband, with a bearded face out of the Mogul period, wearing a turban to match her outfit. She presented me with her book on Lutyens's Delhi and said that she had access any time to the gardens and could get us in. There was an archaeological lady, another from Kashmir, elegant and with a house to be seen. And then a large man appeared and said that he'd worked for me. It was in the early Eighties, when he was a third of the size, and I fancy that it was over the loan [to the V&A] of the votive kneeling figure of the Duke of Burgundy. The years pass and here he is, now a French poet, very successful apparently, who breezes in with Bianca Jagger on his arm. She's got her figure still and her white, pallid skin was heightened by a frame of much-dyed hair. But she's on about her mission to the threatened ethnic groups and about climate change. Mick Jagger married a quite bright woman. Vikram condemns India for trying to wipe out its own history and is worried about the growing number of communists. The room is littered with the odd Begum or multimillionaire – one of them had a hundred factories scattered around the globe. One of Vikram and Jundy's daughters appeared, beautiful and highly intelligent, educated at St Andrews. And so the show went on until, at midnight, we left for the airport . . .

4 DECEMBER

The Queen's dress for her anointing found

I travelled up to London by train thinking how weary I was of this journey and of always going up to London and back. This was the evening of the Hereford Cathedral Perpetual Trust service and party. I read a lesson. The royal personage was Richard Gloucester, a benign man who looks a bit like a 1950s bank manager, along with the usual gathering of Harleys, Clives, Hervey-Bathursts, Cotterells, Darnleys, et al., and hangers-on. The service was much better than last year: a few hymns, which this time were not over-mournful, and splendid singing by the cathedral choir.

I seem to remember that I forked out £70 for this event. The party afterwards was thinner than last year and it'll be even thinner next year: filthy red and white wine, the sweepings of Morocco, and little bits of cheese on top of thumbnail pieces of bread, and that was it. Frances Stainton brought Caroline de Guitaut, who's organising the Buckingham Palace exhibition on the Coronation next year. I told her about them opening a steel filing cabinet in the Abbey and discovering the Queen's white anointing dress by Hartnell. 'I've been looking everywhere for that,' she screamed, so problem solved.

5 DECEMBER

A new Archbishop of Canterbury and thoughts about the monarchy

I made my way to the House of Lords for tea with Richard Luce. Rose was there, pale but still beautiful in black, and an even larger Patrick Cormack. Richard was relieved that they'd appointed a new Archbishop of Canterbury. It had been an appalling task with a committee of nineteen, including far too many from the diocese of Canterbury. At any rate hope springs eternal around this new evangelical, Justin Welby, who has only been a bishop a year and so could find the knives out in a few months. He'd been forced to give in on women bishops but he won't go along with gay marriage. Just the mention of homosexuality sets Patrick off but none of us can understand why the Prime Minister is so obsessed by gay marriage, which flies in the face of the definition of marriage as laid down in the Prayer Book. A civil partnership and a blessing in church would surely fit the bill. Poor Welby comes in at a really awful moment and if he starts attacking the gay community he will reap a lambasting. Ages ago I remember being told that there were nine gay deans – and why ever not? Welby has a Catholic Ignatian spiritual director so he's both ends of Newman's journey simultaneously.

After Patrick left I remained behind and had a long talk to Richard about the monarchy. The pregnancy of the Duchess of

Cambridge has taken over the media and Parliament has had to rush through a bill that gives the firstborn, boy or girl, the automatic right of succession, along with permission for the monarch to marry a Roman Catholic. What are the consequences of this for the hereditary aristocracy? We agreed that the river pageant had been a disaster. The Queen had nearly ended up with pneumonia as there was little provision of shelter. I pointed out that the Queen has failed to play any role in Europe and her family connections cross the Continent but she doesn't know Europe, as she grew up when we were cut off from it by fascist dictators and the war. It is important that the Cambridges should speak at least one European language fluently and that their children should be brought up from very early on to be multilingual. Richard said that he'd feed that into the system.

6 DECEMBER

A chaotic charity concert

On Thursday there was the dreaded Maggie's charity Christmas concert in the Chapel of Cheltenham Ladies College. I'd written the script and Alex James agreed to read with me. It was a very cold day and Alex missed the Gloucester turning and so we drove miles and miles, ending up coming into Cheltenham from the north. The event was chaotic. We were down to rehearse at 6.30 p.m. but by that time they had begun to let the audience in. I was furious. That was stopped. There was a worse than useless young woman in charge – hardly the word for it because she wasn't.

Then the sound people appeared and wired us up. We were meant to stand on the sanctuary steps but the sound didn't work from there! Alex's battery failed and mine, when opened, didn't even have a battery in it. The man in charge of this had no back-ups and offered no apology so, in desperation, Alex read her bits from the sanctuary lectern and I went into the pulpit halfway down the chapel! Any rate, what does one do but one's best and attempt to declaim with commitment and brio? God knows what it was like, but we got through it. Fortunately it was an undiscriminating audience.

There were three contrasting choirs, of which the Cheltenham Bach Choir was the best, doing a stunning rendering of Vaughan Williams's *Fantasia on Christmas Carols*. The event opened with two girls singing 'Once in Royal David's City', walking slowly up the aisle with their hair festooned with purple fairy lights. Hideous. There was Flowers Brass Band, whose over-enthusiastic noise nearly blew us out of our seats. I suppose it had that jollity which overtakes charity events and Christmas, when it really doesn't matter how bad something is and everyone says that it is just marvellous.

19 DECEMBER

Mark Rylance as Olivia

Clive cut my hair at Michaeljohn. I'm letting it grow into the look of an Edwardian actor-manager [it was a failure!]. This was the day of the annual outing for my godchild Charlie Aslet. I'd got two seats for the Globe production of *Twelfth Night*, transferred to the Apollo. We were in the front row of the dress circle. Charlie at ten is an amazing young person, sitting through three hours of Shakespeare and never nodding off but taking in everything. We were allowed in at 1.30 p.m. for a 2 p.m. start. But what was so thrilling was to see the stage as the tire-room with the actors being made up and dressed, especially the men as women. I'd not seen anything like it before. Of course, it was all the result of Janet Arnold's study of historic cut and dress, which was taken up by Jenny Tiramani. Everything was exact – corsetry, ruffs, cuffs, shoes, etc. – it was a revelation to see how that affected the way they stood and moved, and also gestured.

The stage was like the Globe Theatre, with the public sitting on it and, above at the back, the musicians. This was Shakespeare as I wish to see it and hadn't for years as the plays have been buggered up by 'world Shakespeare', political correctness and God knows what else. This was the most glorious *Twelfth Night* and the final scene of miraculous resolution brought tears to my eyes. Mark Rylance as Olivia gave the performance of a lifetime. Just to see him glide across the stage and watch his hand movements was a revelation.

21 DECEMBER

A Christmas visit

To Mucknell Abbey with Michael Tavinor. I took the inmates a dozen bottles of red wine so that they could celebrate Christmas with a glass or two! These visits have become special occasions, Michael excited about building up Corpus Christi as a major feast for the cathedral. In the Middle Ages there was a Corpus Christi cycle of miracle plays for Hereford, so the idea is perhaps to revive them. There was a warm welcome with hugs from Abbot Stuart, followed by the usual sequence of confessions made and absolution given, and then the noon Eucharist in the chapel, which is now better ordered. There was also a group of younger men there, some being what they call 'alongside', testing their suitability to the monastic vocation. These visits are hugely uplifting.

29 DECEMBER

Reflections on the year

The year is over bar the shouting. It is, needless to say, still raining outside and a furrow, through which the water flows down to the lane, indents the drive. The whole garden is awash and floating with water. In that sense it has been a terrible year, particularly when one recalls that we were told to brace ourselves for drought. Instead we've ended up with the wettest year on record.

The media goes on and on about what a wonderful year it has been, what with the Diamond Jubilee and the Olympics, but I don't see it that way. All I see is what I predicted: a year of 'bread and circuses' concealing the fact that our financial plight is no better than when this government came in. Neither side shows a glimmering of any kind of vision as to where we are going. In that sense I am left deeply depressed and still firm in my belief that I won't live long enough to see us come out of the current mess.

However, 2013 beckons, when I will be seventy-eight – which is a serious age and one where eighty seems suddenly very near. I'm lucky in that apart from a few pills I'm in good health; but that can never be taken for granted. Regular gym sessions keep everything going and ensure muscle in old age. But my left knee cartilage has 'gone' and I can no longer jog. I get much more tired and cheerfully go to bed at nine thirty.

2013

3 JANUARY

The Nutcracker *lives on*

I took Penny Graham to Julia's *Nutcracker* at ROH. Peter Wright, as usual, had fiddled with it again but it remained essentially intact. In my view it has settled in as a Royal Ballet icon and it would be very difficult for them to replace it.

4 JANUARY

More on the National Trust and The Laskett

I had lunch with Charles Saumarez Smith, unsinkable and benign. This is his last job, he says: he has about seven years to go until he's sixty-five. He confirmed, rather as I had deduced, that someone on the National Trust Arts Advisory Panel had put the boot in to The Laskett and it was no surprise to learn that it was Giles Waterfield. Why, I know not, for I have never crossed him in any way. Indeed, he did a brilliant job at Dulwich, although he failed to get any of the big jobs that came up after. I suppose that it's a simple case of envy doing terrible things to people.

5 JANUARY

Le Manoir aux Quat'Saisons and the cathedral panto

Jonathan Myles-Lea took me out for a surprise lunch. I didn't know where we were going and we drove for some two hours and passed Oxford. It was to the Manoir aux Quat'Saisons for the best lunch I have probably ever had, seven small but exquisite courses. It was incredibly generous of him and good fun. It celebrated his completion of a picture for the Clives at Whitfield, who had paid him pronto.

In the evening I went to the annual 'panto' dinner of the Cathedral Friends, an amiable hoedown with Sandy Elliott as Sweet Nell of Old Drury and the Dean as Old Parr, etc. The rest can be imagined but it was a cameo of a certain type of good-natured rural society.

6 JANUARY

Esther de Waal entertains

I went for the first time to Esther de Waal's somewhat tumbledown habitation at Rowlestone for a buffet lunch. She is very undomestic, with odd and old plates, tattered napkins, an assortment of cutlery and glasses and the food arriving in a wheelbarrow – Malaysian, I think. The garden outside is a jungle. She never made any attempt to introduce anyone to anyone but I knew a number and most of the men turned out to be clerics of one sort or another. Pudding was some cartons of ice cream which she had forgotten to get out of the freezer and which we chipped at ourselves. But the Wrights were there and so were Eddie Smith, the retired Under Master of Westminster School, and his wife. I'm afraid that I never warm to domestic chaos. It's a flaw in me, I know, but Esther seems totally oblivious to it.

10 JANUARY

The Colonnade Court Garden created

This week the builders returned with great diggers and flattened the old Kitchen Garden. This morning we laid out the new garden. Tom was right: it couldn't be done on the cheap and he had acquired a mass of sandstone at a very good price. So before the Colonnade itself there will be a large paved space, a concourse area. Either side of it there will be the busts of emperors beneath, I think, two of the wooden arches but backed by screens of laurels. A broad walk will lead to the Colonnade and the approach will be flanked by two square parterre beds focusing on large Versailles vases surrounded by low yew hedges and a central planting. The arbour arches, which will straddle gravel walks, will be linked by golden privet hedges. The demolition of the old Kitchen Garden was quite a leap as it was so intimately associated with Julia; but it was high-maintenance and I didn't need the produce. The plan is to make a small vegetable plot elsewhere.

Everything has to become more and more professional as the garden opening develops into a business. Fenella Powell came, with the plan to make her The Laskett Gardens local accountant, for now we have to submit accounts quarterly. It will be a great relief to have it taken from me and it seems sensible, as I'll be seventy-eight in

August, to set up something that can continue to work without me!

II JANUARY

The Duchess of Cambridge's portrait

Ages ago I'd been bidden to the National Portrait Gallery for an event wrapped in secrecy. Hugh Leggatt was presenting something via the Art Fund in memory of Denis Mahon. A postcard from Gay Leggatt also arrived and, as I was in London, I went. I'd concluded that it could only be a portrait of the Duchess of Cambridge and I was right. Who should I come face to face en route with but Michael Kauffman? I hadn't clapped eyes on him for thirty years. We stared, blinked, and then recognised each other. He was taking round a group and complaining that part of the Gallery was shut. He must be over eighty now and a foot shorter. He was one of the 'opposition' at the V&A and it's difficult to forget that. He said to me, 'You look very distinguished,' and that was that.

In the Victorian corridor there was a gathering of Leggatt and NPG Friends with the portrait on an easel. It was an essay in the Annigoni manner but over life-size, just a large, meticulously painted face. It was slated by the critics. I didn't find it that objectionable but it wasn't that interesting or original as a concept either. It made me realise how good Annigoni was, his portraits always having an extra dimension. There was Hugh in a wheelchair, unexpectedly animated and lively, with Gay in attendance. Jenny [his first wife] was also there, now quite bent. There was a speech by Sandy Nairne praising Hugh to the skies for his generosity and his contributions to the museum debate over the years. The fact that he's lived in tax exile for decades was passed over! Then we had Stephen Deuchar of the Art Fund and finally Brian Allen, now a trustee, adding yet more eulogies.

In the evening I met Antonia Fraser, who arrived in off-white embroidered with black and a large art nouveau jewel, at the Festival Hall for the Joseph Calleja concert. The programme billed this as a homage to Mario Lanza and, as I said to Antonia, 'This is a sing-a-long concert.' I don't think Antonia had taken that in but it was a typical Gubbay event, with every pop Puccini aria and an audience that clapped everything hysterically in the wrong place – except the Bizet aria from *Carmen*, which he wasn't any good at. At the interval Antonia said, 'Let's go. I can't stand the clapping.' It certainly wasn't your Wigmore Hall scene and although this Maltese tenor was accorded mega billing, his voice lacked the lyricism of a Domingo. So off we went to The Delaunay in the Aldwych for a gossipy supper. She's thinking of writing about her early life, a good idea. I forgot that she had been engaged to Patrick Lindsay, into whom Brian Sewell had put the boot.

Dalya Alberge, having rung me all excited about the early autobiography and thinking it would be full of revelations, wrote a piece that appeared in the Sunday papers without telling me. Bits were then repeated in the *Telegraph*. I told her that it was not that sort of book and then we got into the present museum scene and I said that it was all ticking PC boxes and never saying anything which might upset anyone. Museums and galleries were obsessed by money-raising and had become a branch of show business.

23 JANUARY

Men's fashion changes

I found that one of my jackets didn't fit me, and also the need for a new, warmer suit, so I decided to go back to Favourbrook in Jermyn Street. Well, I was right, as my chest was an inch and a half larger than last year so my gym training programme is bulking me up! I chose a ready-made jacket to wear in London with jeans and ordered a two-piece dark grey suit to be made with narrow lapels, cuffs and very narrow trousers. Indeed, everywhere I look these days men's jeans and trousers are very, very narrow, so later that day I picked up a very narrow pair in Zara and wondered if I could ever get them on, but I struggled and did. After a slight hesitation as to whether I should be wearing them or not, they settled in – and out on the street every other man was into this skinny look.

In February Joanna Worsley and I took the India tour for which we had made the recce in November 2012.

FEBRUARY

RIP Lettice, Lady Laskett

I arrived back from India on the morning of Saturday 23 February and was met by my driver, Stuart. We had only gone a few miles when the phone rang and it was Fiona in tears, telling me that Lettice had died last Thursday. She and Philip had taken her to the vet and it was discovered that she had a tumour. They brought her home, laid her in a basket by the Aga and she died peacefully not long after.

Just before I left I had a premonition that it might be this year. Lettice was one of our great cats. She arrived a tiny slip of a mottled tortoiseshell with her tail like a piece of string and her whiskers nibbled off by her siblings. She was to grow to a vast size so that two hands were needed to lift her off the ground. She was the most gentle and loving cat that I ever had. Her fur ranged from chestnut to orange. Beautiful. Her presence was always reassuring and undemanding. She barely had a voice, only a croak, but there was always a purr. Lettice was an old lady, thirteen this year, but for me she was a link back to Julia. She looked after me when Julia was no more. Every night as I prepared to go to bed she appeared from nowhere, leapt on the bed, walked slowly the whole way up it and lay full-length along my left side, her huge eyes looking into mine. There she stayed until I'd gone to sleep. Then she would reappear in the morning but quite undemanding. Last year she began to find that she couldn't jump up that high so I put a stool there to help her and then eventually she stopped as even that was too much. But then suddenly she came for the last time about a week before I left for India. Cats are mysterious creatures and looking back I wonder whether this wasn't a purposeful last visit. I adored her and loved to hold her in my arms or have her on my lap. Now no more.

It was in that sense a melancholy return. She lay a stiffened corpse still in the basket, eyes still open, staring up and one paw resting on the edge. I put the blanket cover back and checked that Perkins had seen her dead. He had. Philip came over and a grave was dug not far from Julia's urn and she was lowered into it. I'll have a headstone made, inscribed simply: LETTICE LADY LASKETT BELOVED CAT 2000–2013.

A few days later I discovered that Fiona had placed a sprig of rosemary over the portrait of me holding Lettice in my arms by Paul Brason. I was quite tearful, stepped into the garden, plucked a large sprig and added it. And I wept again. It made me recall the letter I received from a member of the public when Muff died: 'Don't worry. As you approach the gates of paradise he'll be sitting waiting for you and someone will have given him a cushion on which to sit.' Farewell, most loved creature.

24 FEBRUARY

Self-Portrait as a Young Man *is about to be published*

It was very difficult to get copies of the book to give to people or find out who would be at the promised celebratory dinner. But a copy was got to Antonia, who said it was brilliant and a compulsive read [it was dedicated to her]. The *Mail on Sunday* filleting appeared, all sex, celebs and family drama. I shuddered when I saw it but Jonathan Myles-Lea looked at it and said that it's OK as a PR exercise. I dread to think what my poor brother Derek thought of the byline referring to the 'awful' family. But the deed is done and I get a dollop of cash and five million eyes will alight upon it. *The Sunday Times* is to do a profile interview [it didn't] and I'm told that Giles Waterfield has written a favourable review for the *Telegraph*.

Otherwise a nothing week, cold and gloomy but lightened by the advance in the building of the Colonnade and also by a hugely enjoyable church crawl in the north of the diocese with Michael Tavinor. I'd never been to Clun, which is a tiny picture-postcard town with a small river wending its way through it. There we had lunch at a pub and much merriment on this trip as the Dean didn't evoke a response but at the mention of Sir Roy they all lit up! The vicar of Clun and several other parishes had taught Michael at Cuddesdon but wanted to meet me as he'd been vicar of Wilmcote, the early Tractarian church in which Julia and I were married. Touching that that had become part of the building's legend.

4 MARCH

Dinner at Exeter College, Oxford

I went to the Clarendon Building and signed three copies of the autobiography and then gave Chris Fletcher lunch, him elegantly boyish in a suit. In the evening a dinner for about twenty was given in its honour at Exeter College by Sarah Thomas, Bodley's Librarian. It was charming and there was such a marvellous atmosphere around the table. Not everyone could come but lots of friends were there, like Michael Borrie, A.N. Wilson, Sarah Greenall, Jonathan Myles-Lea, the Archers, Felicity Bryan, David Hutt, etc. There were speeches and those around the table were bidden to throw in a word or two. The interview with *The Sunday Times* died, the interviewer having altered the date three times. I've had enough of their discourtesy.

7 MARCH

Publication day

The actual day of publication, although it seems to have dragged on too long already! I went up to Hatchards where I signed about a 150 copies and then over to the Royal Academy for the Manet exhibition, which I had decided to recce before I met up with Antonia. There were a few decent pictures, however it was not a good exhibition but one bent on making an academic point better made in a book. So there were a lot of unfinished canvases and sketches and all of it was strung out with huge gaps between the pictures, one gallery even turned into a reading room, and much use was made of blown-up photographs. Antonia appeared on a stick, having had, the previous day, an injection (one of a number) to her back leading up to an operation in September. She'd lost her cat, Placido, aged eighteen, and was as cut up about that as I was over Lettice. Both of us were therefore somewhat tearful. Took her to lunch at The Wolseley, in which Stephen Fry and Melvyn Bragg surfaced. Antonia revealed that she couldn't stand Hilary Mantel's work; neither can I. I tried to read one of those volumes and gave up, irritated. Antonia's next book is going to be a Book of the Week. Some people have all the luck. But *Self-Portrait*, she said, was a benchmark for her and she admired the fact that there was not one note of self-pity in it.

19 MARCH

The book reviewed and Sophie Wessex

Now, of course, came the reviews of the book, double-page and favourable by the *Daily Mail* on Friday, a single paragraph in the *Sunday Observer* by someone who clearly hadn't read it and a half page in *The Sunday Times* by Lynn Barber. She is someone whom I always regard as potentially utterly poisonous and, although she lurched that way, she ended by calling it a touching memoir. There's been no considered review bar Giles Waterfield's so far, but then reviews of that kind are out.

In the evening was John Swannell's fundraising dinner for the autistic (his son Charlie is one such). He's so engaging, with his cheery smile and owl-like glasses, and I love his gentle, beautiful wife, Marianne. Sophie Wessex was the royal guest, suburban girl made good in a black dress, who read a speech with enough personal touches to make it real. She and Kate Middleton (it began with the dreaded Ferguson) represent the suburbanisation of the monarchy but that, I think, is how it's going to be. I sat between Marianne and Jane Asher, still beautiful, acting and baking cakes. Gerald Scarfe was there, a somewhat scruffy mid-seventies, and inevitably we recalled the exhibition *SNAP!* at the NPG in 1971. The dinner was held in Leighton House and all thirty or so sat at one long table, pretty with large silver candelabra, white flowers and flickering artificial candles. John, with Robert his assistant in attendance, banged away snapping everyone, including me yet again. He told me later that one was good.

20 MARCH

Henry IV remembered

In the evening another grand dinner in the Jerusalem Chamber to mark the 600th anniversary of Henry IV dying there! I sat next to Maurice Saatchi, a huge, smiling man with vast glasses who'd been on the V&A Trustees for years after I'd left. He'd always wanted to meet me as I was the icon that haunted them, but they feared having anyone like me as he'd be uncontrollable. Maurice had lost his wife about eighteen months ago but couldn't come to terms with it. Thoughts of her affected everything. Any belief in ritual, symbol or closure was totally of no use. I told him of what I'd gone through and how, I'm sure, that she would have wanted what Julia wanted for me, to be happy. Afterwards Simon Russell Beale and two other actors did the death scene from the Shakespeare play – very well.

APRIL

Writing in retrospect, Brian Sewell and the garden

The reviews of *Self-Portrait* got better and better, really some of the best for anything that I have ever written: huge pieces by Bevis Hillier in the *Spectator* and Michael Hall in *Country Life*. It is sad that we didn't get any Radio 4 coverage but I refused to do it on *Loose Ends*, a somewhat trashy programme.

On Saturday 23 March in the Divinity School at Oxford I did a double-act with Brian Sewell, whom I'm fond of but only likes talking about one person, himself, and has never run anything, the great divide between us. We could have had a really interesting session of comparing experiences, he having just published his sex-soaked autobiography. But, as things were, repartee and badinage and a lunge into Fiona Bruce on the box gave some colour.

Weatherwise this was a day out of hell. It was freezing cold with snow-sleet and no direct train to Oxford from Hereford. I got up at 6 a.m. and got to Oxford a wreck at about 11.30 a.m., redeemed only by the woman on Worcester Foregate Street station who looked at me and said, 'You made me love museums.'

I have never known such a terrible winter that has gone on and on and on. Almost mid-April and the earliest daffodils just opening and snowdrops still in flower. And of course it has held up the building work in the garden, the cost of which will clean me out in terms of the current account. I'm so far in that there's no way back but the result is magnificent. The Colonnade Court is almost finished but not quite planted up. We decided to plant the parterre beds with marjoram and we all feel happy about that. But the great surprise is the space outside the Court, in which we had planned to plant a circular kitchen garden. The turf went down and suddenly we had a totally unexpected new garden and it was clear that vegetables would be quite wrong there. So I placed the much-moved sundial in the middle – perfect – gave it brick edging and added cross-path stepping stones quartering it. In each quarter there will be good small topiary pieces that were once in the old Kitchen Garden and the whole will be planted with twenty-eight David Austin English roses, 'Charlotte', low spreading with a beautiful yellow flower, the whole edged with Nepeta *fassenii*. We are all amazed at this unlooked-for new garden and also how stunning the Orchard yew hedge looks from this side.

10 APRIL

San Antonio, Texas

I left for San Antonio on 10 April. I'd made it clear that I wouldn't travel other than business class, which of course made all the difference. The place is a fearful disappointment, a cultural wilderness with no receiving house for opera or ballet and virtually no museum. The downtown area is depopulated and what's left of the old Spanish-style small town from the eighteenth century has been heritaged to extinction with winding walkways and phoney fountains and waterfalls and municipal planting and little Spanish-style bridges here and there, as though designed by someone suffering from an overdose of Venice. Along it speed barges full of tourists gawping at what is a rather bad stage set with a backcloth of high-rise buildings. This is the past Disneyfied, a truly awful set at the heart of a sprawling, go-on-forever city. I was virtually on my own on day one so, ever adaptable, typed up this diary and finished reading Jane Ridley's *Bertie*, an excellent biography, but by far the most interesting part was an appendix on the Royal Archives and the fate of both Victoria's and Edward VII's papers, which were either burnt by the cartload or sanitised. We'll in fact never know the truth about so much. The irony is that this mass destruction and sanitisation has done more harm than good to the Royals. If I were doing a biography of Victoria now it would be based on archives other than royal.

In the evening I was collected by the curator of the Tobin Theatre Collection, Jody Blake, a pleasant late-middle-aged small lady with cheerful wrinkled features, and wafted off to a club up in the White Heights for dinner with the amiable Director, Bill, and his wife, Liz, and with Jody's predecessor, Linda. That was quite a lot of fun as we spoke about museums and this and that person from the past.

II APRIL

The day of the lecture

I was collected in the morning by Jody and whisked to the McNay Museum. This began as the bequest of a house, garden and collection from a much-married and apparently unattractive oil heiress. The house was 1920s Spanish colonial but now expanded with a large modern building by a talented French architect, providing gallery and exhibition space and facilities. It had the makings of a good, much-needed museum in this cultural desert. The accent was on the twentieth century but these American museums all repeat each other – they must have one Picasso, one Modigliani, one Renoir, etc., and so the list goes on. They're not in the field for top-notch stuff, so it's all second rate. And I'm tired of white walls and rows of modern pictures exactly spaced. But the facilities were excellent as I set up the lecture.

Jody took me to see the Tobin Collection of festival and theatre stuff. Now that was really interesting, a huge library of rare *fêtes* books, boxes of theatre designs, maquettes, etc. She'd also put on a good exhibition. I went into the stores and she produced boxes with designs by Burne-Jones, Charles Ricketts, Derain, et al. There was an extraordinary box of stuff – photos and cuttings – connected with Cecil Beaton's notorious book *My Royal Past*, with Fred Ashton and others as Edwardian ladies. I wonder how that got loose?

Back to the hotel for a rest, and then the driver failed to turn up at 5 p.m. I was going mad so, at 5.30 p.m., got a cab. It all went well. This was a gathering of Anglophiles and the very rich who support the Tobin Foundation. I'd tempered my coronation lecture and made them laugh, but somehow I don't think most of them had an informed intellect. This was a ritual in the interests of one thing: money. We went afterwards to Tobin's house, which revealed, as indeed did his collection, an idiosyncratic cast of mind. There were drinks and something called a 'dessert reception'. I chatted to everyone and made the usual gracious speech and that was that.

13 APRIL

The Alamo

The well-intentioned Kate, who knows the history of the place, took me to see what was left of two of the eighteenth-century Franciscan mission settlements, extraordinary enclosures in which converted Native Americans lived, with a church and rooms off for the friars. In the afternoon I walked to see the Alamo in downtown, another such settlement but now built up as a national Texan shrine. But both the museum and various information boards filled me in on Texan history, from being a part of the Spanish colonial empire, then part of an independent Mexico, then a struggle between Centralists and Federalists, then an independent state and finally, in 1846, part of the USA. This was heritage myth-making with a consumer vengeance, with much made of the famous siege of Alamo, so there was great attention to firearms, Davy Crockett hats, even Alamo cats and the rest. Much of this has no connection with the America I know. Kate also took me on a tour of the old German district of San Antonio, which is a wonder of delightful late-nineteenth-century domestic architecture, for a time abandoned but now restored.

Geordie Grieg rang and asked me to write about Mrs Thatcher's funeral and was taken aback that I was here [flying home today] so it was not possible!

15 AND 16 APRIL

Bath revisited

I was picked up for Bath and lectured to a sell-out audience on the wonderful series of Jacobean full-lengths of ladies by William Larkin lent to the Holburne Museum. I spent the night in Bath so that I could perform at Toppings bookshop on the Tuesday. The whole day in Bath was a delight because I got to know it just walking around. Even by the Regency period Bath remained quite small and everyone who was anyone must have known who was there. I was recognised at the Building of Bath Museum and taken to see what they were doing to No. 1 Royal Crescent, where they are restoring the whole house, embracing kitchens, bedrooms, etc. It ought to be just what the tourists want. There's a dreadful Jane Austen tourism shop with everyone in costume touting outside. The city should have done something like this but in better taste years ago but they seem pretty hopeless. I went to the Fashion Museum and took Rosemary Harden out to lunch and saw all my clothes rehung up and cared for – as time goes by they get more and more interesting. I told Rosemary that she must come to The Laskett as there will be another massive throw-out precipitated by the exit from Morpeth Terrace [which was up for sale].

19 APRIL

Farewell Patrick Garland

In the evening Patricia Routledge rang me to say that Patrick Garland had died. He had been very ill for a long time and died in hospital. He was my age, seventy-eight. The funeral is next week, done in a hurry as Alexandra has to start chemotherapy as she has cancer of the spine. Not happy news. Patrick was a real link back in time. Julia worked with him doing *Famous Gossips* on TV in the early Sixties, which led on to Jonathan Miller's *Alice in Wonderland* [1966]; the last thing Julia designed for Patrick was *Beatrix* [1992] for Chichester, in which Patricia played Beatrix Potter. He didn't wear well with age, being very pretty when young but all that had long gone. He had an enormous love of and feeling for the literature of this country in all its eccentricity. The great hit with Julia was the famous production of Aubrey's *Brief Lives* [1967] with Roy Dotrice and her landmark set with about six hundred props on it. Julia called Patrick 'Cliffhanger' because he always said that she would be designing his next production but never did. He failed to receive the recognition that he deserved – or the productions either, for he should have worked at the National and RSC. When it came to women he was ruthless. He had lots of them but finally in Alexandra of the menagerie he met his match.

21 APRIL

Farewell Morpeth Terrace

This was the end of an era, having moved there in 1968. After a morass of problems over the sale, it finally went.

This will be the last time that I'll sleep at Morpeth. I'll have to pop in and out but I'm booked into the Lansdowne Club to sleep. The pictures and furniture I want will go on 23 April and be delivered to The Laskett on 25 April.

22 APRIL

The hunt for costume and sitting for John Swannell

This was a long day. It started at 8 a.m. when I took the Tube to Highgate, where I was picked up by John Swannell and then eventually arrived at Angels the costumiers, where we walked miles to get what we wanted – nothing very smart. He was going to snap me as a late Victorian painter seated at an easel in a corner of a cluttered studio – Tennyson wearing a large hat (we could only find one resembling his in beige but John said that he could make it black), Ruskin with a long beard (he said he could lengthen mine), and a bishop with mitre and voluminous cope – all variants of late Victorian photos of the St John's Wood dressing-up school – also, of course, including Julia Margaret Cameron. We tried to find cardinal's robes for me, as in an El Greco, but failed.

So it was all day in John's Highgate house. All the dramas around selling up the London flat had left me exhausted but I wound myself up and off we went with the sittings. He seemed so excited about it all and he's such a genius at this kind of fakery. 'Eat your heart out, Burne-Jones!' he yelled. They will all be in sepia and, I suspect, a bit out of focus [they weren't]. While we were at Angels we got into the military section, where they had real *c.*1900 court dress, so that's another, and Victorian Beefeaters' uniforms. John said that we should do that one in The Tower [we didn't]. This section also had the material to do one of those royal uniform portrait photos with orders and medals like George V or the Tsar – that's three more . . .

26 APRIL

Recreating the past: me as Tennyson

The unsinkable John Swannell texted me to say that the latest portraits are the best yet and he wants me to see them and for us to plot the next. So down he and Marianne came for lunch. And, yes, he was right. They were extraordinary, the ones of me as Tennyson, Ruskin in old age and as a late Victorian painter quite remarkable. I've never seen anything like them but, as it was pointed out, I have an ability to take on the characters in an uncanny way. J and M are both such a joy anyway and we plotted the next series, including me in court dress and peer's cloak in Dore Abbey, a 1920s racing driver, on a penny-farthing with a top hat, etc. John is very, very clever and there's a rapport between us behind this series. What the latest portraits demonstrated is what can be achieved with only a minimum of hired stuff and fudging up the rest. The Tennyson is the most remarkable, quite eerie.

10 MAY

Royal portraiture

Paul Brason came to lunch. What a nice man he is. We hug and he so obviously cares about me, and that's touching. No worry over commissions. He has work to take him to autumn 2014. He was very funny about the Duke of Edinburgh. It was one of the Queen's private secretaries, he learnt, who was responsible for the Queen sitting for Lucien Freud – awful, he said. The Duke and Paul seem to have hit it off, although I loved his doorknob tale. When Prince Michael had sat for him years ago everything had gone well until the Prince went to the door and stopped. He must have been taught that no royal personage ever opened one, as doors had to be opened for them. Paul rushed over and did it. In contrast, seeing this situation arising again with the Duke of Edinburgh, he rushed to open the door at which point the Duke said, 'I'm perfectly capable of opening a door!' Paul aches to rent a really nice house from the NT or some such but hasn't been successful so far. Too late to buy, he says, and he'll just go on painting. After he'd gone I drove into Hereford to Climb On Bikes and bought one, and all the kit. I've never ridden a bike so this is a new adventure. Ady Watts at the gym will find someone to break me in!

From my early forties until the age of seventy-seven I used to jog at least a basic 5 miles three times a week but my left knee showed signs of giving way so to achieve aerobic exercise I decided that I must learn to ride a bike. I'd never had one or learnt to ride one as a child.

14 MAY

An Oldie *Literary Lunch at Simpsons*

I walked to Simpsons in the Strand for The Oldie Lunch, an event I wished I'd never agreed to do. But it was all very different from the last one I did. No high table but round ones, a younger audience too, which was cheering. Richard Ingrams is endowed with a benign, cheery twinkle. I sat on his right. Ian Hislop, who has edited *Private Eye* for thirty years, was also there – was that too long? Yes, I said, it was. All institutions need change and someone who works from a different standpoint. The other speakers were a nice lanky journalist [Peter Stanford] who'd written a book on graveyards and earlier a biography of Frank Longford. Alas he went on too long and Richard Ingrams kept passing him notes asking him to shut up. There was also an old friend, the garden writer Ursula Buchan, whose book was on gardening during the Second World War, i.e. 'digging for victory', and how it was all a myth. I discovered that she was related to Hugh Buchanan, the painter. Ursula had a typed script and she stuck to it – worthy but sleep-inducing – and then came me. I spoke about why I wrote *Self-Portrait* and the short age of the meritocrats and the destruction of the grammar schools. Once I got going the tough points and laughs came and I sat down to a huge of wave of applause.

Afterwards I walked back to the Lansdowne Club via the Man Ray exhibition at the NPG. I was so glad that I caught this. He recorded a whole world of the arts in Paris and New York, etc., at a certain period. Needless to say, all those decades back I didn't know all about that. The result is that I'm always rather amazed when the faces occasionally were of people one had met – Lee Miller for one, who never had any resonance to me other than as Lady Penrose, then Diana Cooper and Ava Gardner and one or two more. Terence Pepper had done a terrific job.

Back and out again, this time to the RA for the launch of one of the satyr-like Fred Hohler's Public Catalogue Foundation's volumes. I presented him with a copy of *Self-Portrait* but left early as suddenly the rooms began to fill with characters from the world I left, only they were often fatter, uglier, older and still going on as though they mattered. Oh God, the sight of them tottering in made me so glad that I avoid gatherings of this kind. Nearly all of them were living off what they had been and not what they are now. The great topic was Penelope Curtis's Tate Britain new hang. I shuddered and departed.

17 MAY

The Hereford Cathedral Nave Dinner

The day of the Cathedral Nave Dinner. This was a really impressive occasion. We entered through the West Door and the sense of spectacle was terrific as it was so very well done, with round tables, purple tablecloths, tall silver candlesticks and flowers. The tickets were £100 a head. It was a sell-out and with the auction raised between £20,000 and £30,000 that evening. There was little that I could fault them on. At my table were Mark and Gillian Archer, Stuart Donachie, John and Anne Foley, 'Chips' and Fiona Fyshe and a couple of others. The Dean and canons acted as wine waiters. I wore my purple and gold maharajah frock coat with an Indian scarf draped around it. There were imaginative touches like the living sculpture and a pair of acrobats, both of which worked within the context, and, of course, the choir singing this and that. It's the best occasion I've seen them do: nine out of ten. Didn't get to bed until 12.45 a.m.

20 MAY

The Chelsea Flower Show centenary

This was not exciting as there was nothing really new. Christopher Bradley-Hole's garden was the best, precisely clipped box and yew cubes and rectangles, with water and cow parsley running between. The Australian garden was an explosion, good in its way, and it won the prize. But the big tent each year has fewer and fewer exhibitors and the paths between them widen as firms contract out as they can't afford it. Rather a lot of photo occasions as I wore my striped blazer! But it was very nice to see old friends – Hugh and Judy Johnson, Arabella Lennox-Boyd, Clive Boursnell, etc.

And then over to give the speech at the opening lunch to what was a huge audience. The speeches began with Alan Titchmarsh launching an RHS appeal to excite the young to enter the profession. Seventy per cent of present vacancies cannot be filled and the young regard it all as drear and unexciting. There was a little too much of Alan as he went on and on. Like Simon Jenkins, he can't keep his head down below the parapet for a time to give us all a welcome rest. The food was awful. I was on Elizabeth Banks's right and Lord Cadogan was on her left. Victoria Wakefield was on my other side; Simon Thurley also turned up. The RHS is still rather over-stuffed with old school county. Elizabeth Banks of Hergest Croft stands down as RHS President this year and Nico Bacon of Raveningham succeeds. His father was KG and they are near Sandringham. *Plus ça change* . . . The RHS seems so self-satisfied with itself that my speech must have come as a shock, but you couldn't challenge it – reality laced with courtly flattery. The RHS hasn't been the driving force of innovation or change for a century. It's a real fat cat with royal-itis.

27 TO 30 MAY

I begin to learn to ride a bike

On Monday my bike instructor Jonty Williams came, a delightful ex-RAF fitness instructor. And so I began to scud up and down the pleached lime avenue. This was a week of horrendous rain, all day the 28th, 29th and 30th.

Thursday was Corpus Christi and I'd agreed to be MC at the cathedral. It was a gathering of Anglo-Catholics, some sixty of us I would guess, in the North Transept. Very moving but quite complex as I had to deal with the humeral veil at Mass and then the procession to the Lady Chapel (the original plan was to go outside but weather was inimical), where we had Benediction. If I do it next time I must site kneelers or wear knee-pads! I took Michael Tavinor to dinner at the Castle House. He was interesting on something that I had not thought about. As parishes are lumped together, everything goes down to the lowest common denominator. Hence the collapse of liturgy. But in the case of Hereford diocese, Catholic Anglicans are uncatered-for except in the cathedral. Also, things are going so rapidly in this direction that no one knows where the new generation of deans will come from. It left me depressed.

31 MAY

The Hay Festival

Antonia Fraser came to lunch and I put on Indian garb and saluted her. Amazing as always, she was swathed in scarves and most of the time wearing very large specs. None the less, there's an enduring charm that is seductive and we always have such a good time together, as she has a beguiling intelligence which appeals to me. So we were happy sitting side by side on a garden bench in the sun, sipping white wine and going over this and that, including why to listen to William Dalrymple was £9, she was £8 and I was £7 at the Hay Festival. She's doing a lot of appearances for *Perilous Question* [her book on the 1832 Reform Bill]. As long as they provide a chauffeur-driven car and put her in a hotel with a swimming pool, she's there. Antonia reckons that *Perilous* will be her last big historical book and she has childhood memoirs in mind.

1 JUNE

I perform at Hay

I was collected at 11 a.m. and was at the Festival at 11.45 a.m. but not on stage till 2.30 p.m., which left me a bit miffed. This event takes place in a huge encampment of walkways, booths, restaurants and auditoria. My event had been moved out of the Sky Arts Studio into the Big Tent. The weather had come full circle and it was sunshine all the way. It was a dialogue with Peter Florence, now large and stubble-encrusted but bright and benign. There must have been over eight hundred in the audience. Peter was exceptionally good at drawing me out and of course there were so many resonances from those in the audience who had also come up through the grammar schools and resented their destruction. This was not a surface dialogue and I was overwhelmed by the warmth of the audience towards me. There were tears in my eyes at the end – and indeed in those of a lot in the audience too, which was made up of just ordinary people who, like me, owed so much to that institution which had set them on the ladder of ascent.

4 JUNE

The Coronation remembered

The great day and it was sunshine all the way. I got to the Abbey by 9.30 a.m. and put on red and black as instructed but found my neckbands were missing. David Burden, my deputy as High Bailiff, gave me a spare set. There was a good atmosphere and, having studied the service sheet, I was glad to see that they had done what I told them to do: borrow a crown and, more importantly, the ampulla. My idea was that it should be carried up to the altar by young people representing the rainbow nature of today's UK. But I guess the idea of them holding it didn't go down, so instead the holy anointing oil was brought up by a motley crew that included a child, a nurse, an ethnic lollipop lady, a teacher, a pensioner, etc. That was quite imaginative, if aesthetically jarring.

There was a pell-mell of people but I dodged out of my stall and said hello to Antonia, looking good in a hat, Sister Judith, David Cannadine, Victor Stock, David Hutt . . . It all went like clockwork and had a real celebratory quality. The royals are a motley crew, and somehow one couldn't help noticing that so many of them looked suburban and there was no co-ordination of look. The Queen, now a little bent at eighty-seven, in white and with a hat with pale blue chiffon roses, very set in expression and not smiling; the Duke's face was well worn but he was there at ninety-two, amazing; the York princesses and the Princess Royal's children look like something from an estate of 1920s semis, 'Mr and Mrs Phillips' and 'Mr and Mrs Tindall' holding hands, which was quite wrong.

None the less, James O'Donnell did his stuff and the Queen came in to Parry's 'I Was Glad', which brought tears to my eyes, and the boys of Westminster School cried out 'Vivat Regina! Vivat Regina

Elizabetha!' There was a good sermon by Justin Welby on service, humility and the role of authority. It was all very Christian, which one knows the Queen would wish for, and very pre-Common Worship, with all the thees and thous. In fact it gave out that the coronation was a Christian ritual and that's what it would be next time. Some other faiths entered in procession at the beginning but took no part. David Cameron read well but indifferently, the Secretary General of the Commonwealth read brilliantly and the rather good poem by Carol Ann Duffy, composed for the occasion, was read poorly by some actress called Claire Skinner, from the Donmar Warehouse. Surely they could have got Judi Dench or Patricia Routledge or Siân Phillips? There was a new anthem and it was wound up with Walton's *Te Deum* from 1953.

We then went to the Cellarium for a drink and I was able to deliver my opening line to the new Archbishop: 'Give my love to your mother,' which rather hit him – so we were into the Portal family and Carola Oman [the connection here was Julia's aunt Carola Oman, Lady Lenanton and Welby's mother, a Portal]. I'm glad, however, that he didn't get his way as leader of the anti-gay marriage lobby in the afternoon. We then all went to College Hall and I was placed on the high table at the end opposite Stephen Lamport, the Receiver General, and next to the Lord Mayor of Westminster, Sarah Richardson, an attractive young woman, and it was all polite conversation. The Duchess of Cornwall was opposite at an angle and after yelling at me 'Hello Roy!', that was it. But she's such a bonus, animated and a bit gung-ho, much easier than Diana. There was the Loyal Toast and then up and away. The Queen passed directly by me and cast a kindly glance and off they went to the Deanery while I and various other Abbey officers were rounded up and taken to stand in a line outside the Deanery door. It opened and out she popped, finding us lot, to her surprise. She smiled at me and I just said 'It was so happy' – and so indeed it was.

In the evening I went to supper with Sarah Greenall in Grosvenor Road and Paul Zuckerman turned up, having been at the Art Fund awards ceremony at the V&A. The other two guests were William Tuckett, a Royal Ballet dancer and now talented choreographer, and his wife who was having a very unhappy time with the Coram Foundation. She's now in her early forties, having been at the Tate. He was something different, tall with hugely intelligent eyes and elegantly curled fair hair but whether by art or nature I couldn't quite decide. Needless to say, we were off to hours of hilarious banter measured by the fact that I didn't get back to the Lansdowne Club until after midnight. Oh the exhilaration of the talented young!

Jonathan's coming back and to supper on Saturday but I do wonder where some younger, sparky people might come from around where I live. The batteries are charged on both sides. So I will always need to come to London to plug into the cut and thrust and wit and creative excitement that they generate.

5 JUNE

MacMillan's Mayerling *and farewell to Johan Kobborg and Alina Cojocaru at the Opera House*

I took Penny Graham to *Mayerling*, still fizzy and dizzy and stylish in her seventies. She'd never been to anything like it before and she was in tears at the end. It was Kobborg and Cojocaru. This was something. One was left gasping at the choreography and what was demanded of the dancers in terms of character commitment and movement. The tension in the audience was almost tangible as the terrible saga reached its ghastly end. The curtain slowly descended, then silence and then the house went mad. Most of the audience was on its feet, cheering, acclaiming and stamping. Vast bouquets of flowers were laid at the dancers' feet and cascades were thrown down on to the stage from above. I haven't seen anything like this since something like Fred Ashton's farewell. It went on and on and on. The audience then sang 'Happy Birthday' to Kobborg. You could see how moved the dancers were as this demand to pay them homage continued for ages. We left after about fifteen minutes and the stamping was still going on. Maybe it still is . . . I couldn't miss evenings like this. I left enchanted, moved, exhilarated and humbled, knowing that I could not live without such magic fixes to the emotions and the mind.

II TO I4 JUNE

Northamptonshire revisited

A Northamptonshire mini-break with a small group gathered by Tania Illingworth and me talking. We stayed at the Stopford Sackvilles' house, Drayton, and had visits to Boughton, Burghley, Milton, Cottesbrook and Coton. I got Stuart to drive me there, a journey wrecked by a major crash on the A14. Drayton is that amazing house with the courtyard and baroque frontispiece by William Talman. I was last there in 1975 filming *Gone, Going, Going* . . . and then it was in a ghastly state of decay. The present incumbent said that he remembered me: he was then a little boy riding a tricycle in the courtyard. It was now very different, wife number two of Charlie Stopford Sackville having been a Pearson and so the entire house was done over by Nina Campbell. Lionel, the father, is still alive, in a wheelchair somewhere in the house (he did not appear), and one wife, Mary, is in another part. A third, now Sue Rathbone, lives in the village. The evening of arrival we had dinner with Mary in her kitchen and laughed at everything. Charlie speaks like some automaton, the result of a ghastly motorbike accident in which his head was virtually torn off and put back on again. They seem a fast-living, fast-loving family. The financial fortunes appear to have been turned around by him. This is a grand house but not overwhelming.

The visits to Boughton and Burghley were indexes of how much things have changed from the early 1970s when I first visited them. Both are institutionalised, Burghley in particular, which is now a Preservation Trust. Victoria Leatham has done a fantastic job putting everything in order but it had lost almost any feeling of a lived-in house. All of this, I suppose, is inevitable to survive but I hated the modern ticket office entrance and the way you had to go round back to front, starting with the kitchens and ending with the state rooms, in reverse to the norm, which was a real shame. Miranda Rock appeared, a delightful woman who has taken on being the resident family.

How lucky I was to have visited both houses when they were still lived in. At least at Boughton you go the right way round but it's all been tidied up into period rooms. Here the Duke has done great things in the gardens, really wonderful, with Kim Wilkie. That is a real contribution, one that goes beyond garden restoration to creating a new modernist minimalist manipulation of land and water. At Burghley they opted for George Carter doing a garden maze of *giochi d'acqua* for the children, harmless but somehow out of key with the grandeur of the place. There was also the inevitable modern sculpture garden.

Milton Hall I last went to in the early Seventies, when staying at Boughton. We all went over and what stuck in my mind was the dining room hung with the most stunning Stubbs pictures of mares and foals. But they had gone and so had the Van Dycks. All this reflected the wind-up of the Fitzwilliam inheritance, divided between two heiresses, Juliet de Chair, who got the Van Dycks and Stubbs, and the Naylor-Leylands, who got the Reynolds and Canalettos. Milton is the original Fitzwilliam house and it's an oddity, one long meandering façade, late Elizabethan one side and the other side classical.

17 JUNE

I learn to ride a bike

Jonty collects me and the bike and off we go to the municipal park in Hereford, which is perfect, with large stretches of rolling green and slopes down which I could safely take off and not, as here, perpetually worry about bashing into something. I had a lingering doubt that this was perhaps all a bad idea but Jonty's such a good teacher, positive, little by little, encouraging. So off I went again on the bike minus pedals and, yes, I did go quite a distance before I slowed up. A couple of those and Jonty put the pedals on. That worried me. But I was instructed to only keep one foot on the left pedal and forget the right but keep the leg out. I fell off but, nothing daunted, went back, got on again and this time sailed away. Then I was to put my right foot on the pedal and then, quite suddenly, he yelled 'Keep pedalling!' and I did and I started to ride the bike. We were all so excited and he was so pleased with me. It was a wonderful feeling. I then did more run downs and, pedalling away, he yelled 'Keep going and turn the wheel', which I did, and I was then cycling back to where we started! It was extraordinarily exhilarating and I just thought 'I'm going to enjoy this.' I went back to The Laskett in a happy haze.

18 JUNE

The Fashion Museum comes and collects

Rosemary Harden came from the Fashion Museum, Bath, to collect another mound of my clothes precipitated by the exit from London. The upstairs guest bedroom and sitting room were covered with piles of designer stuff arranged under suits, trousers, shirts, jackets, etc., and further heaps from Next and Zara. Rosemary said that no one else had collected one fashionable man's clothing for most of a lifetime. She took the lot. One day they will be more than interesting.

28 JUNE

Petertide at the Abbey

This was a long day as I had lunch at the Garrick and then went down to the Abbey for a meeting at 3 p.m., in which Ptolemy Dean explained his musical chairs for accommodation. God knows when the triforium project will actually happen. It's been ongoing since 2000, when I arrived! It's now packaged as the Diamond Jubilee Galleries.

There was a splendid Petertide Mass with a vast set of new vestments and copes, all with huge cross keys in the fabric. John Hall preached the best sermon I'd heard him give, the theme being the unshifting rock which in fact did shift, and being openly definite on the topic of women bishops and gay marriage. Later, at the dinner, much to my surprise he complimented James O'Donnell and Noura on their civil partnership, so at the close I went up to him and said I want to be present at the first gay marriage in the Abbey. He was on top form and such a contrast to Robin Holland Martin, Master of the Fishmongers' Company, who had to present the Abbey with a fish, a piece of post-1945 invented tradition.

I took Fred Hohler to the dinner and he enjoyed himself. We saw the somewhat dire mega-picture of the Queen standing on the Cosmati pavement, which had been damaged with a spray gun in an attempt by the assailant to write 'HELP'. Bob Reiss was on my right, so there was much talk about the grip of the evangelicals. I said that Richard Coles was coming to interview me. Bob said that he was an excellent broadcaster and in a gay relationship. I now begin to worry about these wretched evangelicals. I am still haunted by the fact that in the whole diocese of Hereford only the cathedral caters for Catholic Anglicans. It had been a long and tiring day.

9 JULY

Revd Richard Coles

The Revd Richard Coles came to interview me for the *Church Times*, based on my early autobiography. Quite a jovial, intelligent, bespectacled man in his early fifties, I think, in danger of running flaccid.

12 JULY

Brian Sewell again

This was the last time I saw him, a great miss in my life.

I was driven to the Guildhall in Winchester for a 'performance' with Brian Sewell, which this time worked well. I arrived early and was able to organise the staging. Also, Brian was stuck in a traffic jam somewhere. It was a large hall and some five hundred came, a very full house. We both spoke for just ten minutes and then threw it open to questions from the audience. Although we had varying viewpoints on things, at heart our views were the same. Afterwards there was a book signing, with sales handled appallingly badly by the dreaded Waterstones. We then joined the sponsors for a party and it was all very jolly.

15 JULY

Back at Angels and more sittings

The day of the next John Swannell shoot. We started at Angels, which had surprisingly found a lot of what we wanted. We began with Whistler's Carlyle and quickly chose all we needed – hat, coat, cloak, walking stick, shirt, collar, tie, boots – although failed to notice that although the coat was full of buttonholes, none of them was functional so we had to tape it together. The same dress but with a top hat was to be worn perched on a penny-farthing bike. Two down. Rasputin was also an easy one, with a close long black robe and a gold chain. I just had to look mad. Then came the 1920s racing driver, and much to our astonishment they produced the correct coat and an amazing cap with goggles. Perfect. Then came the Roman emperor and, yes, we were in luck there too, with a short undergarment, lappets, a cuirass with a six-pack, swags of crimson cloak, sandals and a spear.

Then we hit the buffers. All their Charles I stuff was just awful. The plan was to stage the famous Van Dyck triple portrait. We just about put together the doublets, which, with fudging, would pass muster, but it was impossible to find a lace collar with scallops. What they had was made from bits of old crochet. As we were getting ready to leave, who should pop out but Mr Angel himself, an affable man of about sixty. I told him how wonderful everything was, bar the collar, at which point he rushed to rescue us and I traipsed with him down to the lace store. With luck something will arrive tomorrow. We were then told that what we had asked to be set aside for August for a shoot in full court dress and peer's robes had been lent and ruined. But we did find a good peer's crimson velvet and ermine robe.

Back to John's house for an al fresco lunch very sweetly provided by Marianne. And then to work. We kicked off with the most difficult one, me on a penny-farthing. That had already been photographed separately, with the vehicle running through an elegant copse of silver birch trees. I would be superimposed. So John's new assistant Rosie's bike was set up in the garden, jammed between two potted bay trees and with her standing at the other end holding it all up. I got on, with top hat and all, and had to balance myself with one foot or toe on the ground while John snapped away. This was not easy, for I had to be rigidly upright. The same clothes with extra bits were used for a recreation of Whistler's portrait of Carlyle. Everything was right for that and I looked like his double. This was a monochrome essay and again much would be done technically to get rid of the painting behind me and insert two others and add the black band along the back wall. Then came the racing driver, which was a doddle and everyone hooted with laughter. The wheel was a kitchen stool! And with that we came to an end.

16 JULY

Me as Rasputin

Day two and no sign of the Charles I collar so we plugged on with Rasputin. Charlie the hair and wig girl arrived and I was gone over with a false beard, which took ages and a lot of glue and paint. But the result was striking. John said that I looked really evil. It was a long, laborious lead-up to a picture that took virtually no time to take. And then it all had to be taken off. Back to Herefordshire.

18 JULY

Hereford Cathedral

Today seemed to be nothing but the cathedral. They were clearly chuffed that I came to the Hereford College of Art degree ceremony. I think that Richard Heatly is doing a great job lifting the place. Angela Conner and Edmund de Waal were made Fellows, the latter giving a good speech of acceptance. He wanted to come and see me re the V&A [he had been made a Trustee] so I suppose I have to, but I did say that it was all twenty-seven years ago. He's a delightful and talented man, tall and gangling. Then in the evening, drinks in the Deanery garden for cathedral helpers, an affable, kindly, aged and often somewhat tottery lot, but people like this are the backbone of the country, voluntary helpers and charity givers.

JULY

Me on a bike

All through this period I've tended to go to bed early and fall asleep immediately for seven or more hours, then get up early and go off to the gym. Cycling lessons continue. It's a long and laborious process but Jonty's a gentle instructor and slowly but surely I advance. There's so much to master. I still hesitate starting off but I'll get there. Friday 19 July was a turning point, for Jonty hired a tandem and together we went through nineteen miles of country around Ledbury. Wonderful. So on 24 July we moved on to turning corners. 'Trust you to take up what is the most fashionable sport,' someone remarked.

24 JULY

A change of political mood

I begin to think that the Conservatives may get in next time. Somehow there's a mood change. The country has accepted that there's no money and debt has to be paid. Icons of the post-war consensus like education and the NHS are seen to have failed or are dramatically failing. They are no longer viewed as untouchable, but fallible, and, in the case of the NHS, failing in terms of lost human lives and often appalling treatment of the old, ill and frail. Labour is in disarray and the proposal that their financial link with the unions should be dissolved is a real milestone. But there's a feel-good atmosphere at the moment – Andy Murray at Wimbledon, we defeated the Australians at cricket, we won the Tour de France for a second time and the Cambridges have produced an heir to the throne. There's a slight upturn in the economy. It could be a good idea to go to the country before government has to, but alas the Coalition is bound into an agreement that they should go on until 2015.

25 JULY

I am Charles I and Chekhov, and the Coronation exhibition

Up early and off to be picked up by John Swannell at Highgate station. Eventually we get to Angels, which actually produced a very passable Caroline lace collar. The hair and make-up lady comes and sets up and it takes almost two hours to transform me as near as possible into Charles I for a shoot as the famous Van Dyck triple portrait. Much beard and moustache trimming and painting of the same, and much of the hair too before the wig went on. The pearl drop earring rather suited me! But it was a long haul with a mass of make-up. So it wasn't until 1 p.m. that the shoot could begin. John notices every detail. There was much faking up with draped fabric. I seemed to stand there for an eternity as tweaking went on hair, clothes, head and arm positions. But when John got what he wanted, it was just a few snaps and it was in the bag.

All of this had in the main to be got off, or as much of it that would deflect from me being Chekhov! So it was a quick lunch and off we went again. My hair this time was painted, lifted up on the crown and flattened at the sides. I lost my curly moustache and my beard was rounded. So into late nineteenth-century dress and pince-nez. Once I had 'arranged' myself and again been tweaked, it was bang, bang and that was it. By then I was tired but we had to polish off Magritte's *Not to Be Reproduced*, his Surrealist portrait of Edward James looking at his own back in a mirror, my idea, easy to do and witty. One of my books replaced whatever was in the painting. We did it in the upstairs bathroom. All through the day it was yes, I can alter that or deal with this.

In the evening I took Penny Graham to the private view of the Coronation exhibition at Buckingham Palace. It was spectacular, with some very interesting film footage of parts not used or recorded in the official coverage, i.e. what happened in Buckingham Palace on returning. There was an amazing display of original robes and dresses, simply stunning. Would they ever have the nerve to do all this again? That film footage which showed the Royal Family jostling to form a group flashed with a thousand diamonds – tiaras, brooches, orders – was quite breathtaking. All six of the Queen's

Maids of Honour were still alive, and all except Jane Willoughby were there – I said 'Hello' to Jayne Rayne and Anne Glenconner, who must both be over eighty and look pretty good. The anointing dress, which had turned up in a steel filing cabinet in the Abbey, was there. It was the sheer richness of it all that was so overwhelming. Nothing has eclipsed it since. Everything was in more or less pristine condition, except a slight yellowing of some of the white satin dresses.

21 AUGUST

A National Trust visitation

Ben Shipston and Mike Calnan, head of National Trust gardens, came as it had concerned me that as I was approaching eighty the future of the garden remained unsettled. The National Trust wants it but we're stuck with those who voted it down. But this was a constructive meeting as it became clear that one ought to take the fall-back position forward and flesh it out. That meant putting together a group of trustees, each of whom represented a different area of professional expertise: money, legal, running, a garden grandee, etc. Ben Shipston agreed to be one at once. Later I asked Tim Richardson (garden) and Stephen Vakil (finance) and both said that they would be honoured to be such. So that is on its way.

What did emerge was that what had been submitted previously to the National Trust was compiled by one of their houses people and not a garden expert. They said that we needed to draw up a garden profile, indeed they said that The Laskett needed a much higher profile. That request amazed me as the garden has always had such massive coverage. Indeed, when I showed them the scrapbook of press cuttings they were astonished. At any rate the plan was that a

National Trust person would go through the stuff and put together a garden case. I would assemble the material.

9 SEPTEMBER

Tuscan Gardens revisited

I am writing this in a hotel in the Via de' Tornabuoni, Florence, taking a group around some Tuscan gardens on a very short tour. But I longed to see them yet again, and how they had fared and changed since last visited. There were ups and downs. The Villa di Castello was up, the grotto restored and the garden ordered and maintained in a way that it had never been before. That was exciting. The beloved Villa Gamberaia went down a peg or two, as it desperately needed restoring and replanting. The scale has all gone and putting up photographs of how it had looked in the 1920s only made things worse. Sad.

There had been enormous new research on the Villa Medici at Fiesole, indicating that indeed it was designed by Alberti for Giovanni de' Medici. This ought to be in state ownership. And then there's the work of Cecil Pinsent. I was so excited by Le Balze in the 1980s, when it had just been restored, but all I can see now is the man's faults and him as an uneven *pasticheur*. However, at last we saw La Pietra. Harold Acton's parents must have gone mad buying up garden statues on such a scale that the garden in areas is over-populated with them and would benefit from losing some. La Pietra is a series of rooms and vistas and has been beautifully restored and replanted by Kim Wilkie. Some areas of it are better than others, but it's exhilarating all the same.

27 SEPTEMBER

Hidcote revisited

There was a 'works' outing to Hidcote with my PA, Fiona, and the two gardeners, Shaun and Philip. It was a glorious day and it's still a magic garden, although sadly 'killed off' by the excess of visitors. With its shops, restaurant, car parks and other public facilities, any sense that it was once one person's domain has gone. Being 'visited' and 'enjoyed' by such a swarm of people has eroded much.

Afterwards we went along the road to Johnny and Ann Chambers at Kiftsgate and in a way enjoyed it more. There were fewer people and there was Anne sitting by the door taking the money! The modesty of it is appealing. The new Pond Garden is as fresh as a daisy too. There we sat and had tea and consumed an enormous coffee cake.

7 TO 10 OCTOBER

The Netherlands revisited

A short visit to Amsterdam with Jonathan Myles-Lea, who arrived on Sunday 6th. The weather for this time of year was benign and Sunday was of an almost surreal autumn beauty. Off we set for Heathrow on the Monday with Stuart as driver, to find when we got there that the flight had been cancelled. We did eventually get off, after a five-hour wait, on a KLM flight, arriving at where we were to stay at about 6 p.m. This was a place found by Jan van Dorsten's daughter, Anna, which turned out to be accommodation better suited for two mountain goats. It was all vertical staircases and all but stepladders to get into bed. No matter, for they were two one-room self-catering apartments separated by a landing, on the walls of which hung gory pictures of torture.

Winfrid de Munck came and took us both out to dinner. When he can he smokes, but he's a hugely funny and intelligent man, my new Dutch friend who is mad about gardens and loves cats, so what else was needed? He'd read garden history at university under John Dixon Hunt and retained a passion for it, building a library of some three thousand books. But he went off into the new IT of technical translation and publishing and now has a staff of some fifteen; he lives and works in Utrecht.

Next day we went off to the Rijksmuseum and queued before it opened and got in at 9 a.m. This was an outstanding updating of a 1880s historicist building, turning its two vast courtyards into concourse areas with all the mod cons of modern museum-going – café, shop, loos, meeting places, etc.

The museum went up floor by floor according to period, the second floor being the one that had 1500 to 1700 and the 'hall of honour' leading to Rembrandt's *Night Watch*. The walls throughout were painted the same dark blue but the labels were succinct and informative. Somehow the masterpieces began to pall. People surge around them and instinctively one draws away as though they'd been 'killed off'. All of this was summed up by one Japanese guide, who held up in her hand her iPad in front of the *Night Watch*. No one looked at the actual picture but they all looked at the iPad. None the less, it was a joyous visit with so much to see again and enjoy, all hung and displayed in a thoughtful manner. But I was struck by how limited the collections were, set against the mountainous accumulation at the V&A.

We had breakfast, lunch and tea there and just kept going. The pictures we most treasured were two early Haarlem-period de Hoochs, masterpieces of light and open windows and doors, miraculous and ungrand. I hadn't spent a whole day in a museum just looking for a long time so it was back to our digs and a period of restful decompression.

Then in the evening, the van Dorsten family gave us dinner in a very pleasant Italian restaurant. 'I last saw you in 1963, fifty years ago,' said Gertrude. She was the surprise, a new person. My last memory of her was tense-faced and trying to stop Jan doing something or other. What I didn't know was that she had remarried happily, a match that lasted twenty-five years until he died in his sleep. She had taken another degree and is now about to have a collection of short stories published. She's now in her mid-seventies, benign and with a warmth in her eyes, and very much the matriarch. I was so pleased that life had worked out for her and that she was tranquil and creative. I had dreaded meeting an embittered old lady, but not a bit of it.

The daughters, Anna and Emma, were again an utter delight and get on with each other. Anna's husband, a handsome man, was a journalist and went on about the new Queen's South American family. The Dutch, or at least this lot, are surprisingly direct. Instead of saying 'Did you enjoy the Rijksmuseum?' it was immediately 'What are your criticisms?' To Jonathan it was 'Have you got a partner?' But it was all happiness.

On Wednesday we went with Winfrid and his wife Marieke to the great palace of Het Loo. Laura Gatacre had arranged for the head gardener to look after us. William Zelieman remembered me from twenty years ago, when I was filming for the royal gardens series there. It was fascinating to hear the results of the latest research revealing that, for example, as initially restored it was inaccurate. No parterre ever had box hedges like that! They were instead about eight inches high. Struck by the box disease, they were bit by bit being replaced by *Ilex crenata* [that, too, was not a success]. We saw both the Queen's and the King's Gardens as they had been replanted in the new manner. It was fascinating as such a treatment throws huge emphasis on the plants, which will look enormous, soaring above such minute hedging. The ilex calls for cutting twice in a season and they've invented a tiny trimmer with which to do this.

10 OCTOBER

Remembrance

This is the tenth anniversary of Julia's death. It is the first one when I could not go to the 8 a.m. Mass at the cathedral and hear her name mentioned at the altar. No matter, Andrew Piper will do it and, as I told him, she would very much be on my mind when I was MC for the 10 a.m. Eucharist on Sunday 6 October. Somehow that was inevitably very powerful and meaningful for me.

Oh God, how the years fly; and yet it all seems like yesterday but so much has changed: I have, the house has, so has the garden, so has my pattern of life. What am I to make of it all? I'm still seized periodically with grief, particularly if anything like music from one of her operas or ballets is played. I also see the contacts with the past vanish: people like David Walker and Patrick Garland were links in a chain of shared creativity now gone. I plug on with the garden and her wish that somehow it would go on, but I'm painfully aware that without my massive changes the chances would be slimmer than they are. But I'm not there yet.

I'm also aware that I've opened the place up to a far wider circle of people and have joined in as far as I can in the life of the county. All of this seems right to me and I give thanks for it. But I give thanks too for those thirty-two years of marriage, which seem ever more distant. As that old priest said so many years ago, it doesn't matter how great the tragedy, there is within it a blessing to be found if you look for it. I know that to be true.

6 NOVEMBER

A London day of contrast

I went to the Secession portrait exhibition at the National Gallery and found it incredibly interesting. Before that I did a piece for radio with Christopher Frayling about what I did in respect of modern and contemporary design at the V&A. I took Antonia Fraser to lunch at Avenue in St James's. She looked good and fresh but is rightly cautious after her back operation. *Perilous Question* had sold 10,000 copies, so she was well pleased, and she's already on to her childhood memories. Harold remains a huge loss to her and we spoke of the continuance of grief and tried to figure out what the afterlife would be like. In spite of her back she had been to New York for a great event in her role as Widow Pinter. I sense that she feels quite lonely at times. In my case coping with so much domestic helps, all of which she doesn't, I think, do. I'm terribly fond of her and she's all too vulnerable. She'll be in a position to go to things by New Year.

The rest of the day was ghastly. The Lady Mayoress of the City of London, Dr Claire Gifford, had cornered me ages ago to launch a catalogue of the Mansion House sculpture by Julius Bryant, a figure from my past. The event was a mess. We had to be there by 4 p.m., when there was booze, cake and sandwiches, and she and her husband appeared for a spell. The mayoral couple then vanished to a state banquet while we were left stranded until a dinner at 7.30 p.m. God knows who all the people were but at least I had an intelligent conversation with a Wyckhamist journalist on the *Independent*. It went on and on and on. After the dinner there followed a tour of the private rooms, which included the Old Ballroom and an amazing sequence of private rooms with over-the-top rococo stucco work. All of this I thought should be open to the public and the Mayor moved out. This was a Wagnerian occasion, six hours in all. I was not amused.

14 NOVEMBER

I order a racing tricycle

By now I had learnt the hard way that you can't learn balance at seventy-eight. The ever-resourceful Jonty discovered the Tricycle Association, which opened a new period in my life.

I set off with Jonty Williams to Tiddington near Oxford to meet Geoff Booker the trike-maker. Jonty's a delightful person who gradually tells me much about himself and at seventy-eight I'm still intrigued by people. We eventually arrive at a small bungalow in Tiddington, where we're greeted by Mrs Booker, a large, cheerful, smiling lady who immediately offers us tea or coffee. Geoff is in his workshop, a two-storey garage with Tudor leaded windows. Geoff is a man of slight build in his working clothes, a toolmaker of sorts, now retired, and a triker! He had even made a tandem trike for them both.

This was an amazing workshop, full of machinery and parts, everything boxed or in compartments in neat order. At this point Jonty, who had done a cycle mechanics course, took over and the conversation was beyond me – about wheels and hubs and stress on the trike – it was a whole new world to me. Geoff handled and passed on to us to look at some of the precision parts he had made. It was a two-hour session with a large form to be filled in by him with all the details he needed to know. We saw his own trike collection in a separate shed in the garden. Mine will cost about £3,600 so it ought to be a masterpiece! [It was. I am still riding it!]

3 DECEMBER

Art school folly

Monty Don arrives with a film crew for an episode in his craft series. He must be close to sixty, not good looking at all but engaging and with fine eyes. Three young students had been throwing clay pots modelled on one at Hampton Court, which I was to judge. Two of the three were not in a good way, one with Parkinson's and another with MS. Really sad, but also a monument to those with anything wrong with them being put on to pottery! What was sadder was their lack of craft skills, not their fault as they are no longer taught them in art schools. They are told to express themselves! This is ghastly as they can't properly until they have mastered the craft grounding. One lass said that she'd learnt more in the last fortnight through being in Jim Keeling's workshop at Whichford Potteries than in all her time at college!

21 DECEMBER

The winter solstice!

I came up to London on the Thursday in order to read a poem by Longfellow at the Westminster Cathedral Christmas Concert. I took Penny Graham, always good company and an asset. There were drinks with the Archbishop before – a gathering of Catholics high and low, including the Governor of the Bank of England, Mark Carney, who was rather small in stature. I liked Vincent Nichols, hugely welcoming and very good at circulating. We didn't know anyone but it didn't matter. It was great fun.

Then we went in to discover a full house and, after the by now drear monotony of Nine Lessons and Carols, it was quite a relief to come to something different. There was a large stage with an orchestra at the front and the very good choir banked behind. There was much upping and downing of the lights for theatrical effect. It was a *mélange* of carols, parts of which we all sang, Christmas liturgical bits by Poulenc and sections lifted from oratorios by Handel and Bach. There were seven readers and, as John Tusa didn't turn up, the Bank of England Governor was called in. I was number seven and we all read from the pulpit, me using my sub-Gielgudian voice! The Archbishop gave a short address – regrettably read, whereas a few spontaneous words from the heart would have been far better.

22 DECEMBER

Stanley Spencer

I went to see the paintings by Stanley Spencer from the chapel at Burghclere in Berkshire which were on display, all bar the Resurrection scene, at Somerset House. I knew they were marvellous, although I'd never seen them until now. Tears came the whole time: they were so overwhelming – working from the principle that depicting scenes of just daily existence in a hospital with a mental wing (which Spencer did) had more punch than battlefield punch-up and slaughter. I left emotionally knocked out.

31 DECEMBER

The year in retrospect

So, looking back at 2013, I'm lucky to be in the state I'm in. I'm sure that three times a week to the gym is important. I also think that slowing down and coming out of London has been important, and saying 'No'. The flat was on the market at a whopping price compared with what I paid for it in 1983.

It's been a good year but I miss Jonathan, who has gone to the West Coast of the USA, and his bright young friends. Yes, the doctor was right that they energise one in old age and the one thing that I can't stand is boring old people! However, the little early autobiography has had wonderful reviews and garden opening has been a huge success. The Colonnade looks amazing and after initial difficulties with Clive Boursnell over the book [*Remaking a Garden*], that's settled down. I still can't imagine who will buy it. I've settled in to a new rhythm of life for London, and truthfully want much less of it. At the moment I'm putting together my India talks for a February tour. When I get back from that I'll start pulling together the book on Shakespeare's gardens.

The project with John Swannell seems to have run into the ground. The National Portrait Gallery won't exhibit the photographs and we're left wondering how to proceed with them. On the other hand, as they are all of me they could attract a swipe. Who knows? I'm now just an old gent living in the country, and you'd have to be pretty old to remember my museum era.

2014

Jocelyn Burton and Monica Mason

I travelled to London. There were floods everywhere and the
1.14 p.m. train had been cancelled due to problems in the Didcot
area, so it was up via Newport. However, I eventually got to the
Lansdowne Club and thence walked to ROH for Balanchine's
Jewels, to which I took Jocelyn Burton. She arrived dressed like a
Klimt portrait in diaphanous black with asymmetrical gold pat-
terning scattered across it. No lack of work there: she, reflecting so
many in the creative arts, is now dependent on Russian oligarchs.
She'd designed a set of wall sconces for some vast oligarchic mansion
in Moscow but when they were unpacked they were found to be
the wrong colour and she now must supervise their recolouring.
She's finishing a *surtout de table* for the Arts Club, an explosion
of tulips.

Jeffrey Sterling and Felicity Clark were at the next table in the
Crush Bar and, in the second interval, Monica Mason appeared,
which is always a joy. She had with her Tony Dyson, the man to

whom Fred [Ashton] had left the rights of the ballet Julia did with him, *Enigma Variations*. Dyson said that several American companies were interested in it so I gave him my card in hopes! Suddenly at the other table Marguerite Porter sprang up and introduced herself. She had danced the peasant girl with the baskets of cherries in *Month in the Country*, the other ballet Julia designed for Ashton. She was so sweet and so grateful in her memory of Julia that I wanted to cry. I said to Monica how awful the sets and costumes were for *Jewels* and how much better were the ones by Lacroix for the Paris Opera. But Monica told me that it was a take it or leave it package, with no changes allowed. But it's a glorious ballet. I wouldn't miss the uplift of trips like this to London for anything.

8 JANUARY

SNAP! exhibition of modern portraiture at the National Portrait Gallery recalled

First stop the NPG to have coffee with Anne Braybon, who is researching *SNAP!* [staged at the NPG by the Welsh Arts Council in 1971] in connection with the David Bailey exhibition [opening at the NPG on 6 February]. She'd sent me the reviews, which I'd quite forgotten, a litany of shock-horror. She produced photocopies of letters I'd written to Peter Jones of the Welsh Arts Council, which were clear about what I was trying to achieve: to open up the whole subject of portraiture, to bring in cartoon, photography and film. Hockney, Bailey and Scarfe were a pretty strong combination. By having the collaboration of the Welsh Arts Council I was able to distance myself if need be from anything that would upset the still hierarchical and establishment trustees. Also I got someone royal to open it – Princess Alexandra, I think. Anne had a copy of the catalogue, which I haven't got. I'd also forgotten that there was a sound tape of my sitting to Bailey [this doesn't survive].

30 JANUARY

An Abbey meeting

On Thursday there was a pre-Audit Dinner meeting at which James O'Donnell gave a bravura presentation on the music. It costs £2 million per annum to keep that on the road. That was followed by Claire Foster-Gilbert on the new Westminster Institute. There's energy and drive there and it could provide a signal meeting ground in the search for a unifying morality. In the evening there was the usual Audit Dinner and I sat between Guy Weston and the new canon from Worcester.

FEBRUARY

New garden schemes and vestments for the cathedral

This has been a ghastly winter with floods everywhere. The ground is sodden. However, the London flat sold well and as I will be eighty in 2015, this will be last occasion when I will be able to afford to do something major in the garden. So the *thuya* hedge beyond the Yew Garden is to be taken out and that space opened up. It is the area to colonise in the garden and I've done drawings for a grotto-nymphaeum of sorts, into which the lion at present in the Yew Garden will go [it didn't]. The angles of that patch of land are so odd that this piece of 'scenery' can't go that far back. I'm anxious to get water and electricity in but there's an existing pond that has to be got rid of. As usual all this will be done as we go along. It will start with a classical screen based on a triumphal arch, ten feet high and fifteen feet wide. When that is up we can then work out the foreground. I see rocks and ferns. I've also begun inquiries about getting the electricity transformer moved [a blot on the garden for forty years]. Decades ago the Midland Electricity Board would have moved it for nothing but alas, they told me that they could not get the agreement of the owner of that patch of land.

On 27 January Michael Tavinor came to supper and I indicated that he could go ahead on ordering a decent set of green vestments. He brought the fabric samples and we confirmed the choice on 1 February: dark green damask with gold orphreys edged in red and gold braid. And I want a proper set including a dalmatic for the MC and a vestment for the crucifer.

I was asked to finance a project for resiting the font at the west end of Hereford Cathedral but the cost escalated on a scale such that I had in the end to withdraw.

3 FEBRUARY

Commemorating the First World War

This was one of those Abbey suppers where information was transmitted and viewpoints expressed. The gathering consisted of John Hall all in black (where was his Order of the Bath badge, I asked), ebullient, flanked by Jane Hedges, who is to be Dean of Norwich; Clare [Foster-Gilbert], the Lord Mayor of Westminster, bright and stylish; the other canons; Stephen Lamport; Martyn [Atkins] the Methodist; Stephen [Spurr] of Westminster School; and Andrew Tremlett.

There was much discussion as to how to mark 4 August and the

375

outbreak of the First World War. The idea of a vigil with the snuffing of candles in the Abbey was much liked and applauded. There were hopes of transmitting that to parish churches, but I don't see that happening as it would be too expensive. There was much concern that a service to which the Queen was going is to be held in Glasgow after the Commonwealth Games, so that the bunting would have to be swept away overnight. Lively discussions followed but I pointed out that the main commemoration would surely be Remembrance Sunday, that everyone would be away in August and that by Christmas everyone would be fed up with the First World War. Stephen Lamport then read out a list of First World War events which called for special services. All too much and surely, I said, some could be lumped into Commonwealth Day?

We were all there at 9.30 p.m., the witching hour when women in the church and human sexuality sank in Synod.

4 FEBRUARY

Lunch at Christie's

The lunch at Christie's was all male and given by Francis Russell, who usually garners in the dowagers. A gathering like this rather makes me glad that I never ended up in a saleroom. Among the other male guests there was Clive Aslet, Jonathan Marsden, Augustine Ford, Mark Lennox-Boyd (all looking slightly the worse for wear, balding, crumpled and faces now lined) and Philip, brother of Edward Harley, together with four others whom I don't remember. A good lunch of cheese soufflé, venison with veg and a mini *tarte tatin* washed down with good wine. Francis Russell always seems to have the whole art world stitched up. I didn't know that Lloyd Kenyon had a boyfriend – and, in retrospect, who cares? Jonathan

Marsden doesn't have time to breathe, keeping the show on the road at Buckingham Palace and Holyrood, and left early (the Queen had summoned him). And, of course, one or two there were collectors or money men. I couldn't stand going back into that world and, exhausted, I went back to the Garrick Club for a sleep to recover.

18 FEBRUARY

Changes while I go to India

This has been a ghastly winter and I can hardly face any more rain and flood. I leave behind me a battery of workmen as I fly to India. Chris Reeks along with two assistants will move in to patch up paintwork inside, paint the entrance hall dark Victorian green, which will show off the paintings, and also the ante-room, again in a shade of green. Four builders are working on the footings for the greenhouse and dismantling the old garage hidden behind the Colonnade. Two or three more men from Ross Tree Services came to continue clearing the area beyond the Yew Garden. Charlie pointed out to me that one of the juniper *arizonica* in the Spring Garden was leaning at a perilous angle and could fall and wreck the Yew Garden, so down it and two others came. This has been a beastly winter. Gary Grimmitt of Haddonstone sent through a drawing he did from my sketch for the Grotto and I OK'd it. I also asked if he had any more classical bits and pieces with which I could frame the 'ruined' arch.

18 FEBRUARY TO 6 MARCH

India revisited

18–19 FEBRUARY

Hyderabad

To Terminal 5 and eventually on to the 1.35 p.m. flight. There were twelve of us all told, all bar one people who had been on the 2012 trip, a really agreeable lot. I upgraded myself to business class and could therefore sleep. Arriving in Hyderabad, which was warm with a blue sky, we booked in to the Taj Krishna. That evening there was a great al fresco dinner given for us by Joanna Worsley's friends Hassan and Zarah. This was quite an event, with a gathering of Hyderabad cognoscenti and those connected with what we know as heritage. That afternoon we had already been to look at the Charminar. It wasn't exactly restored but it was at last fenced off and cleared of posters and graffiti. That was at least a step in the right direction. Then we visited the great mosque nearby with its tombs of the Nizams. Opposite there was a hospital being done up, one of the numerous buildings designed by the British architect Vincent Esch in the 1920s and 1930s.

But, to return to the party, there must have been fifty of us in all. It began with hours of alcohol and starvation but it was done graciously. Many there were historians of Hyderabad, two in particular who had been trained as members of the British Indian Civil Service. It was a happy evening under the stars with the round tables draped in cream damask and lit by candlelight.

20 FEBRUARY

More Hyderabad; stirrings on conservation

Every journey in India takes an age. The coach lumbered its way through jam after jam. This morning our guide walked us through the old palace area of Hyderabad, once thirteen acres but now, in the aftermath of the abolition of the rulers, reduced to one palace, the Chowmahalla. This, thanks to Princess Ezra, has undergone a facelift. When the Nizam was removed some seventeen thousand people were thrown out of work – a cup of tea alone called for twenty-two servants. But they helped themselves to the contents of the palaces or things were sold off. We wandered through the battered, litter-strewn streets, stopping every so often to stare at what remained of a grand palace façade in an over-the-top classical style and all of limestone mortar. Everything was once up and running until the curtain fell and now all we looked at was ruins. The present Nizam, we learnt, lives in Turkey. God knows where the jewels went. But what had been done in the Chowmahalla Palace represented stirrings about conservation. Amir, who was at last night's party, had been involved in the display of royal textiles, a stunning array of the richest dresses.

After lunch we went to the British Residency, still a sad spectacle but here, too, there are stirrings, including an idea that it should be a museum about the Raj. Much is still there but other parts are in desperate decay.

The day ended with an amazing dinner at the Falaknuma Palace, fabulously restored and a glimpse of what had gone. It went on for two hours and there was too much drink.

21 FEBRUARY

Mumbai

A travel day. Packed and up and out by 7.30 a.m. Hyderabad having been such an untidy dump, the airport was a revelation, several miles of impeccable planting along either side of the approach road leading to a modern, spotless airport. So we got to Mumbai, where the traffic is so bad that it took hours to get to the Taj Hotel. I have a lovely room overlooking the Gateway to India. All we did in the afternoon was drive to the Victoria and Albert Museum, which the group loved: Palladian outside and lacy ironwork within, a restored capsule of Victorian England. There was another good sign nearby: they were restoring the arch into the Victoria Gardens.

22 FEBRUARY

Gothic Mumbai

Saturday and a big walk to see all the Victorian Gothic architecture, which was even more marvellous than I remembered it. Everyone was astonished. We even got into Stevens's Town Hall, which our guide said no one had ever achieved before. This had a stunning central staircase, hall and debating chamber, all in the Gothic style.

In the evening we took the party to dinner at the Bombay Yacht Club, which still serves English food of the 1950s, something vaguely resembling a salad, chicken in unutterable brown gravy with a baked potato in foil . . .

23 FEBRUARY

More signs of conservation and restoration

We began with a walk in the Old Docklands area, visiting St Andrew's Kirk where children were rehearsing a service with a banjo, then on to the Writers' Building, past the Customs House and finally to the huge neoclassical Town Hall, which was all boarded up as it was being restored. Suddenly on this trip conservation and restoration have become the buzzwords. The Horniman Circle is almost fully restored. On to St Thomas Cathedral, where we caught the tail-end of a service with crucifer, acolytes and clergy all fully vested. There were good tombs, in the main by John Bacon of heroic soldiers.

The great event of the evening was staged at the Art Deco Liberty Cinema, whose owner was welcoming and charming and who was the son of a man who, in the 1940s, owned some forty cinemas, all in this 'dream machine' style. The event was staged in the private viewing theatre. Joanna went ahead but had an awful time putting the drinks and supper together as nothing promised had been done. But she's a marvel and so was the technician. The viewing theatre was perfect in every period detail and screened the 1903 and 1911 Durbars and a chunk of the Mountbatten television series when he was the last Viceroy. Dinner followed on the terrace, ending a remarkable evening.

24 FEBRUARY

Lucknow and the Mutiny

Up and off early for the short flight to Lucknow and another Taj Hotel, this time in the classical colonial style. By then I'd had too much food, so had two apples and water for lunch. In the evening I gave my talk on the Mutiny, which they loved, and we had a pretty candlelit dinner on the terrace. The food was fabulous and the chef appeared. I made a speech and we all applauded.

25 FEBRUARY

More restoration

We set off at 9.30 a.m. for La Martinière, which was as weird and extraordinary as I remembered it. Here again restoration was under way. Then on to the Residency, beautiful ruins but somehow the Mutiny and the story of Relief are slipping away. However, the area has huge potential if it is used to bring to life the cantonment. The museum is ghastly.

We had a good Indian lunch with too much food again, after which we went shopping and I bought a glittering *sherwani*. There was then what was billed as a Victorian walk but the traffic was so noisy that we couldn't hear what the guide said. But that ended in a proper bookshop, small and old-fashioned and presided over by a venerated, gracious ninety-five-year-old. Hazan, our guide, saluted him with a gesture of reverence. The man had been running this bookshop since 1942. He had very successful children in the UK: a son a barrister and a daughter a designer.

In the evening we stayed put in the hotel. Six of us met for a drink and followed it with a loquacious supper in the coffee shop.

Beatrix Miller remembered

Beatrix died while I was in India.

I've lost one of my oldest friends and yet I can't mourn. In the last few weeks I've been lighting a candle in the cathedral and praying that God would take her. I'm glad that He did. Every Saturday from about 1990 onwards I would ring her at about 6 p.m. and we would chatter away and scream with laughter. But then, about three years ago, she had a fall in that Mulberry Walk flat and that was the onset of the long run down. She remained bedridden and wouldn't even attempt to get up. Those last twenty-five years remain a complete enigma to me.

She was the one who, all those years ago, spotted me as what was billed a 'Vogue First'. The list was a brilliant one of the movers and shakers in the world of creativity in the late Sixties and Seventies. She sent Cecil Beaton to photograph me and the rest is history. I found her formidable, sitting in that office in Hanover Square, usually disguised behind a pair of dark glasses. On the floor would be spread the next issue, coming together bit by bit as she juggled it around. Always there would be a handful of memorable photographs: Beaton, Bailey, Snowdon, Donovan. These were her golden years with a galaxy of talent: Grace Coddington, Barney Wan, Marina Warner, Pamela Harlech, Bernard Nevill, etc. For a time I was an unlisted contributing editor and wrote quite a lot for *Vogue*. This was the era when Beatrix would give dinners at Mulberry Walk and everyone who was anyone in that Sixties scene was there.

But it's what happened after that was so extraordinary. She was on the Council of the Royal College of Art for a bit but nothing else really. She bought a house in Wiltshire, which she loved but domestically she was hopeless. She couldn't boil an egg. Nor did she even attempt to master new technology. So she sat in that large, gloomy room tapping away at an electric typewriter. One book was to be based on the letters she'd written to her sister in and after the Second World War, during which she was evacuated to Canada. She was in Paris during the post-war fashion ferment and told me that her first lover was a spy. He was the mysterious fifth man in the Blunt–Philby affair. She was always terrified that someone would find that out. She never finished that book. I got Julia MacRae to look at it and edit it but that didn't work as Beatrix didn't want anything cut out. Her other book was to be called *After a Fashion* and God knows how far she got with it. It would have been a great look into that golden era: she was always talking about the letters and papers she had from then.

She promised to leave me Patrick Proctor's watercolour of Cecil Beaton but I would bet that she'd never written that down [she hadn't]. At any rate, I told her nephew Charles Winstanley that I'd help in any way. Beatrix saw me as her literary executor but didn't, I think, put that down either. I wrote offering any help.

Vogue is notoriously mean and Beatrix had never saved or invested so she got miserably poor. She had to sell the country place and was always looking for what else she could dispose of. She was a woman who could have given so much later in life but didn't. She adored her nieces and nephews and was very upset when Charles's marriage collapsed. He asked me about a church service of thanksgiving. Quite wrong, I said. It should be a secular celebration of her in a hotel or somewhere and *Vogue* ought to do it. She was, after all, legendary.

Mercifully, there were 'saints' who tended her: Ingrid Bleichroeder was one and Felicity Clark another, both *Vogue* staff at one time. But Beatrix lived till ninety. I never saw her in her final, bedridden years. I used to fix a date with her to go and then she would cancel it. I don't think that she wanted me to see her like that. I shall miss her.

She was a rock to me. In my days in office I could turn to her for prudent advice when faced with a media crisis. But most of all she was the deeply human and caring woman whom I rang almost daily to talk to in those weeks when Julia was dying.

The Indian tour resumed

26 FEBRUARY

A weird encounter

A good day visiting the Great Imambara, the Picture Gallery and the Palace of Mourning, by pony and trap. The evening, however, was something else. It was billed as an evening with the Nawab of Lucknow. So off we went to a crumbling house in the grotty outskirts. A curtain of flowered fabric was withdrawn, revealing the Nawab. We had been briefed to wear white bonnets in his presence and that we must incline our heads and make a certain hand gesture, which we all duly did. The Nawab was a fat, bespectacled man in black seated on a trunk with his brother next to him. The room was indescribably filthy and dusty. A motley array of chairs, some plastic, were then arranged in a circle facing him. We sat and looked at him and he smiled at us. Mercifully none of us collapsed into fits of giggles. Somehow an awkward conversation was kept going.

The room was his museum, a collection of junk from the lowest provincial saleroom piled up all over the place, in glass-fronted cabinets, on tables and on the walls. A free handout print of the coronation of George VI was then passed round for us to admire. It was weird. Eventually the subject of textiles came up, at which point his brother revealed himself as a fashion designer (it all arose out of Lucknow's fame for embroidery). A bag full of his stuff was produced and it all suddenly got very animated. He had wonderful taste and the fabrics were exquisite. Caroline Windsor bought a superb diaphanous evening coat.

I think we would have given anything to get out of the place but the die was cast, so up a dirty staircase we went onto an equally dirty roof where tables had been laid for us. Female reports on the loos made us shudder. While we ate, the Nawab cautiously moved around but never sat down. We escaped as soon as we could and all of us, on the morrow, had some form of food poisoning.

27 FEBRUARY

Delhi

A flight from Lucknow to Delhi, where we stayed in the Imperial with its marvellous collection of Raj pictures and prints. We did the usual visit to the Red Fort and I gave my lecture on 'Two Ideal Cities: Shahjahanabad and New Delhi'.

28 FEBRUARY

Lutyens's Viceregal Palace

Off we went to the Viceroy's Palace, this time getting in – but not to that much. The basement was full of portraits of kings and queens and viceroys, pictures demoted from the main floor above. I confess to finding the interior disappointing: a vast marble Valhalla going on forever. Then we had to drive all the way round to the back to get into the gardens, where mobs of Indians were also struggling to get in. To begin with I found the gardens a let-down as we were all chugged along a set route and then, quite suddenly, we were at the back of the palace and here, even though much of the water features didn't work, they fully lived to their legendary fame as great gardens, dazzling and immaculately tended and kept.

After lunch we went to the Anglican cathedral designed by Henry Medd. Although there were the usual hiccups about getting in, it is a wonderful building, grandeur in miniature with its echoes of Palladio, Wren and Vanbrugh. In the evening we clubbed together to give Caroline Windsor a sixtieth-birthday dinner.

I MARCH

Freezing Shimla

We left Delhi after a visit to Humayun's Tomb, where again it was noticeable that restoration work was in progress, paid for by the Muslim Gulf states. Then followed the lengthy journey to Shimla, first by plane to Chandigarh and then a car journey up to Shimla, along the usual poor roads with twists and turns and dramatic vertical drops downwards. We had already been told that the plumbing had broken down at the Oberoi Cecil Hotel and that we were to go on to the Wildflower Hotel, forty minutes from the city and higher up. By then it was snowing so we couldn't be got there either, so were put up overnight instead in Clarkes Hotel, a throw back to the 1920s when people took rooms for the social season. Mine had a hall, sitting room, bedroom, dressing room and bathroom. Not everyone was happy at this turn of events after all the *grande luxe*.

2 MARCH

Chaos in Shimla

Today the whole programme went to the wall. It was so cold that I had to buy a padded jacket. However, our guide, Anil, turned out to be highly efficient and we were welcomed to the old Governor-General's house, Barnes Court, the first group ever to gain admittance. It was very little changed, with a huge Durbar hall which also acted as a ballroom with verandas and nooks off it. There was a grand pseudo-Jacobean staircase, a panelled drawing room, a billiard room and dining room. Then on to the Viceregal Lodge by Henry Irwin. The downstairs was devoid of furnishings but there was a grand entrance hall that soared up three storeys, a drawing room, ballroom and state dining room, regrettably with its ceiling lowered. The Lodge is now a women's postgraduate institute. We were lucky to be taken upstairs, where we saw the vicereine's bedroom, etc., all fascinating. The rooms all had balconies affording views over the mountains.

That afternoon we decamped for the Wildflower Hotel because we had to get there before the snow froze. Even then we found the drive blocked by a lorry, so we had to get out and slither over the ice up to the hotel. This was like an English country house and had been built on the site of Lord Kitchener's house, which had been burnt down in 1996.

3 MARCH

Farewell and homewards

We took a train ride with lovely views across the Himalayas and then went on to the Gaiety Theatre, which we found closed but which Anil managed to get opened. It is a really delightful 1880s theatre with an exhibition of photographs of its amateur productions in the early years, things like *The Mikado* and Wilde's *An Ideal Husband*. Both today and yesterday we walked the promenade used by the British in Raj days, and visited Christ Church. Here again there was the novel introduction of taking one's shoes off as one entered. When did this begin?

There was a final gala dinner at the hotel.

26 MARCH

The Prince of the Pagodas *revisited*

In the evening I went to see David Bintley's attempt at a storyline ballet to match Britten's score for *The Prince of the Pagodas*. Some hope! In this version we were transported to Japan. The choreography for the *corps de ballet* was both crowded and chaotic, some of it more suitable for a musical – there were lots of twirling parasols. Scenically there were endless cloths descending and ascending and the plot left one thinking 'Who cares anyway?' Only in the last fifteen minutes was there anything resembling a ballet, with solos and a few *pas de deux*, but by then the ship had already sunk.

The audience seemed mostly 'papered', or rather, full of sponsors and other ballet-world people. But I was pleased to see Monica Mason, who told me that she had been a pagoda (*sic*) in Cranko's version, moving around the stage but unable to see where she was going, looking for a cross on the floor. At that point she opened a 'window' and handed out a mirror! Monica has just had her second cataract operation and can see blue again. Clement Crisp said that there must be somewhere in hell where people must watch versions of *Pagodas* forever!

27 MARCH

The National Portrait Gallery revisited

In the afternoon I wandered through the NPG to look at a small but somewhat disappointing display of early copies of Holbein portraits. The main advance in this area is via dendrochronology and stems all the way back to me letting Dr John Fletcher the dendrologist in to take pieces off Tudor panels. But everything has moved on since then and my two-volume catalogue of the Gallery's early pictures needs rewriting; but I don't want to climb back into any of it.

There was also a small but powerful display of First World War portraits, all sorts but in the main by Orpen, whom, all those years ago, I thought a crashing bore, but now, suddenly, he sprang to life. It was an incredibly moving show and the tears came.

Round the corner to the National Gallery to see their German exhibition. On seeing it, my old question flashed across my mind: 'Is it a book or is it an exhibition?' This was a book and by Room 3 was a bore.

In the evening I went to the new Sam Wanamaker Playhouse at the Globe. What enchantment, a recreation of one of those early indoor theatres lit with candle-filled chandeliers. It is quite small and intimate. I'd never seen *The Knight of the Burning Pestle* but it was a riot – and oh it was such a relief not to have it in modern dress and lifted away from its period! The whole audience was part of the show and we all roared our approval. I was entranced and must go again as it was such an antidote to the RSC and the NT killing off our early drama by wrenching it out of period.

2 APRIL

A new proposal for the garden's future

Lawrence and Elizabeth Banks came to lunch to discuss the future of The Laskett Gardens. They were strongly against the National Trust, an unwieldy organisation whose gardens now all look the same, and strongly advised an independent charity. That would call for a local rep and we talked about this and that person. Elizabeth said that she would send a list. All of this made me think that I ought really to explore this path very fully because I could set everything up. I would, by the time I die, need to find my 'successor'. The whole ground floor of the house should stay as it is. We would need gardeners and someone who would creatively keep an eye on it, with visits several times a year. We went round the garden and they were amazed. All of this made me think seriously of the independent route. They stressed the importance of an *ex officio* member, someone like the Lord Lieutenant or the Dean.

24 APRIL

Beatrix Miller's archive

In the afternoon I went to Beatrix Miller's studio flat in Mulberry Walk and met her niece Helen to work through her papers. What a sad spectacle! It was very run down. More than forty A4 boxes, all the letters, etc. from her *Vogue* era under date, then various separate boxes: letters to her parents from 1939 into the 1950s, invitations, programmes, papers on her house in the country, etc. No sign of the texts of her two adumbrated books, one an edition of her letters to her sister and the other called *After a Fashion*. At any rate I attempted to put what was there in order and went back to the Garrick exhausted.

28 APRIL

Farewell to Beatrix Miller

I went to bed very early as I had to get up at 5.30 a.m. to get to London to deliver the address at Beatrix's celebration at St George's, Hanover Square, with a drinks and canapés reception in Vogue House afterwards. All went well. Another trip down Memory Lane: Zandra Rhodes like a purple dwarf; Anthony Powell large and on a stick; Kaffe Fassett, once so beautiful but now wrinkled; Marina Warner still beautiful and brilliant; Anna Wintour, a pixie face beneath a page-boy cut; Alex Shulman, who couldn't read to be heard and who has now been editor for twenty-two years; glossy Nicholas Coleridge; Jane Stevens, Princess Margaret's sidekick; Felicity Clark, still pretty good; Tessa Traeger, really sweet and wanting to photograph me again; Pamela Harlech letting her helmet of hair at last grow out white; Clive Boursnell his usual benign gypsy self; Nicky Haslam in city gent pinstripe mode, etc.

9 TO 11 MAY

The Heseltines at Thenford

The Heseltines entertain in the grand manner. Michael must be eighty plus and Anne is going to be that age in October but the show goes on. Thenford is a splendid Palladian mansion with a lake and large acreage which Michael has planted up with over three thousand specimen trees. His *furor hortensis* knows no bounds and never ceases. There are ten gardeners and that's not enough really. The walled garden is all hornbeam kiosks, geometric sheets of water, lawn and gravel. There's a William Pye fountain at its centre but not his best. The rest of it is by George Carter, who struggles a bit with this scale of things but it's pretty damn good, with its immaculate box hedging and yew topiary. Further on there's a vast herbaceous border and a cascade with jets in the manner of the Alhambra. There's a lake, chinoiserie bridges, a swimming pool by Quinlan Terry, stables, a tennis court – everything including, inside, Wi-Fi. There's a butler, a cook, waitresses – the list goes on – and at breakfast there are three copies of every newspaper. The dining table is laden with Georgian silver candlesticks, a stunning epergne, the dinner service is Copenhagen botanical and all the glasses have Michael's crest on them. Even the sheets and pillowcases are covered with broderie anglaise . . . Such comfort. And the house overall splendidly decorated, every wall covered with pictures and every horizontal surface littered with *objets*.

But Michael and Anne are delightful people. They enjoy life and they are generous: at every meal more people appear from nowhere. Both are a little plumper but he's hugely agile for his age. Anne's a trifle stiffer. They are a little remiss in introducing people, so one angles for who is who. The gathering this weekend in the main is a gardening one with Kate Rothschild of Exbury, chair of Kew Gardens, and her husband, Marcus; Amanda Ward (Mrs Gerald Ward II, successor to Rosalind Morrison), who's a botanical painter; an economist peer and his wife; John Nott with his Slovenian wife (much more interesting than I thought, although he knew nothing about my sort of world); David Ekserdjian, professor of art at Leicester who did the splendid bronze exhibition at the RA, who was on the National Gallery board and others but who failed to become its director; and Robin Butler and his delightful wife, Jill.

Robin Butler is someone I thought that I would never see again. For me he embodied 'unfinished business'. Shortly after I resigned the V&A Richard Luce asked me (and, apparently, Julia) to lunch at their flat in Ebury Street to meet Robin Butler (and his wife also apparently, according to her memory). It was a kind of sandwich around a table. As I read it at the time it was a kindly act by Richard Luce in the hopes that I might be offered something or other by the man who was head of the Civil Service (Richard Wilding, who was deputy secretary in the Arts Office, had already told me that I would never again find any form of employment within government). I must have misread this lunch as I saw it at the time as giving me the once-over and deciding against me, for I was not (unlike others) offered one thing by government, ever. But maybe that wasn't what it was all about. That encounter had always haunted me, when all I had striven to achieve in the reformation of two of our greatest national institutions was seemingly damned and I was cut adrift at fifty-two with only £12,000 per annum to live on. It wasn't helped either that weekend when, sitting next to Jill Butler, she said to me: 'You're an OM aren't you?' 'No,' I replied, 'I'm just a common knight.'

I love the Heseltines for their energy and delight in life. The garden is astounding and I made the usual suggestions for its improvement! It is all on a huge and ever-expanding scale. Never fewer than twelve sat down to any meal and, with guests, it could rise to eighteen.

This is life on some scale. But they're an inspiration for retaining a glorious enthusiasm.

12 TO 13 MAY

Me as a love-sick Elizabethan, an Edwardian peer and a Beefeater

John Swannell arrived with his new assistant, Rosie. The idea was to reproduce an Elizabethan portrait but it didn't work, and then I remembered the Nicholas Hilliard miniature of the Earl of Northumberland reclining full-length amidst the greensward with hedges nearby. He was also all in black, with a book to hand and a handkerchief. The result when it came was the best of these three – with a jewel-like Pre-Raphaelite quality to the grass and wild flowers.

Next day it was the grand aristo in court dress and ermine and crimson velvet mantle in Dore Abbey. Three good pictures were taken; the one I liked best was that in which I was looking away from camera. And then the Yeoman of the Guard, initially done at Dore but then I rang Jan Lucas-Scudamore and so off we went to Kentchurch, where there was a wonderful, huge old door which was the perfect backdrop. What can be done these days is amazing: the correct blade and tassel at the top of the halberd can be dropped in from another photo!

3 JUNE

Les Carmélites, Grimsthorpe Castle and two arts festivals

Last night I took Antonia Fraser, in a pretty blue and white jacket, to Poulenc's *Dialogues des Carmélites,* an opera I had always wanted to see. It lived up to expectations in a stripped-back production that had already played in several other houses, but it worked well, making use of a large assembly of people put together from those who literally live on the streets. They made up the crowd, shuffling this way and that in a semi-balletic manner. The first half was better than the second. By then the director's inventiveness was flagging.

This has been an appallingly busy period, not all of my own making. Why on earth did I say 'yes' to giving a lecture in Lincolnshire in aid of the St John Ambulance? It effectively knocked three days out of my week. I stayed with Jocelyn Burton's sister, who is one of those ladies on every committee.

The event itself was at Grimsthorpe, that mighty monument to Vanbrugh. Everything there was in tip-top shape in what was a wildly inconvenient building for modern living, all endless long corridors with rooms off. I was put into the Tapestry Bedroom for the night, a room of great splendour. There had been an American marriage in the early twentieth century and, as a result, the whole place was done up rather well. Jane Willoughby was a slight, intelligent figure on a stick (she'd fallen over in London), who seemed ludicrously out of scale for such a vast house with virtually no staff. I saw everything I wanted to see, except two rooms whose doors were ajar and through which I could see that they were stuffed with Lucien Freuds. I was told that any time he was on the rocks she bailed him out. But I don't think that she loved the place. She was just stuck with it and clearly preferred her Scottish house, Drummond Castle, with its vast semicircular parterre.

The Hay Festival this year was a mud bath as the rain fell and fell. I was on the Tuesday together with Clive Boursnell. I didn't expect much of an audience for a garden book [*Remaking a Garden: The Laskett Transformed*] but some 750 turned up and we got a standing ovation. The next day I did Radio 4 *Midweek* with a somewhat whispery Libby Purves, but I was on top form. The book has been well received and its originality recognised. Clive was a star turn on the photographs, really good.

And then there was the Broadway Arts Festival. I could have done without that but Brian Sewell had had to cancel (he was to go into the Marsden where they told him that alas his cancer was too far gone and they couldn't operate) and I stepped in. Adrienne Corri had found someone in Birmingham who probably would have done it, but Brian had stepped in when I had pneumonia in 2008 or 2009 so it was the least I could do. But it meant working the room and lecturing, so it was tiring!

12 JUNE

Althorp revisited

It was the first day of the Althorp literary festival and the weather was glorious. I first came here I think in 1969, and again with Julia when Raine 'reigned'. But this time it's the next generation, Charles Spencer and wife number three, Karen (he's her number two), a svelte Canadian, bright and welcoming. The house had been redecorated and rearranged yet again! But it looked splendid. They to and fro from a house in Los Angeles and between them they have six children so far.

Charles is slightly chubby with a real Spencer face, bright and with a genuine gift for the pen. He loves the place and much has been put in order: the roof and outer walls for a start. But this is sponsorship time, so there are pavilions on the front lawns and rooms set up with silver for sponsored lunches and dinners and a small army of hired cooks, waiters and security men. The sponsors were Christie's, *Harpers and Queen* and Aston Martin, ergo cars were parked in front of the house. It was all very casual and all the others there, bar Jane

Gardam, seemed about thirty. I felt quite ancient amidst all this pretty and sparkling and leggy flesh. Daisy Goodwin, for whom I did *The Diets That Time Forgot*, popped up. There was only one speaker at a time so it was quite a sparse festival. On the second day, Friday 13 June, *Any Questions* is to be broadcast from here.

There was a grand dinner in the evening, twenty-four to thirty at table, with all the silver and white flowers. I sat on my hostess's left and on my left was the ebullient Emma Bridgewater, married to Matthew Rice (son of Pat Albeck and Peter Rice), who sat opposite. I enjoyed her as she was full of energy, with no flagging. Matthew is fifty-seven and she mid-fifties, I suppose. After dinner Charles did a house tour. Architecturally the stables are the thing. The house itself is an oddity, with huge rooms leading on to each other but hung with wonderful portraits, the Picture Gallery itself a dazzling set-piece of Restoration period beauties, for the most part in 'Sunderland' frames. I began to conceive of a book on the country house portrait gallery.

16 JUNE

Preparing for a mega shoot

I spent most of the day with John Swannell at Angels. One of their young girls was in attendance as we put together costumes for a half-length in the manner of Ingres, a romantic figure *c*.1820 with his head turned over his shoulder to the spectator, huge wings to his shirt collar and a swagger cloak; a half-length of a Whig in a wig – velvet coat with large cuffs and cravat; a David Wilkie *c*.1810 Scot in masses of tartan – kilt, socks, jacket, cloak, sporran, etc. – not all matching; and, finally, a Grand Tour aristocrat in the manner of Batoni, but nothing quite like the portrait I had had in mind. Then on to Jan Sewell, the number one make-up and hair lady. All of this was hard work to get everything as right as we could get it.

In the evening Antonia took me to *Tosca* with Bryn Terfel as Scarpia and the new sensation, Sondra Radvanovsky, as Floria Tosca. And she was a sensation, with a marvellous voice aligned to powerful acting abilities.

17 JUNE

The mega shoot

Up to Highgate and a very, very long and concentrated day, beginning with President Lincoln. Jan arrived with Clive Lever, my hairdresser. And so began the demolition of my facial hair or, at least, the bits of it they couldn't use for Lincoln. It was a huge operation and took a long time and I couldn't bear the idea of what I'd look like, having worn a moustache since 1970. Eventually I emerged as Lincoln in a way that I was unrecognisable. The plan is to copy the famous statue in Washington and therefore there was much posing and placing of hands in mid-air, resting on non-existent arms.

Next came a quickie, Lord Kitchener – 'Your country needs you' – but with no white gloves for the right hand. That was done the next day. Jan, who had been amazing on Lincoln, never quite got Kitchener's moustache right but John said he could fix that. Then I was cleaned up and had the shock of seeing myself, not helped by my own hair being pinned down to take a wig. Oh God, what a horror of old age – but then I will be seventy-nine in a few weeks' time and, I suppose, looked at in that light I'm not too bad. Then there was the decision as to what I should do between shoots. The next morning I looked in the bathroom mirror and began to get used to it. But by then Clive had tousled my hair like Chopin's!

However, to revert to the sittings. We banged on after lunch in the garden. Marianne Swannell is a sweetheart and it was proper lunch with chicken and salad, cheese and good bread and little pieces of brownie and a couple of glasses of white wine. And then back to work, recreating that extraordinary photograph of Toulouse Lautrec sitting to himself. Both the afternoon shoots were far easier, although how John is going to turn me into a dwarf I'm not sure. More wig, beard and make-up and pince-nez, then bang, bang and it was done. Happy smiles!

Then came Isambard Brunel. A cloth was set up in the garden with Clive and Rosie propping it up. I love that Howlett photograph of Brunel against a bank of chains. There's a stubborn indifference to looks and the camera's eye, so his clothes are crumpled and worn askew. He has a cigar drooping from one side of his mouth and that amazing top hat. An irresistible persona. Bang, bang and it was over even quicker than any of the others.

What a day! I took John and Marianne out to dinner in Hampstead and collapsed into bed afterwards. There's a wonderful rapport between us. But we need to think of sponsors and the logistics of it, having got Sandy Nairne to say that he would reconsider it.

21 JUNE

Fundraising for St Peter's Church, Ross on Wye

The day of the garden event at The Laskett in aid of St Peter's, Ross. It was Midsummer's Day, perfect weather and the garden at its luxuriant height. It was a sell-out to over two hundred people. Entry was phased so that there was a steady flow, including three local mayors and their consorts with their chains on. It was a touch Riseholme, but no matter, for it was fun and a delight with something happening on and off all over the garden. There was lots of music – a flautist, a group of madrigal singers with a second group near the pleached lime avenue. Then there was a group of the young doing bits of *A Midsummer Night's Dream* around the Shakespeare Monument and Beaton steps, the local ballet school dancing the 'Valse des Fleurs' from *Nutcracker* on the hour in the Colonnade, a painter with an easel in the Rose Garden, the Mad Hatter's Tea Party near the house and a bevy of yet more young carrying baskets of sprays of lavender or local goodies to nibble. There was a Pimm's tent at the top of the drive and tea in the conservatory. It ended at 8 p.m. and by 9 p.m. you wouldn't have known that it had happened. They raised about £5,000. Perfect.

24 JUNE

An old colleague visits

Sue Runyard and her partner, together with a very pleasant gay pair, came to see the garden. She was my PR at the V&A during that awful period in the mid-1970s. She later made a career for herself in the USA at the Getty and then set up her own consultancy, and now she's back in England again. She's still a pretty woman but much larger. It was a delight to see her.

In the evening I went over to Shan Egerton at Hay and we saw the relayed new production of *Manon* from the ROH with Jonas Kaufman. Wonderful music and singing but a horrible production set in the USA, I suppose, with Manon as a kind of Dolly Parton.

LATE JUNE

'Sir Portrait' continues

This morning I went with John to an emporium in the middle of nowhere near Potters Bar, to be fitted with a suit of armour for G.F. Watts's Sir Galahad. This was a bungalow with an encampment of tents and sheds with rows of suits of armour, all of it run by a man called Nick who has six sons. Various attendants came and went as layers of chain mail and armour were put on me. It would have been very easy to have fallen over: the only way to let the stuff be put on me was to cling to the putter-on. It was wildly funny and interlaced with anecdotes of Ian McKellen, who is apparently wonderful to work with on film but a stage nightmare: 'Oh, you can't have that sword. It's *Lord of the Rings!*' But I was well suited and everyone said that I looked good in it.

6 JULY

Trinity vestments

On Sunday the sung Eucharist was prefaced by the blessing of the Trinity vestments I had given to the cathedral. This was a charming event with the recipients lined up and one by one I took each one his or her vestment. The invoice has yet to come! They are beautiful, made of good fabric, lined and generous of cut. The fall and the folds look good and Michael Tavinor told everyone that the backs were to be flipped and the fronts reversed so that hands rested on the lining.

10 JULY

The National Trust again

To fix anything like a delegation coming here at the moment would be a ghastly saga but it did happen. Dame Helen Ghosh and two trustees, Keith James and Orna NiChionna. They went round the garden with the sound guide on a day when it was open for groups and in the evening for a reception by the Welsh Historic Gardens Trust, not to mention a summit meeting about a new septic tank! It all seemed to go well. I said that there were three options: that the National Trust takes it, that a private trust is created or that it is destroyed on my demise. But, they said, there's a fourth option: a trust or organisation that is affiliated to the National Trust. They would come forward with a package. This was a limping step forward and, if agreed, this would go to their September meeting. So there is movement at last.

JULY

A love affair with a trike

I love my trike, and my lessons and rides with Jonty – and those I make on my own – are a great treat. Jonty tells me that my recovery rate is that of a man of fifty and he's astonished how I can take on the steepest hills [not true – but I did in 2017!]. So once or twice a week we have a ride together. I'm still learning about gears and also trying to establish a number of circular routes to and from The Laskett that I can ride on my own. Alas, I shall be in Italy when the Churches Ride and Stride takes place but Jonty's planning a ride to The Laskett all the way from Ledbury [it never happened].

17 JULY

Sir Galahad and the white horse

Up and off early to John Swannell – too early – but eventually we set off for Dorset at 10 a.m. on a glorious summer's day, with a car packed with chain mail and armour and his assistant, Rosie. It was an over three-hour drive but we eventually arrived at what had been Liz Frink's house, with her studio still standing. A great country house had been demolished and bits and pieces of the old stable block had been cobbled together to make a courtyard house with a fountain at its centre. It was very French in feel, with clipped standard greenery in enormous containers placed as sentinels. The interior living area was very open and roomy with a vast kitchen space opening out onto a spacious terrace. This had a stunning view sloping down to three small ponds or lakes surrounded by the good park planting of the old house, and beyond that nothing but distant landscape. Patty Lowe, who must be in her fifties, was hugely welcoming. She loves her garden, her vegetables, her horses, pigs and whatever else. She's also a natural cook and lunch was rustled up out of nowhere. I wish I had that skill!

And then to work. I put on the chain-mail suit and staggered down to location one, where I was piece by piece encased in the armour. The white horse, a sweet, gentle creature, arrived with attendants and did everything we wanted. No sun but we plugged on, me holding the reins, resting my hand on my thigh, the horse bending down, and me, head tilted dramatically to one side, gazing as though glimpsing some vision. That went and on and then I was allowed a breather and the armour was doffed and I sat down while John found setting number two, with a gnarled old tree. The sun came out and off we went again. And then, bang, it was all over.

I was tired. Gordon Robson, Patty's husband, appeared back from London and we all drank too much. Patty produced a gorgeous supper, which we ate on the terrace, and I went to bed, zonked, at 10 p.m.

18 JULY

Cecil Beaton recalled

Up and off we went back via Salisbury to see the Beaton exhibition at the museum in the Cathedral Close. It turned out to be extraordinarily good, a meandering walk through awkward rooms as we journeyed from Ashcombe to Reddish. There it all was, recalling so much I remembered so well, with masses of unseen snaps and photographs and books and scrapbooks and snatches of film. There was not too much on the garden or on the Wiltshire circle, but in the main on Beaton himself and the importations. So lots of Edith Olivier, Rex Whistler, Oliver Messel, Peter Watson, Garbo, Stephen Tennant, et al. The recreated circus bed was as awful, as I always thought it would be. But in its early days much of Ashcombe recalled my own early days of home-making with 'junk' from cheap antique shops. Ashcombe was Sitwell baroque/rococo, Reddish late Victorian splendour laced with a touch of the French eighteenth century. But I was so glad to have seen it, recalling a wonderful period of my life when I learnt so much.

28 TO 29 JULY

The final sittings

I travelled up to London for the final two days' shoot with John
Swannell. Monday was an early start and we gathered at 7 North
Road by 7 a.m., Rosie along with Jan Sewell, queen of wigs and
make-up – and how! The vehicle was piled high with cameras, reflec-
tors, lights, costumes, etc. Everything went smoothly at Hampton
Court and, as John said, planning was all-important. By now I'm
so used to undressing down to my underpants that it comes as an
automatic reaction. Jan shaved my face flat and applied Henry
VIII's whiskers, modelled on the Chatsworth version of the famous
Holbein portrait. For some inexplicable reason Angels had a splendid Henry VIII costume in shades of russet, green and gold. John
set up in the small hall next to the Great Hall and unrolled a carpet
he'd brought with him in front of a late fifteenth-century tapestry. I
arranged myself in the famous pose and then bang, bang, and that
was it. Done. John produced a print the next day, an amazing one,
among the very best so far.

So back we went to 7 North Road for a bite and for me to be
made up as a Batoni gentleman, to be shot in the Soane Museum.
Incredibly, Jan transformed me into a 1770s gentleman – quite
remarkable – and off we went to the Museum. Again John had done
his homework and I found a niche stuffed with antique casts, and
bang, bang, another was done. I suggested that we did the Kneller
Whig in a wig here, a half-length wearing a vast wig, velvet coat and
stock. We found a place on the stairs and I gestured, and bang, bang,
that was done.

Next day we pressed on yet again, starting with the Piero della
Francesca portrait of Federico da Montefeltro *en profile* wearing that

extraordinary hat; then came the Ingres and Jan transformed my old features into a Mr Darcy with tousled Romantic hair. Looking in the mirror, I thought that I ought to stay like it! The finale was a Wilkie-type Bonnie Scot striding through the Scottish countryside. Practically anything goes as Scottish dress at this period, so we just layered it up. I adopted a foot-thrust-forward pose, as though walking through the Highlands, and it all came together. Bang, bang, and that was it.

That evening I took John and Marianne out for a celebratory dinner. It all ended on a high. All we need to do is firm up the NPG, which keeps wavering. They could stage this any time until 23 August 2016, when I'll be eighty-one! I can't understand the endless dithering by Sandy Nairne.

4 AND 5 AUGUST

The First World War remembered

I travelled up to the Abbey for this and took Frances Stainton. As usual there was a great deal of hustle and bustle. Camilla represented the Queen, a leg-up I would have thought, all the royal women being scattered hither and thither at other events and all wearing off-white or cream. The service must have been terribly difficult to compile. We all lit candles and then, one by one, various sections of the congregation blew theirs out. There were four parts to the service, with four candles snuffed by various luminaries. Then came a procession down to the tomb of the Unknown Warrior and, finally, Camilla snuffed out the remaining candle. All of it evolved from Sir Edward Grey's comment about the lights going out all over Europe. Each section had its own sequence of readings, music and prayers. Apart from Sebastian Faulks, the readers were a trifle disappointing, lacking strength and variety. Both pulpits were used and the event was televised, and indeed the snatches that I saw on television were inevitably better than the reality of actually experiencing the service from a fixed viewpoint in the choir.

The commemoration has produced a huge outpouring of events in the form of services and community involvement. I found it all a bit eerie in the light of the ghastly falling apart of the Middle East and the situation in Ukraine. Dominic Sandbrook's piece in the *Mail* on the 5th was brilliant. We should have kept out of it but the drive by politicians in the USA and here to intervene was always disastrous. We are still living with the consequences and we still haven't learnt to keep out. The Middle Eastern mess is a monument to intervention.

7 TO 11 AUGUST

Franco Maria Ricci and the labyrinth at Fontanellato

I've been coming to Masone now for thirty years or thereabouts. It never changes, yet it does. Laura is as pretty and sparkling as ever, always providing a succession of simple and memorable meals from produce bought that day in the nearby town of Fontanellato: *frutta fresca*, pasta with an amazing variety of sauces, *insalata*, *frittate* – it all seems so effortless. Everything here works to a time schedule way out of kilter with my own. People drift in to breakfast at 10 a.m., lunch is at gone 2 p.m. and dinner at 9 p.m. if you are lucky. But it suits me. I don't particularly want to go anywhere. I'm given the so-called presidential suite, sanctified by Giscard d'Estaing, who once stayed in it. It is its own little world of bedroom, bathroom, a working area and a tiny courtyard with a table and chair to sit at. I can do here what I can never seem to do at The Laskett: sleep – ten hours the first night! And then I can quietly sit and read undisturbed. I never seem to be able to do that any more at home, which is always buzzing with a litany of things that have to be done: emails, the post, the gardeners, decisions about this, that and the other, and the obligation to go out and meet the public who come to the garden. I don't really want to go anywhere. I'm just grateful for the quiet and the solitude.

What languages I had have almost vanished. There are other guests, a French publisher and his wife, Pascal and Sandra, and a lady from Lisbon, where she's putting on an exhibition of Franco's art collection before it finds its permanent home in the Labyrinth, which opens next year, 2015, to coincide with the expo in Milan.

We went to look at the labyrinth one evening, one man's folly on a gigantic, mad scale. It is, I suppose, post-Modernist but full of references to historic traditions within the area of the old Duchy of Parma. At the moment I find it slightly forbidding with its vast windowless walls, bastions of brick, although it is soft in colour. Within it is not yet painted but it is clearly a neoclassical repertory of columns and cornices, all at the moment white but that will change. It doesn't exude much fun but then that, too, will change with the arrival of visitors. The second cloistered enclosure is more attractive, with its pergola-like walks on either side backed by the labyrinth's forest of bamboo. This has a chapel like a pyramid (shades of Canova), to which you ascend via a walkway. On one side there are guest rooms and on the other a vast *salle des fêtes* for cocktail parties, dinners and other gatherings, weddings and corporate events of all kinds. I will be intrigued to see how it goes down with the public.

Franco has aged since I saw him last year but his mind is as sharp as ever. The energy is still there and he's almost bought back his magazine, *FMR*. His sign-up to a bank to produce an annual book of substance goes on, although the sales are vastly diminished. His publishing career has no exact parallel in England. Can you imagine

NatWest paying for a book on the history of Birmingham or one on Hogarth? We just don't have that cultural volition or, rather, it goes to the performing arts or exhibitions but not books.

On Sunday I went to Mass in Fontanellato with Laura. The Mass as now performed is a pretty depressing experience, with virtually no vestments: just a stole for the priest and one worn sash-wise for his deacon assistant, a child in a cassock, and all three wearing trainers. They trundled on from the vestry on the south to preside over a baroque altar stationed before the old high altar. All the singing and responses were one long stream of well-meant caterwauling to the music of a girl at a hand organ. Lessons were read by various women from a lectern. There was ringing of bells at the two elevations and the sacrament was administered in one kind only. What a mess!! But I'm hopelessly spoilt by an English cathedral and its choir and ordered ritual. It is difficult to know what to think of it all and where it's going. But I don't think that it can go on like this. Everything depends on Papa Francesco.

However, we drove about twenty kilometres to Castello Torre-chiara, a quite wonderful fifteenth-century castle, beautifully restored and with a suite of rooms covered in frescoes, mostly pro-vincial renderings of *grotesche* but also earlier ones telling the story of a knight's love of Bianca. They were quite extraordinary. He'd built twelve castles and they were all depicted on the ceiling and walls. There he was kneeling before her in adoration, etc.

There was a lovely lunch of *tortelli erbetta*, a local dish, light as a feather, with a salad and a glass of malvasia. After that we went to see the collection of a foundation in a florid nineteenth-century villa with a beautiful *giardino inglese*, with sweeping lawns and fine trees. Inside was a disappointment, in the main boring pictures by Morandi, two murky Renoirs, a few minor Cézanne sketches, that sort of thing. But there were stars like the large Goya of a woman having her hair dressed surrounded by a bevy of people, as in

Hogarth's *Mariage à-la-mode*, a good early Titian, a Ghirlandaio, a Rubens head of a boy cut from the altarpiece of the ducal family at Mantua, a Fuseli – but not much else. I couldn't think that this place had much of a future.

I SEPTEMBER

Retrospective: another National Trust delegation and other reflections

Helen Ghosh said on her 10 July visit that some kind of package would come through from their September meeting. No sign of it yet. Instead there was yet another visitation of the garden by John Sales, Richard Hillier and Richard Barnard of Hillier Landscapes. They came on 20 August and I don't think that any of them had quite seen a garden like this one. The sound guide is a lifeline, and off they go when and where they like. So after coffee, off they sallied. It must have gripped them because we didn't get to lunch until 1.30 p.m. John Sales was amazed how it had changed since he last saw it fifteen years or so ago. All the signs seem good and they were going to present a succinct written report to the trustees of the National Trust in September, Hillier wanting to address them in person. So that's where we've got to.

On 27 August I had my first 'big ride' with Jonty: Much Marcle, Dymock, Eastnor, Ledbury and back to Marcle, in all twenty-two miles and almost as fresh at the end as when I started. I did enjoy it, so totally unlike anything that I have ever done before. So much is a question of priorities and I consider exercise at this time of life edges up to being a number-one priority. Mark at the gym gave me a new exercise programme and I am now into dead lifts. In a real sense I am fitter at seventy-nine than at any other time in my life.

I am doubtful as to whether I will ever write another book [that, of course, turned out not to be true]. A long time was spent considering the Diaries but Felicity Bryan was never that interested as they lack any narrative frame. But why should they have one? I looked at my 1967 to 1987 diaries and realised that I then had a wicked flare, which has now gone. And there's the context of the success of *Self-Portrait* and *Remaking*, a good high on which to end a phase of life. So I'll see through *Shakespeare Gardens* [retitled later as *The Quest for Shakespeare's Garden*] and garden design book reprints if they happen. But I don't lack intellectual focus. Reading up on India is to ascend a mountain, but a refreshing one as it is all new.

All of this I mulled over as I had one of those once in a decade or so clear-ups. Mounds of paper, proofs, etc., were thrown away and things were labelled, put in order and filed. Just to get to the bottom of any desk is a triumph and I have three. I've decided against going back into Elizabethan England. I could have done, but what's the point? [In the end I did.] It's going backwards. I've been mulling over all this for a year because I've never lived without a book on the hob from my mid-twenties onwards.

2 OCTOBER

The Laskett Gardens and the National Trust

So much has happened that it is difficult to know where to begin. First the weather, a golden warm autumn and the driest September since 1910. The gardens closed for the season on Tuesday with a sigh of relief, although I was happy that they gave so much delight to so many. And, at last, the National Trust decision arrived. The Laskett Gardens did not meet the 'high rung of historic and national importance' they set, so the answer was 'no'. I can't conceal a certain anger. They have played me along for four years [it actually went back fifteen years]. Why did Fiona Reynolds say that the National Trust wanted The Laskett and set up a relationship with their West of England manager telling me that all that was needed was a shift in the composition of the Board and it would all change? Why did Simon Jenkins purposefully cross the room at Hay a year or so later to say don't worry, it'll all come right? I have wasted four years of my old age on this. It is difficult not to feel quite bitter about it. Why couldn't they have said all this four years ago? But, they graciously said, if I set up an independent trust they would send a representative to sit on it. Well, sod them. I'm not doing it.

18 OCTOBER

The National Trust's decision

The decision by the Trust came through first by email and then in hard copy: no. This was the second time and the decisions were in reverse from the 2011 one. This time as it had money attached to it that wasn't wanted, whereas last time they wouldn't take it without. Last time overall it was considered of historic interest but this time it met neither their national nor their historic criteria. To say that I felt angry would be an understatement. This has been dragged out over four years, back to 2010. Four years in a sense wasted, but the Trust was what Julia wanted so I pursued it to the end. I just couldn't face any more energy being expended in this direction. In another sense I felt that a lead weight had been taken from me. Let the garden find its own fate. I shall continue to develop it as long as I live but my initial reaction was that when I die I don't want a penny to go towards its preservation. The stipulation in my will now will be that it remain open for one more year so that it can be 'saved'. If nothing happens, let it be stripped of anything that sets it apart as ours: all inscriptions, ornaments, etc., to be removed, sold, given away or destroyed. In a sense I would be doing what Rosemary Verey wanted done to Barnsley on the day she died but didn't do. I couldn't bear The Laskett to be sold as it is. Julia would be horrified. So at the moment the opportunity is there to save the garden. All I know is that I can't stand any more of it.

All of this became public knowledge very quickly as Richard Brooks of *The Sunday Times* rang me about something I'd said on *Desert Island Discs* [which I'd just done for the second time] and then asked me how the garden was as he had published the idea of it as a bequest a few years ago. So he had the lot. It duly appeared in the paper on 12 October and on the Monday it resurfaced in the *Telegraph*, *The Times* and *Daily Mail*. I also appeared on the 1 p.m. news on Radio 4. There was also a deluge of emails and letters and cards, all expressing shock-horror. On Tuesday a reporter came from the *Daily Mail* to do a double-page spread on it. Sarah Greenall came and stayed the night and said that it was the best thing ever for The Laskett that the National Trust deal fell through.

2015

This Diary should not end on a bitter or sour note. I am also aware that I am trespassing close to the present and that brings sensitivities. It is too early to publish my Diary for 2015 more fully other than to include a few entries, enough to give the reader the feeling that things began to right themselves and, in the words of Mother Julian, 'All shall be well'. All my Diaries, for what they are worth, will find a resting place in the Bodleian Library, Oxford, with an embargo until after my demise. I so much want to end on a happy and positive note and 2015 was to prove to be just a miraculous year.

The garden crisis was resolved thanks to Bunny Guinness, who put me on to The Royal Benevolent Fund for Gardeners, known as Perennial. The deed leaving to it the garden with a substantial endowment was settled and signed in the summer.

15 FEBRUARY

Reflection in Jaipur on a tour to Rajasthan

I am sitting in the Taj Hotel in Jaipur, marooned, as the flight has been delayed. Outside, the weather is stunning: blue sky and sun.

And I'm at the end of taking a motley crew to Delhi, Bundi, Nagaur, Jodhpur, Bikaner and Jaipur. But I haven't written this diary for ages. No time, too much happening and I can't remember where I left off.

The negotiations with Perennial have gone well. They came again the week before Christmas and I'm really optimistic about all of this. It is so much better than the National Trust and I think that our next meeting will finally clinch it all. I so much want the Will finalised this year and not to think about it after that, and that everyone should know what is to happen when I pop off.

The *Strong Box* [the provisional title for *Sir Portrait*] is on target and I feel it will be a hit. A brilliant design job has been done and it is so elegant and quirky that I sense, if the price is right, it will 'take off'. We'll see; but it is all buoying.

I had no idea how much work would be involved in doing a Rajasthan tour. Golly, putting those four lectures together knocked me out. There were just too many people on this tour, over twenty, and nearly everyone was ill, either with food poisoning like me or with some form of laryngitis. At times it was like carting around a hospital ward. The numbers had risen because a group said 'either all of us or no one'. The old core was still there: the Windsors, the Hedleys, the Villiers, Peter Ingram, and then the new lot, not all of them my cup of tea, but which included Tom Bower, writing a biography of Tony Blair, and his wife, Veronica Wadley, Boris Johnson's policy adviser (she said that the Conservatives would lose the next election and that Ed Milliband would be Prime Minister, God help us!) and chair of the Arts Council England; Tim Steel, a big-built, benign money-maker (he raised the cash for the Turner Gallery at Margate) and an equivalent large, benign, jolly wife, Sophia, a member of the Hawarden family; Prince Nicholas von Preussen, a character out of a Ruritanian musical together with his partner, Sarah, ex-wife of the Macmillan publishing heir (she was still beautiful). And Joanna Wood, an interior decorator of a kind who makes a fortune, with her partner. She runs a shop at the end of the Pimlico Road and she has just the eye for SW3. But she has no historical knowledge at all and gives herself unwarranted importance. So off we all staggered and, yes, we did get on but – oh dear – so many people ill.

Only one more Indian tour was taken. Joanna was the wife of the explorer Henry Worsley, who died attempting a solo crossing of the Antarctic in January 2016. Although, bravely, Joanna came with me to India again the following month, we both knew that it would be the last occasion.

24 FEBRUARY

Farewell to Sandy Nairne

The steps up to the main concourse area at the NPG were carpeted with gold glitter dust. Good grief, it would have given Kingsley Adams, Director when I joined the place in 1959, heart failure. But now it's a different era as the glitzy world of art, museums and money – above all, money – surged up the stairs for Sandy Nairne's farewell.

Well, he did a fantastic job. John Hayes was dull and safe, Charles Saumarez Smith woke it up again and Sandy carried it on from there. He's done it well for twelve years and decided to call it a day. He's right. You can't go on and on and on. These institutions now cry out for change at the top in a faster-moving world of the arts, no longer genteel backwaters but ones that have to keep fizzing or go under. Heaven knows who all the people were, and who cares anyway? What was rightly striking was how affectionate it was. The NPG has never lost that quality and it is the human attributes of

Sandy that have contributed so much to the success of his directorship.

I dread these gatherings now but I was determined to go. Sandy has always treated me with respect and he's letting a little tribute to me on my eightieth birthday go up [an exhibition of John Swannell's photographs]. But I saw Gerald Scarfe and Jane Asher; Stephen Deuchar; Christopher Frayling, who, surprisingly, said that he'd liked my early autobiography; Patricia Rawlings, who has decided to stay put in her Norfolk mansion; Will Proby, the affable chair of trustees; and Jonathan Marsden. I told Monica Mason how much I admired Wheeldon's *The Winter's Tale* and always wept through the last act. The speeches went on too long. They always do. Rather sweet that there is now an NPG Choir, which added an unexpected touch. Everyone said the right things and the air was suffused with all-round happiness.

9 MARCH

A London week

An odd day, which started out as one series of visits and encounters and ended with another. Suddenly a note surfaced that I was to have lunch with those involved in the future of church buildings. Janet Gough, ex-Christie's, is the secretary, crisp, bright and hopefully a doer. Her chair was Sir Tony Baldry, an overweight, jolly Conservative MP. I said to Janet as I left her after lunch: 'You'll have to push him hard to give any definite action.' He struck me as complacent and the fact that Welby had put him in that role showed, I thought, how low down on his agenda solving the future of some 15,000 Church of England churches, half of which are not wanted, came on his agenda. Baldry didn't have an original idea in his head, except that the V&A ought to do a treasures of the churches exhibition. Waste of time, I said. We've gone past that sort of thing decades back. They are all so limp. All we need is some clear policy enunciated instead of this never-ending nibbling at the edges. I've done my bit, back in 1977 and in 2007, and don't plan to climb back into it in my eighties.

But in the morning I saw the Durand-Ruel exhibition of Impressionists at the National Gallery, dazzling and beautiful, unusual as a theme and crammed with goodies I'd never seen before. I'd no idea how important was his idea of exhibiting series of paintings by one artist. The hang of four of Monet's Poplars in a line was a revelation.

After my ecclesiastical lunch I made my way to the Abbey for Commonwealth Observance, rather jacked up this year with a theme about youth and, unprecedented, all three generations of the Royal Family coming: the Queen, the Duke of Edinburgh, the Prince of Wales and Camilla, and the Cambridges. The Queen continues to shrink and is now a smiling, diminutive old lady, radiant today. The Duke of Cambridge is a tall, sweet young man with a modest, open face and a sense of delight in people. The place was crawling with media as the Duchess of Cambridge was there, tall and elegantly dressed and with one of those ghastly tilted forward mini-hats. But they all seemed in good humour with each other and the event.

There is, however, something valedictory in the air these days. The turn-out shows an intent to switch the spotlight beyond the present reign. Richard Luce looked transparent and didn't take part in the procession. As these events go, this was a good one; we were spared dancing up and down the nave. But one does wonder how long all this will go on.

I managed to get a ticket for Peter Seller's *The Indian Queen* at ENO. Oh dear, but I stuck it through to the end, 7.00 to

10.30 p.m. Purcell's music is wonderful but it had been recast into a saga about the Mayan civilisation and the conquistadores. Ghastly sets, costumes, choreography and lighting. I could see what Sellers was trying to do but spare us another! I'd rather have it in concert form than this pretentious plod.

5 TO 8 MAY

Walsingham revisited

It was inevitable that I should join the Hereford Cathedral pilgrimage to Walsingham. It was a large group in the main of sacramentalists like me. Michael Tavinor wanted me to serve at Mass, although I've never been trained to cope with the priest facing east. We stopped for lunch at Ely. I'd forgotten how enormous that cathedral was and I served at Mass in the vast Lady Chapel – I'd forgotten just how enormous that was too. On we went to Walsingham, a visit close to the one I had made all those years ago. I wondered how I would feel about it now. There is something in the air there that casts a spell which rises above its toy-town quality.

The bedrooms were basic and I got up early to grab the bathroom. There seemed no lack of cash and there was a huge and well-run refectory with, downstairs, a bar. Here one evening there was a gathering of nuns from around the globe, each doing a little dance from her own country, an odd sight with everyone else boozing at the opposite end of the room.

On the first evening there was a gathering of both Anglicans and Roman Catholics in the main church, a service of healing and reconciliation. At a certain moment people were stationed at points along the side chapels ready to place their hands on the heads of any who came forward, and pray for them. There were also two rooms set aside for those who wished to make their confession, one for Catholics and the other for Anglicans. I later sat next to a woman who had made her confession quite unexpectedly and was able to get off her chest something that had troubled her for twenty years. At the close of the service we all went down and were sprinkled with holy water at the well at the west end.

The aura was very much of that of the Society of St Peter and St Paul, very 1920s and 1930s Anglo-Catholic. The walls of the Holy House had inset pieces of stone from various pre-Reformation abbeys and monasteries. The chapel is small and dark within and filled with flickering candles and the smell of incense and the image of Our Lady crowned and cloaked over the altar. Michael said the Mass there too and I served and tinkled the bell.

There's space for that sort of thing and it is where I started. It seems somewhat antiquated now but early on the last day I entered the church when a priest was beginning the Mass at a side altar. There were only two or three of us but I knelt on the hard floor all through it. Sadly Walsingham is Forward in Faith and all the time the place seems to cry out for some women priests. Our Lady seemed curiously isolated in the wrong sense. I can't explain why but that's how I felt.

There was a walk to the Roman Catholic Slipper Chapel and then back at base Mass was said in the small chapel in the grounds, as well as Stations of the Cross. Some of it must have come as a bit of surprise to some of the more middle-of-the-road members of the cathedral congregation but Michael had a wonderful way of drawing us all together. It's a powerful place but it needs to open up as to where we are now. It brought me to the faith and here I am, still there sixty years on.

15 JULY

I am interviewed by Lucy Worsley

Much to my surprise I was interviewed as one of a trinity who had reached eighty. The others were Alan Bennett and Joan Bakewell. This diary entry was written in retrospect, after transmission in August.

The day of the Lucy Worsley interview, which took place in some ghastly dark studio somewhere in South London, God knows where. I was surprised to be asked to do this. I had always concluded, rightly or wrongly, that it was probably Alan Yentob who had kept me off BBC TV for thirty years, except in the early Nineties when he had a sabbatical and *Royal Gardens* slipped through. I hope I am not maligning him, for my first encounter with him remains branded in my memory. It was in a flat somewhere in Notting Hill and there he was, all in black, with his partner, also all in black, by him. I could see that he didn't warm to me but that it would be difficult to scupper a series that had the imprimatur of the Queen.

Over twenty years pass and I'm suddenly asked to do an hour-length interview with Lucy Worsley (whose brilliant first book, a biography of the 1st Duke of Newcastle, I reviewed). How this came about I know not, but it was an accolade so far accorded only to Joan Bakewell and Alan Bennett when they were also eighty – although I was told that Alan did not want his age to be mentioned. The producer was a man called Basil Comely, whom I liked. He loathed Yentob and told me what a creep he was, now chasing after Tony Hall, the new Director-General. Basil has two assistants, nice but not brilliant girls, and they all came to The Laskett to talk about it and what I'd got.

Came the day and Lucy entered the studio wearing a clinging crushed crimson velvet Thirties dress and with her hair in Marcelle waves! I had decided that I must appear bang up to date and went off to Etro and spent a fortune on a cool look, which must have registered as one of the tweets on the programme read 'he even wore trainers'!

It was obvious, because I'd never published a set of Diaries post-1987, that the bulk of the programme would be about the National Portrait Gallery and the Victoria and Albert Museum. And so it was. All sorts of film clips appeared that I couldn't even remember and I had no idea what Lucy would ask me. They'd done their homework. So many people afterwards said they were riveted and that they wished it had gone on for another hour. But we liked each other and it was in its way a flirtatious encounter. I was accorded the role of a trail-blazer and the man who put museums and history on the public map. People loved it, as I said exactly what I thought – and few do these days. Inevitably people like the awful. A.A. Gill had a swipe; but who cares anyway?

Recorded in July, it went out on the evening of my birthday and in its way it was a kind of resurrection. But it's all too late. Television as a medium is a killer and not made for people in their eighties.

Ironically, Alan Yentob has had his comeuppance recently and rightly over Kids Company, of which he was chair. I wish I didn't feel so joyous about his fall and disgrace. But this man had a death grip over the Arts on BBC TV for some thirty years. Certain people like Simon Schama were pushed and pushed by him and few things hurt me more this year than Schama doing a series on British portraiture at the National Portrait Gallery. There he was, a man who barely knew the back of a picture from the front, handling items so very dear to my heart. I couldn't bear to watch it until Brian Allen, a Trustee of the Gallery, said how awful the series had been. I respect Brian. I therefore saw ten minutes of one and, yes, it was truly awful.

6 AUGUST

A retrospective

The year when I will be eighty on 23 August. I am writing this staying with Franco at Masone for the first week in August.

In May I went out to Italy for a couple of days and talked about The Laskett Garden at a conference held at the Acton house at La Pietra outside Florence, at the invitation of the head gardener, Nick Dakin-Elliot. There's something to be written about that place which must be all locked up in the archives there. Arthur Acton was a failed painter who married an American banker's daughter when she was past her sell-by date. Their son, Harold, altered nothing in the interior, which like all those acquired by exiles, consisted of rooms filled with old Italian furniture, all sorts of paintings, mainly religious, and old textiles. This time I found it really creepy and longed to sweep it all away. The garden bore little relationship to the true Italian garden but was rather a pastiche or stage set that seemed to owe more to movie spectaculars. But it was good to see Kim Wilkie again, a lovely and very talented yet modest man who is in charge of its restorations.

Then in July came the Three Choirs Festival at Hereford, the 300th anniversary, not that you'd know it. I did my *Princes and Poems* reading again, this time in Dore Abbey. I had the great good fortune that Siân Phillips was available and she's such a star. I think we gave quite a bravura performance as the clapping went on and on and we had to come back for a further curtain call. I opened the art exhibition for them and attended the civic service, went to *Gerontius* and the Arthur Bliss [*Morning Heroes*] and to the concert sponsored by the Elmley Foundation.

And then also in July there were the final performances of Julia's

La Bohème. The literature promoting this farewell virtually swept Julia's contribution under the carpet and I was terribly upset, suddenly finding myself weeping at such treatment. It was probably the greatest production that she ever did and lasted over forty years. This was a true *verismo* production, utterly wonderful and so loved and still saluted by the critics. I saw John Copley and both of us said why scrap it at all? But they have put both sets and costumes in store so that if the new production flops they can bring it back. So I had a punch-up with the Opera House but buried the hatchet, suggesting that they mount a small exhibition of her designs; this was beautifully done by Jo Elsworth from the Bristol Theatre Collection.

23 AUGUST

My eightieth birthday

As recorded on 17 October.

Being eighty took up a lot of time and energy, but it won't happen again! There were three events. On 22 June there was a drinks party at the NPG for almost two hundred, launching John Swannell's portraits of me exhibited in the concourse area. Jonathan Myles-Lea filmed my speech and put it on YouTube. On 22 August I gave lunch for about a hundred in the country. This was, as I said in my speech, a thank-you to the many who had helped me create a new phase of my life after the loss of Julia. For this I wore two changes of Indian costume, one white and ivory and a second crimson with masses of glitter. The Laskett party had a vaguely Indian theme. Richard Shirley Smith designed the invitation card and two girls added some styling touches with deep claret-coloured cloths alternating with ochre gold ones for the tables, which had turbans at their centre along with scatterings of immortelles and rose petals and gilt chargers. There was also a red carpet scattered either side with rose petals, along which I made my entry.

Sunday 23rd was my actual birthday. I served at the Eucharist in the cathedral and there were Prosecco and cake for the whole congregation. And then the Dean and Chapter gave me lunch. Finally, on 29 September, John Hall, Dean of Westminster, gave a dinner for about thirty in my honour in the Jerusalem Chamber. Here were gathered the 'holy ones' like David Hutt, Pamela Tudor-Craig, Victor Stock, Antonia Fraser and A.N. Wilson – along with those from the Abbey. All these *fêtes* were contrasted and for different constituencies in my life.

For my birthday Patrick Reyntiens gave me a wonderful book of Catholic prayers – not specifically Anglican or Catholic – just prayers for those who express their devotion to God, Jesus, Our Lady and the saints in that way. It is edited by Eamon Duffy and I love the way that it includes items from the Book of Common Prayer, poems by George Herbert, and hymns by Charles Wesley and Isaac Watts. It is now by my bedside.

8 OCTOBER

The Midlands Historic Houses Association

I was cornered into this by Jan Lucas-Scudamore, the chatelaine of Kentchurch. It took place at Chavenage, which is not much of a house but there's a zany brio about its owners, which carries all before it. And it's been lucky finding itself a location for the hit TV series *Poldark*. I was asked to talk about where we are now forty years on from the famous V&A exhibition [*The Destruction of the Country House*] in 1974. So I told them that any new energy about the country house lay now with the private owners. Helen Ghosh had not expressed any adequate word of regret that Clandon had gone up in flames and her main comment over houses was that they had too much 'stuff' and called for beanbags in the rooms for people to bounce on.

It was a full house and I took the opportunity to say that rather than allying themselves with the National Trust they should go in the opposite direction and emphasise what sets them apart from what is becoming a bureaucratic nightmare of correctness. I also sent up a flare that the country parish church will be the focus for any major heritage crisis in this century. What is going to happen to them? And people should remember that in many cases they house their ancestors' tombs and monuments. The Church of England at last, forty years too late, has begun to face up to the crisis of all the rural churches that are not needed. Graham James of Norwich has designated those that will henceforth only function at Christmas and Easter as 'festival churches'. This is sidetracking the truth of the matter, which is a withdrawal of the Church from much of the English countryside.

17 OCTOBER

A retrospective on Perennial

In late summer the deed with Perennial was done, the bequest of The Laskett Garden finalised. The garden and the house go to them along with a large inflation-proof sum. Dealing with Perennial was a revelation. This happened as I was transcribing my earlier Diaries: I was horrified to discover that the National Trust first figured in that narrative as long ago as 1999. So some fifteen years of my life have been spent on and off negotiating with them. The National Trust is like the Stasi and I am appalled in retrospect when I think that first time round Fiona Reynolds was categorical that the Trust wanted the place. And Simon Jenkins crossing the room at a Hay literary festival event and saying 'Don't worry. It'll all come right.' Well, it didn't. Somehow a good angel must have been watching over me, for I now give thanks to have escaped the National Trust and the Labour luvvie, bureaucratic Helen Ghosh. But it was, after all, what Julia wanted and I saw it through to the bitter end. Richard Capewell and Perennial are such a dramatic contrast, kindly, modest, caring. They are a benevolent fund for gardeners, with case-workers on the ground. The present plan is for the running of the garden to pass to them when I am eighty-five, a sensible decision, I feel. I am all for a smooth continuity. Our future meetings will need to flesh things out. My concern is also to put down local roots.

20 NOVEMBER

RIP Fr John Gaskell

I went down by car to Morden College, Blackheath, for the requiem for Fr John Gaskell. He was my confessor for a few years after David moved into Morpeth Terrace. John was like a nightclub chucker-out, very tough. A.N. Wilson also went to him. By the time he took me on he had ceased to be a parish priest but helped out at All Saints, Margaret Street. He was a man with no interest in domestic frills and at both All Saints and in Morden College, to which he finally moved, there were bare boards, a rudimentary bookcase, a wooden chair to sit on, and that was about it! He had been quite a mover in the Affirming Catholicism movement, pro women and also particularly close to pious gay men. His end had been rapid. He was very frail the last time that I saw him, when he went to see David; he declined rapidly and died in hospital.

This was to be a requiem Mass in Morden Chapel; there will also be one later at All Saints, when I shall be in Sri Lanka. Victor Stock presided over a packed congregation with a big turn-out of clergy. Incense was banned as it would have set the fire alarm off! But I'm glad I went as he had been part of my spiritual journey at a particular moment.

31 DECEMBER

Sorrow and joy

I have not written of the death of Michael Borrie this year. He always remained as a kind of silent rock in my life, one whose foundations were in those years when we shared a flat in Lancaster Gate, when we were young suburbanites upping it from where we started, Michael with his job in the Manuscripts Department of the British Museum and me in the basement of the NPG. There was always a hesitancy to him; but one always listened to someone to whom integrity was second nature. He it was, when I was appointed Director of the NPG at the age of thirty-one in 1967, who said, 'Never be seduced by the office you hold [the label on the bottle, as it were], always be yourself. Jobs come and go.' Michael made a good marriage not long after me. Gillian was definite, taller than him, and gave him the framework and decision-making that he needed in life. His career was of the old-fashioned kind. You joined a great institution and, as the years rolled by, you eventually became head of department. No better kind of public servant could be asked for. As the years passed we drifted apart, as we were on different trajectories. But I always retained this sense that here was someone I respected.

Life treated him cruelly. He caught measles from one of his two children, which wrecked his hearing, and he loved music. Then for the last years of his life, he had cancer of the jaw. Gillian's concern for him was both touching and total. This was a man of total modesty, a lovable man and I feel humbled as I write of him. I miss him as a point of reference, a pillar from my past that has now gone.

This was the day on which the news that I had been awarded the Order of the Companions of Honour became public. I was much moved by this. When I returned from Sri Lanka [I had been doing a recce with Joanna Worsley for a tour that never happened] there was the letter and, on reading its contents, I burst into tears. It was so unexpected. Oh, how I wished that Julia had lived to be with me at this moment. And now the news had gone out on a day that found me in Berlin on a not very good four-day tour to see the city and go to the opera. There's an irony to this, as so much of my life has been an expression of someone who, as a child, experienced the war and its aftermath, keenly aware of all things English above all, and nurtured on our glorious insularity – everything from Gloriana to Nelson and then the theatre of Shakespeare, the vision of England purveyed through pictures of market towns and country villages in Arthur Mee's *The King's England*, and so on. So much of this fired me up and then I was quite upset that English painting, apart from Constable and Turner, was looked on with a degree of condescension compared with the giants of the Continent. That set me on a path to rediscover the art of Tudor England and gave me a compulsive love of that heroic era.

EPILOGUE: 2016

I trespass by including one Diary entry from the next year so that this volume can end with a sense of fulfilment and recognition.

26 APRIL

I become a Companion of Honour

I took David Hutt to Buckingham Palace for the investiture, which was a rerun of last time, a bit like an old-fashioned school speech day. Recipients were detached from guests. There was a run-through on how it went and what we did, and then we were off. The setting was the ballroom with the 1911 Delhi Durbar canopy beneath the alcove at one end. What was billed as the Countess of Wessex's string orchestra in a gallery at the back played nondescript pieces from Cole Porter to the Beatles, ending with a Handel march. It lasted about an hour and a half. At the start everyone stood for the National Anthem. Prince William by then had entered, with his staff arranged *en tableau*. I was first off, receiving the highest award, and on cue I advanced, did a neck bow, and the Prince advanced also and hung the Order around my neck. Then a little conversation followed, along the lines of 'you'll be back here again', to which I said unlikely as I'd got the lot now. Then he spoke about the Duchess's involvement with the NPG. This is a sweet Prince, thoughtful, a little shy, and I felt quite moved to have received my award from a man who would reign long after I was dead. As I left I thought of Julia and tears came to my eyes. She would have been so very proud of me.

LIST OF ILLUSTRATIONS

13 With apologies to Maurice Guilbert's photograph of Toulouse-Lautrec, 2014 (John Swannell)

14 In front of the display at the National Portrait Gallery, 2015 (John Swannell)

15 On his beloved trike, 2014 (Jonty Williams)

16 With the painter Jonathan Myles-Lea at The Laskett, 2015 (Jonathan Myles-Lea)

17 With Michael Tavinor, Dean of Hereford, 2015 (Jonathan Myles-Lea)

18 In Indian attire at his 80th birthday party, 2015 (Jonathan Myles-Lea)

19 With the late Felicity Bryan (Felicity Bryan)

CAST OF CHARACTERS

Simon Abbiss
Herefordshire cider-maker.

Abbot Stuart
See Rt Revd Brother Stuart Burns

Jane, Lady Abdy
(1934–2015) Art collector and dealer and society hostess.

Sir Timothy Ackroyd, 3rd Bt
British stage actor and director.

Kate de Rothschild Agius
Art dealer and author; trustee of Exbury Gardens, Hampshire, created by her grandfather, Lionel de Rothschild; Trustee of the Wallace Collection; Chairman of Trustees of the Royal Botanic Gardens, Kew, since 2006; married to financier Marcus Agius.

John Mark Ainsley
English lyric tenor.

Virginia Ogilvy, Countess of Airlie
See under Ogilvy

Dalya Alberge
Freelance arts writer and journalist.

James Aldridge
Garden designer, for seven years one of the gardeners at Highgrove.

Hélène Alexander
Founder and Director of The Fan Museum, Greenwich.

Rosemary Alexander
Founder and Principal of the English Gardening School, Chelsea.

Dr Brian Allen
Art historian, Chairman of the Hazlitt Group; Director of Studies at the Paul Mellon Centre for British Art 1993–2012; Trustee of the National Portrait Gallery 2012–15.

Stephen Anderton
Gardening writer and lecturer; gardening correspondent for *The Times*.

Sophie Andreae
Author and architecture historian; former member of National Trust Council and Trustee of Historic Royal Palaces.

Tim Angel
Chairman of Angels Theatrical Costumiers, London; former Chairman of BAFTA and Governor of the British Film Institute.

Professor Sydney Anglo
Historian, author and Fellow of The British Academy; Emeritus
Professor of History, University of Swansea.

Leonore Cohn (Lee) Annenberg
(1918–2009) American diplomat, businesswoman and
philanthropist; United States Chief of Protocol 1981–2.

Leonora Anson, Countess of Lichfield
Born Leonora Grosvenor, daughter of the 5th Duke of
Westminster; former wife of Patrick, 5th Earl of Lichfield.

Dame Margaret Anstee
(1926–2016) British diplomat; first woman Under-Secretary-
General of the United Nations 1987–92.

Katherine Ara
Painting restorer and conservator.

Mark and Gillian Archer
Owners of Perrycroft, an Arts and Crafts house and garden in the
Malvern Hills.

Antony Armstrong-Jones, 1st Earl of Snowdon
(1930–2017) Photographer; married 1st Princess Margaret (1960),
2nd Lucy Lindsay-Hogg (1978).

David Armstrong-Jones, 2nd Earl of Snowdon
Son of Antony Armstrong-Jones, 1st Earl of Snowdon and Princess
Margaret; styled Viscount Linley until the death of his father in
2017.

Lucy Armstrong-Jones, Lady Snowdon
Second wife of Antony Armstrong-Jones, Lord Snowdon.

Sarah Armstrong-Jones
See Lady Sarah Chatto

Janet Arnold
(1932–98) Clothing historian, costume designer, teacher and author.

Jane Asher
British actress and writer; married to cartoonist Gerald Scarfe (q.v.).

Sir Frederick Ashton
(1904–1988) Ballet dancer and principal choreographer to the Royal Ballet.

Charlie Aslet
Son of Clive Aslet.

Clive Aslet
Writer, historian, countryside campaigner and Editor of *Country Life* magazine 1993–2006.

Clarissa Avon
See under Eden

Sue Ayton
Television agent; co-founder of Knight Ayton Management.

Sir Nicholas Bacon, 14th and 15th Bt
Landowner, philanthropist and businessman; custodian of the family seat, the Raveningham Estate, Norfolk; President of the Royal Horticultural Society since 2013.

Dame Janet Baker
Great English mezzo-soprano.

Sir Tony Baldry
Conservative MP for Banbury 1983–2015.

Christopher Balfour
Former investment banker, chairman of Christie's and friend of Diana, Princess of Wales.

Ann Ballantyne
Conservator of medieval wall paintings; widow of Jim Murrell, conservator of miniatures at the V&A.

Lawrence and Elizabeth Banks
Owners of Hergest Croft Gardens, Herefordshire; Elizabeth was President of the Royal Horticultural Society 2010–13.

Julian and Isabel Bannerman
Garden designers and builders; owners of Trematon Castle, Cornwall.

Lynn Barber
Journalist and author.

Alexandra Bastedo
(1946–2014) British actress; wife of Patrick Garland (q.v.).

Camila Batmanghelidjh
Controversial Tehran-born founder of the defunct charity Kids Company.

Pim Baxter
Director of Communications and, since 2008, Deputy Director of the National Portrait Gallery.

Sir Simon Russell Beale
English stage actor, author and music historian.

Sir Cecil Beaton
(1904–1980) Portrait photographer, stage and costume designer.

Anne Beckwith-Smith
Lady-in-Waiting to Diana, Princess of Wales.

Sir Geoffrey de Bellaigue
(1931–2013) Leading authority on decorative arts, former Surveyor of the Queen's Works of Art and Director of the Royal Collection 1972–96.

Alan Bennett
Leading British author, playwright and actor.

Sally Bercow
Wife of John Bercow, Speaker of the House of Commons 2009–19.

Sir Isaiah Berlin
(1909–1997) Philosopher, historian, essayist, diplomat, academic and man of influence, knighted in 1957.

Marcus Binney
Architectural historian, author, lecturer and broadcaster; co-curator of the *Destruction of the Country House* exhibition at the V&A in 1974; co-founder, with his wife, Anne, of the Domaine des Vaux opera festival, Jersey.

David Bintley
Choreographer, former ballet dancer; Artistic Director of Birmingham Royal Ballet 1995–2019.

Cilla Black
(1943–2015) Singer and television presenter.

Norman Blackburn
Print collector and dealer.

Douglas and Sophie Blain
Owners of Monaughty House and Jacobethan gardens, Radnorshire; Sophie was High Sheriff of Powys 2002–3.

Tony Blair
UK Prime Minister 1997–2007.

Jody Blake
Former curator of the Tobin Collection of Theatre Arts, San Antonio, Texas.

Ingrid Bleichroeder
Executive assistant to Beatrix Miller (q.v.).

Sue Bligh, Countess of Darnley
Herefordshire landowner who has held a number of public
positions; Lord Lieutenant of Herefordshire since 2008.

Betty Lee (Betsy) Bloomingdale
(1922–2016) American socialite, fashion icon and philanthropist.

Geoff Booker
Tricycle-maker, Tiddington, Oxfordshire.

Michael Borrie
(1934–2015) Former Head of the British Library Department of
Manuscripts.

Reg Boulton
Herefordshire artist and engraver.

Clive Boursnell
Photographer of architecture, gardens, landscapes and people.

Tom Bower
Writer and investigative journalist; married to Veronica Wadley (q.v.).

Alice, Lady Boyd
See under Lennox-Boyd

Ian Bradley
Theologian, writer, journalist, broadcaster and Church of Scotland
minister.

Christopher Bradley-Hole
Garden designer and author.

Kathryn Bradley-Hole
Writer and journalist; garden editor of *Country Life* magazine; married to Christopher Bradley-Hole.

Philippa Bradstock
(1931–2017) Artist; former student of Maggi Hambling (q.v.).

Melvyn Bragg, Baron Bragg of Wigton
Author and broadcaster.

Paul Brason
Portrait artist.

Anne Braybon
Photo historian, lecturer and creative director.

Sir David Brewer
Businessman; Lord Mayor of London 2005–6 and Lord Lieutenant of Greater London 2008–15.

Emma Bridgewater
Ceramicist; founder of one of Britain's largest pottery manufacturers; married to Matthew Rice (q.v.).

Viscount Bridport
See Alexander Hood

John Bright
Costume designer; founder of Cosprop, specialists in costume for film, stage and television productions.

Richard Brooks
Writer and journalist; *Sunday Times* Arts editor.

Christopher Brown
Art historian; Director of the Ashmolean Museum, Oxford, 1998–2014.

Edmund and Marian Brudenell
(1928–2016; 1934–2013) Owners and restorers of Deene Park, Northamptonshire.

Elizabeth Bryan (Higgins)
(1942–2008) Paediatrician and pioneer in twin studies.

Felicity Bryan
(1945–2020) Literary agent.

Julius Bryant
Keeper of Word and Image at the V&A; former curator at English Heritage.

Ursula Buchan
Writer on gardening and social history.

Richard Buckle
(1916–2001) Lifelong devotee of ballet, well-known ballet critic and founder of *Ballet* magazine.

Michael Buerk
Journalist, newsreader and broadcaster.

Tim Bulwer-Long
Norfolk bloodstock agent.

David Burden
Former Army officer; Receiver General of Westminster Abbey 1998–2008.

Rt Revd Brother Stuart Burns OSB
Abbot of Mucknell Abbey 1996–2017.

Jocelyn Burton
British silversmith and goldsmith.

John Burton
Architect; Surveyor of the Fabric at Westminster Abbey 1999–2012.

Revd George Bush
Rector of St Mary-le-Bow church, London, since 2002.

Jennifer Crichton-Stuart, Marchioness of Bute
See under Crichton-Stuart

Robin Butler, Baron Butler of Brockwell
Head of the Civil Service 1988–98; Master of University College, Oxford, 1998–2008.

Donald Buttress
Architect; Surveyor of the Fabric of Westminster Abbey 1988–99.

Dame A.S. Byatt (Antonia Susan Duffy)
Novelist, poet and Booker Prize winner.

Claire Byers
Former Creative Director of Alnwick Garden, Northumberland.

Shaun Cadman
Head Gardener at The Laskett.

Simon Callow
English actor, writer and theatre director.

Mike Calnan
National Trust Head of Gardens 1998–2019.

David Cameron
UK Prime Minister 2010–16.

Thomas Stonor, 7th Baron Camoys
See under Stonor

Professor Sir David Cannadine
Historian and author; Chairman of the Trustees of the National Portrait Gallery 2005–12; married to Linda Colley (q.v.).

Richard Capewell
Chief Executive of Perennial, the charity for UK horticulturalists, 1999–2017.

Mark Carney
Economist and banker; Governor of the Bank of England 2013–20.

Very Revd Dr Wesley Carr KCVO
(1941–2017) Dean of Westminster 1997–2008.

Peter Carrington, Baron Carrington of Upton
Distinguished Conservative politician; former Chairman of
Christie's.

George Carter
Garden designer.

Caitriona Cartwright
Stone carver and lettercutter.

Laura Casalis
Italian author; wife of Franco Maria Ricci.

Augustus Caseley-Hayford
British cultural historian, author, broadcaster, curator and lecturer;
presenter for Channel 4 *Genius of British Art* series in 2010, and
subsequently for BBC2 and Sky Arts; Director of the Smithsonian
National Institution of African Art, Washington DC, since 2018.

**Andrew Cavendish, 11th Duke of Devonshire, and Deborah
Cavendish, Duchess of Devonshire**
(1920–2004; 1920–2014) Custodians of Chatsworth House,
Derbyshire.

Camilla, Hon. Lady Cazalet (née Gage)
Daughter of 6th Viscount Gage; wife of Sir Edward Cazalet.

Julian Chadwick
Solicitor, formerly of Penningtons; Chairman of Thomas Eggar
until 2017; Knight of Justice of the Order of Malta.

Revd Professor Owen Chadwick
(1916–2015) Eminent theologian, university teacher and writer;
former Chairman of the Trustees of the National Portrait Gallery.

Johnny and Anne Chambers
Owners of Kiftsgate Court Gardens, Gloucestershire.

Paul Channon, Baron Kelvedon
(1935–2007) Conservative MP and Cabinet Minister; married to
Ingrid, Baroness Kelvedon (1931–2009).

William Chapman
Prime Minister's Secretary for Appointments 1999–2008.

Molly Chappellet
Designer, landscape gardener and author; co-founder with her
husband of Chappellet Winery, Napa Valley.

Rt Revd and Rt Hon. The Lord (Richard) Chartres
Bishop of London 1995–2017.

Sarah, Lady Chatto (née Armstrong-Jones)
Daughter of Princess Margaret and Antony Armstrong-Jones (q.v.).

Anthony Cheetham
Publisher; founder of several publishing companies, including
Century Hutchinson, Orion and Head of Zeus.

Hubert Chesshyre
Former officer of arms; Clarenceux King of Arms and Principal
Herald for the South, East and West parts of England 1997–2010.

William J. Chiego
Museum curator, Director of McNay Art Museum, San Antonio, Texas, since 1991.

Revd Christopher Chivers
Anglican priest, composer and author; appointed Precentor of Westminster Abbey in 2001.

David Cholmondeley, 7th Marquess of Cholmondeley
Film-maker; divides his time between the family seats at Houghton Hall, Norfolk, and Cholmondeley Castle, Cheshire.

Felicity Clark
Journalist and fundraiser; former Director of the Royal Opera House; member of the advisory council of The Royal Ballet School and trustee of the Frederick Ashton Foundation.

Petula Clark
Veteran singer and entertainer.

Kenneth Clarke
Conservative MP; Father of the House of Commons 2017–19.

Sir Timothy Clifford
Art historian; Director of the National Galleries of Scotland, 1984–2006.

Edward Coke, 7th Earl of Leicester
(1936–2015) Patron of the arts who with his second wife, Sarah, restored the family seat at Holkham Hall, Norfolk.

Dominic Cole
Landscape architect; Chairman of the National Trust Gardens
Advisory Panel 2008–15.

Nicholas Coleridge
Writer and journalist; Managing Director and Editorial Director of
Condé Nast Britain 1991–2017; Chairman of the V&A since 2015.

Revd Richard Coles
Musician, broadcaster and Anglican priest.

Linda Colley
Historian and author; married to Sir David Cannadine (q.v.).

Basil Comely
Television producer; former Head of Arts at the BBC.

Angela Conner
Sculptor and artist.

Jasper Conran
Designer.

Diana, Lady Cooper, Viscountess Norwich
(1892–1986) Legendary beauty; ostensibly the youngest daughter of
the 8th Duke of Rutland.

John Julius Cooper, 2nd Viscount Norwich
(1929–2018) Historian and travel writer; son of Lady Diana
Cooper.

John Copley
Theatre and opera producer and director.

Patrick Cormack, Baron Cormack
Conservative peer; former MP for South Staffordshire.

John Cornforth
(1937–2004) Architectural historian; architectural editor of *Country Life* magazine.

Duchess of Cornwall
Camilla Parker-Bowles; wife of HRH The Prince of Wales.

Adrienne Corri
(1930–2016) Actress who first appeared in Jean Renoir's film *The River*, based on a novel by Rumer Godden.

John de la Cour
Former Chair of Hereford College of Arts; Director of the Elmley Foundation, a grantmaking charity in Herefordshire and Worcestershire.

Sylvia, Lady Crathorne
(1942–2009) Wife of Lord Crathorne; charitable fundraiser; Chairman of the Georgian Theatre Royal, Richmond, Yorkshire.

Jennifer Crichton-Stuart, Marchioness of Bute
Adventurer and fundraiser; widow of the 6th Marquess of Bute.

Clement Crisp
Financial Times dance critic since 1956.

Valerie Cromwell (Lady Kingman)
(1935–2018) Former Director of the History of Parliament; High
Sheriff of Bristol 2004–5.

Guida Crowley
(1915–2011) Managing editor of the *Journal of Ethnic and Migration
Studies* 1990–2008.

Nick Curtis
Journalist and art critic; appointed chief theatre critic of the
Evening Standard in June 2019.

Nicholas Dakin-Elliot
Head gardener of Villa La Pietra, Florence, Italy.

William Dalrymple
Historian, writer, broadcaster and critic; lives for most of the year
in Mehrauli, on the outskirts of Delhi.

Gordon and Marilyn Darling
Australian philanthropists and leading arts patrons; Gordon died
in 2015.

Sue, Countess of Darnley
See under Bligh

Marcella, Lady Dashwood
Italian film actress; widow of Sir Francis Dashwood.

Sir Peter Maxwell Davies
(1934–2016) Composer and conductor; appointed Master of the
Queen's Music in 2004.

Lady Kate Davson
Great-great-great granddaughter of abolitionist William Wilberforce.

Ptolemy Dean
Architect and television presenter; appointed Surveyor of the Fabric, Westminster Abbey, in 2012.

Derek Deane
Dancer and choreographer.

Dame Judi Dench
Award-winning British actress.

Stephen Deuchar
Former Exhibitions Director at the National Maritime Museum, Greenwich; first Director of Tate Britain, 1998–2009; Director of The Art Fund since 2010.

Andrew Cavendish, 11th Duke of Devonshire, and Deborah Cavendish, Duchess of Devonshire
See under Cavendish

Monty Don
Horticulturalist, garden writer and television presenter.

Stuart Donachie
Herefordshire plantsman and gardener.

Gertrude van Dorsten
Widow of Jan van Dorsten (died 1985), Dutch academic at the University of Leiden and lifelong correspondent with the author.

Dame Vivien Duffield
Philanthropist; Chair of the Clore Duffield Foundation, founded by her father, Sir Charles Clore.

Dame Carol Ann Duffy
Poet and playwright; Britain's Poet Laureate 2009–19.

Nick Dunn
Horticulturalist, tree expert and author.

Sir Thomas and Henrietta, Lady Dunne
Owners of Gatley Park, Herefordshire; Sir Thomas retired as Lord Lieutenant of Herefordshire in 2008.

James Dugdale, 2nd Baron Crathorne
Fine art consultant; Lord Lieutenant of North Yorkshire 1999–2014.

Tony (Anthony) Dyson
Architect; last lover of Sir Frederick Ashton (q.v.); owner of rights to *Enigma Variations*.

Victor Edelstein
Former couturier to, among others, Diana, Princess of Wales, now an established artist; married to Annamaria Succi Edelstein, also a painter.

Clarissa Eden, Countess of Avon
Widow of Anthony Eden, 1st Earl of Avon, UK Prime Minister 1955–7.

Hugh Edgar
Consultant architect and television butler.

Shan Egerton
Artist and owner of Pen-y-Maes house and garden, near Hay-on-Wye.

David Ekserdjian
Art historian, author and curator.

Judith Elkin
Emeritus professor of children's literature at the University of Worcester.

Revd Canon Sandy Elliott
Former art teacher and canon of Hereford Cathedral.

Jo Elsworth
Director of the University of Bristol Theatre Collection.

Marisa Erftemeijer
Producer at Oxford Films.

Peter Eyre
American-born stage and screen actor.

Samuel Fanous
Head of Publishing at the Bodleian Library, Oxford.

Charles Henderson, 3rd Baron Faringdon, and Sarah, Lady Faringdon
See under Henderson

Kaffe Fassett
Artist and decorative arts designer.

Sebastian de Ferranti
(1927–2015) Businessman and patron of the arts; builder and first owner of Henbury Hall, Derbyshire.

Ralph Fiennes
Actor, film producer and director.

Valerie Finnis
(1924–2006) Plantswoman and flower photographer.

Ann Fleming (*née* Charteris)
(1913–1981) Socialite; wife firstly of Esmond Harmsworth, 2nd Viscount Rothermere; secondly of Shane, 2nd Lord O'Neill; and thirdly of writer Ian Fleming.

Dr Chris Fletcher
Keeper of Special Collections at the Bodleian Library, Oxford.

Dr John Fletcher
Dendrologist; pioneer of dating panel pictures.

Howard Flight, Baron Flight
Businessman; former Conservative MP, elevated to the House of Lords in 2011.

Peter Florence
Director and co-founder with his parents of the Hay Festival.

Lt-Gen. Sir John Foley
Retired Army officer, former Director of the SAS; High Sheriff
of Herefordshire and Worcestershire in 2006; Vice-Lieutenant of
Herefordshire in 2010.

Augustine Ford
Son of scholar and art collector Sir Brinsley Ford.

Sir Bruce Forsyth
(1928–2017) Television presenter and entertainer.

Dr Claire Foster-Gilbert
Founding Director of the Westminster Abbey Institute since 2012.

Robin Lane Fox
Historian, author and gardening writer.

Antonia, Lady Fraser
Historian, novelist and biographer; widow of Harold Pinter (q.v.);
mother of Benjamin and Flora Fraser; sister of Thomas Pakenham,
8th Earl of Longford (q.v.), and Michael Pakenham (q.v.).

Benjamin Fraser
Banker; son of Lady Antonia Fraser.

Flora Fraser
Biographer; daughter of Lady Antonia Fraser.

Sir Christopher Frayling
Writer and educationalist; Rector of the Royal College of Art
1996–2009; Chairman of the Arts Council 2005–9.

Michael Frayn
Playwright and novelist.

Ezio Frigerio
Italian costume designer and art director.

Stephen Fry
Actor, comedian and writer.

Fiona Fyshe
PA to Roy Strong 2009–19.

Patrick Gale
Novelist.

Jane Gardam
Novelist.

Patrick Garland
(1935–2013) Actor, producer, director and writer; married to Alexandra Bastedo (q.v.).

Lesley Garrett
Soprano and media personality.

Marjorie (Mollie) Gascoyne-Cecil, Dowager Marchioness of Salisbury
Noted garden designer; chatelaine of Cranborne Manor, Dorset, and Hatfield House, Hertfordshire.

Robert Gascoyne-Cecil, 6th Marquess of Salisbury
(1916–2003) British landowner and Conservative politician.

Fr John Gaskell
(1928–2015) Priest, noted preacher, spiritual guide and confessor.

Peter and Laura Gatacre
Owners of the Royal Palace and Gardens of Het Loo, near Amsterdam.

Diarmuid Gavin
Garden designer and television personality.

Victoria Getty
Philanthropist and former model; Trustee of the J. Paul Getty Trust since 2003.

Dame Helen Ghosh
Director-General of the National Trust 2012–17; Master of Balliol College, Oxford, since 2018.

Christopher Gibbs
British antique dealer, collector and interior designer.

Robin Gibson
(1944–2010) Art historian; Chief Curator of the National Portrait Gallery 1968–2001.

Prince Richard, Duke of Gloucester
Youngest grandchild of George V and Queen Mary.

John Goodall
Writer and historian; architectural editor of *Country Life* since 2007.

Debs Goodenough
Head gardener of the Prince of Wales's garden at Highgrove, Gloucestershire.

Daisy Goodwin
Writer and television producer.

Mary Gordon Lennox
Lady-in-Waiting to Princess Alexandra, Hon. Lady Ogilvy (q.v.); widow of diplomat Lord Nicholas Gordon Lennox (1931–2004).

Janet Gough
High Mistress of St Paul's Girls' School 1993–8.

Alexander (Grey) Ruthven, 2nd Earl of Gowrie
See under Ruthven

Countess Adelheid (Neiti) von der Schulenburg, Lady Gowrie
See under von der Schulenburg

Camilla Graham
Former Head of Museum Events at the V&A.

Penny Graham
Painter; former student of Maggi Hambling (q.v.).

Candida Lycett Green
(1942–2014) Writer, film-maker and gardener; daughter of Poet Laureate Sir John Betjeman.

Imogen Lycett Green
Author and journalist; daughter of Candida Lycett Green.

Dame Beryl Grey
Retired ballet dancer; President of English National Ballet.

Geordie Grieg
Journalist; editor of the *Daily Mail* and former editor of the *Evening Standard.*

Bunny Guinness
Landscape architect, journalist and radio personality.

Sir John Guinness
Former diplomat; co-founder of the National Heritage Memorial Fund; with his wife, Valerie (1937–2014), custodians of East Barsham Manor, Norfolk.

Miranda Guinness, Countess of Iveagh
(1939–2010) Socialite; former wife of Benjamin Guinness, 3rd Earl of Iveagh.

Caroline de Guitaut
Assistant Curator, Royal Collection Trust.

William Hague, Baron Hague of Richmond
Conservative politician, formerly MP for Richmond, Yorkshire.

Jerry Hall
Texan model; former partner of Rolling Stones rock star Mick Jagger.

Very Revd John Hall
Dean of Westminster 2006–19.

Sir Peter Hall
Theatre and film director; founder of the Royal Shakespeare
Company and former Director of the National Theatre.

Tony Hall, Baron Hall of Birkenhead
BBC Director-General 2013–20.

Maggi Hambling
British painter and sculptor.

Rosemary Harden
Curator of The Fashion Museum, Bath.

Pamela, Lady Harlech
American-born journalist and author; Chairman of English
National Ballet 1990–2000; former Trustee of the V&A.

Philip Harley
Director at Christie's, London; specialist in modern British and
Irish art.

Jerry Harpur
Garden photographer.

John Harris
English historian of architecture and gardens, co-curator of the
Destruction of the Country House exhibition at the V&A.

Philip Harris, Baron Harris of Peckham
Businessman and philanthropist; major donor to the Westminster
Abbey restoration appeal.

Nicky Haslam
English interior designer and socialite.

Mark Haworth-Booth
Historian of photography; curator at the V&A 1970–2004; Senior Fellow of the Royal College of Art.

John Hayes
Director of the London Museum 1970–74 and of the National Portrait Gallery 1974–94.

Jonathan Heale
British children's book illustrator and ceramic artist; wife, Mary, is also an artist.

Karen Hearn
Art historian; Curator of Sixteenth- and Seventeenth-Century British Art at Tate, 1992–2012.

Sir Edward Heath
(1916–2005) UK Prime Minister 1970–74.

Jane Heathcote-Drummond-Willoughby, 28th Baroness Willoughby de Eresby
Chatelaine of Grimsthorpe Castle, Lincolnshire; joint hereditary Lord Great Chamberlain.

Richard Heatly
Principal of Hereford College of Arts 2003–15.

Mark Hedges
Journalist; editor of *Country Life* since 2006.

Drue Heinz
American patron of the literary arts; founder and publisher of the *Paris Review*.

Joan Henderson
(1915–2002) History teacher at Edmonton County Grammar School.

Mary, Lady Henderson
(1919–2004) Writer, linguist and hostess; wife of Sir Nicholas Henderson.

Sir Nicholas (Nico) Henderson
(1919–2009) Diplomat; former British Ambassador to France and the USA.

Jörg Hensgen
Editor at Bodley Head/Random House.

James Hervey-Bathurst
Businessman; custodian of Eastnor Castle and estate; President of the Historic Houses Association 2004–8.

Anne, Lady Heseltine
Supporter of the arts; former Trustee of the V&A and Imperial War Museum; wife of Conservative peer Lord Heseltine.

Michael Heseltine, Baron Heseltine
Conservative peer; former Secretary of State for the Environment; creator, with his wife, of Thenford Arboretum and Gardens, Northamptonshire.

Pamela, Lady Hicks
Younger daughter of Earl Mountbatten of Burma and first cousin of the Duke of Edinburgh.

Marie-Therese Hill
Tour guide with The Ultimate Travel Company.

Shaun Hill
Head chef and proprietor of Michelin-starred Walnut Tree restaurant near Abergavenny.

Ian Hislop
Journalist, satirist and broadcaster; editor of *Private Eye*.

Richard Hobday
Architect, writer and authority on the history of sunlight therapy.

Penelope Hobhouse
Distinguished British garden writer and designer.

David Hockney
Prominent English artist.

Cressida Hogg
Financier; wife of Hon. Henry Legge (q.v.).

Fred Hohler
Former diplomat; creator of the Public Catalogue Foundation; former Chairman of Governors of St Paul's School, London.

Revd Grant Holmes
Vicar of St Mary's Church, Marshalwick; partner of Very Revd
Jeffrey John (q.v.).

Alexander Hood, 4th Viscount Bridport, 7th Duke of Bronté
Investment banker; descendant of William Nelson, elder brother of
Horatio Nelson.

Sir Simon Hornby
(1934–2010) Former Chairman of WH Smith.

David Howard
Horticulturalist; former Head Gardener to the Prince of Wales at
Highgrove.

Elizabeth Jane Howard
(1923–2014) Bestselling English novelist.

Ken Howard
Artist; President of the New English Art Club 1998–2003.

Geoffrey Howe, Baron Howe of Aberavon
(1926–2015) Conservative peer; former Chancellor of the
Exchequer; Margaret Thatcher's longest-serving Cabinet Minister.

Caro Howell
Director of the Foundling Museum, London; married to Will
Tuckett (q.v.).

Erica Hunningher
Garden writer, lecturer and editor.

Douglas Hurd, Baron Hurd of Westwell
Conservative politician, Foreign Secretary 1989–95.

Susan, Lady Hussey, Baroness Hussey of North Bradley
Lady-in-Waiting to the Queen.

Revd Canon David Hutt
Former Canon and Steward of Westminster Abbey; Sub-Dean of
Westminster 1999–2005.

Tanya Illingworth
Tour Leader with The Ultimate Travel Company.

Richard Ingrams
Journalist; co-founder and former editor of *Private Eye*; founding
editor of *The Oldie*.

Revd Prebendary Gerard Irvine
(1920–2011) High Anglican vicar of St Matthew's Church,
Westminster.

Keith Irvine
(1928–2011) Eclectic interior designer who trained with John
Fowler; married to author and former fashion designer Chippy
Irvine.

Jeremy Isaacs
Television executive; former General Director of the Royal Opera
House, Covent Garden.

Derek Jacobi
Distinguished actor and stage director.

Howard Jacobson
Novelist and journalist.

Bianca Jagger
Nicaraguan social and human-rights activist; former wife of Mick Jagger.

Sir Mick Jagger
Rock musician; lead singer of the Rolling Stones.

Rt Revd Graham James
Bishop of Norwich 1999–2019.

Keith James
Businessman; Chairman of the National Trust Advisory Board in Wales.

Marie-Sygne James, Baroness Northbourne of Betteshanger
French-born wife of Lord Northbourne.

P.D. (Phyllis) James, Baroness James of Holland Park
(1920–2014) Distinguished crime writer.

Robin Janvrin
Courtier; Private Secretary to the Queen 1999–2007.

Keith Jeffery
Former Adviser for External Affairs at the Arts Council.

Dame Jennifer Jenkins, Lady Jenkins of Hillhead
Chairman of the National Trust 1986–90.

John and Lesley Jenkins
Owners of Wollerton Old Hall, Shropshire, childhood home of
artist Lesley.

Roy Jenkins, Baron Jenkins of Hillhead
(1920–2003) Politician; first Leader of the Social Democratic Party.

Sir Simon Jenkins
Journalist and author; former Chairman of the National Trust.

Elton John
Singer-songwriter; married to David Furnish (q.v.).

Very Revd Jeffrey John
Dean of St Albans; partner of Revd Grant Holmes (q.v.).

Hugh Johnson
Doyen of wine writers; with his wife, Judy, restored and enlarged
the gardens at Saling Hall, Essex.

Paul Johnson
Journalist and popular historian; married to Marigold, wit, former
parliamentary candidate and campaigner.

Sir Mark Jones
Art historian and numismatist; Director of the V&A 2001–11.

Natasha Kaplinsky
Journalist, television presenter and newsreader.

John Kasmin
Art dealer and collector.

Roger Katz
General Manager of Hatchards 1991–2010.

Michael Kauffman
Art historian; director of Courtauld Institute 1985–95.

Jonas Kaufman
German operatic tenor.

Mary Keen
Lecturer, writer and garden designer.

Katharine, Duchess of Kent
Wife of Prince Edward, Duke of Kent; Catholic convert, music teacher and charitable patron.

Nicolas Kent
Chief Executive and Creative Director, Oxford Films.

Robert Kime
Antique dealer, designer and interior decorator.

Sir John Kingman
Distinguished mathematician; widower of Valerie Cromwell (q.v.).

Miles Kington
(1941–2008) Journalist, musician and broadcaster.

Tim Knox
Director of Sir John Soane's Museum 2005–13 and of the Fitzwilliam Museum, Cambridge, 2013–18; Director of the Royal Collection since 2018.

Robert Lacey
Historian and biographer.

Lady Lucinda Lambton, Lady Worsthorne
Architectural writer, broadcaster and photographer.

Sir Stephen Lamport
Receiver General of Westminster Abbey, formerly Private Secretary to the Prince of Wales.

George Lascelles, 7th Earl of Harewood
(1923–2011) Music director, author, governor of the BBC (1985–7) and President of the British Board of Film Classification 1985–96. His wife, Patricia Lascelles, Countess of Harewood (1926–2018), was a former violinist and model.

Andrew Lawson
Garden photographer.

Victoria, Lady Leatham
Antiques expert and television personality; chatelaine of Burghley House 1982–2007.

Evgeny Lebedev
Russian-born media tycoon, supporter of the arts and charity campaigner.

Sir Hugh Leggatt
(1925–2014) Art dealer and heritage lobbyist.

Hon. Henry Legge
Youngest son of Raine Spencer (q.v.); married to Cressida Hogg (q.v.).

Edward Coke, 7th Earl of Leicester
See under Coke

Barbara Leigh-Hunt
British actress; widow of actor Richard Pasco.

Alice Lennox-Boyd, Viscountess Boyd of Merton
Horticulturalist; former President of Cornwall Garden Society and garden adviser to the Royal Horticultural Society; wife of Simon Lennox-Boyd, 2nd Viscount Boyd of Merton.

Hon. Christopher Lennox-Boyd
(1941–2012) Scholar and authority on prints; owner of Sanders antique print shop, Oxford; brother of Lord Boyd of Merton and Sir Mark Lennox-Boyd.

Hon. Sir Mark and Arabella, The Hon. Lady Lennox-Boyd
Former Conservative government minister and his wife, a well-known landscape designer; owners of Gresgarth Hall and Gardens, Lancashire.

Michael Leonard
Artist, illustrator and portraitist.

Quentin Letts
Journalist and theatre critic.

Clive Lever
Hairdresser.

Diane, Lady Lever
Widow of Lord (Harold) Lever.

Jeremy Lewis
(1942–2015) Veteran publisher, writer, biographer and journalist; deputy editor of *The Oldie* and popular figure in the London literary world.

Leonora Anson, Countess of Lichfield
See under Anson

Marguerite Littman
American-born socialite and philanthropist; friend of Diana, Princess of Wales.

Bob Lockyer
Former executive produce for dance programmes at the BBC.

Konrad Loewenstein
Roman Catholic priest, member of the traditionalist Priestly Fraternity of Saint Peter; son of Prince Rupert and Princess Josephine Loewenstein.

Prince Rupert and Princess Josephine Loewenstein
(1933–2014) Merchant banker; financial manager of the Rolling Stones; widow, Princess Josephine Loewenstein, is a former ballerina, socialite and friend of Princess Margaret.

Andrew Logan
Sculptor, performance artist, portraitist and jewellery-maker.

David Lough
Author and historian; Artistic Director of Penshurst Festival, Kent.

Jan Lucas-Scudamore
Custodian of the Scudamore ancestral home, Kentchurch Court, Herefordshire.

Richard Luce, Baron Luce
Former Conservative Cabinet Minister, Minister for the Arts 1985–90.

Dame Vera Lynn
(1917–2020) Veteran singer, the 'Forces' Sweetheart' during the Second World War.

Revd Alan McCormack
Rector of City St Botolph without Bishopsgate and St-Vedast-alias-Foster in the City of London 2007–15; Chaplain to the Lord Mayor of London; Assistant Priest at St George's, Hanover Square, since 2017.

Revd Michael Macey
Vicar of Boxmoor, St Albans; previously Minor Canon and Precentor at Westminster Abbey.

Neil MacGregor
Art historian; Director of the National Gallery 1987–2002 and of the British Museum 2002–15.

Wayne McGregor
Choreographer and dance director.

Sir Ian McKellen
Distinguished actor of stage and screen.

Catharine MacLeod
Curator of Seventeenth-Century Art at the National Portrait Gallery, London.

Julia MacRae
Publisher; editor of *The Story of Britain* and *The Spirit of Britain*.

Caroline Magnus
Owner of Stokesay Court, Shropshire.

Sir Laurie Magnus
Financier; Deputy Chairman of the National Trust 2005–13; Chairman of Historic England; Trustee of English Heritage.

Sir Denis Mahon
(1910–2011) Scholar, connoisseur and collector of Italian art.

Sir Noel Malcolm
Journalist, historian and scholar; Sub-Warden of All Souls College, Oxford.

Peter Mandelson, Baron Mandelson
Labour MP for Hartlepool (1992–2004) and Cabinet Minister under Prime Ministers Tony Blair and Gordon Brown.

Sir Jonathan Marsden
Art historian and curator; Surveyor of the Queen's Works of Art
and Director of the Royal Collection 2010–17.

Mary Anna Marten
(1929–2010) Former owner of Crichel House, Dorset; collector,
traveller and supporter of the arts.

Dame Monica Mason
Former ballet dancer, teacher and Director of the Royal Ballet
2002–12.

Vivien Merchant
(1929–1982) Actress; first wife of Harold Pinter (q.v.).

Sir Oliver Millar
(1923–2007) Surveyor of the Queen's Pictures 1972–88.

Beatrix Miller
(1923–2014) Legendary editor of *Vogue* 1964–84.

James Miller
Fine art consultant; former Deputy Chairman of Sotheby's.

Jonathan Milton
Headmaster of Westminster Abbey Choir School 2002–18.

David Montgomery
Celebrated portrait photographer.

Sir Peter Moores
(1932–2016) Heir to the Littlewoods empire, patron of the arts and owner of Compton Verney House, Warwickshire.

Rosalind, Lady Morrison
Chatelaine of Madresfield Court, Worcestershire; first wife of Gerald Ward (1938–2008), businessman, farmer and close friend of the Prince of Wales; 1984–99 married to Sir Charles Morrison (1932–2005), Conservative MP for Devizes.

Timothy Mowl
Architectural landscape historian.

Dame Iris Murdoch
(1919–1999) Distinguished novelist.

Dermot Murnaghan
Broadcaster and journalist.

Peter Murphy
Icon painter and teacher.

Simon Murray
Senior Director of Strategy, Curatorship and External Affairs at the National Trust since 2014 (previously Chief Operating Officer).

Jeremy Musson
Architectural historian, writer and broadcaster; architectural editor of *Country Life* 1998–2007.

Robert Myers
Landscape architect and garden designer.

Jonathan Myles-Lea
Accomplished painter of country houses, historic buildings and landscapes.

Sandy Nairne
Historian, writer and curator; Director of the National Portrait Gallery 2002–15.

James Naughtie
BBC radio presenter.

Orna NiChionna
Deputy Chair of the National Trust since 2014.

His Eminence Vincent Nichols
Cardinal of the Roman Catholic Church since 2014; Archbishop of Westminster since 2009.

Alexander Nicoll
Head of Internal Communications, Church of England, since 2001.

Lila de Nobili
(1916–2002) Italian stage designer, costume designer and fashion illustrator.

Rt Revd Philip North
Traditionalist priest; Rector of Old St Pancras 2008–15; Bishop of Burnley since 2015.

Marie-Sygne James, Baroness Northbourne
See under James

John Julius Norwich
See under Cooper

Sir John Nott
Former Conservative MP for St Ives, Cornwall; businessman and author; wife, Miloska, is an Anglo-Slovenian fundraiser.

Diane, Lady Nutting
Chairman of the Georgian Group 1999–2014; chatelaine of Chicheley Hall, Buckinghamshire.

Michael Nyman
Composer, musician and librettist.

Revd Mark Oakley
Canon Chancellor of St Paul's Cathedral; former Rector of St Paul's Church, Covent Garden.

James O'Donnell
Organist and Master of the Choristers of Westminster Abbey.

Princess Alexandra of Kent, The Hon. Lady Ogilvy
Wife of Sir Angus Ogilvy; first cousin of the Queen.

Sir Angus Ogilvy
(1928–2004) Businessman; husband of Princess Alexandra of Kent.

James Ogilvy
Son of Sir Angus Ogilvy and Princess Alexandra of Kent.

Virginia Ogilvy, Countess of Airlie
Wife of the Earl of Airlie; Lady of the Bedchamber to the Queen
since 1973.

Julia Trevelyan Oman, Lady Strong
(1930–2003) Distinguished theatre, television, ballet and opera
designer; wife of Sir Roy Strong.

Onora O'Neill, Baroness O'Neill of Bengarve
Philosopher and politician; President of the British Academy
2005–9.

Mirabel Osler
(1925–2016) Garden writer and designer.

Rupert Otten
Creator, with his wife, Antoinette, of Monnow Valley Arts Centre
in the Welsh Marches.

Sir Michael Pakenham
Diplomat; younger brother of the 8th Earl of Longford (q.v.) and
Lady Antonia Fraser (q.v.).

Thomas Pakenham, 8th Earl of Longford
Writer, historian and arborist.

Steven Parissien
Architectural and cultural historian, author and curator; Director
of Compton Verney Art Gallery and Park 2009–18.

Camilla Parker-Bowles
See Duchess of Cornwall

Brendan Parsons, 7th Earl of Rosse
Eldest son of Michael and Anne Parsons, the 6th Earl and
Countess of Rosse; half-brother of Antony Armstrong-Jones (q.v.);
custodian of the family seat, Birr Castle, County Offaly.

Richard Pasco
(1926–2014) British stage, screen and television actor.

John Patten, Baron Patten
Former Conservative Cabinet Minister.

Anna Pavord
Garden writer and journalist.

Jane Percy, Duchess of Northumberland
Businesswoman; with her husband, Ralph, 12th Duke of
Northumberland, redeveloped the Alnwick Garden at Alnwick
Castle; first female Lord Lieutenant of Northumberland (since
2009).

Dame Siân Phillips
Veteran Welsh actress.

John Physick
(1923–2013) Official historian and Deputy Director of the V&A.

Harold Pinter
(1930–2008) Playwright, screenwriter, director and actor; husband
of Lady Antonia Fraser (q.v.).

Revd Canon Andrew Piper
Precentor of Hereford Cathedral.

Mary, Lady Carew Pole
Wife of Sir Richard Carew Pole; Lady-in-Waiting to Princess Anne; former President of the Royal Cornwall Show.

Sir Richard Carew Pole, 13th Bt
President of the Royal Horticultural Society 2001–6; resident at the family seat, Antony House, Cornwall.

Olga Polizzi
Hotelier and interior designer; former Westminster City Council councillor.

Marguerite Porter
Choreographer, actress and former principal ballet dancer.

Michael Portillo
Former Conservative Cabinet Minister.

Anthony Powell
Costume designer for stage and screen.

Carla, Lady Powell
Socialite and former model; wife of diplomat and cross-bench peer Charles Powell, Baron Powell of Bayswater.

Dr Sean Preston
Consultant gastroenterologist.

Prince Nicholas von Preussen
Guinness heir and direct descendant of Queen Victoria and German Emperor Wilhelm II.

Rt Revd Anthony Priddis
Bishop of Hereford 2004–13.

Prince Michael of Kent
Grandson of George V and paternal first cousin of the Queen.

Princess Alexandra of Kent
See The Hon. Lady Ogilvy

Sir William Proby, 3rd Bt
Former Chairman of the National Trust and Chair of Trustees of the National Portrait Gallery; resident at the family seat, Elton Hall, Cambridgeshire.

Libby Purves
Journalist, radio presenter and author.

William Pye
British sculptor, known particularly for his water sculptures.

Charles Quest-Ritson
Garden writer, translator and historian; former Director of the Royal National Rose Society.

Anthony Quinton, Baron Quinton of Holywell
(1925–2010) Philosopher; President of Trinity College, Oxford, 1978–87, and Chairman of the British Library Board 1985–90; presenter of the BBC Radio 4 *Round Britain Quiz*; married to Marcelle Wegier (1930–2017), accomplished American writer, translator and sculptor.

Peter Radford
Former Olympic athlete who had been confined to a wheelchair as a child; former Chair of UK Athletics; Professor of Sport at Brunel University.

Sondra Radvanovsky
American-Canadian operatic soprano.

Patricia Rawlings, Baroness Rawlings of Burnham Westgate
Conservative peer and former MEP; owner, with Paul Zuckerman (q.v.) of Burnham Westgate Hall, Norfolk.

Lady Jane Rayne
Philanthropist and charity patron; daughter of the 8th Marquess of Londonderry; widow of property developer Max Rayne; later wife of historian and biographer Robert Lacey.

Nancy Reagan
(1921–2016) First Lady of the USA 1981–9.

Peter Rees, Baron Rees of Goytre
(1926–2008) Conservative politician.

William Rees-Mogg, Baron Rees-Mogg
(1928–2012) Journalist and writer, former editor of *The Times*; Chairman of the Arts Council and Vice-Chairman of the BBC.

Gareth Rees-Roberts
Acoustic guitarist.

Revd Dr Robert Reiss
Former Sub-Dean and Canon Treasurer at Westminster Abbey (retired 2013).

Vanessa Remington
Art historian, writer and Curator of Paintings at the Royal Collection.

Dame Fiona Reynolds
Director-General of the National Trust 2001–12; Master of Emmanuel College, Cambridge, since 2012.

Patrick Reyntiens
Leading British stained-glass artist.

Dame Zandra Rhodes
Fashion designer.

Franco Maria Ricci
Italian art publisher.

Matthew Rice
Designer, illustrator and author; married to Emma Bridgewater (q.v.).

Sarah Richardson
Lord Mayor of Westminster 2013.

Tim Richardson
Journalist, confectionery historian, and writer on gardens and theatre; married to Claire Whalley (q.v.).

Tony Ridler
Swansea-based graphic designer and gardener.

Bob Ringwood
English-born Hollywood costume designer.

Angela Rippon
Television journalist, newsreader, writer and presenter.

Jill, Lady Ritblat
Barrister and patron of the arts; Trustee Emeritus of The Design Museum, London; wife of property developer Sir John Ritblat.

Andrew Roberts
Historian and journalist.

Sir Hugh Roberts
Art historian and curator; Director of the Royal Collection and Surveyor of the Queen's Works of Art (1996–2010).

Geoffrey Robinson
Former Labour MP; owner of the *New Statesman* 1996–2008.

Gordon and Patty Robson-Lowe
Owners and restorers of Elizabeth Frink's former home, Woolland House, Dorset.

Miranda Rock
Daughter of Lady Victoria Leatham (q.v.); Director of Burghley House Preservation Trust.

Malcolm Rogers
Art historian, curator and portraiture expert.

Richard Rogers, Baron Rogers of Riverside
Noted British architect; married to Ruth, Lady Rogers, chef and owner of the Michelin-starred River Café, London.

Kenneth Rose
(1924–2014) Royal biographer and *Telegraph* diarist.

Sir Norman Rosenthal
Curator and art historian; former Exhibitions Secretary of The Royal Academy of Arts.

Caroline Ross-Pirie
Television producer.

Brendan Parsons, 7th Earl of Rosse
See under Parsons

Jacob Rothschild, 4th Baron Rothschild
Investment banker.

Kate de Rothschild
See under Agius

Patricia Routledge
Distinguished British actress.

Revd Prebendary Pam Row
Chaplain of Hereford Cathedral.

J.K. Rowling
Author; creator of Harry Potter.

Baroness Rosalind Runcie
(1932–2012) Classical pianist; wife of Archbishop of Canterbury
Robert Runcie.

Sue Runyard
Author; former Head of Corporate Communications and PR at
the Royal Botanic Gardens, Kew.

Francis Russell
Deputy Chairman of Christie's UK.

Alexander (Grey) Ruthven, 2nd Earl of Gowrie
Conservative politician, Arts Minister 1983–85; former Chairman
of Sotheby's and of the Arts Council; married to Countess
Adelheid (Neiti) von der Schulenburg (q.v.).

Ned Ryan
(1933–2009) Irish businessman; close friend of Princess Margaret.

Maurice Saatchi, Baron Saatchi
Businessman, co-founder with his brother of advertising agency
Saatchi and Saatchi; Trustee of the V&A 1988–96; Chairman of the
Conservative party 2003–5.

Anya Sainsbury, Lady Sainsbury of Preston Candover
Retired ballerina and patron of the arts; wife of Lord Sainsbury
(Baron Sainsbury of Preston Candover, President of Sainsbury's;
businessman and politician).

Norman St John Stevas, Baron St John of Fawley
(1929–2012) Barrister and Conservative politician.

John Sales
Former National Trust Head of Gardens.

Marjorie (Mollie) Gascoyne-Cecil, Dowager Marchioness of Salisbury
See under Gascoyne-Cecil

Robert Gascoyne-Cecil, 6th Marquess of Salisbury
See under Gascoyne-Cecil

Coral Samuel
Philanthropist and supporter of the arts.

Sir Charles Saumarez Smith
Cultural historian and writer; Director of the National Portrait Gallery 1994–2002 and of the National Gallery 2002–7; Secretary of the Royal Academy of Arts; married to jewellery designer Romilly Saumarez Smith.

Gerald Scarfe
Cartoonist, married to actress Jane Asher (q.v.).

Countess Adelheid (Neiti) von der Schulenburg, Lady Gowrie
Wife of Lord Gowrie (q.v.).

Most Revd and Rt Hon. Dr John Sentamu
Bishop of Stepney 1996–2002; Bishop of Birmingham 2002–5; Archbishop of York since 2005.

Sir Nicholas Serota
Art historian and curator; Director of Tate 1988–2017.

Brian Sewell
(1931–2016) Art critic.

Jan Sewell
BAFTA Award-winning hair and make-up artist.

William Shawcross
Writer and commentator; Chairman of the Charity Commission 2012–18.

Jane Sheffield
Lady-in-Waiting to Princess Margaret; former wife of Sir Jocelyn Stevens (q.v.).

Julian Sheffield
Businessman; brother of Jane Sheffield (q.v.).

James Sherwood
British-based American businessman; married to Shirley Sherwood (q.v.).

Dr Shirley Sherwood
Writer and collector of botanical art; married to James Sherwood (q.v.).

Ben Shipston
Director of Operations at the National Trust.

Alexandra Shulman
Journalist; editor-in-chief of British *Vogue* 1992–2017.

Philip Sidney, 2nd Viscount De L'Isle and Isobel, Lady De L'Isle
Owners of Penshurst Place, Kent.

Lois Sieff
(1923–1982) Enthusiast and supporter of the arts.

Donald Sinden
(1923–2014) Distinguished screen and stage actor.

Sister Judith SCS
Chaplain to the staff at Westminster Abbey.

Sir Reresby Sitwell, 7th Bt
(1927–2009) Patron of the arts and culture; married Penelope (née Forbes) in 1952.

Ian Skelly
Writer and BBC Radio 3 presenter.

Claire Skinner
Television actress.

Wayne Sleep
Dancer and choreographer.

Lt Col. Sir John Smiley
Nephew of Sir Cecil Beaton (q.v.).

Sir Tim Smit
Dutch-born businessman, ecologist and horticulturalist, co-restorer of the Lost Gardens of Heligan and co-founder of the Eden Project, Cornwall.

David and Lucy Abel Smith
Art collectors and champions of fine craft, sculpture and the decorative arts.

Christopher Smith
Chief of Staff to Archbishop of Canterbury Rowan Williams (q.v.).

Eddie Smith
Former archivist of Westminster School.

Dame Maggie Smith
Distinguished actress.

Richard Shirley Smith
Painter, engraver and illustrator.

Fortune Smith, Duchess of Grafton
Mistress of the Robes to the Queen.

Jon Snow
Journalist and television presenter.

Lucy Snowdon
See Lucy Armstrong-Jones

Tony Snowdon
See Antony Armstrong-Jones

Dame Mary Soames
(1922–2014) Writer; youngest child of Sir Winston Churchill.

Valerie Pitts, Lady Solti
Patron of music and culture; widow of conductor Sir Georg Solti.

Anne, Lady Somerset
Historian and writer.

Peter Soros
Hungarian-American investor and philanthropist.

Charles Spencer, 9th Earl Spencer
Younger brother of Diana, Princess of Wales and stepson of Raine Spencer (q.v.); married to Canadian social entrepreneur Karen (née Villeneuve) since 2011.

Raine, Countess Spencer
(1929–2016) Socialite stepmother of Diana, Princess of Wales, and Charles Spencer (q.v.).

Hilary Spurling
British journalist and biographer.

Frances Stainton
Artist and Conservative councillor; served two terms as Mayor of Hammersmith and Fulham.

Lindsay Stainton
Author and museum curator.

Sarah Staniforth
Expert on heritage conservation; trustee of English Heritage and
The Landmark Trust; formerly Museums and Collections Director,
Historic Properties Director and Head Conservator of the National
Trust.

Graham Stansfield
(1940–2018) Composer, musician and literary agent.

David Starkey
Historian and radio and television presenter.

Tim and Sophia Steel
Owners of Norton Court, Kent.

Jeffrey Sterling, Baron Sterling of Plaistow
Businessman and Conservative peer.

Sir Jocelyn Stevens
(1932–2014) Publisher and cultural administrator, Chairman of
English Heritage 1992–2000; married to Jane Sheffield (q.v.)
1956–79.

Revd Victor Stock
Rector of St Mary-le-Bow 1986–2002; later Dean of Guildford.

Thomas Stonor, 7th Baron Camoys
British peer and banker; first Roman Catholic Lord Chamberlain
since the Reformation; married to Elizabeth, née Hyde Parker.

Charlie Stopford Sackville
Custodian of Drayton Park, Northamptonshire, since 1997.

Sir Tom Stoppard
Prolific playwright and screenwriter.

James Stourton
Art historian and former Chairman of Sotheby's UK.

Janet Street-Porter
Journalist and broadcaster.

Alexander Sturgis
Art historian and museum director; Director of the Holburne Museum, Bath, 2005–14; currently Director of the Ashmolean Museum, Oxford.

Dame Joan Sutherland
(1926–2010) Acclaimed operatic soprano.

Deborah Swallow
Museum curator and scholar; Director of the Courtauld Institute since 2004.

John and Marianne Swannell
Celebrated portrait photographer and his wife, a former model.

Lucy Swingler
Television director and producer.

Very Revd Michael Tavinor
Dean of Hereford since 2002.

Dr Claire Taylor, Lady Gifford
Consultant haematologist, co-founder of the City Music
Foundation and Lady Mayoress of the City of London, 2012.

Philip Teague
Gardener at The Laskett.

Robert Tear
(1939–2011) Welsh tenor.

Charlie and Virginia Temple-Richards
Custodians of Sennowe Park, Norfolk.

Sir Bryn Terfel
Welsh bass-baritone opera and concert singer.

Rachel de Thame
Gardener and presenter of *Gardeners' World* for BBC2.

Sarah Thomas
Director of the Bodleian Libraries and Bodley's Librarian 2007–13.

Julian Thompson
(1941–2011) Chairman of Sotheby's 1982–7; leading expert on
Chinese porcelain.

Colin Thubron
Travel writer and novelist.

Simon Thurley
Architectural historian and broadcaster; Chief Executive of English
Heritage 2002–15.

Morag Timbury
(1930–2018) Scottish bacteriologist, virologist and writer; close friend of John Hayes (q.v.).

Jenny Tiramani
Costume stage and production designer; Principal of the School of Historical Dress, London, since 2012.

Alan Titchmarsh
Gardener, broadcaster and gardening journalist.

Claire Tomalin
Author, biographer and journalist.

Steve Tomlin
Managing Director of Reclamation Services, architectural salvage, Painswick, until 2011.

Carl Toms
(1927–1999) Theatre, opera, ballet and film set and costume designer.

John Tooley
General Director of the Royal Opera House, Covent Garden, 1970–88.

Tessa Traeger
Photographer specialising in still life and food.

Joe Trapp
(1925–2005) Director of the Warburg Institute 1976–90.

Gaynor (Gay) Tregoning
Second wife of Sir Hugh Leggatt (q.v.).

Very Revd Andrew Tremlett
Dean of Durham since 2016; previously a Canon Residentiary of
Westminster Abbey, Rector of St Margaret's Church, Westminster,
Archdeacon of Westminster and Sub-Dean of Westminster Abbey.

Will Tuckett
Choreographer for the English National Ballet and the Royal
Ballet; married to Caro Howell (q.v.).

Pamela Tudor-Craig
See under Wedgwood

Audley Twiston-Davies
Businessman; former owner of the Mynde Park Estate, near
Hereford.

Jenny Uglow
Historian, biographer, critic and publisher; former editorial
director of Chatto & Windus.

Ed Vaizey
Conservative MP; son of economist Lord Vaizey and author
Marina Vaizey.

Stephen Vakil
Financier.

Rosemary Verey
(1918–2001) Influential gardener and garden writer.

Santo Versace
Businessman; elder brother of Italian fashion designer Gianni Versace.

Hugo Vickers
Writer, journalist and broadcaster.

Edmund de Waal
Artist, ceramicist and author; son of Esther de Waal.

Esther de Waal
Scholar, speaker and retreat leader; mother of Edmund de Waal.

Veronica Wadley
Chair of Arts Council London and board member of Arts Council England; first female editor of the *Evening Standard* 2002–9; in 2012 appointed senior adviser to London Mayor Boris Johnson; Chair of the London Music fund 2012–16; married to Tom Bower (q.v.).

Gillian Wagner
Writer and philanthropist; former Chair of Barnardo's, the Thomas Coram Foundation and the Carnegie Trust.

Terry Waite
Humanitarian and author; Church of England envoy to Lebanon, held captive 1987–91.

Victoria Wakefield
Plantswoman, designer of the garden at Bramdean House, Hampshire; Royal Horticultural Society Committee member; Chelsea Flower Show judge.

Richard and Susie Walduck
Hertfordshire landowners.

David Walker
(1934–2008) Costume designer for theatre, opera and dance.

Peter Walker, Baron Walker of Worcester
(1932–2010) Conservative Cabinet Minister; Secretary of State for Wales 1987–90.

Robin Walker
Conservative MP since 2010; son of Peter (q.v.) and Tessa Walker; married to businesswoman Charlotte Keenan.

Amanda Ward
Artist; widow of Gerald Ward (1938–2008), businessman, farmer and close friend of the Prince of Wales.

John Warde
Farmer and landowner; former custodian, with his wife, Anthea (1947–2018) of the family seat, Squerryes Estate, Kent (now run by their son, Henry Warde).

Anne Wareham
Garden writer; co-owner of Veddw House Garden, South Wales.

Marina Warner
Cultural historian and writer.

Giles Waterfield
Art historian, curator and novelist.

Merlin Waterson
Architectural historian; former Director of Historic Properties, National Trust.

Professor David Watkin FRIBA, FSA
(1941–2018) Architectural historian.

Very Revd Derek Watson
Dean of Salisbury 1996–2002.

Justin Webb
Journalist and BBC radio presenter.

Pamela Tudor-Craig, Lady Wedgwood
(1928–2017) Scholar of medieval art.

George Weidenfeld, Baron Weidenfeld of Chelsea
(1919–2016) Publisher and philanthropist, founder and Chairman of Weidenfeld & Nicolson.

Mark Weiss
Art dealer; authority on sixteenth- and seventeenth-century Northern European portraiture; founder of the Weiss Gallery, London.

Most Revd Justin Welby
Archbishop of Canterbury since 2013.

Sophie, Countess of Wessex
Wife of Prince Edward, youngest son of the Queen.

George Garfield Weston
Chief Executive of Associated British Foods, founded by his
grandfather, Willard Garfield Weston; board member of the
Garfield Weston Foundation.

Guy Weston
Businessman and philanthropist; grandson of Willard Garfield
Weston, founder of Associated British Foods; Chairman of the
Garfield Weston Foundation.

Dame Vivienne Westwood
Fashion designer.

Claire Whalley
Film-maker; co-founder and Managing Director of What Larks!
production company; married to Tim Richardson (q.v.).

Huw Wheldon
(1916–1986) Broadcaster and BBC executive.

Alan Whicker
(1921–2013) Journalist, television presenter and broadcaster.

David Vines White
Somerset Herald of Arms in Ordinary at the College of Arms,
London.

Lisa White
Former Chairman of the National Trust Arts Advisory Panel.

Bill Wiggin
Conservative MP for North Herefordshire since 2001.

Richard Wilding
Former head of the Office of Arts and Libraries.

Kim Wilkie
Landscape architect.

Jonty Williams
Hereford cycling coach.

Paul Williams
Exhibition designer.

Peter Williams
Television producer; President of Canterbury International
Festival.

Revd Dr Rowan Williams, Baron Williams of Oystermouth
Former Archbishop of Canterbury; Master of Magdalene College,
Cambridge, since 2013.

Very Revd Dr Robert Willis
Dean of Canterbury.

A.N. Wilson
English writer and columnist.

Caroline Windsor
See under Windsor-Clive.

Gabriella, Lady Windsor
Daughter of Prince and Princess Michael of Kent.

Ivor Edward Other Windsor-Clive, 4th Earl of Plymouth, and Caroline, Countess of Plymouth
Custodians of the family estate at Oakly Park, Shropshire.

Dame Anna Wintour
Editor-in-chief of *Vogue* since 1988 and Artistic Director of Condé Nast since 2013.

Joanna Wood
Interior designer.

Glyn Woodin
Former banker; founder of Mustard Catering.

Christopher Woodward
Director of the Garden Museum, formerly the Museum of Garden History, London.

Joanna Worsley
Traveller and tour guide; widow of polar explorer Henry Worsley.

Lucy Worsley
Historian, author, curator and television presenter.

Sir Peter Wright
Dancer and choreographer.

Dame Frances Yates
(1899–1981) Historian, writer and scholar.

Alan Yentob
BBC TV executive and presenter.

Chris Young
Editor of *The Garden*, the Royal Horticultural Society magazine, since 2010.

William Zelieman
Head Gardener at Het Loo Royal Palace and Gardens in The Netherlands.

Philip Ziegler
Biographer and historian.

Paul Zuckerman
Financier; Treasurer of the Art Fund 2004–15.

Astrid Zydower
(1930–2005) Sculptor.

INDEX